LEADING US OUT OF DARKNESS

Garry McGiboney, Ph.D.

eLectio Publishing
Little Elm, TX
www.eLectioPublishing.com

Leading Us Out of Darkness
By Garry McGiboney, Ph.D.

ISBN-13: 978-1-63213-316-8
Published by eLectio Publishing, LLC
Little Elm, Texas
http://www.eLectioPublishing.com

Printed in the United States of America

5 4 3 2 1 eLP 20 19 18 17 16

The eLectio Publishing editing team is comprised of: Christine LePorte, Lori Draft, Sheldon James, Court Dudek, and Kaitlyn Campbell.

OTHER BOOKS BY GARRY MCGIBONEY

The Psychology of School Climate

Lessons for Leaders and Governing Boards

The Private Side of Public Education

Crisis Management Planning

For those living in darkness, the light is in your heart.

I will bring the blind by a way that they knew not; I will lead them in paths that they have not known; I will make the darkness light before them.

-Isaiah 42:16

CONTENTS

Prologue

Growing up in a small country church provided me with the opportunity to experience the richness, meaningfulness, and importance of music during worship services. It was common for the congregation to sing as many as five hymns during the course of the service. The beauty of the experience was highlighted by the participation of everyone in the church singing each hymn, regardless of age or singing ability. And everyone sang with joy and fellowship. It was a powerful spiritual experience and a central focus of worship.

Many times after church services my mother hummed some of the hymns as we drove home. She talked about her favorite hymns and frequently pointed out particular lines in a hymn that she thought were beautiful and inspirational. She viewed hymns as poems put to music, and she told me I should take the time to read hymns for the pleasure of enjoying the inspirational messages and stories. My mother also told me to look at the bottom of each page of the hymnal and note the name of the hymnist, because that was the name of a very special person—a person who was sharing a part of his or her soul through the hymn.

Many years later, I did read the lines of hymns and I started to pay attention to the names of hymnists. When I asked several people if they knew the names of hymnists who crafted beautiful hymns I found that very few knew any of them.

I started reading and enjoying the beauty of the messages in hymns and I developed a keen interest in the people who wrote and composed the hymns. I wanted to know more about them. I started by reading dozens of hymnals from many sources, but I found that it was difficult to find information about many of the hymnists, even though their hymns were very well known and could be found in numerous hymnals. It took a few years to research their lives and the stories behind the hymns. Narrowing down the selection of hymnists was difficult. This book could be a thousand pages long, but the length needed to be reasonable for readers, so the hymnists selected were those whose hymns appear most often in hymnals.

In this book, the reader will find a collection of almost 400 brief biographies of hymnists from medieval days to contemporary times. The personal stories are interesting, compelling, inspirational and at times heart rending.

There are also common themes in many of the hymns that were composed by the hymnists. References to fear, hope, and inspiration are found not only in the hymns but also in the biographies of the hymnists, as well as in the Bible and in our daily lives. Therefore, the first three chapters of the book include a study of fear, hope, and inspiration and how they are linked together.

Introduction

Hymnists are a special lot. They put words and meaning to our spirit, our needs, and our hopes.

-Anonymous

Their stories and lives are seldom considered or known, yet their works and influence are felt almost every day somewhere in the world and have been for numerous generations. They are the hymnists and their gift to the world of the past and for the future are poems and hymns. To many people, they are important to our hopes, inspiration, and spiritual healing.

The oldest known hymn is the *Phos Hiliron,* which is also called the *Hail Gladdening Light.* Trying to discover the music that accompanied the hymn has proven difficult for scholars but it is commonly believed now that the music was from a Byzantine Chant. The hymn was part of daily Vespers and was sung at each worship service, as it is today in some churches. St. Basil the Great (329-379 AD) wrote about the beauty of *Phos Hiliron* when it was sung in great cathedrals. He said that the words and music filled the heart with joy, redemption, reassurance, and hope.

Other hymns on the list of antiquity include *Let All Mortal Flesh Keep Silence* (3rd century); *Te Deum* (probably the 4th century); *The Song of Miriam from the Book of Exodus* (5th century); *Be Thou My Vision* (from ancient Ireland in the 5th century); *The Vision of the Lord* (ancient Hebrew in the 5th century); and *Savior of the Nation* (4th century by St. Ambrose of Milan).

These and countless other hymns have survived wars, famines, plagues, the Dark Ages, revolutions, the rise and decline of church attendance, contemporary debasement of religion and anything related to worship, and many other follies and frailties of mankind. The hymns survived because of dedicated hymnists and the meaningfulness of their words to a world that always faces turmoil and challenges to faith and hope.

Hymnists are the poets of the spirit, the leaders of light who pull us from the dark and who show the way back to clarity and purpose in our lives.

Rejoice in their inspirational stories and learn more about the people who bring their gifts to us each time we sing their hymns. Explore how the hymnists help us cope with fear, search for hope, and find inspiration.

LEADING
US OUT OF
DARKNESS

Chapter One
Fear

Only when we are no longer afraid do we begin to live.

–Dorothy Thompson

Fear enters our lives almost every day in some way. For many people fear is a constant debilitating presence that prevents them from fully developing their intellectual and social potential. Fear controls their lives. Jiddu Krishnamurti said, "What is needed, rather than running away or controlling or suppressing or any other resistance, is understanding fear; that means, watch it, learn about it, come directly into contact with it. We are to learn about fear, not how to escape from it." That is the theme in many hymns, such as ***In Christ Alone***.

There are many types of fears. The major fears are obvious, but there are lesser fears, but even those fears are enough to sink us into fits of depression, self-doubt, and anxiety. These "little" fears impede our ability and opportunity to learn from unpleasant experiences and keep us from enjoying our successes. Often the little fears take on more importance than they should. For example, something seemingly insignificant as handling a public speaking engagement adequately can bloom into a terrifying fear. This is illustrated by the results of Gallup Polls conducted over the last twenty years. It shows that most people fear public speaking more than almost anything else, and, in fact, fear it so much that they will do almost anything to avoid speaking in public—even to the detriment of their careers. These manmade fears can be turned into a healthy preparation for challenging times or events, for a certain measure of fear often times helps us prepare more fully. Recognizing this can be the difference between a helpful fear and a harmful fear. As a hymn says, "far, far above thy thought His counsel shall appear, when fully he the work that wrought that caused thy needless fear." (***Give to the Winds Thy Fears***)

It is important to recognize that there are two elements of fear: the fear that is necessary and helpful and the fear that is harmful. Gavin de Becker's book, ***The Gift of Fear***, dramatically and effectively highlights the good and necessary aspects of survival fear: "You have the gift of a brilliant internal guardian that stands ready to warn you of hazards and guide you through risky situations." Regarding the second type of fear, de Becker has a theory about that too: "Linking an unwarranted fear to its ultimate terrible destination usually helps alleviate that fear. Though, for example, you may find that public speaking can link to death, you'll see that it would be a long and unlikely trip." De Becker's advice is deeply seeded in logic, but oftentimes fear whips logic into submission, as Samuel Butler said, "Fear is the static that prevents me from hearing myself." Counteracting the negative power of fear is often the theme of hymns, such as ***A Mighty Fortress is Our God*** and ***And Can It Be That I Should Gain***.

It may come as a surprise to many people, but confronting fear can be enlightening and gratifying. Henry Ford wrote, "One of the greatest discoveries a man makes, one of his great surprises, is to find he can do what he was afraid he couldn't do." This positive attitude toward fear starts the journey and that first step is encouraged by several hymnists like Ruth Duck and Civilla Martin (***His Eye is On the Sparrow***). Getting to the point where a person can confront fear can be a long journey, and during the journey, that person will need hope, inspiration, and reassurance.

The Bible describes two types of fear. One type is of a beneficial nature and is useful, and for that reason should be encouraged. According to the Bible, it is the fear of God. This is a guiding fear, a respectful fear, a fear that is essential for learning. Hymns have described the fear based on biblical verses. *Psalms 111:10* is an example of this: "The fear of the Lord is the beginning of wisdom; a good understanding of all that they do [His Guiding Commandments]; his praise endureth forever." Additionally, *Proverbs 1:7* states that the fear of God is a necessary entry to wisdom and discipline: ". . . the Lord watches over those who fear him, those who rely on his unfailing love." In return for the healthy fear, "The Lord is a friend to those who fear him." (*Psalm 33:18*) "The Lord confides in those who fear him. He teaches them his covenant." (*Psalm 25:14*)

There are other comforting words of assurance from the Bible embedded in the fear of God and are in hymns such ***Amazing Grace.*** One of the most reassuring things is that it's spoken as if from a caring and protective parent, when in *Psalm 103:13* it states, "The Lord is like a father to his children, tender and compassionate to those who fear him."

Although one type of fear can be spiritually healthy, the other type of fear is destructive and must be overcome. Brendan Francis captured the destructive nature of fear when he said, "Every man, through fear, mugs his aspirations a dozen times a day." In the face of destructive fear, the Bible says, "This is my command—be strong and courageous. Do not be afraid or discouraged" (*Joshua 14:27*). "Don't be afraid. Just have faith" (*Mark 5:36*). Hymns such as ***Guide Me, O Thou Great Jehovah*** and ***It is Well With My Soul*** echo these themes.

What is the fear that grips people the most and is most destructive? While the fear of death and public speaking always rank at the top of anyone's list of fears, the question has to be asked -Why? The death fear is obvious though its presence varies greatly from person to person, but the fear of public speaking is very revealing. It illustrates the fear of self-expression and the importance of social acceptance. The fear of public speaking is representative of a fear of public embarrassment, of being humiliated, of exposing oneself and having that exposure lead to a negative experience that lingers in our memory for a long time. It's the type of memory that picks away at the fabric of our self-esteem, our self-worth, our happiness. Fear can dampen our spirits and challenge our faith, which creates more conditions for fear to control us. According to Charles Stanley, "Fear stifles our thinking and actions. It creates indecisiveness that results in stagnation. I have known talented people who procrastinate indefinitely rather than risk failure. Lost opportunities cause erosion of confidence, and the downward spiral begins." Hymnists understand that people will struggle with fear because many of them have the same challenges. That is why hymns like ***Fear Not, I Am With Thee*** can be so powerfully supportive: "Like a star of glory lighting up my way; through the clouds of midnight this bright promise shone, I will never leave thee."

The main character in Yann Martel's powerful book, ***The Life of Pi***, has to deal with fear every day for months, as he is trapped on a makeshift life raft with a Bengal tiger. The journey is a study in fear, and Pi begins his own difficult journey through his soul as he looks deep into the essence of fear. When he looked into the eyes of the huge Bengal tiger every day, he was looking into the heart of fear.

> *I must say a word about fear. It is life's only true opponent. Only fear can defeat life. It is a clever, treacherous adversary, how well I know. It has no decency, respects no law or convention, and shows no mercy. It goes for your weakest spot, which it finds with unerring ease. It begins in your mind, always. One moment you are feeling calm, self-possessed, and happy. Then fear disguised in the garb of mild-mannered doubt, slips into your mind like a spy. Doubt meets disbelief and disbelief pushes it out. But disbelief is a poorly armed foot soldier. Doubt does away with it with little trouble. You become anxious. Reason comes to do battle for you. And then you are reassured. Reason is fully equipped with the latest weapons technology. But, to your amazement, despite superior tactics and a number of undeniable victories, reason is laid low.*
>
> *You feel yourself weakening, wavering. Quickly you make rash decisions. You dismiss your last allies: hope and trust. There, you've defeated yourself. Fear, which is but an impression, has triumphed over you.*

Note the importance of the line, ". . . you've defeated yourself. Fear, which is but an impression has triumphed over you." To triumph over self-defeating fear, hymnists remind us that "he promised never to leave me."

Thomas Carlyle wrote: "The first duty of man is to conquer fear; he must get rid of it; he cannot act till then." How can we challenge fear, take it on face-to-face and win most of the battles? How can we avoid being the type of person whose only moment of happiness is the temporary absence of fear? How can we possibly prevail against the fear that "has many eyes and can see things underground"? (Miguel de Cervantes) The answer lies in hope. Hope is at the center of many hymns. It was hope that helped several hymnists endure personal tragedies, resulting in hymns such as ***Awake, My Soul and With the Sun***; ***Commit Thou All Thy Griefs***; ***In Heavenly Love Abiding*** and many others.

When hope is present, fear can be conquered. Hope is the salvation of mankind because hope provides the light showing the way to success and fulfillment and out of the darkness of doubt and fear. A person can survive almost anything as long as hope survives. In the book, ***Unbroken***, by Laura Hillenbrand, hope was the only thing left for the men that survived an airplane crash, several days drifting in a lifeboat, and then years in a torturous war prison camp.

An equally powerful account of surviving fear through hope is found in Viktor Frankl's compelling book, ***Man's Search for Meaning***, a true story of how he and others survived the brutal Nazi death camps during World War II. When facing unimaginable fear Frankl explained, "When we are no longer able to change a situation, we are challenged to change ourselves. Those who have a 'why' to live, can bear with almost any 'how'." When writing about hope and fear, Frankl said, "Those who know how close the connection is between the state of mind of a man—his courage and hope, or lack of them—and the state of immunity of his body will understand that the sudden loss of hope can have a deadly effect." The hymn ***Lighten the Darkness of Our Life's Long Night*** captures the power of hope and its essential quality for life: "Lighten the darkness of our life's long night through which we blindly stumble to the day; shadows mislead us; Father, send Thy light to set our footsteps in the homeward way."

Chapter Two
Hope

Hope is a waking dream.

–Aristotle

Fear and its impact frequently dominate individuals, communities, institutions, organizations, and nations that have lost hope. Fear and hope are unquestionably related. Hope can minimize fear; hope can replace fear; hope can conquer fear. Also, however, the inverse is true. Fear can minimize hope; fear can replace hope; fear can crush hope.

In the 17th century, the philosopher Baruch Spinoza wrote about the inescapable relationship between fear and hope: "Fear cannot be without hope nor hope without fear." The constant interplay and struggle between the two either energizes people or overwhelms them. Some who have succumbed to fear often say, "Hope is a myth; the reality is fear."

Chad Davis said when he feels that everything seems stacked against him and fear creeps into every corner of his soul, "There is a strong little voice somewhere deep down inside that shouts from underneath all of that emotional rubble and says, 'Don't give up, Chad. Keep going; keep fighting.'"

Hope can hold fear at bay. In the book *Hunger Games* written by Suzanne Collins, there is an exchange between President Snow, who controls the nation through fear, and one of the other characters, Seneca, that illustrates the power of hope as they talk about "the games."

> President Snow: *Seneca . . . why do you think we have a winner?*
>
> Seneca Crane: *What do you mean?*
>
> President Snow: *I mean, why do we have a winner? I mean, if we just wanted to intimidate the districts, why not round up*

twenty-four people at random and execute them all at once? It would be a lot faster. [Seneca just stares, confused]

President Snow: *Hope.*

Seneca Crane: *Hope?*

President Snow: *Hope. It is the only thing stronger than fear. A little hope is effective. A lot of hope is dangerous. A spark is fine, as long as it's contained.*

Seneca Crane: *So. . .?*

President Snow: *So, contain it. [Hope]*

Note the powerful statement: "Hope is the only thing stronger than fear." Some of the most powerful dictators in world history understood this, and they also understood that "a little hope is effective and a lot of hope is dangerous." So, they made certain that the natural hope that springs from mankind's will to live and survive was not fueled by anything that inspired them beyond the basic level of hope, such as writing, reading, art, singing, and spiritual gatherings.

A little hope motivates people to keep moving, to keep producing, and to keep others from capitulating to depression and hopelessness. Several hymns illustrate that hope emerges from even a small flicker of light, such as ***Great is Thy Faithfulness***; ***The Solid Rock***, and ***Love Come Down***. The hope that centers on the belief that life somehow and in some way will improve is powerful. That's what dictatorial leaders have known for decades, and that's the mystery of how their leadership survives without crushing everyone around them from the beginning of their reign. These types of leaders at all levels know that if hope expands and grows beyond the basic level and becomes the spark of inspiration then dictatorial leadership will be threatened.

Antoine De Saint-Exupery, the author of ***The Little Prince***, wrote, "It is only with the heart that one can see rightly; what is essential is invisible to the eye." The importance and essence of hope in our heart are rightly captured in this line from the famous book. Hope and the quest for hope are basic to living and the conquering of fear, or, at least, the controlling of fear and this is the focus of some hymns: "His eye is on the sparrow, why should I feel discouraged" (***His Eye is On The Sparrow***).

Psychologist Abraham Maslow wrote extensively about motivation and the hierarchy of needs that must be met before advancing toward the higher state of self-actualization - where an individual focuses on problems outside of self and can discern fact from fiction and can manage or even conquer fear. A self-actualized person is comfortable with creativity and pushing the limits of social convention, and, for the most part, lives a life free from debilitating fear.

Maslow's needs hierarchy includes five levels: physiological (including fear), safety (including fear), love/belonging (despite fear and dependent on hope), esteem (in the absence of fear), and self-actualization (understanding the role and nature of both destructive and beneficial fear as well as the essential elements of hope in all forms). At the basic level of the hierarchy are the essential survival needs of food, shelter, water, and clothing. Maslow opined that no one can move to the higher levels of self-awareness, perception, and ultimately self-actualization unless or until the basic needs are met.

Hope, however, is also a basic element of man's needs, because hope is as essential to the quality of thought and life as food, shelter, water, and clothing. Hope is essential to carry people through times when the basic necessities are difficult to find. How can hope be left out when a person is desperately seeking the basic needs? In fact, hope is so vital to the mental and physical health of a person, it should be included in all five levels of Maslow's hierarchy. What keeps a person looking for food, shelter, water, and clothing when none of those are easy to find and when the struggle and the suffering to meet those needs are a daily, hourly fight? Hope mingles with survival instincts that prevent the person from allowing death to tempt him; that keeps him from giving up. Pearl S. Buck wrote, "We must have hope or starve to death." We are assured of this and comforted, also, by hymns like ***God is On The Move.***

To dramatically illustrate the importance of hope to survival psychologists devised an experiment. In the psychological experiment in 1957, a lab rat was put into a container of water and the top was sealed, leaving the animal in darkness. The staff measured the time it took for the lab rat to give up its fight and willingly sink to the bottom. The researchers created the same scenario but created a small hole in the lid of the container top so that a sliver of light shone through. The lab rat fought longer and stronger in the container with the light shining through the lid. When the water-filled container had no lid and light filled the container the lab rat struggled even longer. With light in the darkness, even at the basic levels of despair, life will fight on. We sing about this frequently in church with hymns like ***Song of Hope*** and ***My Hope is in You.***

There is no clear measure of hope, or what it looks like, or how it moves and motivates, but there are many examples and illustrations that hope exists and is a basic and essential human need, and there is ample evidence that hope can master fear. Robert Fulghum, the author of the popular book ***All I Ever Really Needed to Know I Learned in Kindergarten***, wrote, "Hope always triumphs over experience and fears." Hymnists agree and put words in hymns to show how hope can conquer fear: ***My Hope is You; God Will Take Care of You; Hope Will Rise*** and others.

There is an undeniable relationship between fear and hope. Fear can conquer individuals and nations. Fear can undermine ambition and self-value. But not so easily when hope abounds. The presence of hope does not mean the absence of fear; just like the presence of courage does not mean the absence of fear, for what is courage if one is not fearful. Hope is the mother of inspiration and the enemy of fear. The fight against fear begins with hope and hope is the genesis of inspiration. Ultimately, it is the presence of inspiration that fuels the hope that combats the fear. It is the heart of inspiration that provides the tools of war against fear. If there are moments completely absent of fear, it is during moments of inspiration. Samuel Johnson wrote, "The natural flights of the human mind are not from pleasure to pleasure, but from hope to hope." The road from fear to hope is called inspiration.

Words can inspire hope, such as from motivational speeches, poems, and hymns, but words are not enough. The words must come alive in the heart and soul. The 17th-century English writer, John Bunyan, wrote, "Let your heart be without words then your words without heart." Words without heart are no match for fear.

The wonderful news is that the gift of hope can be found in words that are crafted and nurtured by the soul with a touch of divine inspiration.

Chapter Three
Inspiration

Try to be a rainbow in someone's cloud.

–Maya Angelou

Inspiration is as essential for life as food, water, and air because inspiration is hope's nutrition. Inspiration is around us every day, but we often don't recognize it. We miss many moments of inspiration. The most obvious example is inspiration in God-given moments—the sunrise with streaks of orange and soft reflections off of billowy clouds; a star-filled and cloudless warm summer night; the perfect and delicate design of a full bloom rose; the perfection of a nautilus seashell; a child's smile, and so many other miracles and minor miracles of inspiration.

Our lives are filled with so many challenges, fears, and distractions that inspiration does not seem so apparent. We become desensitized to inspiration, and we forget the promise of inspiration as the fuel for hope. *Jeremiah 29:11* reminds us that we should continue to look for inspiration: "For I know the plans I have for you, declares the Lord, plans for welfare and not for evil, to give you a future and a hope." Hymns such as ***All Things Bright and Beautiful*** remind of this.

The Bible and numerous hymns are filled with verses of inspiration and the link to hope and reassurance; so is literature. The poet Langston Hughes wrote, "Hold fast to dreams for if dreams die life is a broken-winged bird that cannot fly." Dreams are the seeds of inspiration, and dreams are inspired by hymns such as ***Be Thou My Vision*** and ***All Creatures of Our God and King***. These are hymns that encourage us to see and live the dream of hope and faith.

Without inspiration, we drag through life in a stupor and miss so many opportunities, so many beautiful moments, and so many potential moments of hope and strength. Strength to carry on in the face of stormy times comes from inspiration and inspiration comes from the recognition that we sometimes have to walk on hot coals of adversity and strength-sapping challenges, but lest we forget like Maya Angelou wrote, "We delight in the beauty of the butterfly, but rarely admit the changes it has gone through to achieve that beauty."

In addition to the sources of inspiration all around us in the beauty of nature, the voice of opportunity and blessings, words of inspiration and hope from the Bible, and literary works, there is another source of inspiration that is often overlooked—the inspiration in hymns.

Hymns are a bountiful source of inspiration, but too often during worship services singing hymns becomes a perfunctory duty to many parishioners. That is regrettable because the words are powerful, poetic, and are waiting to wash over our spirits as waves of inspiration. The music and the words move through and fill the air waiting to land softly on our hearts and in our souls, but too often we let them drift, with no invitation to nurture our inspiration.

The words of the hymnist sow love, forgiveness, faith, hope, grace, and joy—in other words, inspiration. Without the poems of hymns worshippers around the world would not feel the power to immerse their soul in the inspiration of God's message of light against darkness. We all need that light of inspiration, especially during difficult times when we go through each day in the dim light of fatigue, depression, and burdens.

Abraham Lincoln often found inspiration in hymns. It is said that Lincoln's favorite hymn was Isaac Watts' ***When I Can Read My Title Clear***.

> *When I can read my title clear to mansions in the skies, I'll bid farewell to every fear and wipe my weeping eyes. Should earth against my soul engage and fiery darts be hurled, then I can smile at Satan's rage and face a frowning world? Let cares, like a wild deluge come, and storms of sorrow fall! May I but safely reach my home, my*

God, my heaven my all. There shall I bathe my weary soul in seas of heavenly rest and not a wave of trouble roll across my peaceful breast.

Let us each lift the light of hope higher and help darkness find the light. Let us each embrace the inspiration that can touch our lives and souls in profound ways, in everlasting ways, in ways that inspire us to seek and comfort those who have lost touch with hope and inspiration and who live in darkness.

See the beauty of promise in the verses of modern hymns as well as those dating back centuries. Use the verses of inspired hymnists and poets who bear their souls for each of us so that we may shine a light so bright that fear shrinks away and hope lives.

Each day of each month of each year holds promise even during our most difficult times. Sometimes it only takes a moment of inspiration or reassurance to make it through a day or hour that is so painful it almost seems insurmountable and interminable. That small spark of inspiration may come from the beauty and simple words of a hymn, as hymnists lead us from the darkness and help us find the light.

Chapter Four
The Hymnists

Ackley, Alfred Henry

Henry was born in 1887 in Spring Hill, Pennsylvania. As a young boy, Alfred displayed considerable interest in music and began to develop musical skills as he grew older. He attended school locally until the family moved to New York City. Alfred's father paid close attention to his son's musical talents, and being a trained musician himself, he provided professional musical training for Alfred. Alfred's talents expanded and his father determined that Alfred needed more professional training than he could provide, so Alfred was sent to London to attend the Royal Academy of Music.

Entry to the Royal Academy of Music was difficult, but in an audition, it was immediately clear that Alfred was very talented and well-trained. Alfred's special skill was with the cello, and he quickly became a master cellist. He loved to play a variety of musical scores, including hymns. It was during the time that he began enjoying hymns that he also discovered an interest in theology. After completing his work at the Royal Academy of Music, Alfred enrolled at the Westminster Theological Seminary in Maryland. He combined his musical talents with his study of theology.

After completing his studies at the Westminster Theological Seminary, Alfred was ordained a Presbyterian minister at age twenty-seven. He was a minister first in Wilkes-Barre, Pennsylvania, and later at Elmhurst, Pennsylvania, before moving to Escondido, California. In California, Alfred met the famous evangelist, Billy Sunday, and traveled with Billy on the revival circuit. Billy encouraged Alfred to write hymns and he helped him with the themes of a few hymns. Alfred often said that Billy was a role model for him and at times a father-figure.

Beginning when he was a young man, and throughout his career and life, Alfred never stopped writing songs of all types, including hymns. Many of them were published, but after his death, more songs were found unpublished. Altogether it appears that Alfred wrote well over 1,500 songs and hymns. Several of Alfred's hymns were inspired by events, feelings, or circumstances. Arguably his most famous hymn is ***He Lives***, which remains very popular today around the Christian world. Alfred was inspired to write the hymn on Easter in 1932. In the days leading up to Easter, Alfred enjoyed the emerging signs of spring, with the return of birds, the appearance of jonquils, and the first greening of the trees. These observations combined with a question put to him (actually it was more of a challenge by one of his Jewish friends) that cast doubt on the resurrection of Jesus inspired Alfred to think of the best way to express the certainty and the power of resurrection. Alfred's response was life itself, how spring each year and every year resurrects from the "death" of winter. His best method of communication and inspiration was through verse; consequently, he began composing a hymn that would answer any doubts about the resurrection in an inspirational manner. The result of Alfred's efforts was the world-famous hymn, ***He Lives***. The hymn became incredibly popular and within a short period of time, it could be heard in many churches.

Alfred's reputation grew far beyond his wildest dreams. Even so, he remained humble about his hymns and his talent. Alfred continued to write and worship and was very active until he became seriously ill. After a brief illness, Alfred died in Whittier, California in 1960 at the age of 73.

(References: *Alfred Henry Ackley*, Hymntime.org. Retrieved 2013; *Alfred H. Ackley*, Hymnary.org. Retrieved 2013; *Alfred Henry Ackley*, Ackley Genealogy, Retrieved 2013)

Adams, Sarah Fuller

Sarah was born in 1805 in High Street, Old Harlow, Essex, England. Her father was Benjamin Flower, the founder, editor, and owner of the *Cambridge Intelligencer*, a popular and respected journal. One of her siblings became well-known, also. Her sister Eliza Flower became a successful composer. Sarah was a precocious child who enjoyed music, poetry, and especially plays. She dreamed of being an actress and later determined that acting was her destiny. However, Sarah had health issues throughout her life that curtailed her activities and particularly circumvented her acting career aspirations. Although she showed promise as an actress, she could not handle or cope with the rigorous practices necessary for stage plays; her physical endurance would not allow it. Sarah did have one glorious moment on the stage; she played Lady Macbeth, and apparently very successfully, for the critics gave positive reviews of her performance. Since Sarah did not have the physical stamina for the actress life she turned full-time to writing. She showed a gift for poetry and she was encouraged by her friends and family to be a poet. Many of her poems were published in several newspapers and magazines. Two of her most famous poems that sealed her reputation as a poet were ***Viva Perpetua*** and ***The Flock at the Fountain***. Sarah also wrote several hymns, many of them were included in Reverend William Johnson Fox's publication *Hymns and Anthems.* Her hymns were frequently sung at her church, the South Place Unitarian Church in Finsbury, London. Of her many poems and hymns, one became legendary and remains so today. She wrote the hymn ***Nearer, My God, to Thee***. This hymn is considered one of the most famous hymns of all time and remains one of the most frequently sung hymns in worship services.

Sarah traveled frequently with her family and friends. During one of her visits to other cities, Sarah met and soon thereafter married the popular, dashing inventor and engineer William Adams. Her popular poems and hymns and his successful inventions and engineering successes made them a well-known and socially sought-after couple. The world-famous poet Robert Browning was a friend of Sarah. Her portrait was painted by the famous Scottish painter Margaret Gillies, whose reputation had grown throughout Europe and America. She met and corresponded with Charles Dickens, Williams Wordsworth, Leigh Hunt and other famous people. Often times Sarah teamed up with her famous friends on causes that benefitted children and expanded educational opportunities for girls and young women.

Sarah continued to write even when her health became a serious concern to her husband and friends. She never complained but it was obvious from her weight loss and a persistent cough that she was not well and she was growing weaker each week. William sought medical advice from around the world and took Sarah to coastal climates that he thought would give her relief from her difficulty breathing. Despite her courageous battle and William's efforts, Sarah died from tuberculosis in 1848 in St. Martin-in-the-Fields, Middlesex, England at the age of forty-three.

Her legendary hymn ***Nearer, My God, to Thee*** became destined for immortality when the eight musicians aboard the sinking *Titanic* played the hymn as the last selection before the ship broke up and sank.

(References: *Sacred Poets of the 19th Century*, 1907, Alfred H. Miles. Retrieved through Bartleby, 2014; *Sarah Flower Adams*, The Canterbury Dictionary of Hymnology. Retrieved 2014; *Sarah Fuller Flower Adams—Beautiful Poetess*, 2011, Reflections Issue #504, Al Maxey)

Akers, Doris Mae

Doris was born in 1923 in Brookfield, Missouri. Her family was large; she had nine siblings. When Doris was young her family moved to Kirksville, Missouri.

Doris was a lovely child who was always smiling and singing. She loved music and she loved to perform for her siblings and friends. Doris taught herself how to play the piano and learned to play by ear. But she was more than a child trying to learn a few songs; instead, Doris had a natural talent for music and a gifted ear for songs. At Bethel A.M.E. Church in Kirksville, Doris learned how to sing and play gospel music. By the time she was ten years old she had written her first song, ***Keep the Fire Burning in Me***.

Doris enjoyed performing and decided to make that her career. When she was a teenager, Doris formed a singing group with her siblings called *Dot and The Swingsters* that included her brothers Edward, Marian, and Donald. They performed a variety of songs and hymns in churches and community centers for a few years before each one decided to pursue other interests.

Against the advice of her mother, Doris moved out of her parent's house and was on her own at age twenty-two. She had saved money so that she could pursue a music career. Doris moved to Los Angeles where she was spotted singing in a church by a talent agent and was signed to a contract with the *Sallie Martin Singers,* a group that was at the time famous across the nation.

Doris was more than a musical talent, she was a life-long learner and curious about more than just composing and singing. She wanted to learn about all facets of music, including the business of music. Her interest in business methods evolved after watching Sallie Martin solve complicated business problems.

Two years after joining the *Sallie Martin Singers,* Doris left the group and started her own group when she was twenty-four years old. She soon published her first hymn, ***I Want a Double Portion of God's Love.*** With the team of Dorothy Simmons and Hattie Hawkins, they had many successful recordings. Doris would later release several of her own recordings to much fame and rewards. She won back-to-back Gospel Composer of the Year Awards. Her most famous hymn was ***Lord, Don't Move the Mountain,*** which sold over one million records. She also became the director of the *Sky Pilot Choir* which went on to make records and perform on radio and television.

Doris was a prolific writer and performer. She was at one time known as "Miss Gospel Music," not only for her own success but also because many of her compositions made stars of other performers, often selling millions of records for those recording artists. Doris often credited her faith and God's grace for her success. She explained one time that her work was inspired by divine intervention. As an example, she said that one of her most popular songs, ***Sweet, Sweet Spirit,*** came to her during a prayer session with one of her choirs, just before a church service began.

Growing tired of the growth and congestion in Los Angeles, Doris moved to Columbus, Ohio, after almost forty years in Los

Angeles. She lived her final years in Minneapolis, Minnesota, where she died in 1995 at the age of seventy-two. Just prior to her death, Doris was honored by the Smithsonian Institute as "the foremost black gospel songwriter in the United States." Shortly after her death, Doris was inducted into the Gospel Music Hall of Fame.

(References: *Doe and Dove—The Doris Akers Singers Story*, 2005, Opal Louis Nations; *Doris Mae Akers*, Encyclopedia of American Gospel Music, 2013, W.K. McNeil. Retrieved 2015; *The Golden Age of Gospel*, 1995, Horace Clarence Boyer)

Alexander, Cecil Frances

Cecil was born in Dublin, Ireland in 1823, as the third child and youngest daughter to Major John Humphreys, who held the high position of land agent for the 4th Earl of Wicklow. Cecil was a very active and precocious child. She was very talkative and inquisitive about books, gardens, and many other topics. Her parents often directed her to books to satisfy her energetic curiosity.

From her love of books, she discovered a fascination with poetry. Cecil tried writing poetry and found that she had a talent for writing even at a very young age. With encouragement from her father and training from other poets, Cecil wrote several poems, particularly narrative poems that were widely read and admired. Her poetry became so well known that Lord Alfred Tennyson once said that he would have been proud to have written her poems. He especially admired her poem ***The Burial of Moses***.

Cecil turned to writing hymns when she saw the link between poetry and hymns. By 1840, at age seventeen, she was so gifted that some of her hymns were included in the Church of Ireland hymn books. During her lifetime, she composed over 400 hymns. Her book ***Hymns for Little Children*** had an incredible sixty-nine editions. Some of her hymns like ***All Things Bright and Beautiful***; ***There is a Green Hill Far Away***, and the Christmas carol ***Once in Royal David's City*** are still known around the world. Her hymn ***There is a Green Hill Far Away*** became a very popular hymn during World War I, because of the hope it conveyed.

Cecil married Reverend William Alexander who later became the Archbishop of Armagh, Ireland, and Primate of Ireland. They were married for forty-five years.

In addition to her devotion to hymns and poetry, Cecil had a kind heart for families living in poverty. She often ministered to the poor. She was widely admired for her work with the families, as well as her advocacy for them. Cecil saved much of the money she made from poems and hymns so that she and her sister could establish a school for the deaf, the Derry and Raphoe Diocesan Institution, which was the first school for the deaf in that area of the country. The school provided education, health care, and inspiration for the deaf.

When Cecil died in 1895 at the age of seventy-two, she was mourned by a world of grateful Christians and numerous people who benefitted from her kind and generous heart. Her funeral was attended by hundreds of admirers.

(References: *Voices in Ireland,* 1994, P.J. Kavanagh; *Poems of Cecil Frances Alexander,* Poemhunter.org. Retrieved 2014; *A Life of the Hymnwriter Cecil Frances Alexander,* 1995, Valerie Wallace)

Alford, Henry

Henry was born in 1810 in London, England. Henry was destined to be a clergyman because he was born into a family of clergymen—going back five generations. Each generation produced an Anglican minister. Henry's father was the Curate of Steeple Ashton in Wiltshire, England. Henry was proud of his father but he was very close to his mother. His world was crushed after his beloved mother died at a young age. For several years, Henry's grief deepened over the loss of his mother; at times he was inconsolable. His recovery was slow and painful, as he took the long, lonely journey from grief and depression. Henry later attributed the genesis of his healing to his retreat into reading; it was the only relief he felt from grief.

Henry was a gifted child whose intellectual talents were recognized and encouraged by his father. Henry read every book in the house and spent considerable time in the local church's library. He was an extraordinary student at the school. His teachers found it difficult to challenge him intellectually. Also, Henry learned to write at an early age and showed remarkable literary skills. He wrote several Latin poems (odes) before he was ten years old. Henry became fascinated by the stories of the ancient Jews. Consequently, before he entered secondary school he had written a long history of the Jewish heritage.

Henry's intellectual prowess led to his early admission at Trinity College at Cambridge. Both his intellect and insight were remarkable. Henry became the top student at the college. Due to his growing reputation at Trinity, based on the unusually high quality of his work, he was named a theological scholar at age seventeen and was named a Fellow of Cambridge at age twenty-four.

Henry was ordained into the Anglican Church at age twenty-five and immediately became the Vicar of Wymeswold in Leicestershire, England. He remained there for eighteen years. During that time, he was also a lecturer at Cambridge University. His reputation as a scholar and minister spread across England and Europe. Henry's interests included poetry and metaphysics which led to his membership by invitation in the Cambridge Camden Society and the Metaphysical Society.

After a few years at Wymeswold, he accepted the position of Vicar at Quebec Street Chapel in Marylebone, England, which was part of greater London. Quebec Street Chapel had a large congregation, but when word got out that the famous Henry Alford was coming to the church the membership increased rapidly. Four years later Henry was named Deanery of Canterbury, a high office in the Anglican Church.

Henry continued to write poetry, hymns, scholarly papers, and he edited publications for the Anglican Church. He also edited the works of the famous writer and poet John Donne.

Henry's many talents included illustrations in books such as ***The Riviera***. His other publications were also popular, such as ***The School of the Heart***; ***The Abbot of Muchelnaye***; ***The Greek***

Testament and many others. Henry's book ***The Four Gospels*** pleased both the public and scholars, which was very rare during that era. Of his many hymns, perhaps the most popular then and in modern times are ***Come, Ye Thankful People Come*** and ***Ten Thousand Times Ten Thousand***.

Despite his hectic and demanding schedule, he found time to translate the ***Odyssey*** and became the first editor of the *Contemporary Review*, which became a popular periodical. With publications too numerous to list and accomplishments that are remarkable, Henry's legendary reputation rests largely on his eight-volume edition of the ***New Testament in Greek*** which contained the readings of the main manuscripts and research of the finest scholarship of the time, including his own research. In some theological studies even today, over 150 years later, scholars cull through the eight volumes to glean information for research. The eight volumes took him twenty years to complete.

Henry remained active with his remarkably diverse interests until his death in Canterbury, Kent, England in 1871 at the age of sixty-one. He wrote his own epitaph for his cemetery marker: "The inn of a pilgrim traveling to Jerusalem." Henry was buried at St. Martin's in Canterbury. He is considered one of England's greatest intellectual and creative giants.

(References: *Henry Alford,* Cambridge Alumni Database, University of Cambridge. Retrieved 2015; *The Gospels in Hymns,* 1950, Albert Edward Bailey)

Ambrose of Milan

Ambrose was born in 340 in Augusta Treverorum, Belgica, Gaul as the second son of a Prefect, Aurelius Ambrosius the Praetorian Prefect of Gaul (a magistrate or imperial viceroy). When Ambrose's father died the family relocated to Rome. There Ambrose lived with his mother and sister, who was a nun. The older siblings had already moved to Rome prior to their father's death.

In Rome, Ambrose was raised in privilege and wealth, because his mother's family was wealthy and because his father made numerous friends in powerful positions before his death the family still carried much political influence. Because of his family's political power and wealth, the palace that he lived in was frequented by politicians, scholars, and clergymen. Most of them were seeking power and/or influence since Ambrose's widowed mother was a woman of great influence through her wealth, intellect, political acumen and integrity. A word of support from her could expedite a suitor's career. Ambrose's older siblings were as righteous as their mother and both received sainthood, as would Ambrose later in his life.

Ambrose benefited from the finest education a student could receive in Rome. He had a parade of Rome's best and finest tutors and teachers. Ambrose was intelligently gifted, being blessed with a photographic memory. His intelligence, his good looks, and his charming personality were considered by many to be the gifts of the gods. A myth arose about him that would become legend. The legend claims that a swarm of bees came through an open window and descended upon Ambrose's face when he was just a few days old. But instead of attacking the defenseless baby, they flew away and left droplets of honey on his face. Ambrose thereafter was considered a gift to Rome and that is why Saint Ambrose's symbol includes bees and beehives.

Ambrose's education was geared to allow him to follow his father as a Prefect. At a young age, the Prefect Probus insured that Ambrose was appointed to the Rome Council and a few years later sponsored him as Consular Prefect (similar to a regional Governor) of Liguria (northwestern Italy, bordering France and Emilia. Emilia-Romagna was one of the wealthiest and most developed regions in Italy). He governed the region from Milan which was second only to Rome as a seat of power and wealth. Ambrose was a beloved leader. He developed an interest in the church and theology and tried to rule based on the principles of benevolence. Ambrose became so popular with the citizens of the region that it led to an awkward situation for him.

In an unusual set of circumstances, he became the Bishop of Milan. A furor erupted between the Catholics and the Arians when the Bishop of Milan died. The conflict threatened the stability of the entire region. When the Bishop of Milan died, who was an Arian, the conflict between the two groups over the selection of the next Bishop evolved into a crisis. Ambrose stepped into the fracas to resolve the issue. He went to the podium to offer mediation but his speech was repeatedly interrupted with the growing chant, "Ambrose—Bishop of Milan". He refused the offer because he had no theological training or experience. He was, in fact, a Catholic, but the Arians trusted him explicitly. Therefore, much to his dismay, he was selected Bishop of Milan by a united proclamation of the Catholics and Arians. Despite the confidence showed in him from both sides, Ambrose went into hiding to avoid the appointment. He thought his selection would be forgotten and someone else would be appointed. Instead, the Catholic and Arian leaders petitioned the assistance of the Roman Emperor Gratian who sent an edit to Ambrose appointing him Bishop of Milan after he received training. The Emperor made it clear that the training would begin immediately and would be intense and brief. Accordingly, Ambrose was baptized, ordained and consecrated Bishop of Milan. All of this happened in only one week.

As soon as he became Bishop, Ambrose adopted an ascetic lifestyle, arranged for his wealth to be distributed to the poor, except for a portion for his sister Marcellina, and he donated the land he owned for sale to raise money to care for the poor. He called upon his brother to handle the financial care of their family. Ambrose's sacrifice raised his popularity to unbelievable heights. Many people began calling him a saint for his noble gestures and his kind and giving heart. In addition to being a leader, he was also a teacher.

Ambrose became the teacher of several young prodigies during his time as Bishop. One of his students was Augustine, who Ambrose converted and baptized. Augustine would later become St. Augustine of Hippo and the legendary author of *The City of God*.

Ambrose developed an interest in the music of worship. He encouraged and helped develop the style of chanting in which one side of the choir responds alternately to the other side of the choir. This was called the antiphonal chant. He also composed hymns, including Christmas hymns. Ambrose became a theology scholar as well. His literary writings are considered even today as masterpieces of Latin prose.

As a devoted Bishop, Ambrose's popularity gave him enormous political influence. Even the Emperor of Rome respected Ambrose's power of popularity and called on him often for advice. Ambrose established the medieval concept of a Christian emperor as a dutiful son of the church "serving under orders from Christ," and therefore subject to the advice and strictures of the Bishop.

Ambrose remained in Milan for several years and only retired to Bologna, Italy after Emperor Theodosius took power. Theodosius did not hold Ambrose in high regard; in fact, he considered Ambrose a threat to his power. Ambrose also spent time in Florence before returning to Milan after Theodosius left Rome. Ambrose lived the remainder of his life in his beloved Milan where he was revered and honored in many ways.

He continued to speak out for the poor and offered them aid until his death in 397 at the age of fifty-seven. The Catholic Church later named Ambrose a Saint. Ambrose's body can be viewed in the Church of St. Ambrogio in Milan.

(References: *Lives of Saints,* 1991, Michael Butler Walsh; *The Life and Times of St. Ambrose,* 1935 F. Homes Defarrari; *The Penguin Dictionary of Saints,* 1993, Catherine Rachael John and Donald Attwater)

Augustine of Hippo

Augustine was born in 354 in Algeria, Africa, which was at the time part of the Roman Empire. His family was divided in their religious beliefs, with his mother being a devout Christian while his father was a Pagan. Although his father converted to Christianity as he was dying, in Augustine's early years he was a witness to outrageous verbal fights between his parents over their religious differences. Despite their well-known verbal fights, his family was close and very supportive of each other.

Augustine's family was high in the social order and seemed wealthy and popular in the community. Because of the family's social standing, Augustine's first language was Latin. He was taught at home until the age of eleven, when he was sent to a bordering school in M'Daourouch (then called Madaurus), a small city near Thagaste, Algeria (a Roman colony). He received an education rich in thought, religious survey (including Paganism and Christianity), and languages.

Although Augustine was raised in a religiously conscious family, he followed a hedonistic lifestyle with other youth who recognized no religion and very few morals. Augustine was influenced by his classmates in a negative way and was a follower until he and his friends stole fruit from a vendor for no particular reason one day. Augustine immediately regretted this transgression; consequently, he took more control of his own life and decisions and was less prone to follow the crowd.

Always a prodigious reader, his maturing intellect was influenced by the writings of Cicero, a Roman politician and philosopher, and Plotinus, a neo-Platonist. At the age of seventeen, Augustine moved to Carthage to study rhetoric, in the tradition of Cicero. He adopted the Manichaean religion, which he knew ran contrary to Christianity and would trouble his mother. Augustine faithfully practiced his faith, but he read extensively about other cultures and religions.

Augustine took a teaching position and taught grammar at Thagaste in 373. Two years later he moved to Carthage to teach rhetoric, but that did not last long because the students were unruly and disrespectful of him and showed no interest in his teaching. Augustine sought the advice and guidance of more experienced teachers, but they offered him no assistance. Consequently, he moved to establish his own rhetoric school in Rome in 383, which was successful and influential.

Throughout his life, Augustine's mother continued to urge him to embrace Christianity. He rejected her efforts until a turning point in his life led to his conversion to Christianity—he met Ambrose, Bishop of Milan. Ambrose greatly influenced Augustine both in spirit and intellectually. Ambrose's compelling personality, searing intellect, saintly presence and demeanor provided Augustine with a model to follow that would lead to his conversion to Christianity. In 387, Augustine accepted Christ and was immediately baptized. Once he became a Christian, he delved deep into reading what was available about Christianity. Through his studies and prayer, he developed his own beliefs about philosophy and theology. Augustine determined that religion was essential for civilization, and it was the element that held civilization together. He believed that without religion and faith, beliefs, guidance, and structure provided through it, civilization would break down. That is primarily why he became gravely concerned about the decline of the Roman Empire. He worried that civil disorder would prevail and Paganism or some other belief would destroy Christianity.

In response to his fears he conceptualized and wrote the legendary and almost mythical book the ***City of God***, which later would become the genesis of the Catholic Church. Augustine's ***City of God*** is a masterwork of philosophy, spirituality, religion, social order, intellectual structure, and social insight.

Due in large part to his publications, teaching ability, and leadership, he became the Coadjutor of Hippo and later full Bishop, which is how he became known as Augustine of Hippo.

Augustine lived a long and productive life. His influence was felt throughout the Christian world, and his writings, hymns, and treatises are still popular today. His book the ***City of God*** has remained in print for over 1,500 years.

Augustine died in 430 at the age of seventy-six. Augustine was declared a saint in the Catholic Church and in the Anglican Communion. He is credited with the original teachings on salvation and divine grace. More than 350 of his sermons have survived, and many of them have been the inspiration for hymns. He wrote poetic hymns, and he sometimes used the themes of the hymns in his sermons.

References: *Augustine of Hippo,* 2000, Peter Brown; *The Anti-Pelagian Christology of Augustine of Hippo,* 2012, Dominic Keech; *Works of St. Augustine of Hippo,* Catholic Encyclopedia. Retrieved 2013; *Augustine for the Philosophers,* 2014, Calvin Troup)

Babcock, Maltbie Davenport

Maltbie was born in 1858 in Syracuse, New York, into a wealthy family. Maltbie came from a long line of descendants prominent in the settlement of Portsmouth, Rhode Island. Also, his relatives were prominent in college education and religion, with several leaders in each field.

Maltbie was a strong, smart, active and gregarious boy who was involved in activities of some type each day. He was easily bored, so he was always looking for something to do. He was very athletic and loved the competition of baseball and swimming, and he enjoyed hiking and climbing mountains and trees. Also, he was an excellent student in public school and very popular with other students and the teaching staff. Maltbie was expected to attend college and he was eager for the college experience.

He enrolled at Syracuse University where he was very successful. Maltbie's brilliance, gregarious nature, and creative genius truly blossomed at the university. He played on the baseball team, won awards for public speaking, and participated in musical productions and plays. He was also a member of the prestigious Psi Upsilon Fraternity. Maltbie developed an interest in religion and began a lifetime of reading and studying all things related to religion, theology, and the Bible. Maltbie graduated with highest honors in 1879 at the age of twenty-one.

After graduating from Syracuse University he attended Auburn Theological Seminary in New York where he completed his theology degree in less than three years. After graduation, Maltbie was invited to become the pastor of Lockport Presbyterian Church in Lockport, New York. The congregation had never heard anyone like him before. The power, intellect, and spirituality of his sermons became legendary. Word of his abilities spread rapidly across the state and eventually into other parts of the country.

Due to his growing reputation, Maltbie became the minister of the prestigious and world-known Brown Memorial Presbyterian Church in Baltimore, Maryland. He wrote remarkable sermons, but he also wrote hymns and poems. Maltbie's restlessness included an intellectual curiosity about many things and from that he brought new ideas into his sermons, hymns and poems. Within just a few years at Brown Memorial, Maltbie had become famous worldwide for his brilliant sermons and oratorical magic. He also worked tirelessly to provide support to poverty-stricken families and supported fundraising events to meet the needs of local families as well as missionary needs abroad.

After three years at Brown Memorial, he was offered the senior minister position at the prestigious Brick Church of New York City, where they offered him a $30,000 annual salary—a very high income in that era. Members of Brown Memorial as well as the Baltimore City community pleaded with Maltbie to stay. John Hopkins University in Baltimore offered him an endowed professorship if he remained at Brown Memorial. Despite the outpouring that touched his heart and soul, Maltbie was thrilled by the new challenge so he accepted the position in New York City.

Known to only a few people, Maltbie struggled through much of his life with bouts of severe depression, some of which were almost debilitating. In fact, at age thirty-two he sunk into a serious depression that threatened his career if not his life. Somehow he was able to keep it a secret and his productivity and sermons showed no signs of his internal turmoil.

Maltbie's career took an unexpected and tragic turn in 1901 when he was forty-two years old. That year he went on a trip to the Holy Land with several lay persons and other theologians. While in Jerusalem he contracted a bacterial infection that was dreadful to endure. He fought pain, fever, nausea, and depression. At times, Maltbie was delirious with pain and suffering. Having battled depression much of his life, the depression coupled with almost unbearable physical pain was more than he could endure. Maltbie took his own life while he was being treated at the International Hospital in Naples, Italy. It was later determined that he had brucellosis, a bacterial infection that is spread from unpasteurized dairy products.

Maltbie was buried at Oakwood Cemetery in Syracuse, New York after a memorial that included some of the most prominent people in the state and country. At the funeral, which was attended by over a thousand mourners, his wife read a poem that Maltbie wrote entitled ***This is My Father's World***. His wife told the grieving crowd that when Maltbie needed to take a walk around the beautiful Niagara area with its expansive vistas, he would tell her that he was "going out to see my Father's world." He was just short of his forty-third birthday when he died.

In 1905 in memory of Maltbie's life, Brown Memorial Presbyterian Church installed a magnificent stain glass window that depicts several figures from nature.

(References: *A History of Brown Memorial Presbyterian Church 1870-1995*, 1995, Jane T. Swope; *Funeral of Reverend Dr. Babcock*, The New York Times, June 13, 1901. Retrieved from archives 2014; *Sacred Glass: The Tiffany Windows of Brown Memorial Park Avenue Presbyterian Church*, 2005, Joan Feldman; *Christian Hymnody in 20th Century Britain and America*, 2001, David W. Music)

Baker, Henry William

Henry was born in 1821 in Vauxhall, Surrey, England. He was born into a famous family as the eldest son. His father was Vice Admiral Henry Loraine Baker, who became a national hero for his distinguished service at the Battle of Guadeloupe in 1815 (the last battle of the Napoleonic Wars between France and England). Henry's grandfather was well known, also. He was Sir Robert Baker of Dunstable House, Surrey, and Nicholashayne (south of Wellington, England) who was conferred a baronetcy in 1796, which Henry inherited upon the death of his father in 1859, as the third baronet, so he became Sir Henry Baker.

As a youth, Henry was very studious and serious-minded, probably because of the orderly family tradition. He also enjoyed boating, music, and many other activities. Being the eldest son, he faced high expectations from his parents, and he tried very diligently to live up to those expectations socially and intellectually.

Henry attended Trinity College at Cambridge to study theology, and after graduating he was ordained in 1844. Shortly thereafter, he accepted the position of Assistant Curate of Great Hockesley, near Colchester, Essex. There he impressed his superiors and colleagues with his dedication, intellect, and insight. He greatly enjoyed his seven years there.

In 1851, he became Vicar of Monkland Priory Church in Herefordshire, England. His service there allowed him to explore his enjoyment of music, and it was during that time he began in earnest to write hymns. Also, from 1860 to 1877, Henry was editor-in-chief of the Anglican hymnal ***Hymns Ancient and Modern***, to which he contributed hymns, tunes, and translations. This historic hymnal was widely popular, selling an incredible 60 million copies. Henry's most acclaimed hymns were ***Oh, What If We Are Christ's*** and ***There is a Blessed Home***.

After suffering from uneven health for over two years, Henry died in 1877 at the age of fifty-six. It was reported by his life-long friend, John Ellerton, that Henry's dying words were from one of his famous hymns: "Perverse and foolish oft I strayed, but yet in love He sought me, and on His shoulder gently laid, and home, rejoicing, brought me."

Henry was buried at Monkland in the churchyard of the parish. A stained glass window in the church where he worked and worshiped is dedicated to his memory.

(References: *Church Hymnal: By Permission of the General Synod*, Church of Ireland, 1900; *Henry Williams Baker*, 1999, Dictionary of

National Biography; *Henry Williams Baker,* Hymnary.org. Retrieved 2014; *Henry Williams Bake*r, Cyberhymnal.org. Retrieved 2015)

Baring-Gould, Sabine

Sabine was born on January 28, 1834, in the parish of St. Sidwell, Exeter, England as the first son of Edward Baring-Gould and his first wife, Sophia Charlotte. Sabine was named after a great-uncle, the Arctic explorer, Sir Edward Sabine.

In his youth, Sabine had very little formal education, because the family spent much of the time traveling around the world. Sabine's exposure to the world's cultures, traditions, religions, and languages became his education. Sabine was a very intelligent and studious youth, and although he did not have a formal education, his performance on entrance exams allowed his admission at Cambridge University.

Sabine's knowledge from his visits to several countries served him very well at Cambridge. He was an extraordinary student who excelled in languages, the classics, and philosophy. Sabine earned a Bachelor of Arts degree with honors. He then enrolled at Clare College, Cambridge, where just two years later he received a Master of Arts degree.

At various times in his career, he was an English Anglican priest, architect, hagiographer (a biographer of saints), antiquarian (collector of antiques), archeologist, novelist and eclectic scholar. He became a prodigious writer. His publications include more than 1,240 hymns, articles, and books.

Sabine reached immortality with one hymn. He wrote the words to ***Onward, Christian Soldiers***, which is one of the most famous Christian hymns ever written. Sabine found inspiration for the hymn when he was trying to create a song for children to sing as they traveled together from a community event to a church event. Sabine found what he needed while reading a reference in the New Testament to followers and believers being a soldier for Christ—*Timothy* 2:3. The music for the hymn was composed by Arthur Sullivan. ***Onward, Christian Soldiers*** has been played in many famous settings, including on board the British warship *HMS Prince of Wales* during one of the legendary meetings of Winston Churchill and Franklin D. Roosevelt. In fact, it was during that event that Churchill and Roosevelt were both brought to tears by the power of the hymn in that setting with two nations and hundreds of soldiers and sailors singing the hymn at sea. Churchill and Roosevelt reported that it was difficult to adequately describe the power of that moment.

The hymn was also played at President Dwight D. Eisenhower's funeral and at many other funerals of famous people. The hymn has found its way into the modern culture; it is heard in several major movies, including *Elmer Gantry, A Canterbury Tale, MASH,* and many others. It has also been played on numerous television shows.

Sabine died in 1924, at the age of eighty-nine, after a long and productive life of writing hymns that were rich with insight and inspiration, but he will forever be remembered for ***Onward Christian Soldiers***.

(References: *Who's Who,* Volume 59: p. 91, 1907; *Early Family Correspondence of Sabine Baring-Gould,* 2010, Ron Wawman; *Sabine Baring-Gould,* Time Magazine, June 1957; *Sabine Baring-Gould,* Oxford Dictionary of National Biography, Retrieved 2015)

Bartlett, Eugene

Eugene was born in 1885 in Waynesville, Missouri on Christmas Eve. His family soon moved to Sebastian County, Arkansas to live with relatives. The family lived in a humble dwelling with few provisions, but they were deeply religious and generous with their time to the community.

Eugene was baptized at a very young age. He was a good student and from a very early age dreamed of a career in music. He learned to play three musical instruments and tried his hand at writing music while he was still in his teens.

After he graduated from high school, Eugene applied to Hall-Moody Institute in Martin, Tennessee, which later became the University of Tennessee at Martin. Because of his stellar academic record in high school, his work in the community, and his ability to play and write music, he was awarded a scholarship. In college, he majored in music with hopes of becoming a music teacher. After graduating from the University of Tennessee at Martin, Eugene enrolled at William Jewell College in Liberty, Missouri where he received training as a music teacher.

Through hard work and continuous self-improvement, Eugene became one of the finest music teachers in the south, and his reputation grew as he traveled around the southern states teaching music and training teachers of music how to teach music in more effective and innovative ways. He provided music lessons in several states with a focus on voice development, sight reading, and composition. Many times he was invited to schools of music to improve music instruction. Eugene also had a love of gospel music and over time developed a devotion to gospel music and the creation of hymns that influenced several church music programs.

The demand for his services and teaching skills grew so rapidly that Eugene could not keep up his hectic schedule. He decided that it was time to reduce his time on the road and settle into a more stable lifestyle.

Eugene wanted to remain in music, so he looked for a job in that field. He took a job at the Central Music Company where he learned about the music publishing business. After acquiring the knowledge and experience necessary to understand how the music publishing industry operated, he convinced two friends to partner with him to start the Hartford Music Company in Hartford, Arkansas. The company published music lessons, songs, hymns, and other music materials. His own book of hymns sold over 15,000 copies in the first year of publication. Over time, the Hartford Music Company became one of the country's most important gospel music publishing companies. He also became the editor of the music magazine *Herald of Song*.

Due to his phenomenal influence on the gospel music publishing world, Eugene was a founding father of what would be called the "Southern Gospel Music Movement," not only because of his prolific composing of hymns, but also because his company recognized and encouraged talented musicians such as Albert Brumley who wrote hit songs like ***I'll Fly Away*** and ***Turn Your Radio On.***

Although he enjoyed his business, Eugene's first love remained the composition of hymns. He wrote more than 800 of them, and he influenced his son to be a composer of gospel music, also. Unfortunately, many of Eugene's songs have faded from memory and recognition, but one remains an endearing tribute to his love of life and gospel music, ***Victory in Jesus,*** which he wrote while recovering from a serious stroke at the age of fifty-four.

Eugene was essentially bed-ridden after the stroke. He was physically weak and his speech was impaired, but his mind was active and creative. Eugene greatly missed working, and he worried about his company. Even though he was gravely ill and had understandable reasons for slipping into depression, Eugene fought on. The source of his strength was his endearing love of music and his faith. Determined to improve and under the most challenging physical and emotional stress, Eugene continued to compose hymns until his death in 1941 at the age of fifty-six in Siloam Springs, Arkansas.

In 1973, Eugene was inducted into the Gospel Music Association's Hall of Fame.

(References: *E.M. Bartlett 1885-1941*, The Encyclopedia of Arkansas History. Retrieved 2014; *The Songbook Gospel Movement in Arkansas*, 2001, David Deller; *Close Harmony of Southern Gospel*, 2002, James Goff)

Bateman, Christian Henry

Christian was born in 1813 in Lower Wyke, Yorkshire, England, to John Frederick Bateman and Mary Agnes (La Trobe) Bateman. He had three brothers and two sisters. Christian's family members were long-standing contributors to the needs of the Lower Wyke community. The family's life was simple but filled with activities and interactions with neighbors and other family members. They were regular members of the local Moravian Church.

Christian was an intelligent and thoughtful child who adored his parents and siblings. He loved to read and explore the surrounding countryside with his brothers. Christian's education was mostly from what he learned at home and in the church. He decided at a young age that his primary interest was religion, but he also developed an interest in languages and literature while studying religion in the Moravian church.

Upon completion of his church-based education, Christian served as minister at the local church in Wyke. At the age of thirty, he became the minister of the Richmond Place Congregational Church in Edinburgh, Scotland. Thereafter, he served as a minister in churches at Hopton, Yorkshire, and Reading.

Christian was always seeking a deeper understanding of scripture and faith, so he was a tireless reader who used what he read to broaden his message to his congregations. He took Holy Orders and served as Curate of St. Luke's Penymyndd, Hawarden for seven years. During that time, Christian also wrote and composed hymns, such as ***The Sacred Song Book***, which was later published as ***Sacred Melodies for Children*** and as ***200 Sacred Melodies for Sunday Schools and Families***. Other versions of his work appeared as ***The Children's Hymnal and Christian Year,*** which contained over 250 hymns. It is estimated that altogether his various song/hymn books sold over six million copies. Countless numbers of adults and children have enjoyed singing many of Christian's songs, particularly ***Come Children, Join to Sing,*** which was changed to ***Come Christians, Join to Sing.***

Christian was very proud of the hymns and the positive effect they had on children. He was often seen with tears in his eyes when he heard children singing his hymns.

Christian died in 1889 at the age of seventy-six in Carlisle, England. He died with family and friends present at his bedside. A children's choir sang ***Come Children, Join to Sing*** during the eulogy which was attended by hundreds of women, men, and children who adored Christian and his many hymns.

(References: *Making Preaching Less of a Chore and More of a Joy,* 2007, Richard Niell Donovan; *Genealogy for Christian Henry Bateman,* Genealogy Bank. Retrieved 2014; *Christian Henry Bateman 1813-1889,* Hymntime.org, Retrieved 2015; *British Hymn Writers and Composers,* 1977, Andrew Hayden and Robert Newton)

Bayly, Albert Fredrick

Albert was born in 1901 in Bexhill on the Sea, Sussex, England. As a young boy living near the sea and watching ships come and go at the nearby docks, he was influenced by the life of the sea and those who made a living working with the sea. Albert loved ships and frequently built his own small model ships.

He was a bright student in school but he was frequently distracted by his love of the sea. Albert was a frequent visitor to the docks, and he enjoyed talking with the sailors and sneaking on to anchored ships for brief visits. He also enjoyed music and took up a few instruments casually. He seemed to have a natural talent and ear for the music of various types. However, Albert from a young age intended to become a shipbuilder.

At age fifteen, he attended school at the Royal Dockyard School in Portsmouth to be a shipwright (shipbuilder). Upon completion of the training he worked in the shipyard for a few years, but he discovered that he had other interests. His keen mind was always exploring many different things. He wanted more intellectual challenges.

Albert told his parents that he wanted to go to college. With their encouragement, he completed an application to enroll at London University. To everyone's surprise, he was accepted. Within four years he earned a Bachelor of Arts degree and during that time he developed an interest in religion and philosophy. After his successful studies at London University, he attended Mansfield College, Oxford University where he continued his studies in religion. All the while Albert remained active with his music. His first published hymn was included in *More Hymns and Spiritual Songs* which was a book of hymns by an Episcopal publisher.

After receiving his Master of Divinity degree, he was ordained a Congregationalist at the age of twenty-eight, and for the next forty years, he served as a minister in Sussex, Lancashire, East Yorkshire, and finally at Essex.

Albert retired from active ministry in 1972 and moved to Chelmsford, England where he was an active member of the local church and community. He planned and participated in several musical plays and productions, often writing the scripts and composing the music. Albert worked in the local church and community until his death in 1984 in Sussex at the age of eighty-three.

During his lifetime, Albert composed dozens of hymns that covered text from the Old Testament as well as other areas of spirituality, including favorites such as ***What Does the Lord Require***. However, Albert is most known for a series of "***Rejoice***" hymns which are found in most Christian hymnals around the world.

(References: *Rejoice O People: Hymns and Poems of Albert Bayly*, 1964, Albert Bayly; *Albert Bayly-What Does the Lord Require*, UMC History of Hymns, 2011, Henry Waters; *Albert Bayly*, Hymntime.org. Retrieved 2015)

Bell, John Lamberton

John was born in 1949 in Kilmarnock, Ayrshire, Scotland. He and his family enjoyed music and frequently sang songs together around the dinner table and after dinner in the gathering room.

John was a spirited and loving child who enjoyed running around the countryside and befriending almost everyone he met. He also greatly enjoyed singing and listening to music of all types. He decided at a young age that he wanted to be a music teacher. That was his goal until he turned seventeen years old.

During the year of his seventeenth birthday, John experienced a call to the ministry. He felt like the Holy Spirit touched his life and inspired him to minister to people about the word of God. He attended the University of Scotland where he planned to study liberal arts, theology, and music. However, John was too restless to settle into the routine of university classes. He was particularly disappointed in his music classes because he found them dull, listless, and solely academic with no connection with the ministry. Also, the religion classes were too academic and less spiritual than he expected. John was used to the spiritedness and beauty and vitality of music and worship.

After his junior year at the university, he left to do volunteer work in a socioeconomically depressed neighborhood near London. He was shocked at the poverty, depravity, and lack of basic services to meet the needs of the citizens, especially the children, in the neighborhood. With his gentle and caring spirit, he realized that he must follow his calling, so he went to Amsterdam as an associate minister for a couple of years before returning to the university to study theology so he could move into the ministry full-time. He wanted to combine advocacy for those in need while spreading the word of God. He completed his bachelor's degree and master's degree at the University of Glasgow. While at Glasgow he was elected President of the Students' Representative Council and also served as Rector of the University.

After he received his master's degree he was ordained by the Church of Scotland and accepted a position as one of only two youth pastors for the Church of Scotland in a region with hundreds of churches. At times, he felt overwhelmed with the responsibilities of working with so many churches. He often turned to music for solace.

A few years later he moved full-time into music and worship with the Wild Goose Resource Group. He was a Convener of the Church of Scotland's Panel on Worship and because of his expertise in hymnology, he was also a Convener of the Committee on Revision of the Church Hymnary.

John has written many hymns that can be found in hymnals around the world. His hymns have been translated into at least ten languages. John has appeared in countless churches, appeared on many stages, led numerous charity drives to raise money and clothing for economically disadvantaged families, and he has participated in numerous British Broadcasting Company radio productions as a regular contributor to *The Thought for the Day* radio program.

John has received many honors including awards from the Presbyterian Church of Canada and the Royal School of Church Music, with the latter bestowing Fellowship status to John. The University of Glasgow awarded him an honorary doctorate degree.

His most recently published book is ***Ten Things They Never Told Me About Jesus: A Beginner's Guide to a Larger Christ***.

John continues to live in the Iona Community in Scotland, a community famous for its liberal philosophy, creativity, and on-going support of humanitarian efforts.

(References: *John L. Bell,* GIA Publications. Retrieved 2015; *An Interview with John Bell of the Iona Community,* reformedworship.org. Retrieved 2015; *John Lamberton Bell,* The Hymn, 2007, Gray and Nancy Wicklund)

Benson, Louis Fitzgerald

Louis was born in 1855 in Philadelphia, Pennsylvania. He was raised in a family with a strong and devoted sense of responsibility, faith, and industry.

At a very young age, Louis showed signs of intellectual brilliance and dedication to hark work and thriftiness. His father encouraged these traits and pronounced when Louis was just a young boy that he would be a success in anything he endeavored. Louis tried to live up to his father's expectations. He excelled in grade school and secondary school. After secondary school, Louis attended the University of Pennsylvania where he graduated with honors at the age of nineteen.

After graduation, Louis began the practice of law in Philadelphia, where he became very successful. He also had a spiritual side that continued to mature and take form in his heart and soul. He had long talks with his father about faith and theology. It became obvious to both his father and friends that in his heart Louis wanted to study theology. So, with the encouragement of his father, Louis enrolled in theology studies at the Princeton Theological Seminary, where his father was a trustee. Louis completed his studies in 1886 and was ordained and served in the Church of the Redeemer (a Presbyterian church) in Germantown, Pennsylvania for over six years.

During his time in the church, Louis became enamored with written works on theology and hymns. He also loved to read articles about faith, Bible study guides, and other related written materials, and he began writing, but much of his interest was in collecting written material. This new found interest motivated him to leave the Church of the Redeemer to accept a position at the Presbyterian Board of Publication and Sabbath-School Work in Philadelphia, where his work focused primarily on editing hymns and hymnals.

Throughout the Presbyterian world, there were very few if any hymnals that were not at that time edited by Louis. He became a renowned scholar and writer in the field of hymnology. Louis' library of hymns and rare and antique works totaled over 9,000 volumes - all of them were carefully cataloged in chronological order. Many of these works would have been lost if not for Louis' devotion to retrieving, restoring, and collecting the priceless works.

Louis' fame expanded each year. He was in demand for lectures all around the country, and several times served as Stone Lecturer at Princeton Seminary, a rare honor. He served on the Board of Christian Education for the Presbyterian Church for several years, and he held other influential positions as well.

Louis found time during his many duties to compose hymns. Many of them had a lyrical nature that made the selection of accompanying music easier to compose. His most famous hymn was ***The Sun Is on the Sea and Shore*** which Louis said was inspired by a visit to the Atlantic coast where he walked on a beach at sunrise in 1897 while visiting friends. When Louis went back into his friend's beachside cottage, he composed a draft of the hymn.

After a brief illness, Louis died in 1930 at the age of seventy-five. He was mourned by hundreds of people who attended the funeral to express their appreciation for Louis' life and the expression of his faith through his hymns.

(References: *Louis F. Benson, Hymnologist,* 1955, Morgan Phelps Noyes; *Stewards of Our Heritage,* 2002, Virginia F. Rainey; *Louis F. Benson, the 1895 Presbyterian Hymnal,* 1999, Paul Richard Powell)

Bernard of Clairvaux

Bernard was born in 1090 in Burgundy, France. His parents were in the exclusive order of highest nobility in the region and country—Lord of Fontaines and Aleth of Montbard. There were seven children in the family. Bernard was one of six sons and the third oldest of the children.

His early years were spent enjoying the vestiges of a privileged life in his beloved home and community. However, shortly after his ninth birthday, his parents sent him to a school run by the secular Canons of Saint-Vorles at Chatillon-sur-Seine, France. Bernard was homesick for several months but he developed a great love of world literature and read at every opportunity. His love of literature led him to discover a gift for thoughtful study. Bernard's introduction to the Bible as literature generated an insight into the ancient text that won him the admiration of his teachers. Bernard was fascinated by the Bible story of the Virgin Mary, who he later referred to in several of his written works as the "Queen of Heaven."

As his intellectual development blossomed, so did his theological curiosity and devotion. Bernard sought admission to and was accepted into the Cistercian order, a religious order of monks and nuns. Upon his acceptance in the Cistercian order, he found comfort in the atmosphere of the spiritual study of the monks and nuns.

Bernard showed natural leadership and planning ability; consequently, three years later, he was charged with creating a new abbey in the remote Val d'Absinthe, an isolated glen southeast of Bar-sur-Aube. Bernard named the abbey Claire Vallee, which later became known as Clairvaux.

Bernard's influence and reputation extended far beyond Clairvaux. The abbey drew monks and nuns from across France, as word of Bernard's preaching prowess spread. At the age of thirty, he was present at the first general chapter of the order convoked by Stephen of Citeaux, and it was the influence of the young Bernard that carried the chapter toward the regulations of the Charter of Charity, which Pope Callixtus II later confirmed. Bernard outlined the concept of the Rule of the Knights Templar that became the model for Christian nobility.

His fame grew so quickly and significantly that upon the death of Pope Honorius II, Bernard was selected to judge between the rivals for Pope. His high profile sometimes worked against. Bernard became tangled in the internal strife within the Catholic Church and was accused of inciting the Crusades and for the failure of the Crusades. In reality, he had little if any influence on the Crusades.

During his active and busy life, Bernard found time to write several hymns. Some of them survived through the centuries, but many of them did not. Of the hymns that were found, ***Jesus, the Very Thought of Thee*** is the most popular. He wrote the hymn while at Clairvaux.

Bernard's work ethic and devotion to his work were lauded by his friends and colleagues. He seldom missed worship services and he seemed to always be available if friends or worshipers needed assistance. He sometimes sacrificed his own health to help others. Bernard became sick in 1152 and never fully recovered his strength. He died at the age of sixty-three in 1153.

Bernard's reputation grew even more after his death. He became the first Cistercian to be placed on the Calendar of Saints, and he was canonized by Pope Alexander III in 1174. In 1830, Pope

Pius VIII bestowed upon Bernard the rare and prestigious title of "Doctor of the Church."

(References: *Bernard of Clairvaux: Selected Works*, 2005, G.R. Evans; *Saint Bernard of Clairvaux*, 1954, T. Merton; *Saint Bernard—His Life and Teaching*, 1971, O.J. Egres)

Bianco da Siena

Bianco was born in 1350 at Anciolina in Val d'Arno near Tuscany, Italy. Not much is known about his family, other than the family moved to Siena, Italy sometime around 1359.

In Siena, Bianco learned about music and wood carving, and he loved both. When he was still very young, he became a talented wood carver. It was a physically demanding job for an adult, and much more challenging for a young boy. Nevertheless, he remained a wood carver for many years. However, there was another side to young Bianco—he loved poetry and music, and he pursued both when he could.

Due to his interest in spirituality and religion, many of his poems and music were inspired by those themes. Bianco's interest in religion led him to join the Jesuates which was founded by Giovanni Colombini and was dedicated to following the rule of St. Augustine. Bianco wrote several poems that were translated into many languages and composed into several hymns. His hymns were frequently used in worship services locally and throughout Italy and other parts of Europe.

Bianco wrote poems for hymns and he often wrote poems for friends, relatives, and colleagues. Experts claim that he wrote more than 120 poems, but that is a conservative estimate. It is more likely that he wrote at least 300 poems. Bianco loved to compose hymns from his poems; he enjoyed watching his poems "come to life" in music. His hymn ***Come Down, O Love Divine*** has for centuries been a favorite among Christians.

Bianco had uneven health during his life. There were times when he suffered from unidentified pain, but he seldom complained. Bianco became gravely ill and died in Venice, Italy in

1399 at the age of forty-nine surrounded by his friends and colleagues.

(References: *II Bianco da Siena,* 2013, Silvia Serventi (translated 2014); *Medieval Italy: An Encyclopedia,* 2004, Christopher Kleinhenz; *An English Speaking Hymnal Guide,* 2005, Erik Routley)

Bliss, Philip Paul

Philip was born in 1838 in Rome, Pennsylvania - a rural part of the state. Philip's family was poor and lived in a log cabin. They worked thc land to survive. Nevertheless, they found time to pray and worship in a small rural Methodist church. Philip's father was a devoted Methodist who led his family in prayer every day of the year. His father loved music and encouraged his children to enjoy music, also. He found that Philip had an unusually beautiful voice with superb range for someone his age. Philip loved singing; it became a passion to him.

Philip had no formal education because the family lived in rural areas and had to work all day in the field to survive. What he learned was what his mother taught him. The "textbook" was the Bible. Philip was fascinated by the stories in the Bible and the parables that Jesus told. The parables would have an influence on Philip for the rest of his life.

When Philip was young the family moved to Kinsman, Ohio in an effort to find better living conditions, but soon thereafter they returned to Pennsylvania in Espeyville and settled in a tiny house that was once in the middle of farmland. The family's small farm grew vegetables. Selling vegetables was their only means of income. Philip at a young age, like the rest of the family, was responsible for selling their vegetables. He walked from town to town and house to house trying to sell vegetables. This difficult work and experience, nevertheless, gave him the opportunity to meet a lot of different people and hear many stories. Also, it was not uncommon for him to hear music from someone's house. When he was almost ten years old he heard a live piano for the first time.

He walked up to a house to sell vegetables and someone in the house was playing the piano. Philip was struck by the beautiful sound and determined then and there that he wanted to learn how to play the piano and learn how he could make music his career.

Incredibly, Philip left home when he was only eleven years old to live on his own. He loved his family but he knew that if he stayed with them his life would be that of a poor farmer. Philip slept wherever he could and worked at dozens of jobs, most of them backbreaking manual labor jobs. He found that work in timber camps and sawmills were the most reliable so that is where he stayed. Philip was wise enough to look for timber camps and sawmills that were near a school because he wanted an education. After work and before work he would attend classes.

Philip learned to read and he found that his math skills were unusually good compared to the other students at the timber camps and sawmill schools. He enjoyed school so much that he decided he wanted to become a teacher. When he found out what he had to do to be qualified to teach he set out on that path. By the age of seventeen, with a remarkable work ethic and uncommon intelligence, Philip had met the requirements to be a teacher. Soon thereafter he became a teacher in Hartsville, New York during the school year and worked on a nearby farm during the summer.

Philip also wanted to develop his singing skills. In pursuit of singing lessons, he met J. G. Towner who would have a great influence on Philip both as a singing teacher and as a mentor. J. G. immediately recognized Philip's singing talent as well as his ability to teach, so he and others encouraged Philip to become a music teacher. He applied for and was offered a teaching position at Rome Academy in Pennsylvania. It was there that he met Lucy Young whose family was involved in music. Philip and Lucy married and it was Lucy and her family that encouraged Philip to develop his musical talents. By then he was also composing music.

Philip faithfully attended church at Lucy's Presbyterian Church and participated in the music activities and programs. Lucy's grandmother was so impressed with Philip's musical abilities and his good nature that she loaned him $30 (a great deal of money then) to attend the Normal Academy of Music in New York City for six weeks. When he returned home he was considered an expert and was in great demand as a music teacher.

Philip and Lucy moved to Chicago to broaden their prospects. In Chicago, Philip's hymns became well known and widely played. He went on a concert tour before being drafted into the Union Army during the Civil War, but the war ended before he saw any military action. He then went on more concert tours but they were not well attended and he missed home, so he accepted a job at Root and Cady Musical Publishers. He worked there for eight years and during that time learned a lot about music, composing, and publishing. Philip's employers recognized his talents as a musician and teacher so they asked him to entertain and teach the children of the company's employees.

At a revival event one evening Philip met Dwight Moody who encouraged him to be a singing evangelist and to publish his hymns under his own name instead of the publishing house's name. Shortly after that chance encounter, Philip started a career as a singing evangelist and published his hymns and other songs under his name. His fame grew far and wide and he made considerable money from royalties stemming from his compositions. Philip was at the height of his career when tragedy struck.

He and Lucy were traveling by train when the train derailed into a ravine. Somehow Philip escaped the wreck but when he discovered that Lucy was not with him he went back into the flaming carnage to find her. They were never found. Philip and Lucy were two of the ninety-two people who died in the Ashtabula River Railroad Disaster. Philip was only thirty-eight years old and Lucy was only thirty-two years when they died.

When the wreckage of the train was being removed several days after the accident, a travel trunk belonging to Philip was found undamaged. Inside the trunk were the lyrics to a hymn that would become famous, ***I Will Sing of My Redeemer.*** Later the tune was added by James McGranaham.

Many of Philip's hymns and songs are popular today, including ***Almost Persuaded; Hallelujah, What a Savior; Let the Lower Lights Be Burning; Wonderful Words of Life; It is Well with My Soul*** and many others. His songbooks include ***The Charm; The Song Tree; The Sunshine; The Joy, Gospel Songs;*** and two versions of ***Gospel Hymns and Sacred Songs.***

From a poor family in rural Pennsylvania and from raw talent and determination Philip became famous worldwide. During his short life, he wrote some of the most memorable hymns ever written.

(References: *Hymns and History: An Annotated Survey of Sources,* 1997, Forrest M. McCann; *Memoirs of Philip P. Bliss,* 1877, Daniel Webster. Retrieved from A.S. Barnes and Company 2015; *Hymns of Our Faith,* 1964, William Jensen Reynolds; *P.P. Bliss 1838-1876,* STEM Publishing. Retrieved 2015)

Bode, John Ernest

John was born in 1816 in St. Pancras, Middlesex, England. His father worked in the General Post Office and was well respected in the community. John's parents strongly valued family, education, and worship above all else. They insisted that John have the best education possible, and when he showed intellectual acumen at a young age, they encouraged his intellectual and creative development.

He attended Eton Academy and the Charter House. John's academic work was superb and earned him acceptance at Christ Church University at Oxford where he earned a Bachelor in Arts degree. He was the recipient of the Hertford Scholarship in theology and received a Master of Arts degree in theology. John was soon thereafter ordained at the age of twenty-five and was offered the position of Rector of Westwell, Oxfordshire. He thrived in that position and his reputation as a pastor and theologian grew.

A few years later, John accepted the position of Rector of Castle Camps in Cambridgeshire. It was during his time at Castle Camps that he wrote several hymns and poems. He also cataloged his sermons and lectures. John's creative and scholarly works were published as the ***Bampton Lectures*** and ***Ballads from Herodotus***. He also published several of his hymns in the popular ***Hymns from the Gospel of the Day for Each Sunday and Festivals of Our Lord***, with the most popular being ***O Jesus, I Have Promised*** which can be found in almost every Christian Hymnal today. John's poems were published as ***Short Occasional Poems***. The subjects of his poems ranged from the spiritual to poems about his beloved daughter and two sons. John also wrote the script for his children's confirmation service, which was later published in the famous book ***Psalms and Hymns by the Society for the Propagation of Christian Knowledge***.

Despite suffering from chronic health issues, John continued to preach, lecture, and write up until his health deteriorated further in 1874, the year he died in Castle Camps, Cambridgeshire, England at the age of fifrty-eight. He was buried at the All Saints Church there.

(References: *John Bode*, Dictionary of Hymnology, 1907, John Julian; *The Gospel in Hymns*, 1950, Albert Bailey; *John Ernest Bode*, hymntime.com. Retrieved 2013)

Bonhoeffer, Dietrich

Dietrich was born in 1906 in Wroclaw, Poland (then known as Breslau, Poland). Dietrich had eight siblings, including a twin sister. He was born into a family of wealth and education. His father was the famous psychiatrist and neurologist, Karl Bonhoeffer. Dietrich's mother was the granddaughter of the theologian Karl von Hase and the world famous painter Stanislaus Kalekreuth. Some of Dietrich's siblings had stellar careers of their own. One of his brothers was a chemist who made groundbreaking discoveries.

Dietrich, beginning at a very young age, was an intellectual phenomenon. He excelled in all subject areas and was conducting his own scientific experiments when he was in grade school. At the college preparatory school his teachers, who were highly trained and credentialed, admired Dietrich's intellectual abilities, insight, and creative thought.

After secondary school, he attended the University of Berlin where he graduated with degrees in theology and philosophy. Dietrich moved to the United States for the purpose of postgraduate studies at the Union Theological Seminary in New York. He studied under the famous theologian/philosopher Reinhold Niebuhr. Reinhold greatly influenced Dietrich and challenged him to more fully develop his intellect, his writing skills, and his social consciousness. Dietrich followed Reinhold's advice. He studied more diligently and he improved his writing and research skills. He also taught Sunday school at the Abyssinian Baptist Church in Harlem where he became enamored with African-American spiritual hymns, which influenced some of his later hymn work when he returned to Germany. The enthusiasm, spiritual depth, sincerity, and commitment he saw in the predominantly African-American church made him realize the power of belief and how infrequently ministers inspire congregations to live and worship with their full heart and soul.

Dietrich went to London, England to serve as minister at the German Lutheran Church and later at the German Reformed Church. When Dietrich returned to Germany he was asked about his experiences in the United States, to which he said he learned about religion and worship from many perspectives, learned what true spirituality can mean, learned how ministers can inspire, and learned that religion alone cannot solve racism.

Upon his return to Germany, Dietrich found that Nazism was spreading rapidly. He very quickly and fervently became an outspoken critic of Adolf Hitler's Nazism. Only a few days after Hitler was appointed Chancellor, Dietrich went on national radio to deliver an address criticizing Hitler and warning Germans about the path of Nazism. As a clear sign of what was to come, his radio address was cut off in mid-delivery by Nazi officials.

Dietrich was not intimidated by the Nazis. In fact, he publicly urged all church leaders to denounce the policies of Nazism, but while he found many supporters among the church leaders he also found several intimidated and frightened church leaders.

Depressed by the worsening conditions in Germany he went to London, England to serve as minister at the German Lutheran Church and later at the German Reformed Church. His friends and relatives encouraged Dietrich to remain in England, but he wanted to return home to Germany despite the deteriorating social conditions of his country.

Dietrich became a lecturer of theology at the University of Berlin and he was given a leadership role in the World Alliance for Promoting International Friendship (which later became the World Council of Churches). He also continued to express his alarm over the growing influence and domination of Nazism. As Nazism's brutal racism and persecution of the Jews became more apparent, he spoke out against the "madness" and pleaded with the churches to unite against the tactics of Nazism.

When he was physically threatened by Nazi officials, Dietrich left Germany and went to Switzerland and later accepted an invitation to teach at the Union Theological Seminary in New York. He was not happy in New York, so again against the advice of his family and friends, he returned to Germany where he accepted a teaching position at the University of Berlin. Dietrich continued to speak out against Nazism. His resistance to Nazism had immediate consequences. His post at the University of Berlin was eliminated. Despite harassment and threats, Dietrich remained in Germany.

Dietrich worked with the underground resistance to Nazism until he was arrested and sent to a Nazi concentration camp in 1943. He tried to comfort the other victims in the camp through prayer, but he was beaten and starved. Dietrich was told that he was found guilty of treason and sentenced to death. He was stripped and paraded before other prisoners to be hanged. Dietrich was bold and brave throughout his life, and witnesses to his execution said he held true to his beliefs until his life ended at the age of thirty-seven. Tragically, his death came only two weeks before the Allied forces liberated the concentration camp.

Dietrich's many hymns and writings are found in hymnals and scholarly works throughout the world. His famous hymn ***By Gracious Powers*** is in most Christian hymnals.

(References: *Dietrich Bonhoeffer: Reality and Resistance,* 2005, Larry Rasmussen; *Dietrich Bonhoeffer: Did You Know?,* 1991, Mark and Barbara Galli; *The Tragedy of Dietrich Bonhoeffer and Hans von Dohnanyi,* 2012, Elisabeth Sifton and Fritz Stern; *Bonhoeffer: Pastor, Prophet, Martyr, Spy,* 2010, Eric Metaxas)

Bowring, John

John was born in 1792 in Exeter, England to a wool merchant family that was deeply involved in politics and religion. As a young boy, John was precocious and interested in almost every aspect of his environment. He wanted to know how things worked, why people acted the way they did, why the sky was blue and much more. John did not challenge everything in a rebellious manner, he simply questioned everything with a series of "Why" questions.

John was educated in a Unitarian school, but at age thirteen he started working with his father in the merchant world. John was not just a child doing busy work and running errands; instead, his father recognized that John was intelligent and possessed an agile and perceptive mind, so he did meaningful and necessary work in the business for his father.

Even though he worked many hours each day, John continued his education by reading and attending lectures in the community. He became a well-informed student of literature and Eastern European languages, becoming fluent in several languages before his twentieth birthday. John loved the study of languages, and it is believed that he was familiar with 100 languages and could speak at least a few sentences in almost all of them. He became very skilled at identifying languages, as merchants and sailors from around the world came into port.

John also enjoyed writing. With his vast knowledge of languages, he was skilled at translating literary works from many languages into English. He also became well-known for his own poems, hymns, and scholarly works. John's scholarly works included: ***Specimens of the Russian Poets***; ***Batavian Anthology***; ***Ancient Poetry and Romances of Spain***; ***Specimens of the Polish Poets***; ***Serbian Popular Poetry***, and ***Poetry of the Magyars***.

John's reputation brought him the opportunity to become editor of the *Westminster Review*, a widely known and respected publication. It was through his work with the *Westminster Review* that he gained national attention for his political and economic views, support of parliamentary reform, public education, and Catholic freedom. John's popularity grew so much that he entered Parliament and was soon thereafter named the head of a commission to study economic commerce between England and several other countries, including France, Italy, Syria, Germany, and Switzerland. Additionally, he was appointed Governor of Hong Kong, was knighted Sir John Bowring and named a Fellow of the Royal Geographical Society. All the while, he kept writing poems, hymns, and translations, including a translation of the ***Manuscript of the Queen's Court***, a comprehensive and scholarly collection of Czech medieval poetry.

John wrote several hymns, but many of them he never published. His most well-known hymns include ***In the Cross of Christ I Glory*** and ***Watchman, Tell Us of the Night***, which are still included in many Christian church hymnals around the world.

John remained active in politics and literature until his health declined in the late 1860s. He died in 1872 at the age of eighty in Claremont, England.

(References: *Sir John Bowring*, Oxford Dictionary of National Biography. Retrieved 2015; *A Portrait of Sir John Bowring and His Family*, 1994, George Frederick Bartle; *Sir John Bowring—Aspects of His Life*, 1993, Joyce Alice Youings, editor)

Brandy, Ernest William

Ernest was born in 1801 (estimated) in New York, New York. Very little is known about his family or personal life.

He worked in a New York church as an administrator and lay minister and where he became a champion for destitute families. Ernest provided food and clothing to poverty-ravaged families in the notorious slums at the New York City waterfront. He was appalled and shocked by the conditions of the people living there; he was particularly haunted by the women and children living in such squalor and dying of disease, violence, and malnutrition.

Ernest gave up his promising career and comfortable position at the church and joined the Salvation Army for the sole purpose of working in the waterfront area of New York that would become known as "Hell's Kitchen." Ernest felt that it was God's calling to him and he followed. His work with the families in Hell's Kitchen became the inspiration for one of the more enduring and beloved hymns of all time - ***Where He Leads Me***. He felt God clearly led him to provide spiritual and physical comfort to the families; Ernest went where he was needed the most, doing the work that filled his heart and soul and God's mission for him.

For most of his life, Ernest lived in obscurity. He never sought attention or credit for his devotion to the families on the waterfront. He would write other hymns, but most of them were never found. Ernest seemed content to write and sing hymns for the poor, as he led them in daily worship. He spoke out against companies that provided no jobs or support for the families and he had to solicit support from churches and charities to find enough food and clothing to help the families. Most of the work he did on his own since he was not affiliated with a church or denomination.

It is commonly believed that Ernest never strayed from his mission to make life better for the women and children who suffered the most. That is where God led him. Although there are no records to verify the date of his death; it is believed that Ernest died in New York City in 1900, which means that he was probably in his nineties at the time of his death. The location of his burial site is unknown.

(References: *Ernest William Brandy,* Dictionary of North American Hymnology. Retrieved 2013)

Bridgers, Luther Burgess

Luther was born in 1884 in Margaretsville, North Carolina. Luther's father was a minister and a traveling revival meeting evangelist. His father's family had ministry lineage dating back as far as the 17th century when Lawrence Bridger was the Rector of St. John the Evangelist Church in England.

Beginning when he was a young boy, Luther accompanied his father through several towns and cities to witness and sometimes participate in revivals. Luther saw some revivals with only a few dozen people attending and yet there were times when thousands of people participated in the revivals. Luther's father told him that if he saved one soul his efforts were not in vain.

Luther was also influenced by the importance of the music in worship, especially as he saw his father bring a fever pitch to revivals when favorite sacred hymns added drama and power to his message of salvation.

Luther loved music and his gregarious nature endeared him to family, friends, and teachers. Although Luther was an average student in local school, he was encouraged by his father and mother to attend college, so he enrolled at Asbury College in Wilmore, Kentucky. There he met his future wife, Sarah Jane "Sallie" Veatch. They would have three sons.

After college, Luther was ordained in the Methodist Episcopal Church South. Luther's first church assignment was in Perry, Florida. He loved the church and the community and they returned his affection in many ways, but Luther was not comfortable using the church setting as the vehicle for delivering God's word. He longed for the excitement of the revival circuit and the power and excitement of the revival meetings. After only one year in Perry, he took up the revival evangelism that he loved. His revivals drew very large crowds, which resulted in numerous invitations for him to set up revivals across the south. Luther said he had so many invitations he could have been on the road every day of the year. He traveled throughout Georgia, North Carolina, Florida, Alabama, Tennessee, South Carolina, and Mississippi. Luther became famous for his sermons and his beautiful voice. Luther had a talent for writing hymns, also. In fact, he wrote several hymns including the world-famous hymn ***He Keeps Me Singing***, the hymn he is most known for writing.

By the time his fame soared, Luther had three small children. Luther disliked being away from them so he cut back his schedule in order to enjoy being a husband and father. However, it was while he was away from his beloved family on March 26, 1911, at a revival when an unimaginable tragedy occurred. His wife decided to take the three sons to visit their grandparents in Harrodsburg, Kentucky. While there a fire broke out in the small frame home, killing everyone, including Sallie and three small boys. When a friend told him the news, Luther dropped to his knees to pray. He was completely devastated, but he said prayer saved his sanity.

It was falsely reported for several years that Luther wrote the famous hymn ***He Keeps Me Singing*** in response to the tragic loss of his young family, but that is not entirely true. The hymn was written before that incident. However, there is no doubt that the hymn took on new meaning. Congregations and revival attendees could not hold their emotions back when he sang the hymn, knowing that his family was close to his heart each time he sang the hymn's powerful words. Luther found comfort in prayer and work. He worked harder than ever before because during idle times he was haunted by the loss of his family.

In 1914, Luther was named General Evangelist by the Methodist Episcopal Church South which was an important recognition of his work and influence. He continued his revival work until after World War I when he decided to join the missionary efforts by the Christian world to reach out to families in Russia, Poland, Czechoslovakia, Belgium, and other countries that had been devastated and displaced by the war. In the war zones, Luther saw widespread physical and spiritual hunger. He had intended to go on a few short missionary trips, but he was moved by the needs of the countries and the lost families; consequently, he decided to extend his missionary work by several months. Because of his fame, his dedication, and his hard work with the missionary efforts, he was an inspiration to thousands of people who volunteered to help with the missionary work.

Upon his return to the United States, Asbury College awarded Luther an honorary doctorate degree for his work. Luther went back to the revival circuit until 1932 when he accepted pastor positions in churches in the Atlanta, Georgia area. Due primarily to declining health, Luther retired in 1945 and moved to Gainesville, Georgia where he died in 1948 at the age of sixty-four.

His hymn ***He Keeps Me Singing*** has been recorded by several recording artists and the hymn remains one of the most beloved hymns in the Christian world.

(References: *The Death of Melody Man*: Luther B. Bridgers, 2012, Christianity.com. Retrieved 2015; *Luther B. Bridgers*, wordwisehymns.com. Retrieved 2015; *Luther B. Bridgers - He Keeps Me Singing*, Library.timelesstruths.org. Retrieved 2015)

Brooke, Stopford Augustus

Stopford was born in 1832 in Glendoen, Ireland, as the oldest of four sons and four daughters to Richard and Anna Brooke. At the time of Stopford's birth, his father was Curate of the Glendoen parish and his mother's father was the Rector of Glendoen.

Stopford was expected to follow the career path of his father and grandfather, but as a sickly and quiet child, those expectations did not seem realistic. His younger siblings showed much more promise. However, as he grew older Stopford began to mature and his health problems diminished each year until by the time he reached his teen years he was a healthy and handsome young man with an engaging personality and sharp intellect.

Stopford attended a local school for a short period of time. Then he was sent to boarding school at Kidderminster Grammar School after his father observed that Stopford was not intellectually challenged by the local school. Kidderminster was a rigorous academic-focused school that encouraged Stopford's intellectual development, which helped prepare him for college. He excelled at all school work. His intelligence and studious nature placed him at the top of his class.

Stopford could have attended almost any college, but he wished to attend Trinity College in Dublin because of his growing interest in the study of divinity. Stopford was a prize-winning student at Trinity, winning a prize for divinity and another for English verse. He received a Bachelor of Arts degree. Stopford remained at Trinity and two years later received a Master of Arts degree.

Stopford had great respect for his father and grandfather and their dedication to the evangelical churches, but he began to question the evangelical precepts. In fact, his first publication was about his admiration for Reverend Charles Kingsley who supported a liberal Christianity that advocated social responsibility as an article of faith for Christians. Stopford's article in the *Dublin University Magazine* was a public declaration of his beliefs, and he held true to those concepts throughout his life.

Stopford was ordained in 1857 at the age of twenty-five. He accepted a position as curate at St. Matthew's at Marylebone which was one of the most deprived sections of Ireland. It was there among the poor that his sense of social consciousness and the role of Christianity strengthened. In addition to providing spiritual support for the poor, he also provided food and shelter and aided F. D. Maurice's attempt to offer classes at Queen's College for the education of working men.

In 1859, Stopford moved to St. Mary Abbots in Kensington in the position of a curate. During his time at St. Mary Abbots, his reputation as a brilliant preacher blossomed in the city, then the region, and eventually throughout Ireland.

Stopford always enjoyed music, poetry and he loved to write. A well-known publisher, Henry King, received word of the talented young man and attended one of Stopford's sermons. Henry was so impressed with Stopford that he insisted on meeting him. The two met and found many common interests. At the time, Henry was looking for someone capable of writing a biography of the great pastor Frederick William (F. W.) Robertson whose published sermons were extraordinarily well received across Ireland and Europe. Henry did not think Stopford had the time to take on such a task, in addition to his duties as a popular curate, but Stopford was fascinated by the challenge and subject. Stopford said that he could accomplish the task; consequently, Henry commissioned him to write the biography. Stopford worked tirelessly on the biography. He drew upon hundreds of references and interviews. The result was a brilliant biography that received great acclaim for himself and F. W. Robertson.

As his reputation grew, Stopford was made Chaplain to Queen Victoria. The Queen was so enchanted with his abilities and social and religious beliefs, she wanted to make Stopford the Canon of Westminster, but the Prime Minister did not approve of Stopford's position on social issues.

Stopford moved to a chapel on York Street and remained there for several years. After he retired, Stopford continued to write poems, hymns and other works and his fame never diminished, even after his death in 1916 at the age of eighty-four.

Stopford's hymn ***Let the Whole Creation Cry*** remains one of the most popular Christian hymns. It's interesting to note that George Bernard Shaw used Stopford as the model for the character of Reverend James Mavor Morell in his book *Candida*.

(References: *The Life and Letters of Stopford Brooke,* 1917, Lawrence Pearsall Jacks; *Christian Hymns,* 1999, Joanne Shattock; *Be Still, My Soul,* 2014, Randy Petersen)

Brooks, Phillips

Phillips was born in 1835 in Boston, Massachusetts. Phillips was considered by many to be one of the greatest American preachers of the 19th century. His sermons became legendary.

Phillips was born into a well-educated and respected Boston family. Through generations of Christian worshippers, he was raised in a world of Christian beliefs and devotion. Three of his five brothers became ordained ministers.

As he was growing up, Phillips was a serious-minded child who enjoyed reading and learning. He seemed to thrive on the intellectual challenges that his mother and father provided him. Phillips attended the finest Boston private schools, including the Boston Latin School, where he excelled in every subject. He applied for and was accepted at Harvard University. When he was attending Harvard University, Phillips developed a strong interest in all aspects of theology. His professors marveled at his insight and intellectual maturity at such a young age. Many of his professors wanted him to spend his career at Harvard as a professor. But Phillips wanted to experience the world, so he took a teaching position at his alma mater, Boston Latin School. However, he was not a very effective teacher, and to his shock was fired from his job.

Phillips was disappointed by the setback, but he decided to gather himself and make a new start, so he pursued his interest in theology at the Episcopal Theological Seminary in Alexandria, Virginia. At the age of twenty-five, Phillips became a priest and later a Rector of the Church of the Advent in Philadelphia where his social consciousness and activities fully developed. When he saw unequal or mistreatment he spoke out against it. He was respected for his strong beliefs and he was a powerful theologian, but his stance on social justice was not always well received by those who did not oppose slavery.

Phillips never shied away from what he believed was God's love for all mankind, so his efforts to help freed and escaped slaves seemed like the work of God. He strongly favored the position of the North in the American Civil War and he was an admirer of

President Lincoln. From the pulpit and in speeches, he frequently spoke in favor of President Lincoln's efforts to free the slaves and reunite the country. Phillips was devastated by Lincoln's death. He gave a stirring and a widely quoted sermon on the death of Abraham Lincoln.

Phillips' influence and reputation as a minister grew, and he was asked to become the Rector of Trinity Church in Boston. It was Phillips who helped design the world famous Trinity Church in Boston's Back Bay. During this time, he was a prolific writer of verse, sermons, treatises, and hymns.

At the age of fifty-six, Phillips became the Episcopal Bishop of Massachusetts. His sermons, delivered with majestic language, a trumpet voice and emphasized by his 6'-4" height, were legendary. Also, for many years, he was overseer and minister of Harvard University, but he frequently declined invitations to be a professor of Christian Ethics at Harvard.

Many famous people sought Phillips' advice and counsel. It was well documented and widely reported that Phillips converted Helen Keller and Anne Sullivan to Christianity. When Helen and Anne visited Phillips they were doubters, not non-believers as was reported at the time. Phillips was patient with them and did not pressure them in any way. He used passages from the Bible, logic, examples from life, and inspiration to reach the spiritual needs of Helen and Anne. They accepted Jesus as their savior and remained devoted Christians for the remainder of their lives.

During the height of his incredible career, with a world-wide reputation, Phillips died unexpectedly at the age of fifty-eight in 1893. His death shocked the world and was a devastating loss for the Boston community. His funeral was spectacular in its planning and execution. All denominational leaders came together, and Harvard University students carried the coffin on their shoulders. The funeral was attended by many of the country's most famous people.

Although Phillips was legendary during the 19th century and into the 20th century, and to this day is revered in Boston, he is most widely known today for one of his hymns that became legendary in its own right, and to this day is one of the world's most beloved Christmas hymn carols. Phillips wrote ***O Little Town of Bethlehem.***

(References: *Celebrating the Saints,* 2001, Robert Atwell and Christopher Weber; *Phillips Brooks,* Cyberhymnal.org. Retrieved 2014; *Phillips Brooks,* Touchstonemag.com. Retrieved 2014)

Buck, Carlton C.

Carlton was born in 1907 in Salina, Kansas to a family with humble origins and God-fearing beliefs.

Carlton was a serious-minded child who adored his siblings and greatly respected his parents. His kind heart and gentle nature endeared him to family and friends.

Carlton worked diligently in school and was interested in attending college, even at a young age, but he also wanted to explore his spirituality. Consequently, he decided to attend Biola University (La Mirada, California, sixteen miles from downtown Los Angeles) where he became a student at the Institute for Spiritual Formation, a Christian, evangelical, and academic community within the university. He also attended Talbot School of Theology, located in California and Whittier College and the Los Angeles Bible Seminary, both in California. He earned a Bachelor of Arts degree from the seminary, and Carlton received a Master of Arts degree from San Gabriel College.

After college, he became an ordained minister. Carlton served as pastor at the First Christian Church in Arlington, California. He also served other First Christian churches in California and Oregon until he retired from the ministry in 1960.

Carlton enjoyed research and writing. His publications include: ***At the Lord's Treasury***; ***At the Lord's Table***; ***Communion Thoughts and Prayers***; ***Devotion Time Verse***; and ***Quiet Time Verse***. He also composed over 100 hymns, including ***All Praise to God for Song***; ***Till the Morning***; ***We Want to Know, Lord*** and many others that can be found in hymnals around the world. He was often asked to compose hymns for special occasions such as weddings and anniversaries.

Carlton remained active with his writing and in his community of worship until his health declined in his mid-80s. Carlton died in 1999 in Oregon at the age of ninety-two.

(References: *The Presbyterian Hymnal Companion,* 1993, Linda Jo H. McKim; *Carlton C. Buck,* hymntime.com. Retrieved 2014; *Carlton C. Buck,* Hymnary.org. Retrieved 2014; *Songs by Carlton C. Buck,* SongSelect by CCLI, 2015)

Cameron, Catherine Bonnell Arnott

Catherine was born in 1927 in St. John, New Brunswick, Canada. She was the daughter of a well-known minister, Dr. John Sutherland Bonnell.

As a young girl, it was obvious to all that Catherine was very intelligent, inquisitive, and talented. She had a gift for writing and especially enjoyed writing poetry. Catherine enjoyed attending church and singing hymns. She appreciated the poetic nature of hymns but she thought some of the music and the poetry within the hymns did not match very well together, so she worked on the idea of matching the words to the music.

Catherine excelled in all academic endeavors. After success in her secondary school, she attended McMaster University, a research university in Hamilton, Ontario, Canada, and is considered one of Canada's top universities. Catherine earned a Bachelor of Arts at McMaster University. After marrying and moving to Claremont, California, she continued her studies at the University of California, where she received a Master of Arts and a Ph.D. in sociology with a specialization in family problems.

Catherine had a distinguished career as a professor of social psychology at the University of La Verne, near Los Angeles, California from 1971 to 1992. Her work in the field of social psychology is nationally and internationally known and admired.

She is the author of numerous professional publications, but she is also known worldwide for her hymns, including the very popular ***O Christ, Who Came to Share Our Human Life*** and ***God Who Stretched the Spangled Heaven.*** Catherine said that she spent several months working on ***God Who Stretched the Spangled Heaven.*** She sought the perfect linkage between the words and the music. She wanted to also convey the dangers of the Cold War, which was at a critical and potentially devastating point.

Catherine is retired but remains active in many endeavors and volunteer projects.

(References: *Catherine Cameron,* 1967, Michael Hawn, Hope Publishing; *Worshipping God with Science,* 2011, Ruth Bancewicz; *Praying Twice: The Music and Words of Congregational Song,* 2000, Brian Wren)

Campbell, Alexander

Alexander was born in 1788 in County Antrim, Ireland, as the first child of Thomas and Mary Campbell. He was educated in the local community schools and later attended Glasgow University.

Alexander immigrated with his mother and younger brothers and sisters to Washington, Pennsylvania to reunite with his father who had immigrated to Pennsylvania two years earlier to take the position as Presbyterian minister. Prior to moving to America, the elder Campbell was a minister in Belfast, Ireland. Alexander's father was an inspirational and thought leader for many people in his congregation and throughout the region; however, he would come to famously reject Presbyterianism.

Alexander studied religion and was ordained. He joined his father's leadership in the church, which he would later lead. Alexander and his father questioned many of the traditions of the Presbytery, such as the baptism of infants and the baptism of anyone by any means other than total immersion in holy waters. This and other beliefs were more akin to Baptist beliefs so their church merged with the Redstone Baptist Association. But his views about the creeds and traditions of the Baptist faith and his public questioning of them led to his split with the Baptist. There was no longer an affiliation with any other churches.

After he separated from the Presbyterians and Baptists and created a different path of worship with his congregation, Alexander found a kindred spirit in Barton W. Stone and their congregations merged to form the Disciples of Christ. Together they created the American Christian Missionary Society that led to the founding of Bethany College. Alexander wrote ***The Declaration and Address of the Christian Association*** that became well-known for its emphasis on all Christians working together. Alexander would later take those principles and ideas to help launch the American Restoration Movement which led to the organization of the Christian Association Church at Brush Run, Pennsylvania.

In addition to his work with the Disciples of Christ Christian Church, Alexander was the President of Bethany College for over twenty years and was instrumental in its growth and academic and theological reputation. He also became a respected expert on the New Testament. Among his many academic papers, he published a translation of the New Testament that was widely referenced.

Alexander's national reputation grew as he never shied away from debates about theology, religion, worship, baptism, or any other topics. Alexander famously debated with Bishop Purcell of the Roman Catholic Church and later with Reverend Rice of the Baptist church.

Under his influence, the Disciples of Christ Christian Churches sprang up rapidly around the United States and Canada. During this time, Alexander wrote articles, papers, treatises, and hymns. His most famous hymn was ***When You Do This Remember Me,*** which is a powerful message of reconciliation.

Just as the movement of the Disciples of Christ was growing rapidly the momentum was slowed significantly with the onset of the American Civil War. Alexander was heartbroken by the devastation of the war and the death toll of the war, as well as the almost total annihilation of towns, communities, cities, and churches. Although the devastation of the war never threatened the strength of his faith, it did affect him in many other ways, including his health. Alexander remained active until failing health confined him to his home where he died in 1866 at the age of seventy-eight. Disciples of Christ Christian Churches across the United States and Canada together mourned the loss of Alexander and his spiritual leadership.

(References: *The Philosophy of Religion of Alexander Campbell,* 2013, Caleb J. Clanton; *The Encyclopedia of the Stone-Campbell Movement,* 2005, Douglas Foster; *Campbellite and Restoration Traditions in the South* [previously published in Bibliography of Religion in the South, 1985 by Charles Lippy], 2000, Anthony Ash—Dissertation)

Carmichael, Amy Wilson

Amy was born in 1867 in the very small village of Millisle, Country Down, Ireland. Amy was the oldest of seven children. Her father was a miller and her mother was a devoted and influential wife and mother. Her parents were deeply religious and were devout Presbyterians. The family struggled to survive but her parents made life as comfortable as possible for the children.

There was a small school in the community that included all grade levels, but most of the children had to work around the house or in the local mill and could not attend school full-time. When the mill owner died the mill and the school shut down. Amy's family was forced to move to Belfast so her father could find work.

In Belfast, the family continued to struggle, but Amy had access to an education and the family attended worship services when they could. Amy loved attending church, and she enjoyed the music and fellowship at the worship services and during the other activities of the church. As she grew older, she helped the teachers of the mill school with the youngest girls. After working at the mill, Amy tutored the younger girls. She read to them and helped them with math. Amy was instrumental in linking the mill school with the local churches. The churches provided support to the school through donations of resources like books, paper, and pencils.

Amy received religious training at the church she attended and she was encouraged to pursue her dream of expanding church activities for the children of mill workers. She followed that dream and was one of the founding members of the Welcome Evangelical Church that truly welcomed everyone including the mill children. The church decided to sponsor education programs for girls, which was unusual at that time and in that era. The girls were called "Shawlies" because they all wore shawls. The church grew so rapidly that they ran out of space. Due to her continued efforts and determination, Amy was able to raise enough money to erect a building large enough to seat over 500 people. It was called "Welcome Hall."

Helping others was Amy's mission in life, and it came naturally to her. In Belfast, she learned of the growing need for missionary work. With the understanding and support of her mother, Amy went on a missionary trip to Japan. While in Japan, she worked hard and enjoyed the work but she developed health issues believed to be her on-going battle with neuralgia. After fifteen months in Japan and suffering from ill-health, she returned home to recover.

Despite her health issues, Amy continued her missionary work which took her to India. She met the famous Reverend Thomas Walker who was leading the missionary work that was especially aimed to help young girls who were prostituted at young ages. Amy created the "Woman's Band" which became a safe haven for the young girls of India that fought religious and state-sponsored exploitation of young girls.

In Hindu temples, young girls were dedicated to the gods and forced into prostitution to earn money for the priests. Fighting this horrendous practice put Amy at risk of her own safety. Undaunted by the risks, she founded the Dohnavur Fellowship in order to raise money to continue her work. Dohnavur is in Tamil Nadu in southern India. It became a safe haven sanctuary for as many as 1,000 children—children who probably would not have survived childhood because of the sexual abuse they would have been exposed to otherwise. It should be noted that Amy's work at Dohnavur and the idea for the sanctuary started when a young girl escaped from a temple and found her way to Amy. Her name was Preena. Amy could not believe Preena's story of temple prostitution but soon found out that all of it was true. Amy provided shelter and protection for Preena, and she refused to allow temple priests to take the young girl back to the temple. Amy documented her work against the horrible treatment of children in her book ***The Gold Cord***. Another book, ***Things as They Are: Mission Work in Southern India***, became an international bestseller in 1903. Much of Amy's work went unnoticed by the rest of the world until the book was published. Because of her work and bravery, Amy was recognized and honored by Queen Mary.

At age sixty-four, Amy was injured in a fall, and thereafter, her always tenuous health declined further; however, she continued to write even though she could not travel without great physical pain. Amy composed hymns and poems and published several more books: ***Windows***; ***Though the Mountains Shake***; ***His Father Said***; ***If***; ***Edges of His Ways***; ***God's Missionary*** and many others. It is estimated that she wrote thirty-five books. Almost all of her books were about her missionary experiences. Due in large part to Amy's international exposure of temple prostitution, India banned the practice in 1948.

Amy died in 1951 at the age of eighty-three while living in India. She lived in India for over fifty-five years. Many of the children she saved from abuse attended her memorial service. There was no headstone placed to mark her grave. Instead, a bird bath was placed over her grave by the children who were spared from a horrible fate by Amy's dedication, courage, and kindness. A small marker was added with only one inscription: "Amma"—Tamil for "mother." To this day, over sixty years after her death, children in India take care of the bird bath.

The memory of Amy's devotion to children has become legendary in India, but very few people in other parts of the world know her story or remember her name. For a short period of time, a book by Derick Bingham highlighted Amy's life and brought renewed interest in her work. The book, *The Wild-Bird Child,* was published in 2004.

(References: *A Chance to Die: The Life and Legacy of Amy Carmichael,* 1987, Elisabeth Elliot; *Amy Carmichael: A Life Abandoned to God,* 1998, Sam Wellman; *The Wild-Bird Child: A Life of Amy Carmichael,* 2004, Derick Bingham)

Carmines, Al

Al was born in 1936 in Hampton, Virginia. Early in his life, it became clear to his parents and others that Al had many talents, but he excelled in music. Although many of his friends and family thought his career would be in music, Al had many other interests that he wanted to explore in college.

He attended Swarthmore College. Al enjoyed the intellectual stimulation of the classes and the supportive nature of the professors. The study of religion and theology stimulated Al's spiritual and intellectual growth. After receiving his Bachelor of Arts degree in English and philosophy, Al entered the Union Theological Seminary in New York City. He was a remarkably gifted student. The professors wanted him to remain at the seminary as a professor, but Al wanted to experience life outside of the college setting.

After he completed his college work and was ordained, Al became the minister at the Judson Memorial Church in New York. Not only was he an inspirational spiritual leader, he used his musical talents to enhance the worship services. He composed music for the church.

Al also organized a Bible study group that met on a regular basis. That Bible study group grew very popular and attracted hundreds of people and led to an expansion of worship services in the region. In fact, the Rauschenbusch Memorial United Church of Christ evolved from the Bible study group. Al also taught at the Union Theological Seminary and was an award-winning professor, both as a respected and gifted professor, but also because of his lyrical and musical productions and works.

Al started the Carmines' Judson Poets' Theater, which became a successful venue for Off-Broadway plays. He wrote several plays and the music to many of them. He won acclaim for his work, including a Drama Desk Award for Lyrics and the Lifetime Achievement Obie Award.

At the height of his career, Al suffered a cerebral aneurysm that left him partially disabled. He labored through physical therapy for several months, but he never fully recovered. Al died in 1985 at the age of forty-nine.

Before he died, Al said, *"If you want to know how to live, go to church. If you want to know how your life is in its deepest roots, also go to the theater."*

(References: *Al Carmines*, Wikipedia.org. Retrieved 2015; *History of Hymns—umcdiscipline.org*. Retrieved 2015; *Al Carmines*, hymntime.com. Retrieved 2014 and 2015; *traditionalmusic.com*. Retrieved 2015; *The Life and Influence of Al Carmines—The Pastor and the Musician*, Off Broadway Times, 1986)

Carter, Russell Kelso

Kelso was born in 1849 in Baltimore, Maryland. His family was a well-respected and educated family that insisted on obedience to God and family. Kelso's strict and supportive childhood instilled self-discipline and self-confidence in him throughout his life.

Kelso was a serious-minded child who excelled in everything he attempted. He was an excellent student, athlete, and musician. He was an extraordinary student who participated in sports, drama, and other clubs and activities at the high school. After completing high school with honors, he attended the Pennsylvania Military Academy (PMA). He was a top student in the classroom and in all sports. He was considered a scholar and star athlete.

Kelso earned a bachelor's degree in civil engineering, and so impressed the administrative and teaching staff at PMA that he was offered a position there to teach mathematics and engineering. Kelso taught at PMA for three years and then abruptly resigned and moved to California to raise sheep. He confided in his closest friends that he was burned out and mentally exhausted after spending his entire life up to that point working and striving to be successful almost every minute of every day.

After three years working on a farm, Kelso returned to PMA and taught mathematics and engineering. He studied chemistry and developed a course sequence for students interested in chemistry which allowed the academy to offer a degree in chemistry. Kelso was appointed Chair of the Civil Engineering Department at the academy and remained in that position for almost eight years. During his tenure at the academy, he studied music and theology on his own. It was not commonly known that Kelso had decided he wanted to become a minister.

He abruptly left the academy and became an ordained minister in the Methodist Church. He worked in the ministry for a short period of time before he studied to become a physician. His last career move was to medicine where he worked successfully in private practice for several years.

Throughout his various careers, Kelso was a prolific writer of articles, songs, hymns, and books on many topics including theology, mathematics, science, and music. He published five books about faith healing, seven books about Christianity and science, one book about missionary work, two books about medicine, four novels, and three hymnals. Kelso also wrote the music and words for fifty-two hymns and the music for another sixty-nine hymns. Arguably his most well-known hymn is ***Standing on the Promises***, which is in almost every Christian hymnal.

Kelso continued to practice medicine and write until his death in 1928 at the age of seventy-nine in Catonsville, Maryland. Kelso is remembered for his remarkable intellect, his broad interests and skills, and his faith.

(References: *Kelso Carter*, 2009, Daniel Mount and Levi Johnson; *Standing on the Promises*, Kregel Publications, 2012; *Kelso Carter*, Healingandrevival.com. Retrieved 2015; *Kelso Russell Carter*, Cyberhymnal.com. Retrieved 2015; *K.R. Carter*, Sharefaith.com. Retrieved 2015)

Cartwright, Colbert Scott

Colbert was born in 1924 in Coffeyville, Kansas. Colbert's father, Lin D. Cartwright, was a Disciples of Christ minister at the First Christian Church in Coffeyville. The family moved to Chattanooga, Tennessee. That is where Colbert grew up from age four to sixteen. When he was sixteen, the family moved to St. Louis, Missouri.

Colbert grew up wanting to follow in his father's footsteps as a minister. He was a good student in school, especially in secondary school where he excelled in all subjects and graduated with honors. After graduating, Colbert was accepted at Washington University in St. Louis. He enjoyed the university and was a superb student, earning election to the honor societies of Phi Beta Kappa and Phi Sigma Iota. Colbert earned a Bachelor of Arts degree. Due to his academic prowess, he was accepted at Yale University Divinity School where he earned a Bachelor of Divinity degree and a Master of Sacred Theology degree.

After being ordained, he became the minister at several churches including the First Christian Church in Lynchburg, Virginia; Pulaski Heights Christian Church in Little Rock, Arkansas; Central Christian Church in Youngstown, Ohio; and South Hills Christian Church in Fort Worth, Texas. After ministering at those churches Colbert served for ten years as area minister in the Trinity-Brazos Area in Fort Worth, Texas. He also served on the Board of the Southern Regional Council for five years. Additionally, Colbert was president of the Little Rock (Arkansas) Ministerial Association, an organization whose purpose was to unite all Christian churches, regardless of race.

Colbert was a stalwart leader in the civil rights efforts beginning in the 1950s when he preached a sermon supporting the decision of *Brown vs. Brown*, the landmark desegregation court case of the United States Supreme Court. His sermon was published in an Arkansas newspaper and generated considerable controversy, both negative and positive. Regardless of what people thought about his support of the Court's decision, he was hailed as a progressive Christian who advocated for all children.

Colbert was a prolific writer and became a frequent contributor to local newspapers and journals such as *The Christian Century; Christianity and Crisis; Progressive; New South; The Reporter,* and others. He also wrote several hymns and helped produce a hymnal for the Disciples of Christ. Colbert's most famous hymn is ***Be in Our Midst, O Christ***, which is in most Christian hymnals around the world. In addition, Colbert wrote scholarly works and published two books on the Disciples of Christ history and practices. He also wrote about the life and work of Bob Dylan, the legendary musician, which was published in England with positive reviews and sales.

Colbert's lifelong work was recognized in many ways and with numerous awards, including an honorary doctorate degree conferred on him by Texas Christian University. The Disciples of Christ recognized his lifelong dedication to worship and his service to the church and communities where he provided spiritual leadership and scholarship.

Colbert remained active in retirement until his health declined. He died at age seventy-one in 1996 in Ft. Worth, Texas.

(References: *Colbert S. Cartwright,* University of Arkansas Archive Manuscript Collection. Retrieved 2013 and 2015)

Cherry, Constance

Constance was born in 1953 in Michigan. She has served as director of music and as pastor in several churches. She holds a Bachelor of Arts in music from Huntington College, a Master of Music from Bowling Green State University, and a Doctor of Ministry in Christian Worship from Northern Baptist Theological Seminary.

One of her hymns, ***When Will People Cease Their Fighting***, appears in six major hymnals. Constance created the ***Worship Architect*** website which provides information about her and her work.

She is an experienced professor, worship leader, musician, and pastor, having served in local church ministry and academic teaching positions for thirty years.

While a young woman she received a lifetime call to serve Christ through serving His church. Constance was ordained in the United Methodist Church. For many years, she served as a full-time minister of music in large churches where she directed multiple types of choral groups and instrumental ensembles, prepared worship services, and provided leadership for the many dimensions of the multi-faceted church music program.

A growing interest in formal worship studies drew her eventually to pursue doctoral studies at Northern Baptist Theological Seminary (Chicago area). There she studied with Robert E. Webber who was not only Constance's professor but also the supervisor for her doctoral thesis, "Discovering Your Vision for Worship: Teaching Worship Services in an Interdenominational Seminary Setting."

Constance's call to ministry expanded into teaching seminary full-time at Winebrenner Theological Seminary, Findlay, Ohio, and serving nearby congregations as pastor.

Presently, Constance is Professor of Worship at Indiana Wesleyan University, Marion, Indiana where she directs degree studies in Christian Worship. Also, she has served on the faculty of The Robert E. Webber Institute for Worship Studies (IWS) located in Jacksonville, Florida. Additionally, she has taught worship at institutions of higher education in several countries, most recently in the Master's program at the *Evangelische Theologische Faculteit* (Evangelical Theological Faculty) in Leuven, Belgium.

She has three published books and several articles in numerous magazines such as *Worship Leader, The Hymn, Reformed Worship, Worship Arts,* and *Creator*. Constance also writes hymns. Once when asked how she started her hymn writing career, Constance said, "In 1980 I took the course, 'Hymnology' with esteemed scholar Dr. Hugh T. McElrath at Southern Baptist Theological Seminary. I had begun the Master of Church Music degree program. This course really changed my life. During the semester, Dr. McElrath convincingly addressed our class of eighty students with these words, 'Every one of you should be writing hymns.' I took him seriously and began to write hymn texts. Now, decades later, I have hymns in seven major hymnals published since 1990. In 2001, Hope Publishing Company published a solo collection of my hymns."

A native of Michigan, Constance enjoys traveling, playing the piano, walking, and fellowship with family and friends.

(References: *Constance Cherry,* theworshiparchitect.com. Retrieved 2015; *Selecting Worship Songs,* 2011, Constance Cherry; *Constance Cherry,* Hymnary.com. Retrieved 2015; *Rev Constance M. Cherry,* Indiana Wesleyan University. Retrieved 2015)

Chisholm, Thomas Obadiah

Thomas was born in Franklin, Kentucky in 1866 in a rural country log cabin where he lived with several siblings and his parents who were tenant farmers.

Thomas received his education first grade through tenth grade in a very small rural school with only two rooms. All of the students regardless of age and grade were taught in the same building and frequently using the same textbooks.

Thomas was small for his age and in frail health throughout most of his childhood. Nevertheless, he worked hard at school and at home and earned the respect of his parents, siblings, friends, and teachers for his intelligence, determination, and positive attitude. Thomas seldom complained and was known for his happy and charming demeanor.

He was the most gifted student in the school and mature for his age, although he was small and frequently ill. Thomas frequently helped other students and became an unofficial tutor. The small rural school had trouble keeping teachers, so with his intelligence, excellent school work, work ethic, and maturity, Thomas was offered a job as a teacher at the school when he was only sixteen years old. He worked in the small school for over five years.

With the teaching experience and his interest in literature and writing, he took a job as associate editor of *The Franklin Favorite,* which was a well-known and locally popular weekly newspaper.

Thomas' work afforded him the opportunity to meet and interact with a lot of people, and he began attending the local church.

One evening when he was twenty-seven years old he attended a revival being held by the legendary minister Dr. Henry Clay Morrison (who later became the President of Asbury College). Thomas was converted that night due to the influence of Dr. Morrison.

Thomas moved to Louisville, Kentucky and became the editor of the *Pentecostal Herald*. He renewed his friendship with Dr. Morrison who encouraged him to become a minister. Thomas was excited about the possibility of being a minister, so he studied with Dr. Morrison. Under the tutelage of Dr. Morrison, Thomas was ordained a Methodist minister. He then became the minister of the Scottsville Methodist Church in Scottsville, Kentucky.

Fighting poor health most of his life, his health declined further and he was forced to leave the church. Looking to improve his health, Thomas moved to a farm in Winona Lake, Indiana. As his health improved he became a full-time insurance salesman after moving to Vineland, New Jersey. When he was trying to regain his health he had a lot of idle time, so Thomas became a prolific writer of poems and he never stopped writing until he entered a nursing home near the end of his life.

Over his lifetime, Thomas wrote over 1,200 poems with almost 800 published. Many of his poems became hymns. Thomas is famous for writing one of the most popular hymns ever written—one that is probably played somewhere every day of the year. The hymn is the legendary ***Great is Thy Faithfulness***. Thomas explained the inspiration for the hymn: "My income has not been large at any time due to impaired health in the earlier years which has followed me on until now. Although I must not fail to record here the unfailing faithfulness of a covenant-keeping God and that He has given me many wonderful displays of His providing care, for which I am filled with astonishing gratefulness."

Despite a life-long battle with uneven health, remarkably Thomas lived until 1960 when he died at the age of ninety-four in Ocean Grove, New Jersey.

(References: *Amazing Grace: Illustrated Stories of Favorite Hymns,* 1999, Kenneth W. Osbeck; *Thomas Chisholm,* Berean Bible Heritage Church. Retrieved 2014; *Great is They Faithfulness—The Story Behind the Hymn,* Gaither.com. Retrieved 2014; *Thomas Obadiah Chisholm,* Reflections, 2012, Al Maxey)

Clark, Thomas Curtis

Thomas was born in 1877 in Chicago. His father was a minister in the Son of Disciples of Christ who encouraged him to study and read everything he could about a variety of subjects. This led to Thomas' love of literature and especially poetry. He read every poem and book of poems he could find in the school library, the community library, and in his father's church's library. Thomas tried writing a few poems and greatly enjoyed the experience, but he was reluctant to share them until much later.

Thomas excelled in school and showed a talent for writing and music composition. He became interested in hymns from his experience in his father's church. Thomas began to pay close attention to the details of the hymns sung in church and he became interested in the hymn composers. He noticed that many of the lyrics in hymns were poetic, and he found out later that many hymns are poems composed into a hymn. He was hooked; he wanted to write poems and hymns.

Thomas attended Indiana University where he earned a Bachelor in Arts degree. He was a very successful student in college and his poems caught the attention of professors and other students. Some of them were published in the university's magazine of arts. Thomas wanted to learn more, so he enrolled in the University of Chicago, where he continued his studies in music and writing.

After college, he looked for work because he was not making any money from his poetry. He found a teaching job in

Washington, Indiana, but he did not stay long. Thomas found jobs as a singer in evangelist revivals and as a tuner in the piano business. None of these were satisfactory to his creative needs or his personal budget. He finally found a job he liked as assistant editor of church school literature at the Christian Board of Publications in St. Louis, Missouri. From there he moved to a job on the *Christian Century Quarterly* editorial staff. Thomas enjoyed his work and the job allowed him to pursue his musical and poetry interests; in fact, he started composing hymns from his poems.

In 1943, he submitted one of his poem hymns to a contest that he thought he had no chance of winning. However, his hymn ***Thou Father of Us All*** won the Hymn Society of America's nationwide contest. This award brought attention to his other works and he enjoyed national attention thereafter.

Thomas was a prolific writer. He wrote hundreds of poems, published many books, and published over sixty hymns. His books included ***Poems and Songs; Friendly Town; Love Off to the War and Other Poems; Lincoln and Others; Poems of World Brotherhood; A Child's Thought of God; The New Patriotism; Poems of Justice; Poems for Special Occasions***, and others. His poem about Abraham Lincoln became extremely popular around the United States and the world.

When he was asked why he did not follow his father's wish for him to be a minister, Thomas said, "It was my father's wish that I enter the ministry, but when I entered religious publishing he was gratified. In my poems, I have simply put into verse the Christian convictions that were bred in me through twenty years of listening to his preaching. Every poem I have written has been inspired by deep faith and confidence. I take no credit, for it has been his voice speaking in all my writing. During all my years with him, I never heard one expression of doubt that God's will would finally prevail."

Thomas continued writing and publishing until his health declined in his early 70s. He died in 1953 at the age of seventy-six.

(References: *The Story of Our Hymns,* 1952, Armin Haeussler; *Who is Thomas Curtis Clark,* 2014, Richard Jean So and Hoyt Long—University of Chicago; *Thomas Curtis Clark,* Ancestry.com. Retrieved 2014)

Clausnitzer, Tobias

Tobias was born in 1619 in Thum, Saxony, Germany which is near Annaberg.

There are conflicting stories about Tobias' youth and family. Apparently, although it has not been verified, he received an education primarily from the local church. And because he was identified as an unusually intelligent child he was selected by the church to receive private tutoring with expectations that he would attend a university and become a minister.

Tobias was accepted at Saxony University, but he did not remain there very long. He studied at two or more other universities before settling in at Leipzig University where he earned a Master of Divinity degree.

Soon after he graduated he was appointed Chaplain of a Swedish Army regiment. He quickly became well-known within the ranks of the Swedish Army for his kindness, attention to the soldiers, his spirituality, and his sermons. Tobias' powerful sermons became legendary. He was summoned by General Friedrich Henrich Ernst Graf von Wrangel, General Field Marshall of the Prussian Army, to give a sermon at a field service in Upper Palatinate in Bavaria to recognize the conclusion of the Peace of Westphalia which ended the Thirty Years' War in the Holy Roman Empire and the Eighty Years' War between Spain and the Dutch Republic. Tobias' sermon earned high praise by the General and many others that attended the service. He also was invited to give the sermon at St. Thomas' Church in Leipzig on Reminiscere Sunday (the second Sunday in Lent) on the accession of Christina as Queen of Sweden (she had become Queen upon the death of her father when she was only six years old, but Queen Christina officially took her charge as Queen when she turned eighteen years old). Christina was enthralled by Tobias' sermon, so much so that she wanted a written copy of it.

Tobias became the First Pastor of a Weiden, Bavaria church (believed to be a Lutheran church). There he remained until his death. Tobias published several sermons, treatises, and hymns. Apparently, none of his sermons survived the years; however, some of his hymns did. The famous hymn ***Blessed Jesus, at Thy Word*** was bequeathed to his church. He also wrote ***Lord Jesus May They Grief and Pain.***

Tobias was one of Sweden's most well-known and loved religious leaders. Many members of government and royal families attended his church to hear his sermons, but he always found time in his busy schedule to tend to the needs of people in his church and community.

Tobias worked tirelessly with total devotion to his faith, his congregation, and his church until his death in 1684 at the age of sixty-five while living in Leipzig.

(References: *Tobias Clausnitzer,* 1907, Dictionary of Hymnology, John Julian; *Tobias Clausnitzer,* Cyberhymnal.org. Retrieved 2015)

Cober, Kenneth Lorne

Kenneth was born in 1902 in Dayton, Ohio to parents who were soon after Kenneth's birth assigned to Puerto Rico for missionary work. Kenneth grew up in Puerto Rico observing people living in desperate and abject poverty. During that time, he watched his parents convey the message of God to the people of Puerto Rico and provide food and shelter for them.

Kenneth adored his parents and greatly admired their dedication to their work and beliefs. Through their beliefs, music, reading activities, community activities (where he learned a lot about the Puerto Rican culture), and spending time together, the family remained very close.

Kenneth received much of his education at home from his parents, but he also attended a public school with Puerto Rican children. He learned the Puerto Rican history, language, and culture, but he also learned about other cultures and religions. Kenneth enjoyed living in Puerto Rico with his parents, but he wanted to attend a university in the United States.

When Kenneth turned seventeen, he enrolled at Bucknell University in Lewisburg, Pennsylvania. There he was active in college activities, especially music activities, events, and programs. Kenneth wanted to be a minister like his parents, so after he completed his bachelor's degree at Bucknell he attended Colgate Rochester Divinity School in Rochester, New York. Soon after receiving his Master of Divinity degree he accepted a pastorate at the First Baptist Church in Canandaigua, New York. A few years later he moved to Lafayette Avenue Baptist Church in Buffalo, New York where he unwittingly became the center of controversy at the church in 1941.

After the United States entered World War II in response to the Japanese bombing of Pearl Harbor, Kenneth gave a pacifist sermon that essentially criticized the United States' leaders for entering into a war with Japan and other countries. He was widely and wildly criticized and some within his congregation wanted him to step down from the pulpit and leave the church. But he was not forced to leave, unlike other ministers who lost their jobs by taking a pacifist position during World War II. Kenneth remained at the church for several more years.

Kenneth ministered to congregations in New York, Rhode Island, and Connecticut until he accepted the position as director of the Division of Christian Education for the Baptist Convention. Kenneth remained there for over seventeen years.

In the 1960s, Kenneth frequently joined the desegregation marches in the Deep South and was threatened many times. Despite the threats, he continued to participate in the Freedom Marches and he spoke out against racism and violence. Kenneth received a personal letter from Dr. Martin Luther King, Jr. thanking him for his support and his courage.

During his career, Kenneth had several publications including ***Teaching Seniors***; ***The Church's Teaching Ministry***; ***Hymnbook of***

Christian Worship; Evangelism in the Sunday Church School, and many others. Kenneth also wrote several hymns, but his most familiar is ***All Is Well,*** a hymn that can be found in almost every Christian hymnal around the world. ***All Is Well*** was inspired by his belief that all men are created equal and that God's grace extends to all mankind.

Kenneth retired and moved to Penney Farms in Florida where he was active in local church and community activities until his death in 1993 at the age of ninety-one.

(References: *Kenneth Cober,* Dictionary-Handbook to Hymns for the Living Church, 1978, Donald Paul Hustad; *Kenneth L. Cober,* The Canterbury Dictionary of Hymnology. Retrieved 2014; *Evangelism in the Sunday Church School,* 1955, Kenneth Cober; *The Papers of Martin Luther King, Jr. Letter to Kenneth L. Cober,* 1997, Clayborne Carson)

Cole-Turner, Ronald

Ronald was born in 1948. Ronald from a young age had a compelling interest in his spiritual life and a natural curiosity about life and science. This led him to a life of exploration in literature, science, theology, and philosophy.

Ronald excelled in all subjects in elementary and secondary school and earned a scholarship to Wheaton College where he received a Bachelor of Arts degree in Literature with honors. Following his interests, Ronald applied for graduate school at Princeton University and was accepted at the Theological Seminary. His level of brilliance was uncommon even among exceptionally intelligent students and faculty members. Many of his classmates and professors encouraged him to develop his intellect by remaining at Princeton for post-graduate studies. Ronald followed their advice and received a Master of Divinity degree and continued his intellectual and spiritual journey throughout his life.

He was ordained as a minister in the United Church of Christ. A few years later he earned a Ph.D. in Systematic Theology from Princeton. For several years and currently Ronald has worked at the

Pittsburgh Theological Seminary. He is the H. Parker Professor of Theology and Ethics.

Ronald was a founding member of the International Society for Science and Religion (currently serving as vice president) and has served on the advisory board of the John Templeton Foundation and the Metanexus Institute.

He is a prolific researcher and writer. Ronald is the author of ***Transhumanism and Transcendence: Christian Hope in an Age of Technological Advancement***; ***The New Genesis: Theology and the Genetic Revolution***; the co-author (with Brent Waters) of ***Pastoral Genetics: Theology and Care at the Beginning of Life*** (which was awarded the prize for Outstanding Books in Theology and Science from the John Templeton Foundation); the editor of ***Human Cloning: Religious Responses and of Beyond Cloning; Religion and the Remaking of Humanity***, the co-editor of ***God and the Embryo: Religious Voices on Stem Cells and Cloning***, **editor of *Design and Destiny: Jewish and Christian Perspectives on Human Germline Modification***, and editor of ***Technology and Transcendence*** (in press). He is also the author of the popular baptism hymn, ***Child of Blessing, Child of Promise***.

Ronald has received numerous awards for his scholarly research and publications.

(References: *Ronald Cole-Turner,* Biography, Pittsburgh Theological Seminary. Retrieved 2014; *Ronald Cole-Turner,* ResearchGate. Retrieved 2014; *Ronald Cole-Turner,* Great Lecture Library. Retrieved 2015); *Ronald Cole-Turner,* Libraries Australia Archives. Retrieved 2015)

Cosnett, Elizabeth

Elizabeth was born in 1936 in Liverpool, England. She was a precocious and charming child who loved music and being around people. Elizabeth had several friends and she was very active physically and intellectually. She loved to discover new things, but she especially enjoyed reading.

Elizabeth was an excellent student in all of her school work and she also participated in school activities. She graduated with honors from Calder High School.

She continued her education at St. Hugh's College at Oxford, where she earned a Bachelor of Arts degree. Elizabeth wanted to teach, so she taught grammar for over ten years at a Liverpool high school. While teaching she enrolled at the University of Liverpool to work on a master's degree. Elizabeth earned a Master of Arts degree. Her master thesis paper won acclaim for its study of poets as hymn writers.

In 1969, Elizabeth joined the faculty of the Liverpool Institute of Higher Education (formerly known as St. Katharine's College) and taught literature. She remained at the Liverpool Institute of Higher Education for over twenty-seven years.

During her teaching career, she published several poems and hymns. Her work first gained widespread attention in 1985 when several of her hymns won honors at the British Broadcasting Center's (BBC) Song of Praise competition. Elizabeth received more honors at the BBC's Song of Praise competition in 1988. Following those honors, some of her hymns were included in various hymnals across Great Britain.

Visitors to churches in Britain heard Elizabeth's hymns and brought them to the United States and Canada where they were published. Many of her hymns became popular, such as ***Can We by Searching Find Out God***; ***Shaping Spirit, Move Among Us***; ***We Bring our Children, Lord, Today*** and ***When Candles are Lighted on Candlemas Day***.

After her retirement, Elizabeth remained active with her writing and she served in many roles, often volunteering to help churches and communities. For three years she served as Executive President of the Hymn Society of Great Britain and Ireland. She served as a churchwarden at City Centre Parish Church of St. Nicholas, where she was also a bell-ringer.

Elizabeth died on January 10, 2015, at the age of niety-one in her home in Birmingham, England.

(References: *Elizabeth Cosnett,* Dictionary of Hymnology. Retrieved 2013; *Hymns for Everyday Saints,* 2001, Elizabeth Cosnett; *Elizabeth Cosnett,* Obituary, January 10, 2015, Birmingham Mail)

Coxe, Arthur Cleveland

(Arthur later added the "e" to his surname and he used his middle name, Cleveland, more than his first name.)

Cleveland was born in 1818 in Mendham, New Jersey. His family moved to New York, New York when he was two years old. His father was a famous Presbyterian minister, Reverend Samuel H. Cox. His maternal grandfather was also a well-known and respected theologian, Reverend Aaron Cleveland. Cleveland wanted to follow in his father's footsteps but often felt inferior to that possibility even though he showed early signs of an extraordinary intellect.

As Cleveland grew older he became a very gifted student. He excelled in all of his school work and he showed an early talent for writing and music. He enjoyed writing poetry, and he learned to play various musical instruments. Cleveland benefitted greatly from the private tutorship of Professor George Bush, who prepared Cleveland for college.

Cleveland attended the University of New York and graduated in 1838 at the age of twenty. During his freshman year, he published his first poem, which was enthusiastically received by the publisher. After completing college, he immediately enrolled in the General Theological Seminary. After graduation, he took Holy Orders when he was only twenty-three years old. Cleveland began his distinguished career as the Rector of St. John's in Hartford, Connecticut. From there he became the minister at Grace Church in Baltimore, Maryland and later minister at Calvary Church in New York City. Cleveland was a gifted minister and a guardian and mentor to his congregations. He was also involved in missionary work, especially in Haiti where he served as de facto bishop until one was appointed. Cleveland enjoyed writing, including the composition of hymns, poems, and scholarly works. He wrote ***Advent; Christian Ballads; Athanasian; Halloween and Other Poems; Saul—a Mystery; Writings of Hawthorne***, and other popular publications. Cleveland was also a theology scholar, having published ***Criterion; Apollos - or the Way of God***; and ***The Institutes of Christian History***. His book ***Christian Ballads*** went through several editions and is considered a classic in American literature. He was offered several positions around the country, and at one time was offered a bishop position in Texas. Cleveland, however, enjoyed his life and career in New York. In 1865, he accepted the position of Episcopal Bishop of the Western Diocese of New York. Cleveland received honorary doctorates in divinity from St. James College, Hagerstown, Maryland in 1856; from Trinity, Hartford, Connecticut in 1868, and from Durham University in the United Kingdom in 1888. He also received an honorary doctorate of laws from Kenyon College, in Ohio in 1868. Cleveland continued to write and he remained active in church and even in debates with Catholic theologians up until the time of his death in 1896 at the age of seventy-eight. He is buried in Geneva, New York.

(References: *The Gospel in Hymns*, 1950, Albert Edward Bailey; *American Hymns Old and New: Notes on the Hymns and Biographies of the Authors and Composers*, 1980, Charles William Hughes; *Dictionary Handbook to Hymns for the Living Church*, 1978, Donald Paul Hustad)

Croly, George

George was born in 1780 in Dublin, Ireland. His father was a physician and community leader and his mother was also active in community activities and efforts to support families.

George's father and mother emphasized education for their four children. George was a good student, but he did not excel in his schoolwork. Nevertheless, he enrolled at Trinity College in Dublin and was very successful. George responded positively to the intellectual challenges at the college and he enjoyed college activities and developing friendships. He received Bachelor and

Master of Arts degrees at Trinity College, where later in his life he would be awarded an honorary law degree.

Having studied theology, George was ordained at the age of twenty-four and took a job as Curate of the Diocese of Meath. His father died unexpectedly, leaving George responsible for his mother, one brother, and two sisters. George moved the entire family to London, hoping that a ministry would be more likely there. However, he received no offers so he turned to his writing skills to make money for the family.

George's first article was accepted in the popular *Literary Gazette* where he would become a regular contributor. George also provided articles to *Blackwood's Magazine* and the magazine *Britannia*. His reputation in the literary world, at first, grew slowly but then his literary prowess expanded rapidly after several of his articles were published. He became a theater critic for the *New Times*, wrote poems and plays, novels and treatises. At one point, he also served as a foreign correspondent for several newspapers and magazines. George, however, was best known for his successful novels, ***Salathiel***; ***Wandering Jew***, and ***Marston***.

George's career took an unexpected turn when he was asked to fill in for the Vicar of the parish of Romford, Essex, who had become seriously ill. This experience convinced George that his heart was in parish work and not literary work. Later he gained his own appointment as Rector of St. Stephen Walbrook in London. George loved serving there, but the parish was in serious financial trouble when he took it over, and it was located in one of the worst slums in London. It was almost completely absent of a viable congregation and the building was in ill-repair. George was not discouraged, however. He worked hard to gain the trust and interest of people near the parish and beyond the parish. George's efforts were successful. His powerful sermons, his engaging demeanor, and bright spirit attracted people back to the church. He even published a new hymnal that was just for his church, ***Psalms and Hymns for Public Worship***. Worshippers soon filled the church and all repairs to the church were completed in just a few years due to donations and work from the congregation. George was proud of the parish and the congregation. He remained there until his death twenty-five years later.

George accomplished a lot even as he suffered through personal tragedies in his life. His twenty-three-year-old son died in the Battle of Ferozeshah (a long ago and mostly forgotten battle between the Sikhs and the British in Punjab, India) and he lost his nine-year-old daughter just a few months after his wife died. He seemed to express much of his sadness and the spiritual relief within his hymns, but only one of his hymns survived—***Holiness Desired***.

George continued to expand the congregation and he created many activities to encourage the congregation to participate in and support the church. He was a tireless, committed spiritual leader who was always available anytime he was needed. George seemed like a saint to his congregation.

George died unexpectedly in 1860 at the age of eighty as he was out walking near his home. As he desired, George was buried at St. Stephen's. His funeral was attended by hundreds from his congregation and by many other admirers.

(References: *The Story of Christian Hymnody*, 1961, Ernest Ryden; *George Croly*, Dictionary of Hymnology, 1907, John Julian; *George Croly*, Britannica.com. Retrieved 2013)

Crosby, Frances Jane (Fanny)

Fanny was born in 1820 in the small village of Brewster, New York, as the only child in a Puritan family. Fanny was born healthy but developed an infection from a cold and became gravely ill. Her eyes became infected and the popular treatment of the day was to put mustard poultices on the eyes for hours at a time. There is some debate whether the treatment caused her blindness, or if it was a congenital condition.

Even though she was blind, Jane was very active and gregarious. The young vivacious girl was called Fanny by her family and friends. Fanny's family had ties to Harvard University and to families who came to America on the *Mayflower*.

Unfortunately for the family, Fanny's father died the same year she was born, so Fanny was raised by her mother and maternal grandmother, both of whom were very dedicated to Christian principles and study of the Bible.

Her mother and grandmother did not allow Fanny to feel limited by her blindness. Fanny was made to memorize as much of the Bible as she possibly could, as they read passages to her. There were times when Fanny could recite extremely long passages from the Bible, and many of the entire books of the New Testament. She was exposed to world literature and music at a very young age, and she wrote her first poem when she was only eight years old. The poem was about her blindness.

Fanny was very intelligent and creative in many ways. She often surprised her mother, grandmother, and teachers with the depth of her insight, intelligence, and creative mind. To encourage her poetry and interest in music the family hired a music teacher to give Fanny lessons twice a week. The music teacher suggested to Fanny's mother that the young girl would enjoy church music and the experience may heighten her interest in music. Following this suggestion, Fanny's mother and grandmother took her to the Methodist Episcopal Church in town and marveled at Fanny's fascination and delight over the hymns.

Much of Fanny's education was at home, with teachers coming to the house, but when she turned fourteen years old she was enrolled at the New York Institution for the Blind (NYIB), a residential school, where she would remain for almost ten years. There she received a broad and well-rounded education and she learned to play the piano, organ, guitar, harp, and violin. It was during this time that Fanny discovered a love of and talent for writing. Her first publication was a poem she wrote about dishonesty. Her teachers at NYIB thought the poem was excellent if not also controversial. Without her knowledge, a group of the teachers sent the poem to publishers. P. T. Barnum loved the poem and published it in *The Herald of Freedom* magazine. This was the beginning of a long career of writing, including publications in the most popular newspapers and magazines in the country.

After leaving NYIB at the age of twenty-three, she was recruited by a group of lobbyists working in Washington, D.C. to assist them with efforts to persuade Congress to dedicate money for the education of the blind. Fanny's influence grew rapidly, and she made history, being the first woman to speak in the United States Senate when she read a poem that advocated the cause for the education of the blind: "O ye, who here from every state convene illustrious band! May we not hope the scene you now behold will prove to every mind instruction hath a ray to cheer the blind."

Fanny continued her advocacy for the blind across the country, including audiences with Congress members, state legislatures, and others. Her advocacy work seemed boundless and time-consuming, but she never stopped writing poems, prose, and hymns.

Her book ***A Blind Girl and Other Poems*** was a national sensation. She also published four other books of poetry and hymns. In her career Fanny wrote over 8,000 hymns, making her one of the most prolific hymnists in history. Over 100 million copies of her hymns have been made and the number keeps increasing each year.

During her lifetime, Fanny was famous beyond her wildest dreams. Her name was recognized in almost every household in the United States. The news media referred to Fanny as the "Queen of Gospel Song Writers". Fanny's hymns became so popular and filled so many hymnals that publishers began to exclude some of her works. In response to this, Fanny used over 200 pseudonyms so her hymns would be included. Late in her life, she expanded her advocacy work to address the needs of people and families living in poverty.

Sadly, as her writing productivity diminished with age, her living conditions deteriorated, despite her fame and the widespread use of her hymns. Apparently, she received very little compensation for her published hymns and poems. Many publishers took advantage of her and did not pay her the royalties she earned.

With encouragement from friends and supporters, Fanny wrote her autobiography, which was published in 1904. Though she received very little money from book sales, the book reestablished her legacy which allowed her to improve her living conditions and live in more comfort and security.

After being ill for several months with multiple ailments, Fanny died from a cerebral hemorrhage in 1915 at the age of ninety-four. The quote on her grave marker reads: "She hath done what she could!"

(References: *Fanny J. Crosby: An Autobiography,* 2008, Fanny J. Crosby (originally published in 1912) Hendrickson Classic Biography; *The Story of the American Hymn,* 1921, Edward S. Ninde (reproduced by Abingdon Press through Wholesome Words 2014); *The Life and Ministry of Frances Jane Crosby,* 2014, Christian Hall of Fame Series by Ed Reese)

Crum, John Macleod Campbell

John was born in 1872 in Mere Old Hall, Cheshire, England to a modest family that valued family and friends.

John was the youngest of the five children, but he was strong and had a determined personality. He was a natural leader and to some friends of the family, John acted like the oldest child. His family grew to admire John's intellectual and practical abilities. John enjoyed learning and much of what he learned came from his insatiable appetite for reading. He also enjoyed music and activities at the local church.

The minister of the Mere Old Hall Church saw the potential in John and encouraged him to pursue his education and enter the ministry. This suggestion fascinated John because up to that point he never seriously considered the possibility that he could rise to that level of intellectual acumen. He studied diligently for the exams and spent many hours taking exams that he made up to prepare him for the college exams. By then he desperately wanted to attend college.

Not only did John do well on qualifying exams for college, he exceeded all expectations. He was enrolled at the New College at Oxford. After some initial struggles to adjust to college life and high academic expectations, he settled in and excelled in all of his classes and subjects. It was soon obvious that John was a gifted student. His gregarious nature endeared him to his classmates and the professors. He graduated from New College with honors.

John was ordained as a deacon in 1897 and as a priest in 1900. During this time, John continued at New College and earned his Master of Divinity degree. He became the Assistant Curate of St. John the Evangelist in Darlington, England, and he remained there for almost four years. During his time at St. John he started to write poetry and hymns. He moved to a position as chaplain to Francis Paget who was Bishop of Oxford. John learned a lot from the Bishop about theology but also about leadership—what it meant to maintain a stellar reputation as a model to members of the congregation. John then accepted a position as assistant curate in Windsor, England and then as Vicar of Mentmore.

After his reputation grew while at Mentmore, John was honored with the position of Rector of Farnham, where he remained for over fifteen years. John fulfilled his lifetime ambition when he was appointed Canon of Canterbury in 1928. He loved the work at Canterbury and enjoyed each of the fifteen years he was Canon.

Throughout his service career John wrote poetry and hymns; however, his first published hymn was not until 1924 when ***Road Mending on the Sacred Way*** was published. That was followed by another successful and well-known hymn, ***What Mean Ye by These Stones***. John also published books, including two popular books, ***The Original Jerusalem Gospel,*** and ***St. Mark's Gospel—Two Stages of Its Making***.

Even after retirement, John was a mentor to countless spiritual leaders, who often sought his advice about a number of issues. He also continued to write until his health declined.

John died in 1958 at Farnham, Surrey, England at the age of eighty-six. Several hundred people attended the memorial service for John and sang his hymns.

(References: *John M. Crum,* Cyberhymnal.org. Retrieved 2014; *The Seventh-day Adventist Hymnal,* 1996; *Too Deep for Words; A Theology of Liturgical Expression,* 2002, Clayton J. Schmit)

Davis, Frances W.

Frances was born in 1936 in Winnipeg, Manitoba, Canada. Her family was very close and spiritual. Her parents encouraged her interest in music and she learned to play several musical instruments when she was young.

Frances was a superb student in school, gaining honors for her school work and projects. She also participated in several school activities and was an active member of musical productions. Frances played different musical instruments in the productions and often helped arrange the music.

After completing secondary school, Frances enrolled in the University of Manitoba where she earned a Bachelor of Arts degree when she was only twenty-one years old. While attending classes at Manitoba she was involved in extracurricular events. She was recognized for her musical talents and gregarious personality. Frances composed music and she was also a gifted writer. After completing her work at Manitoba she attended the University of Toronto. Frances completed her Master of Arts degree in 1962. Her Master thesis, "A Theory of Feminine Fiction" created a stir on the campus and was widely quoted in articles and opinion pieces across Canada.

Frances began her career as an Anglican teacher, but she also wrote poems, stories, and music compositions. She was involved with the music at St. George's Church in Ste.-Anne-de-Bellevue, Quebec, Canada and there she met Robert Fleming. They worked together on hymns, with Frances writing the lyrics and Robert the music. It was this teamwork that led to the internationally famous and long-enduring hymn ***Let There Be Light***, which was composed and published in 1968. With the turbulence in the world at that time and the desperate desire for peace in a world filled with war, including the Viet Nam war, the timing of the hymn captured the hearts of millions of people and it became an instant classic. The opening lyrics struck at the heart and soul of many people: "Let there be light; let there be understanding; let all the nations gather; and let them be face to face."

Frances said in an interview with Michael Hawn of United Methodist Church Disciples Ministries that the famous hymn had a special meaning: "I remember that I was very much swept up in the peace movement at the time, and was very excited by Robert's very simple and powerful musical setting. We sang the hymn a lot at St. George's, where Robert was the music director and I sang in his choir, long before the hymn was formally published."

Frances' influence on worship music and social issues continued throughout her career and well into semi-retirement. Frances at the age of eighty continues to write poetry, stories, and hymns.

Frances' co-composer and friend, ***Robert Fleming***, was born and raised in Prince Albert, Saskatchewan. He attended the Royal College of Music in London, England and there studied with famous composers Arthur Benjamin and Herbert Howells. Robert then attended the Royal Conservatory of Music in Toronto. Robert was the music director for the National Film Board and later a professor at Carlton University. Tragically, Robert died in 1976 when he was only fifty-five years old.

(References: *Frances Davis,* Dictionary of North America Hymnology. Retrieved 2014; *Let There Be Light,* 2002, Michael Hawn, UMC. Retrieved 2014; *Robert Fleming,* The Canadian Encyclopedia. Retrieved 2014)

Davison, Fannie Estelle Church

Fannie was born in 1851 in Cuyahoga Falls, Ohio. Her family was well educated and her father's business was successful and prominent in the community. Fannie lived a comfortable and quiet life filled with church, school, and community activities. She loved the small community of Cuyahoga Falls.

Her world fell apart, however, when she was ten years old. Her beloved father was killed in an accident. The family struggled with the loss and in his absence they tried to overcome the tragedy and keep the family business running, but it did not run efficiently.

A couple of years later Fannie's mother met and married hotelier Henry Warner and the family relocated to Carthage, Missouri. Fannie completed her education at the local school and went to work.

Even as a young child Fannie enjoyed poems and singing and even wrote a few hymns and poems before she was eighteen years old. She continued to write hymns and poems throughout her life.

She met and married Asa Davison who was a court reporter and they moved to Chicago, Illinois to advance his career. Later they would settle in Madison, Wisconsin and raise two children.

Fannie was reluctant to do so, but her husband encouraged her to submit her poems and hymns for publication. To her surprise, they were well received. Fannie's hymns were first published by the Fillmore Brothers Music Publishing House in Cincinnati, Ohio in several small hymnals that were sold to churches around the country. Fannie's hymn ***Purer in Heart, O God*** became a favorite and remains so today. Her hymns appeared in three hymnals that were very popular for decades, *Songs of Gratitude, Joy and Gladness,* and *The Voice of Joy.* Many of her other hymns were well-known during her lifetime and can be found in modern hymnals.

Fannie suffered from poor health at an early age due to chronic respiratory problems, probably asthma. She had episodes when she was bedridden for several days as she struggled to breathe. She sought special treatment for her health problems in Chicago, but she became too weak to benefit from the treatment. Fannie rallied a few times, but then her respiratory distress would return which weakened her body. She died in Chicago, Illinois in 1887 when she was only thirty-six years old.

Fannie was buried in Carthage, Missouri.

(References: *Handbook for Spiritual Hymns*, 2003, Myron K. Sauder; *Fannie E.C. Davison*, 1999, Eric Spencer; 2012 *Hymnic Anniversaries*, 2011, Carl P. Daw)

Daw, Carl P., Jr

Carl was born in 1944 in Louisville, Kentucky. His father was a Baptist pastor who frequently moved to various churches throughout Tennessee when Carl was a young boy. His father was an enigmatic and charismatic minister who loved being a messenger of the faith. Despite all of the many moves, the family remained close.

Carl had a compelling interest in learning and reading as well as in music and worship. He was influenced by his father to value spiritual development and education, as well as the importance of music in worship services.

Carl was a good student in elementary and secondary schools which gave him the opportunity to gain admission to academically challenging Rice University, where he showed his intellectual prowess. Carl thrived at the university and was greatly admired by his classmates and professors. After earning a Bachelor of Arts degree at Rice University, Carl was accepted at the University of Virginia where he earned a master's degree and a Doctor of Philosophy degree. After he received a Ph.D., Carl taught English for almost eight years at the College of William and Mary.

Although he was considered a top professor and was very popular with the students, he longed to enter the seminary, which he did at the University of the South. After he was ordained, Carl served as Assistant Rector of Grace Church in Petersburg, Virginia before working almost ten years as Vicar Chaplain at St. Mark's Chapel at the University of Connecticut. He left there to serve several churches in the area near Aliquippa, Pennsylvania and served as executive director of the Hymn Society of the United States and Canada.

During his career, Carl has composed many hymns and written several books and articles. Carl's hymns appear in many denominational hymnals in the English-speaking world. Also, some of his hymns have been translated into Spanish, Japanese and Chinese, as well as other languages. Over seventy of his hymns are currently in print around the world, including four books of hymns, ***A Year of Grace; To Sing God's Praise; New Psalms and Hymns and Spiritual Songs***, and ***Gathered for Worship***.

Carl continues to write hymns as well as articles about liturgy and music. He reviews materials for the *St. Luke's Journal of Theology, The Anglican Theological Review,* and for *The Hymn*. Carl serves as a curator of hymnological collections and adjunct professor of hymnology at Boston University School of Theology.

Carl has received numerous awards. For recognition of his career-long successes, he was named a Fellow of the Royal School of Church Music in 2011.

(References: *Carl P. Daw, Jr.,* Boston University School of Theology professor profile. Retrieved 2015; *Companion to the United Methodist Hymnal,* 1993, Carlton Young; *Carl P. Daw, Jr.,* Hope Publishing Company. Retrieved 2015; *Carl P. Daw, Jr.*, 2007, Nancy Wicklund Gray)

Dearmer, Percival (Percy)

Percy was born in 1867 in Kilburn, Middlesex, England, to a family that was blessed with creative talents and skills. Percy's father was a professional artist and an art teacher. Percy's mother also enjoyed art, as did his siblings.

Percy's father encouraged him to pursue several interests so he could decide which vocation would be best for him. Percy attended Streatham School in Kilburn and was an excellent student. He participated in school activities and community activities. Percy had a wide range of interests including art, music, and literature.

After completing Streatham School he attended Westminster School for a short period of time before transferring to a residential school in Switzerland in order to receive an international education. He returned to England to attend Christ Church at Oxford University where he earned a Bachelor of Arts degree.

Percy developed an interest in his spiritual evolution which led him to seek a career in the ministry. After studying theology on his own and in his local church, Percy was ordained into the priesthood at the Rochester Cathedral (England's second oldest Cathedral) in Essex. It was during this time that he began courting a writer, Jessie Mabel Prichard White. They married and her influence on Percy was immediate and profound. She encouraged him to write and further develop his considerable intellect.

Percy and Jessie had two sons who both served in World War I. One of them, Geoffrey, became well known for his poems describing his experiences in the war. He was one of the most popular of a group of poets commonly referred to as the "War Poets." It's worth noting that Geoffrey lived to be 103 years old and is remembered as a cherished poet in Great Britain.

Percy lost his other son, Christopher, to the trenches of World War I, but he also lost his beloved wife to World War I. She died while serving in an ambulance in Serbia as a volunteer. Percy was a Chaplain for the British Red Cross during World War I in Serbia with his wife. He was with her when she died from injuries and enteric fever. Percy was devastated by the loss of his wife and son. Many of his friends said that his faith in God was tested during his years of grieving.

Even though he continued his ministry and writings, it was evident to his friends that he was struggling with the loss of his loved ones and the damage to his spirit.

Percy's most famous publication was ***The Parson's Handbook***, which is a liturgical manual for ministers and other religious leaders. Among many other messages, the manual conveys the need for worship services to be sacred, uplifting, and spiritual, but also proper, based on the fundamental principles of the Catholic Church and proper English courtesy and manners.

Percy also wrote many poems and hymns, some of which are still in hymnals around the world. He also wrote the ***Book of Common Prayer*** out of his concern that people did not know how to pray and also for his annoyance at some ministers who seem to have lost the basic meaning and purpose of prayer. Percy believed prayer should not be verbose or a grand oration but instead should be simple, heartfelt and intended to feed the soul.

Percy's fame and respect for his work grew steadily, which led to him being named Third Vicar of St. Mary-the-Virgin Church in London, England. While he was there he continued to compose hymns and he went through several revisions of ***The Parson's Handbook***, providing updates and extended explanations of existing points and chapters.

Percy published ***The English Hymnal*** and the ***Oxford Book of Carols*** with Ralph Williams. The Oxford book attempted to bring back the tradition of medieval English melodies and lyrics. The two writers also published a book of hymns titled ***Songs of Praise***, which is most famous for one hymn it provided to the world, ***Morning Has Broken*** - the almost legendary hymn that became known not only in churches but also in the music world.

While that hymn found its way into our modern culture in the social revolution of the 1960s with the singer, Cat Stevens, there was another hymn that remains a stalwart in churches, ***A Great and Mighty Wonder***.

When he left St. Mary's-the-Virgin, Percy did community volunteer work, continued to write and was Professor of Ecclesiastical Art at King's College in London for over twelve years.

Percy died suddenly from a heart attack in 1936 at the age of sixty-nine. His ashes were interred in the Great Cloister at Westminster Abbey which is a rare tribute reserved only for those held in the highest esteem by Great Britain.

(References: *Percy Dearmer: A Parson's Pilgrimage,* 2000, Donald Gray; *Percy Dearmer,* Oxford Dictionary of National Biography. Retrieved 2013; *Percy Dearmer 1867-1936,* World Categories Identities. Retrieved 2013)

Doddridge, Philip

Philip was born in 1702 in London, England to a well-known family. His father was a successful businessman in oils and pickles and his grandfather was the Rector of Shepperton, Middlesex, who later became a leader in the non-conformist movement.

Philip was the youngest of twenty children, and as much as it could be possible with that many children, he was considered the favorite of his mother, the redoubtable Elizabeth Doddridge. Philip's mother read to him starting long before he could read. They read the Bible together from both the Old and New Testament and from those readings taught him that the Bible is not only a spiritual guide but also a historical masterpiece. He was very close to his mother and was devastated when she died shortly after his eighth birthday. He grieved for several months, and for the rest of his life he talked frequently about his loving mother and he often dedicated his publications to her.

The family's prosperity afforded him the opportunity to learn from a private tutor until he was old enough to enter a private school, the same grammar school where his maternal grandfather was once master. Philip was ten years old when he entered the Kingston-Upon-Thames grammar school where he excelled in academic work and music. He was happy there but only two years later tragedy struck again when his father died unexpectedly. Without a guardian and with a considerable inheritance, he was assigned a guardian by the name of Downes, for which little is known, who moved young Philip to another private school at St. Albans.

Philip grieved for his parents and his former life, but he grew to like St. Albans because of the influence of a Presbyterian minister, Samuel Clark. Philip became interested in the church and developed friends at the school and in the community. In the meantime, Philip did not know that his guardian was draining all of his inheritance. When he discovered that Downes was gone he also found out that his inheritance was gone too—all of it. Suddenly, Philip was a destitute and orphaned thirteen-year-old with no family to depend on. Fortunately for Philip, the minister Samuel Clark took him in and raised him like a son. He encouraged Philip's interest in the ministry and music and guided his education.

Philip became a gifted writer and musician. His intellectual prowess was seen by all and he was encouraged to pursue a career in law, but Philip's interest was primarily in theology due in large part to the influence of Samuel Clark.

Philip entered the Dissenting Academy in Leicestershire, with encouragement and support from Samuel Clark. Philip was ordained as a nonconformist minister. His first independent career position was at the newly formed Northampton Academy which was later named the Daventry Academy and many years later evolved into New College, Hampstead, and eventually New College London, a center for training Congregational and then United Reformed Church ministers. While working at the Northampton Academy he also served as the minister of the Northampton Independent Church congregation.

Philip became very popular both as a brilliant scholar-teacher at the Academy and as an enthusiastic and thoughtful minister who carefully crafted each sermon. He also began writing and composing music. Philip became a prolific writer and hymn composer. His works became so well-known and respected and his sermons so much admired for the scholarly yet practical messages that he was awarded a Doctor of Divinity degree from Aberdeen University.

Philip's lectures became so popular that students from other universities and academies filled his classes, with as many as 250 students present to hear him lecture about philosophy and theology. He had a special attraction to the writings of the philosopher Spinoza.

Even when he was busy beyond reason with the Academy and the church, he still managed to find time to write. His book ***The Rise and Progress of Religion in the Soul*** was widely popular. It was translated into seven languages. His other famous books were ***The Family Expositor; Life of Colonel Gardiner*** and a ***Course of Lectures on Pneumatology, Ethics, and Divinity***. Additionally, Philip found the time and creativity to write over 400 hymns. Most of his hymns were aligned to the themes of his sermons, so the hymns preceding and following his sermons were sharing the same message.

Philip's health was always a problem, and it is remarkable that he accomplished so much even during times when he was weak and fighting headaches, respiratory problems, and other ailments. He became gravely ill while sailing to Lisbon in September of 1751 to visit friends and lecture at colleges in the area. He received medical treatment there but he was too sick to return home. Philip never fully recovered. He finally succumbed to what many experts believe was tuberculosis at the young age of forty-nine.

News of Philip's death shocked the world because he was young and so greatly admired. Philip was buried at the British Factory in Lisbon where his grave and tomb remains a popular site for visitors.

The power of Philip's work influenced the Christian world and continues to do so over 260 years later.

(References: *Philip Doddridge,* Oxford Dictionary of National Biography. Retrieved 2013; *Dissenting Academies in England,* 2009, Irene Parker; *Philip Doddridge,* Encyclopedia Britannica. Retrieved 2013; *Philip Doddridge,* The Banner of Sovereign Grace Truth, September 1998, G. Ella)

Dorsey, Thomas Andrew

Thomas was born in 1899 in Villa Rica, Georgia. His father was a Baptist preacher and his mother gave piano lessons. With that combination of influences, Thomas learned about religion and the spiritual side of life at the same time he learned to play the piano.

At a very young age, Thomas showed unusual talent as a piano player and singer. He loved music and he enjoyed all of the activities at his father's church. However, at age six he moved to Atlanta and remained there until he turned sixteen.

While he was in Atlanta he learned about blues and jazz music, which he loved. Thomas wanted to have a music career and he thought blues and jazz music could be his ticket to fame. He and others recognized his talent for music composition, but to be a professional he knew he had a lot to learn about writing and composing music, so he moved to Chicago to attend the Chicago College of Composition and Arranging.

To make money, Thomas played in nightclubs and at "rent parties" where individuals would hire him to play in homes or apartments during parties. These experiences allowed Thomas to be creative and try a variety of approaches to music. It was during this time that he combined blues and jazz with gospel music. In fact, many give him credit for being the "father of gospel music." He created the Wild Cats Jazz Band, a blues and jazz band that became the talk of Chicago.

Even though his religious upbringing was on his mind and in his heart, he strayed away from his commitment until he suffered a nervous breakdown and had to return to Atlanta, Georgia to recover. Under the watchful eye of his mother, he improved but not enough to return to his music. Thomas' mother told him that he should give up blues and jazz and return to church music exclusively.

Gradually, over a three-year period of time, Thomas fought his way out of a debilitating depression and returned to Chicago where he recommitted himself and joined the Pilgrim Baptist Church in Chicago. It was there that he found his spiritual, creative, and music home. Thomas became the church's choir director and remained in that position for over forty years.

Thomas recognized the values and importance of a strong and dedicated music program in the church, and to advocate for that he created the National Association of Gospel Choirs and Choruses. This led to Black-owned publishing companies that became essential for Black musicians and composers to get their works published. Thomas formed the Thomas A. Dorsey Gospel Song Music Publishing Company, a publisher of inexpensive gospel blues music.

He curtailed his blues and jazz work and turned almost exclusively to gospel music shortly after the death of his wife and newborn child, both of whom died during childbirth. It was during this dark time that he composed the famous hymn ***Precious Lord Take My Hand.*** In an interview many years later for *Atlantic Magazine*, as reported in a PBS special program, Thomas explained what happened: "Back in 1932 I was thirty-two years old and a fairly new husband. My wife, Nettie and I were living in a little apartment on Chicago's Southside. One hot August afternoon I had to go to St. Louis where I was to be the featured soloist at a large revival meeting. I didn't want to go. Nettie was in the last month of pregnancy with our first child. But a lot of people were expecting me in St. Louis. In the steaming St. Louis heat, the crowd called on me to sing again and again. When I finally sat down, a messenger boy ran up with a Western Union telegram. I ripped open the envelope. Pasted on the yellow sheet were the words: 'Your wife just died.' When I got back, I learned that Nettie had given birth to a boy. I swung between grief and joy. Yet that night, the baby died. I buried Nettie and our little boy together, in the same casket. Then I fell apart. For days I closeted myself. I felt that God had done me an injustice. I didn't want to serve Him anymore or write gospel songs. I just wanted to go back to that jazz world I once knew so well. But still I was lost in grief. Everyone was kind to me, especially a friend, Professor Frye, who seemed to know what I needed. On the following Saturday evening, he took me up to Malone's Poro College, a neighborhood music school. It was quiet; the late evening sun crept through the curtained windows. I sat down at the piano, and my hands began to browse over the piano keys and the words and music flowed out. That inspiration became ***Precious Lord Take My Hand.***"

Thomas' other famous hymn is ***Peace in the Valley,*** which can be found in almost every Christian hymnal. Countless famous singers have recorded both songs, including Albertina Walker, Elvis Presley, Mahalia Jackson, Aretha Franklin, B. B. King, Clara Ward, Dorothy Norwood, Jim Reeves, Roy Rogers, and Tennessee Ernie Ford, Johnny Cash, etc.

Thomas has a copyright on over 1,000 musical works, of which 250 are hymns. Thomas was the first Black elected to the Nashville Songwriters Hall of Fame and the first inducted into the Gospel Music Association's Hall of Fame.

Thomas remained active and productive up until his death in 1993 in Chicago at the age of ninety-four. Thousands attended his funeral and procession to Oak Woods Cemetery. He was buried next to his beloved wife and baby who were buried together sixty-one years earlier.

(References: *Obituary: Thomas Dorsey,* January 26, 1993, The Independent; *The Rise of Gospel Blues: The Music of Thomas Andrew Dorsey in the Urban Church,* 1992, Michael Harris; *How Sweet the Sound: The Golden Age of Gospel,* 1995, Horace Clarence Boyer; *Thomas Dorsey,* New Georgia Encyclopedia, Ian Hill. Retrieved 2013; *This Far by Faith,* 2003, PBS. Dialogue retrieved 2015)

Duba, Arlo

Arlo was born in 1929 in Platte, South Dakota into a family that valued education and worship.

Arlo was a quiet and studious boy who enjoyed school and who loved to read. After secondary school, he attended the University of Dubuque in Iowa where he majored in music and Bible. Arlo was an extraordinarily talented and gifted student at the university. His professors encouraged Arlo to pursue post-graduate studies at a university that would suit his intellectual and creative talents. Arlo wanted to study theology, so he applied for admission to Princeton Theological Seminary. Due to his stellar record of work and based on recommendations from his professors at the University of Dubuque, he was accepted at Princeton.

Arlo enjoyed the intellectual stimulation at Princeton. He earned a Master of Arts degree and soon thereafter a Doctor of Philosophy degree from Princeton Theological Seminary with a primary emphasis on theological language. After completing his work at Princeton he continued his studies at the Liturgical Institute in Paris, France.

Arlo was ordained as a Presbyterian minister but his professional life was spent in higher education as he held several positions beginning as the assistant director of the Princeton Seminary Choir, then Chaplain and Associate Professor of Religion at Westminster Choir College, and then as director of the Chapel and Lecturer in Liturgics. He served on the Psalter Committees for the United Methodist Church and the United Presbyterian Church.

Many of his hymns can be found in hymnals around the world. His writing of ***How Lovely Lord, How Lovely*** was composed with Hal Hopson's ***Merle's Tune*** to create one of the most popular hymns of today.

Arlo is currently Professor of Worship Emeritus and retired Dean of the University of Dubuque Theological Seminary. He lives in Hot Springs, Arkansas, where he continues to write.

(References: *Arlo Duba,* Hope Publishing Company. Retrieved 2014; *Interview with Dr. Arlo Duba,* The Covenant Network of Presbyterians, recorded on January 27, 2011; *Arlo Duba,* TheThoughtfulChristian.com. Retrieved 2014; *Keeping Vigil,* 1998, Princeton Theological Seminary, Barbara A. Chaapel)

Duck, Ruth

Ruth was born in 1947 in Washington, District of Columbia. Ruth's family lived near Annapolis, Maryland.

Ruth showed signs of a keen intellect at a very early age. In fact, during her fourth-grade year, Ruth wrote a paper entitled, "I Want to be a Missionary." However, she was shy and introspective. Ruth's introverted nature extended into her teenage years, where she found that her belief and faith in God and the Holy Spirit sustained her through difficult times.

In high school, she enjoyed the visual arts and even contemplated a career in that field. However, she feared that she would not be able to sustain a living in the visual arts, so she decided to major in piano. Ruth ran into another challenge, however, when she found that she was too nervous and self-conscious to perform in public. After much contemplation, she decided to major in English.

Ruth's love of theology and her strong beliefs in God and the potential good in people led her to study theology. Ruth received a Master of Arts in theology at Notre Dame University and a Doctor of Theology and Liturgy at Boston University School of Theology in 1989.

She became an ordained minister in 1974 and served several churches until 1989 when she took a teaching position at Garrett-Evangelical Theological Seminary. She became a professor of worship. Ruth continues to teach, lecture, and lead workshops on worship and hymnody.

Many of Ruth's hymns are in hymnals around the world and have been translated into at least six languages. Her hymns include ***A Mighty Fortress is Our God***; ***All the Earth is a Temple***; ***Arise, Your Light is Come***; ***Colorful Creator, God of Mystery***, and others.

In an interview about her world renowned hymns, Ruth said she and her parents enjoyed music and poetry. Ruth revealed that her first song was in Girl Scouts when she was working on a songwriter badge. She said, "I'm a text writer. My family started my reading with poetry."

Ruth is the author of almost 200 hymns, and she has been described as one of the world's most gifted hymnists. In addition to her reputation as a poetic hymnist, Ruth's academic works are equally impressive.

Also, Ruth served as President of the North American Academy of Liturgy in 2007 and served on the Academy Committee from 2006-2009.

Ruth is a life-long learner, teacher, and spiritual inspiration for many.

(References: *Worship for the Whole People of God,* 2013, Ruth Duck; *Ruth Duck,* 2012, Music for the Church - GIA Publications, Inc.; *Hymns, Psalms, and Spiritual Songs,* 1990, Westminster John Knox Press; *Everflowing Streams: Songs for Worship,* 1981, Ruth Duck and Michael Bausch)

Dudley-Smith, Timothy

Timothy was born in 1926 in Manchester, England. His parents ensured that all of their children received a good education, and they encouraged them to work hard at school so they would be prepared to attend college.

Timothy was a gifted student throughout elementary and secondary school, showing a high level of intellectual prowess. He attended Tonbridge School where he was an award-winning student.

Timothy could have attended any college of his choice, but after visiting Pembroke College in Cambridge, he decided that was where he wanted to be. Timothy was a model college student with a thirst for knowledge and a deep understanding of all academic subjects, but he greatly enjoyed religion and theology. He graduated from Pembroke College with honors.

Timothy was ordained as a deacon at the age of twenty-four and priest only one year later. He served as a priest in many places over several years. In 1973, he was named Archdeacon of Norwich, and there he remained until 1981 when he became the Bishop of Thetford for the next ten years. During that time, he also served as President of the Evangelical Alliance.

When Timothy was a student at Pembroke College, he and the English Christian leader and Anglican cleric, John Stott, who was named as one of the top 100 leaders in the world by *Time Magazine,* became close friends. After John's death in 2011, Timothy was asked to write a biography of his friend. He wrote a two-volume biography that was greatly admired and won the John C. Pollock award for Christian Biography.

Throughout his career, Timothy has been a prolific hymnist. He is probably most widely known for his hymn ***Tell Out, My Soul***. Timothy is an honorary dignitary of the Hymn Society of Great Britain and Ireland, and the recipient of numerous awards. His most cherished moment was when he was awarded the Order of the British Empire in 2003 for services to hymnody.

In 2003, his collected works ***A House of Praise*** was published to critical acclaim. The book became very popular in Great Britain and throughout Europe, the United States and Canada.

Timothy continues to collect awards and recognition well into retirement. Durham University recognized Timothy's extraordinary career with an honorary doctorate degree. He has been writing hymns for over thirty years, and he still writes several new hymns each year. Altogether, his number of hymns now exceeds 300 published in over 250 different hymnals throughout the world.

(References: *Timothy Dudley-Smith,* Hope Publishing. Retrieved 2015; *Transcript of Interview with Timothy Dudley-Smith,* 2006, The Royal School of Church Music. Retrieved 2015; *Companion to the United Methodist Church,* 1993, Carlton Raymond Young)

Dunstan, Sylvia

Sylvia was born in 1955 in Canada. She always attributed her love of music to the influence of her grandparents who strongly encouraged her to study music. Her parents supported her, also, but the direction Sylvia took in her famous and productive career of composing music was sparked primarily by her grandparents.

Sylvia was an excellent student in school, although she was somewhat hesitant to participate in school activities due to a lack of self-confidence, but she found her passion and gift when she started writing and composing music while in secondary school. She learned about composing music from the convent of nuns near her home. There she met Sister Miriam Winter who encouraged Sylvia to write hymns. Sister Winter and the other nuns taught Sylvia about Scripture, so many of her hymn compositions were based on Scripture.

As much as Sylvia loved composing hymns, she often struggled with the music, so eventually, she shifted her focus to writing lyrics.

Sylvia attended college at York University where she earned a Bachelor of Arts degree in music. She wanted to expand her knowledge of religion and theology so she entered graduate school. Sylvia earned master degrees in both theology and divinity from Emmanuel College in Toronto.

At the age of twenty-five, she was ordained by the Hamilton Conference of the United Church of Canada. She took a job as a prison chaplain and remained there for over ten years. Then she became the minister at Malvern Emmanuel United Church in Scarborough, Ontario. During this time, despite her very busy schedule, she continued to write lyrics for hymns, many of which were published in hymnals around the world. She also occasionally sang with folk music stars such as Ray Repp.

Sylvia's reputation soared after being invited to the Hymn Society Conference in 1990 where her hymns were highlighted. This led to the publication of her ***In Search of Hope and Grace***, a book of verse and lyrics that includes her most famous hymn, ***All Who Hunger***. She was working on another book when she became ill and learned that she had liver cancer.

Sadly, Sylvia died four months after the shocking diagnosis at the age of thirty-eight, in 1993. Several hundred people attended her funeral where many of her hymns were sung. Her beautiful book ***Where the Promise Shines*** was published after her death.

Even though she died at a very young age, Sylvia is considered one of North America's finest hymn composers of all time. Her books are still in print and many of her hymns are in hymnals around the world.

(References: *Sylvia Dunstan,* GIA Publications, Inc., Press release. Retrieved 2015; *Sylvia Dunstan,* Ancestry.com. Retrieved 2015; *In Search of Hope and Grace,* 2005, Sylvia Dunstan; *Sisters in Song,* 2013, Leslie Clay; *Sylvia Dunstan,* touchstonejournal.ca. Retrieved 2015)

Edgar, Mary Susanne

Mary was born in 1889 in Sundridge, Ontario. Her parents encouraged Mary's love of music and being outdoors. She and her parents were avid campers, and Mary's enjoyment of the beautiful area she lived in lasted a lifetime.

Mary was a very studious young girl who enjoyed school. She attended Barrie High School where she excelled in all academic areas and participated in several school activities and plays.

Mary was accepted into Havergal College in Toronto where she earned a Bachelor of Arts degree. Mary enjoyed learning; consequently, she took several courses at the University of Chicago and frequently attended lectures at Columbia University. Her interest in religious studies took her to the National Training School of the Young Women's Christian Association (YWCA) where she earned a degree in religious studies.

Mary became involved in the work of the YWCA in Canada which led to a lifetime devoted to educating and supporting young girls. Mary was the secretary and administrative assistant for Girl's Work in Montreal before she became the director of Camp Oolahwan in the Laurentian Mountains. Her dream was to open a camp for girls in Canada that would focus on Christian values, education, self-confidence, self-reliance, and self-motivation for girls.

The first step toward that dream occurred when Mary purchased a large tract of land on Lake Bernard in Canada near her birthplace of Sundridge. She used all of the money she had so conscientiously saved so she could seek fulfillment of her goal to help young girls grow and thrive. She named it Glen Bernard Camp.

Glen Bernard Camp opened in 1922 with thirty-eight girls in attendance. Its popularity grew exponentially after that. Mary developed it and was the camp director for over thirty-five years. Her devotion to the work was also seen in her commitment to the Canadian Girls in Training Program; the Girl Guides of Canada; the Ontario Camping Association, and the Canadian Camping Association.

Mary was also a prolific writer. She wrote books, plays, and hymns. Mary's most famous hymn is ***God Who Touches Earth with Beauty***. The hymn is in virtually every hymnal published since she wrote it, and it has been translated into several languages around the world. Her books include ***Wood Fire and Candlelight***; ***Under Open Skies***; ***The Christmas Wreath of Verse***, and ***Once There was a Camper***. Her most popular and cherished poem is ***A Magic Store***.

Mary continued to work until her death in 1973 in Toronto at the age of eighty-four. Her papers are archived at Queen's University and are a popular source of information and inspiration to students and others.

(References: *Mary Susanne Edgar*, Queen's University Archives. Retrieved 2015; *History of Glen Bernard Summer Camp*, Glen Bernard Summer Camp.com. Retrieved 2015)

Edwards, David Lawrence

David was born in 1929 in England to a well-educated family that valued education and Christian values.

He attended King's School at Canterbury where he excelled in all academic subjects and was a prize-winning writer and orator. He was a scholar of almost legendary proportions at Magdalen College, Oxford where he earned a Bachelor of Arts and Master of Arts degrees. David was selected as a Fellow of All Souls College, Oxford for seven years.

After studying at Westcott House College, Cambridge he was ordained as a priest at age twenty-six. His first position was as an Assistant Curate at St. John's in Hampstead and later Assistant

Curate of St. Martin-in-the-Fields. David also served as editor of the Student Christian Movement Press for several years.

Due to his professional reputation, his scholastic accomplishments, and his influence on others, he became the General Secretary of the Student Christian Movement. In this respected position, his published works drew more attention and praise. His hard work and intellectual prowess led to his appointment as Dean of King's College, Cambridge while he continued serving as a Six Preacher of Canterbury Cathedral.

David's illustrious career also included being Canon of Westminster Abbey and Rector of St. Margaret's, Westminster, as well as serving the House of Commons as Chaplain to the Speaker of the House of Commons and Sub-Dean of Westminster Abbey.

Among many honors, the Archbishop of Canterbury conferred upon him the Lambeth degree of Doctor of Divinity in 1990. In 1995, Queen Elizabeth II appointed David an Officer of the Order of the British Empire.

In addition to writing over sixty books, including ***Poets and God***; ***The Church That Could Be***; ***A Concise History of English Christianity***, and many others on a variety of topics, he has also written several hymns, including the popular ***Fill the World With Love***; ***When You Do This, Remember Me***, and ***You Have Called Me***.

David continues to write occasionally and offers advice and guidance to many who still seek his opinions. He is a legendary figure in Great Britain.

(References: *The First 2000 Years*, 1998, David Edwards; *Glimpses of God*, 1995, David L. Edwards)

Ehrenborg-Posse, Elizabeth

Elizabeth was born Catherine Elizabeth Ehrenborg in 1818 at Raback in Skaraborgs County, Sweden. She went by the name of Betty.

Betty's father, Casper Ehrenborg, was a Member of Parliament and her mother, Anna Fredrica Carlqvist, was a writer. Her father was a well-respected member of the community and a caring father, although he was somewhat distant with the children at times. Betty's mother was gregarious and creative and very interested in literature. Betty inherited her mother's interests and began writing poetry at a very young age.

Betty was educated in the local schools and received additional education at home, primarily from her mother, even though she learned a lot about governance and leadership from her father because he talked about his work when the family was at the dinner table.

Betty's interest in poetry led to a curiosity about hymns when the family worshiped in the local church. She also became interested in theology. That combination of interests would later lead Betty to teach young people about worship and writing hymns. After finishing her local education, Betty moved to England to study at a seminary for six months. When she returned home, she helped create a Sunday school that grew in popularity and influence to the point that she was credited with being the founder of the Swedish Sunday School. Betty became the director of teacher training at the Deaconess Institute. When that school closed she started her own school.

Betty married Johan August Posse, and that is why she is often referred to as Elizabeth Ehrenborg-Posse; however, she never used that combination of names. Instead, she lived as Betty Ehrenberg. Betty and her husband worked together to publish a regional newspaper, ***The Watchman*** (*Waktaren*). At the same time, Betty's interests in the Christian education of children and hymns and songs for children continued to occupy her time. Betty was fluent in four languages, including English. She translated several English songs for the Swedish children and published the songs in Sweden under the title of ***Spiritual Songs for Children***. The children loved the translated songs. Christian educators, parents and others found that through the songs many of the lessons of Christianity could be taught to children. Inspired by the positive response, Betty published another work of translated songs and hymns for children, but this time, she included some of her own hymns, including ***For God So Loved the World*** and ***When Christmas Morn is Breaking*** and many others.

Betty continued her busy schedule and composition of hymns and poetry until she became ill. After being ill for several months, Betty died in 1880 at the age of sixty-two. At her funeral, a children's choir sang several of Betty's hymns.

(References: *The History of Nordic Women's Literature*, 2012, Anne Brugge; *Elizabeth Ehrenborg-Posse*, 2001, Glenn Belcer; *Elizabeth Ehrenborg-Posse*, 2000, Dictionary of Hymnology Archives; *The Hymns of Elizabeth Ehrenborg-Posse*, Hymnary.org. Retrieved 2014)

Ellerton, John

John was born in 1826 in Clerkenwell, Middlesex, England to a family steeped in religion. His family members were Evangelical and John's father was a leader in the Evangelical community. John and his siblings grew up in a spiritually devoted family that was loyal to the church, family principles, and hard work.

John showed an early interest in church music and learned to read music when he was young. He also participated in numerous church activities, especially activities that focused on music. John learned to play the piano and other instruments but his musical interests were in writing and composing hymns.

After breezing through elementary and secondary school he entered King William's College on the Isle of Man. It took John time to adjust to being away from home but he soon began to enjoy the intellectual stimulation of the college and the college's music program. He participated in several music events and activities at the college. After two years at King William's College, he transferred to Trinity College at Cambridge where he received both his Bachelor and Master degrees in the Arts. While at Trinity he became acquainted with the theologian Frederick Maurice who sparked John's interest in theology and the value that hymns bring to spiritual messages and sermons. After taking some theology classes at Trinity College and studying further under Reverend Maurice, John was ordained.

With his education, training, and musical talents he became the Curate of Easebourne, Sussex, England. Two years later he took a position as lecturer at St. Peter's in Brighton, England. While in Brighton he published ***Hymns for Schools and Bible Classes***, which was well received by the churches in the area and later throughout England. He also published ***Church Hymns*** and ***The Children's Hymn Book***. The publication of the hymn books brought attention to his skills and talents. John became Chaplain for Lord Crewe (Bishop of Durham) for a few years and then Vicar of Cheshire.

John maintained his work with hymns and theological studies, but he also became interested in education when he saw many young people and workers without any education. John's interest in education led to his appointment as Chairman of the Education Committee at the Mechanics Institute, where he taught English and Bible History. While John was Chairman he made progressive changes in the institute that helped it thrive and dramatically improve—to the point that many considered it one of the best education institutions of its kind in England.

John was offered the position of Rector of Hinstock Parish in Shropshire, England and although he found it difficult to leave the Institute he could not turn down the Rector position. Four years later John was asked to take over the rector position at one of London's largest parishes. He worked hard and some said too hard to meet the needs of the parish and its congregation. The amount of work led to a physical and mental breakdown. John asked for a transfer and he was moved to Pegli, Italy for over a year where he worked briefly as a chaplain. When he returned to England he was assigned to a small parish in White Roding.

Although this was a difficult time for him, John continued to write and compose hymns. Music was his comfort; his love and joy. He began experiencing additional health issues, but he valiantly continued to work until his health deteriorated and he became disabled.

John died in 1893 in Torquay, Devonshire, England at the age of sixty-six surrounded by family and friends.

During his life, John wrote or translated 100 hymns, including the famous ***Savior, Again to Thy Dear Name***. Many of them are in modern day hymnals.

(References: *Hymnal Companion to the Lutheran Book of Worship*, 1981, Marilyn Kay Stulken; *John Ellerton*, Dictionary of Hymnology, 1907, John Julian; *Our Hymnody*, 1937, Robert Guy McCutchan; *The Story of Christian Hymnody*, 1961, Ernest Edwin Ryden)

Elliott, Charlotte

Charlotte was born in 1789 in Clapham, Surrey, England, to a wealthy family that was religious and supportive of community service projects of the local church. Charlotte lived in Clapham for thirty-two years, before her family moved to Brighton, England.

Charlotte's early exposure to the spiritual and philanthropic world influenced her throughout her life, but she was very sensitive about her chronic physical illnesses, and she lacked self-confidence despite the reassurances and support of her parents, especially her father. Her father was a well-known and respected silk merchant. Although he was a busy and hard-working man, he was also a loving and caring father and husband. He doted on his three daughters and two sons.

Despite her early experience with religion and the encouragement of her father and mother, Charlotte often felt as though she was not worthy of God's grace; she could not be as pure of thought as her beliefs demanded. Also, her physical ailments limited her ability to attend church on a regular basis, which grieved her and worsened her guilt and poor self-concept. She tried to express her concerns to her parents, who reassured her that she was living a good life. She even shared her worries with the local minister, who advised her to pray more.

Charlotte did find relief from her internal misery through expressions in poetry and deeply felt hymns. She loved all types of literature and music. She would read and write for hours while humming music tunes. There were times when Charlotte was too weak to leave her bed and she seldom left her house after her physical condition worsened sometime near her twentieth birthday. Charlotte was essentially an invalid thereafter.

Even though she struggled with pain and immobility, she continued to write poems and hymns. She published almost 150 hymns, but there were many others she did not publish. Charlotte's most famous hymn is ***Just as I am, Without One Plea***, which came from a time in her life when she felt the most helpless and worthless.

Her brother, Reverend Henry Elliott, often tried to console Charlotte and it was with that he shared a dream he had to help children. It was Henry who conceived the idea of St. Mary's Hall, a school of higher learning for daughters of the clergy. There was an outpouring of support, including fundraising activities such as bazaars. The entire Elliot family and many community members participated in the bazaars and other events, but Charlotte did not, even with the encouragement of Henry. By this time, her health was deteriorating even further and she had the added burden of guilt and depression, because she wanted to help her brother's noble cause and plans but she could not. She helped in a small way to plan the first bazaar, which was an important event to start the fundraising campaign, but she could not do anything else to help. The night before the bazaar, she sank to the depths of feelings of uselessness and depression. The well-known minister, Dr. Cesar Malan, was visiting that evening and she shared her feelings with him. He told her to review her spirituality, to look deep into God's plans for her, and to remember that God accepts people, "just as they are." While the bazaar was scheduled to take place the next day, her thoughts during the night before the bazaar flooded her mind and stirred her spirit. She had an epiphany—God's grace is too powerful and his gifts are too meaningful for her to succumb to the negative feelings that possessed her. If God's gift to her was writing and composing instead of physical participation, then she would use His gift. That is what Dr. Malan was trying to tell her the previous evening. That is when she wrote one of the most popular and powerful hymns in the Christian world, ***Just as I am, Without One Plea.*** It is found in virtually every hymnal in the English-speaking world and has been translated into over fifty other languages.

Charlotte also published books, poems, and other hymns. Her book ***Psalms and Hymns for Public, Private, and Social Worship*** was a bestseller in the religious community for several years. There were thirteen editions of the book.

Despite her physical condition and long physical and spiritual suffering, Charlotte found comfort and relief in her God-given talents of writing. She lived until 1871 when she died at the age of eighty-two. At the time of her death, she was working on the 13th edition of her bestselling book.

(References: *The Complete Book of Hymns,* 2006, William J. Petersen and Ardythe Petersen; *The Story of Just As I Am,* 2007, Lorella Rouster; *Charlotte Elliott,* Dictionary of Hymnology. Retrieved 2014; *Wonderful Words of Life Songbook,* 1985, William H. Goddard)

Escamilla, Roberto

Roberto was born in 1931 in a small town near Monterrey, Mexico, at the Texas border. He was an excellent student in school and was devoted to his family and friends. Roberto enjoyed reading and music, and he found that attending church was very motivating and in some ways reassuring and comforting.

Roberto's spiritual awakening coincided with the development of his gift for music and his interest in writing hymns and other forms of music. He was inspired to write hymns that expressed gratitude for life and God's grace on life. Roberto wanted to write a hymn that encouraged people to see the miracle of life and enjoy being alive. From that desire, he wrote the world-famous hymn ***When We Are Living***.

Roberto wrote the hymn during a very difficult personal time in his life: "I learned the one original stanza of ***When We Are Living*** when I was a very young boy. An anonymous writer wrote the Spanish words, based on the beautiful text found in *Romans 14:8*. I thought that this was a profound theological statement about the meaning of life being determined by our belonging to God, the Giver of life and death. In my early fifties, I went through a rather difficult time in my life. It was during this period of time that I was inspired to write the second, third, and fourth stanzas of this hymn. I had some crucial decisions to make regarding my career, and the future was very uncertain. It was then when I truly realized the idea of giving and receiving, of sorrow and joy, and through these contrasting forces was inspired to finish writing the hymn. Whether we suffer or rejoice, ultimately we are to be Christ-like, concerned about the hurts of others. It is because we belong to God that we can transcend all circumstances and rejoice in serving others in God's name."

Roberto continues to worship and serve God in several ways.

(Reference: *The Festival of Hymns*, 2000, Hal Hopson)

Faber, Frederick William

Frederick was born in 1814 in Calverley in the West Riding of Yorkshire, England. His father was the local Bishop of the Church of England and his grandfather was the Vicar.

Fred was a precocious child, and it was evident early on that he possessed a keen intellect and love for music. Fred attended elementary school at Bishop Auckland, but most of his early years were spent at Westmorland, England where he attended the Harrow School for over five years. He was also a very thoughtful child, and as he grew into his teen years, he became a serious student of religion, classical literature, and music.

Fred's academic success in secondary school led to an opportunity to enroll in Balliol College at Oxford University, a prestigious institution. Not long afterward Fred was offered a scholarship at University College at Oxford, which was a rare accomplishment. At Oxford, Fred's intellect and scholarly work became almost legendary. He graduated with high honors. Fred also won the famous Newdigate Prize for his poem, ***The Knights of St. John***. Fred's scholarly work was so distinguished while at University College, he was named a Fellow of the College after he graduated.

Not all was well with Fred, however. He was enduring an internal struggle with his beliefs. Prior to entering the college, he was steeped in Calvinist beliefs, but in college, he learned about Anglo-Catholic principles. Fred was influenced by John Henry Newman, who was a popular and powerful Vicar of the University Church of St. Mary the Virgin. There were times that Fred was so conflicted by his internal and spiritual struggle that he would travel to the Lake District and corral his feelings by writing poetry, some of which became the basis for hymns. While at the Lake District one year he met and befriended the poet William Wordsworth, who would later encourage and influence Fred's poetry and composition of hymns.

After a very difficult internal struggle, Fred abandoned his Calvinistic beliefs and received Holy Orders in the Church of England at the age of twenty-five.

For a few years, Fred earned his living as a tutor. His reputation as an effective tutor grew, and he was in great demand which allowed him to travel. During his travels, he learned about other religions, cultures, churches, music and countries. Eventually, he published a book that he dedicated to his friend, Wordsworth, ***Sights and Thoughts in Foreign Churches and among Foreign Peoples***.

Fred was offered and accepted the position of Rector in Elton, England. His time there was not easy, for many times the local Methodists attended his church to mock him and discourage his work. He endured and eventually his intellect, integrity, and patience won over the Methodist and other worshippers and earned him the respect of the community.

A few years later Fred left Elton to join John Henry Newman and the Catholic Church. Along with others, he created a religious community called the Brothers of the Will of God in Staffordshire,

England, and built the Church of St. Wilfrid. This was a difficult task because it was the only Catholic Church in the region. To add to his stress, he was instrumental in adding a school for young children. Fred was so overwhelmed by work that his retreats to write poetry in his study did little to relieve the stress. He became so gravely ill from the demands of his work that he received Last Rites. Much to his surprise and that of his fellows, Fred slowly recovered and returned to his work. He credited his recovery to the Blessed Mother. For the rest of his life he was devoted to the Blessed Mother, which led to his translation of St. Louis de Montford's ***True Devotion to Mary***, a French classic that had never been translated into English.

Scholars believe that Fred's chronic health problems were similar to Bright's disease—a chronic kidney disease. Despite his uneven health, Fred continued writing, preaching, and traveling up until his death in 1863 at the age of fifty.

During his relatively short life, Fred published several religious works, poems, and hymns. It is interesting to note that one of his uncles was Geoffrey Faber, co-founder of the publishing house known as Faber and Gwyer and later became Faber and Faber, a major international publishing house of literary and religious works, where T. S. Eliot was an editor.

(References: *Fredrick William Faber,* Catholic Encyclopedia. Retrieved 2013; *Frederick William Faber,* 2007, Melissa J. Wilkinson; *English Hymns of the 19th Century: An Anthology,* 2004, Richard Arnold)

Farjeon, Eleanor

Eleanor was born in 1881 in London, England. She was the daughter of Benjamin Farjeon, a popular novelist of his era, and Maggie Farjeon, who was also a novelist. Both of his parents were involved in all elements of the social and intellectual world of literacy.

Eleanor was not thought to be destined for a distinguished career, because as a child she was small, timid, sickly, and showed no particular aptitude of any type. She did learn to love books early in life, but she was so timid and so often ill that she received her education at home.

Eleanor, who was called "Nellie" by her family, enjoyed retreating to the attic with her books. She was content to be in the quiet, secluded confines of the attic for most of the day. However, as she matured and soaked in the literary atmosphere in her family, she slowly blossomed into a writer, which was strongly encouraged by her father.

She described her family and childhood in her autobiography, ***A Nursery in the Nineties.*** Later, Eleanor became a poet, biographer, hymnist, and playwright. Interestingly, her siblings had creative talents, also. Her two younger brothers were writers and her older brother was a composer. She adored her brothers and she came to enjoy the daily activities and interactions of her family as she matured socially and physically. Eleanor especially enjoyed family vacations and family holidays. Some of her stories and poems were inspired by her family and their vacations and holidays. For example, a family holiday in France inspired her to create a story of a troubadour, later rewritten as the wandering minstrel of her most famous book, ***Martin Pippin in the Apple Orchard***.

Eleanor's writing career led to many awards, and her works were so endearing to children across generations that the Children's Book Circle presents an annual award in her honor—the Eleanor Farjeon Award for children's literature. In addition to her literary work, Eleanor enjoyed writing music. Her song ***Morning Has Broken*** became a Christian hymn legend and later became a popular modern day song that sold millions of copies for a pop singer. Her children's book ***The Little Book Room*** has remained in print since its publication in 1950.

Eleanor remained active throughout her life and despite her childhood illnesses and frequent episodes with poor health she lived a full life. She died in London in 1965 at the age eighty-four.

Her children's books and her hymn ***Morning Has Broken*** remain popular around the world.

(References: *Eleanor Farjeon—British Writer,* Encyclopedia Britannica. Retrieved 2014; *The Eleanor Farjeon Award,* Children's Book Circle.org. Retrieved 2014; *Eleanor Farjeon Family Collection,* Dunedin Libraries. Retrieved 2015; *A Book for Eleanor Farjeon—A Tribute to Her Life,* 1966, A.J. Walek)

Farquharson, Walter

Walter was born in 1936 in Rosetown, Saskatchewan, Canada. He had a very active childhood that included studious work combined with outdoor activities that centered on winter snow treks in the fields and mountains and summer exploration in the woods, streams, rivers, and meadows.

Walter was a good student who excelled in all academic work. He also showed creative skills and precocious thinking and logic skills. Walter was inquisitive about many subjects. After secondary school, he attended the University of Saskatchewan where he received a Bachelor in Arts degree. Afterward, Walter decided that he wanted to enter the ministry, so he enrolled at the University of Saskatchewan's St. Andrew's College of Divinity. Walter earned a Bachelor of Divinity degree. He was ordained but he wanted to further his studies so he did post-graduate work in Edinburgh, England where he also accepted a position as assistant minister at Morningside Parish Church. Walter soon thereafter accepted a position back in Canada as the minister of the United Church of Saltcoats in Saskatchewan where he remained until he retired twenty years later. Walter wanted to set an example for his congregation about commitment to the community, so he sought and accepted a teaching position at the local high school where he taught English for several years while maintaining his full schedule as a minister.

In his spare time, Walter worked on composing hymns. Many of his hymns were set to music by his friend Ron Klusmeier, who had a talent for musical scores and dramatic musical cadence. Three of Walter's hymns were included in the hymn Book of the Anglican and United Churches of Canada in 1971. His hymn ***Men Go to God When They are Sorely Placed*** was published in the Australian hymn book for the Anglican, Methodist, Presbyterian, and Roman Catholic usage. Later, several of Walter's hymns were included in various Christian hymnals in the English-speaking world. His hymn ***Walls That Divide*** is a popular hymn that is frequently sung in churches around the world. In addition to his church duties and work on hymns, Walter was Moderator of the United Church of Canada from 1990–1992.

In his retirement, Walter continues to write hymns, does community work, and until recently occasionally gave sermons.

(References: *Songs of the People of God: A Companion to the Australian Hymn Book,* 1982, Wesley Milgate; *Walter Farquharson,* Dictionary of North American Hymnology. Retrieved 2014; *Walter H. Farquharson,* 1998, Lambert Surhone, Mirian Timpledon, and Susan Marseken; *Christian Hymnody in 21st Century Britain and America,* 2001, David W. Music)

Fawcett, John

John was born into poverty in Lidget Green, Bradford, England in 1739. John Fawcett and his family had a very difficult life. They struggled to survive. Their abject poverty created health problems for each member of the family. John watched helplessly as his siblings struggled and his parents wasted away. His parents died, leaving John an orphan when he was only twelve years old. At that young age, he was on his own with no support from friends or family.

John was a gregarious boy who made friends with other children very easily and he was comfortable around adults. He knew and understood that in his town and in nearby villages, if not throughout most of the country during those difficult times, many adults had disinterest in children except as possible laborers, so he was always very respectful and helpful to them and willing to do any type of work. In his desperate attempt to find work for food, he came across a tailor who needed help in his small shop. Quick to recognize his good fortune, John went straight to work doing every type of work possible in the tailoring shop. No task or duty was too small or too difficult for John. Soon he was delighted to accept the tailor's offer of an apprenticeship. A successful apprenticeship would give him the chance to escape the grasp of harsh poverty. He would never have much money as a tailor, but he would have a skill and food. To John both were a God-send.

After long days of work, John liked to walk through town. One evening he heard people talking about a preacher who was "the voice of God." John was intrigued. He asked about the preacher and learned that it was George Whitfield, who was to become arguably the best-known 18th-century preacher in Great Britain and America. Whitfield's revivals stretched across the Atlantic to America. His series of revivals in America and Great Britain later became known as "The Great Awakening". John went to one of Whitfield's revivals, and he was mesmerized by Whitfield. As the result of attending the revival, John began attending a Baptist church, and he became very active in the church. His charisma, good heart, and study of the Bible entered him into the hearts of the preacher and the congregation. He was asked by the preacher to speak from the pulpit a few times, and it became obvious to all that John was a natural—he combined the word of the Bible with stories.

Over time, John became an excellent young assistant to the preacher. Eventually, he became an ordained preacher. His reputation grew within his church and small community. When he was twenty-five years old, a small church in Wainsgate invited him to be its preacher. John and his wife eagerly accepted the invitation. Wainsgate was a small and poor town. The congregation could not afford to pay John very much, so they compensated by providing him and his wife with farm products. John and his wife loved the people of the town and their love was returned by the people. John was with families during their darkest hours, and he asked for nothing in return. When he and his wife had children the meager income became troubling. In a few years his skilled sermons became well known, and at the age of thirty-three, he was offered the job as a preacher of the large and influential Carter's Lane Baptist Church in London. For the first time in his life, he would have a very comfortable income and a quality style of living. John gratefully accepted the job at the London church; his wife and children were equally excited. They packed up their belongings and had a long farewell with their beloved community members. As they were leaving their beloved small town and the families that they cared so deeply for, they stopped and looked at each other and asked, "What are we doing?" They admitted to each other that they did not really want to leave their friends and the families that were the center of their lives, and who depended on them for so much more than spiritual guidance. Consequently, they turned around and returned to Wainsgate. John and his wife were welcomed back by the community with such warmth and excitement that he was inspired to set his feelings to writing. The result was the hymn ***Blest Be the Tie***. Over the course of his life, John wrote more than sixty hymns. Many of his hymns focused on community, devotion, and duty to help others as evidence of God's grace.

Because of his family's tie to the community, they never left Wainsgate. John continued his spiritual leadership at the tiny church for fifty-four years, being paid not much more than the equivalent of $40 a year.

John died in his beloved community of Wainsgate in 1817 at the age of seventy-seven. In 1912, a plaque commemorating John's many years of service and dedication was placed in the New Testament Church of God in Bradford, England.

(Reference: *Life Truths*, Winter 2009, LifeWay Christian Resources, Curtis Honts (editor); *John Fawcett—Hymn Writers of the Church*, 2012, Christian Classics Ethereal Library Calvin College. Retrieved 2014; *The Hymns and Hymn Writers, An Annotated Edition*, 1911, Charles Sumner Nutter, Boston University School of Theology Archives. Retrieved 2014)

Featherstone, William Ralph

William was born in 1848 in Montreal, Canada. Apparently, his family worked in the mercantile business, but that has never been confirmed.

William was active in the Wesleyan Methodist Church in Montreal, which was later renamed St. James United Church, and there are some records indicating that he was involved in the music programs in the church, as well.

There are no records of his literary skills except one poem survived and that was only because of another person, Adoniram Gordon, who would later found Gordon College and Gordon-Conwell Theological Seminary. Adoniram came across one of William's poems in a forgotten and obscure publication several years after William's death. One story claims that William as a young boy sent a copy of the poem to his grandmother who was living at the time in Los Angeles, California. She was so impressed with the poem that she sent it either to a small local newspaper or a weekly journal or magazine. It is commonly believed that William wrote the poem when he was only twelve or fourteen years old. Adoniram was a talented composer and musician who wrote songs and hymns. Adoniram immediately saw William's poem as a powerful hymn and he put it to music as the famous hymn ***My Jesus I Love Thee***. It is unlikely that anyone would remember William if not for Adoniram's eye for creative work and his ability to put poems to music. There are no records containing William's other poems, and details of his death, including the exact year, are obscured by time, but it is believed that he died during or near 1875 at the age of approximately twenty-seven years in Montreal, Canada, of unknown causes.

William may have lived an obscure life, but he is immortal for the words he wrote in ***My Jesus I Love Thee***.

(References: *Companion to the Song Book of the Salvation Army*, 1988, Gordon Harry Taylor, The Campfield Press; *Hymns of Our Faith*, 1964, Broadman Press, William Jensen Reynolds; *William Featherstone*, Cyberhymnal.org. Retrieved 2015)

Ferguson, Manie

Manie was born in 1850 in County Carlow near Dublin. Her large family worked and lived off of the land. They traded farm animals and bartered for food and personal belongings with fellow citizens.

Manie had no formal education, except when her mother read to her from the Bible. Manie stayed close to home and did not marry until late in life, compared to the age that most women married during that era. At age thirty-three she married Theodore Ferguson who was a minister. He did not have a church; instead, he participated in the circuit of revivals and ritual services.

Manie and Theodore, who Manie called TF, decided that they should take a risk and travel to the United States find a better life, but they were not certain where to relocate in the United States. TF heard about the California gold rush and he convinced Manie to leave her small world and go with him to Los Angeles. When they arrived in Los Angeles they were shocked to see the living conditions and the lack of churches and worship opportunities in the area. They founded the first religious mission in Los Angeles which soon became known as the Peniel Mission, which meant the Face of God.

The Peniel Mission welcomed all non-believers and believers of any denomination. Manie and TF struggled many times to keep the Mission open, and they seldom kept any donations for their own personal use. Initially, they used the Masonic Hall on Spring Street (near 416 North Main Street) in downtown Los Angeles but after only a few-months they were forced to move. The only place they could find for the Mission was the basement of the Nadeau Hotel on the corner of Spring Street and First Street. A year later as the hotel's business grew they were asked to leave.

Manie and TF could not find any space available for free and they had no money. They finally had to settle on space in a church that had caught fire and was abandoned until the congregation could gather enough money to fully restore it. So Manie and TF opened the Mission in the only part of the church that was not damaged by fire. The Mission then relocated to rented rooms at 107 North Main Street.

In the first eight years, the Mission relocated six times before establishing a permanent location when in 1894 a substantial endowment was given them by George Studd, an English sportsman. With this donation, they were able to expand the Mission and in doing so were able to solicit more donations and contributions.

In 1899 a Methodist Church legend, Dr. Phineas Bresee, joined the Mission and with his experience and leadership, plus the Studd donation and other support, they opened a permanent facility on South Main Street in Los Angeles. It was during this time that Manie discovered her love of and talent for writing poems; she also had a talent for composing hymns from her poems. Manie had a natural talent for capturing spiritual meaning and reconciliation through hymns. Her poems and hymns focused on recovery, the grace of God, forgiveness spoken by Jesus, and mankind's need to help others through the word of God. Manie wrote hundreds of poems and hymns, but she is probably most famous for her hymn ***Blessed Quietness***. Her hymn ***Christ in the Storm*** is also one of her most popular hymns. Both of these hymns can still be found in most Christian hymnals.

Manie and TF continued to work at the Mission, and during their lifetime, they helped many other missions open in California and other parts of the United States. They suffered through many challenges including leadership battles with other members of the Mission's board, but through it all, they helped thousands of lost souls.

TF died in 1920. Although she deeply mourned the loss of her husband, Manie continued to work at the Mission and write poems and hymns until her death in 1932 at the age of eighty-two in Los Angeles.

The *Los Angeles Times* referred to Manie as "Mother Manie" to honor her decades of work with the poor and homeless people of Los Angeles.

(References: *Women Hymn Writers of the 19th Century*, 1998, Keith Schwanz; *Manie Ferguson*, Ancestry.com. Retrieved 2015; *Manie Ferguson*, Timeless Truths. Retrieved 2015)

Foley, William Brian

Brian was born in 1919 in England. His family supported each other and were very religious. Brian's siblings shared a strong bond that prevailed throughout their lives.

Brian was educated at the local small public school where his interest in reading and writing began to take shape. He was a conscientious student, and he showed an early interest in music affiliated with worship. Brian loved singing in church and was fascinated by the church organ and how music was written, read, and played.

Brian's interest in religion and his dedication to worship plus his aptitude for scholastic work led him to enter St. Mary's College–Crosby in Merseyside near Liverpool, England. He excelled academically, finishing first in his class in several subject areas. Later he attended St. Joseph's College at Upholland in Lancashire, England to study theology. Upon completing his theology studies, Brian was ordained a priest in 1945, near the end of World War II. He became the parish priest of Clayton Green, Chorley, Lancashire, England and helped the community with all worship, family, and personal matters. He guided the community's recovery from the terrible loss of human life from World War II (the community of Chorley played an important role in World War II, being the home of the Royal Ordnance Factory - one of the largest ammunitions manufacturers in Great Britain). Brian brought more music to the worship services to ease the stress of the congregation as they grieved the loss of loved ones as well as their sense of spiritual loss.

As his interest in worship music developed over the years, and partly in response to how congregations reacted to worship music, Brian expressed openly and privately his concern about the trend in hymns. He longed for the "plainsong", which is a body of chants used in the liturgies of the Western Roman Catholic Church. He wanted the church to return to the more traditional Roman Catholic hymn style. To express his support for this style, Brian wrote fourteen hymns in the old tradition music style. The response was immediately favorable, and they were all included in the 1971 *New Catholic Hymnal*.

Brian's most famous hymn is ***Holy Spirit Come, Confirm Us***, which he wrote in 1960 after presiding over a Sacrament of Confirmation (a ritual to complete the process of initiation into the Christian community). He was inspired to write a hymn that captured the essential and fundamental meaning of Confirmation. He pursued his love of music for the rest of his life.

Brian was active in his faith community until his death in 2000, at the age of eighty-one. His hymns, his support of his congregations, and his devotion to making his communities responsive to the needs of others endeared him to thousands of people.

(References: *An English-Speaking Hymnal Guide*, 2005, Erik Routley and Peter Cutts; *Brian B. Foley*, Praise, 1999. Retrieved 2015; *Brian Foley*, The Canterbury Dictionary of Hymnology. Retrieved 2015)

Fortunatus, Venantius Honorius

Venantius was born in 530 in Ceneda, Italy. Venantius' family moved to Aquileia when he was young to avoid the turmoil that developed after the death of King Theoderic.

Even at an early age, it was clear that Venantius was very intelligent and curious about theology, science, and music. He became serious about his spiritual development. With the influence of his friends, sometime before adolescence, he was converted to Christianity.

Venantius excelled in all academic studies, and later entered a university-like school in Ravenna. Venantius became ill while at Ravenna of an unknown physical ailment, resulting in partial blindness in one eye and almost total blindness in the other. He struggled with his studies and his self-reliance because of his disability. Venantius' life became traumatic and uncertain, but he found comfort being with his friends. His friends helped him study by reading to him. With his extraordinary memory, he memorized everything that was read to him, and he could recite what he learned while taking exams.

Venantius' life changed unexpectedly and dramatically due to what he called a miracle when he anointed his eyes with sacred oil that was taken from the St. Martin of Tours lamp used during religious services. The sacred oil was brought to him by friends upon their return from a pilgrimage to the church in Tours. Within two or three days after anointing his eyes with the sacred oil, his vision began to improve in both eyes. Within a week, his vision was restored. Venantius and his friends beheld the cure as a miracle; consequently, he made a pilgrimage to St. Martin of Tours in 565 to pay homage to the sacred site.

With his sight restored he hastened his studies in the classics, theology, and language. He was especially interested in the Greek language, works, and culture. The Greek influence on him can be seen in his writing. Upon the completion of his studies, Venantius was ordained and later became the Bishop of Poitiers. He became famous for his sermons, writings, hymns, and poetry. Members of his congregation, theologians, musicians, scholars, and politicians visited him frequently throughout his life seeking his knowledge, counsel, and to ask for favors. People of humble status would travel hundreds of miles to see Venantius; they wanted to see this legendary religious leader who had experienced a heavenly miracle.

His writings were published and well-known, but more importantly his hymns became part of the liturgy of the Catholic Church, including the ***Pange Lingua Gloriosi Proelium Certaminis,*** a hymn that later inspired St Thomas Aquinas's ***Pange Lingua Gloriosi Corporis Mysterius.***

Venantius' influence and reputation spread across the continent, and he remained a source of wisdom, inspiration, and insight until his death.

Venantius died in 600 (or between 600 and 605, according to historians) around the age of seventy. Even though he was never canonized, he has for centuries been called a saint; in fact, Venantius is often referred to as St. Venantius Fortunatus.

(References: *Venantius Fortunatus,* Catholic Encyclopedia, Volume 6. Retrieved 2014; *Venantius Fortunatas—French Poet and Bishop,* Encyclopedia Britannica. Retrieved 2014; *The Career of Venantius Fortunatus,* Tradition, Volume 41, 1985 p. 49-78)

Fosdick, Harry Emerson

Harry was born in 1878 in Buffalo, New York. He was a precocious child who had broad interests in a number of things. Whatever attracted his attention, he quickly learned about it.

After excelling in all academic subjects at every grade level, Harry enrolled at Colgate University and graduated with honors at age twenty-one. He then entered Union Theological Seminary and upon graduation became an ordained Baptist minister at age twenty-five. Shortly thereafter, he became the minister at Madison Avenue Baptist Church in New York. Harry's sermons drew attention for their intellectual and spiritual power, but also because of his opinions about the conflict between the fundamentalist and the modernist. There was a great debate in the Protestant Society of America, and Harry did not shy away from the controversy. His liberal ideas and opinions were not well received by the more traditionalist ministers and theologians.

Although he remained the minister at Madison Avenue Baptist Church, he was also a guest minister at the Presbyterian Church in Manhattan and at Riverside Church in Morningside Heights in Manhattan, which was an inter-denominational church.

His involvement and reputation quickly rose to national attention due to a sermon he gave at the First Presbyterian Church on May 21, 1922, called "Shall the Fundamentalist Win?" The sermon defended the modernist views and claimed that the Bible was not literally the word of God. This brought him national attention and controversy. Even though he was a Baptist, the controversial sermon was at a Presbyterian Church so the National Presbyterian Convention instructed the local Presbytery to conduct an investigation. It is interesting to note that the person charged with conducting the investigation was John Foster Dulles, who would later become the legendary Secretary of State under President Dwight D. Eisenhower. At the time of the investigation, John Foster's father was a nationally known and widely respected liberal Presbyterian seminary professor. Harry escaped censure by resigning from his First Presbyterian Church position and he also left Madison Avenue Baptist Church.

Despite the controversy, several churches offered Harry minister positions, and he accepted the ministry at the recently completed Park Avenue Baptist Church where John D. Rockefeller attended. The church was near Columbia University overlooking the Hudson River. The new church was opened in 1930 when Harry's picture was on the cover of *Time Magazine*. The church became a community center with a gymnasium, library, theater, dining rooms, and classrooms for all types of classes for all ages.

Harry became a national spokesman against racism and prejudice. Harry thought that a major role and responsibility of the religious community was to support communities and individuals and to speak out against racism. Harry continued to write and publish liberal, socially conscious sermons and articles.

Harry was not always controversial; he respected and enjoyed the traditions of worship, especially the music. He loved the music of the church and became interested in how hymns were composed. Harry's creative nature found purpose and joy in penning several hymns, including the popular ***God of Grace and God of Glory***. He also enjoyed literary success. His book ***A Guide to Understanding the Bible*** was a bestseller in the religious community and was also considered an excellent scholarly account of Hebrew beliefs. Those two publications made Harry well known across the country, but many people remember Harry for something else. He reviewed, edited and gave his heartfelt and very public approval to the first edition of *Alcoholics Anonymous* (AA) in 1939. That was a turning point in the treatment of alcoholism and the AA movement.

Harry remained productive and influential throughout his long life. He died in Bronxville, New York in 1969 at the age of ninety-one.

(References: *Harry Emerson Fosdick,* Obituary, New York Times, October 6, 1969; *The Living Days,* 1956, Harry Emerson Fosdick; *Harry E. Fosdick: Preacher, Pastor, Prophet,* 1985, Robert Moat Miller)

Frostenson, Anders

Anders was born in Loshult Parish, Sweden in 1906. He was the oldest of five children. Anders was a very dutiful and serious-minded boy. When he was very young, Anders learned to read and he became fascinated by different languages. On his own and without help from anyone else he began a study of languages and literature. Consequently, by the time he entered Lund University he was already well-versed in several languages and had read literature from around the world. At the university, he added an interest in theology while maintaining his studies in language and philosophy. He also developed an active interest in collecting hymns from traditional Swedish worship.

After earning a Bachelor of Arts degree, he was ordained a priest and soon thereafter began his career at the Gustav Vasa Church in Stockholm, Sweden. He worked there a few years and then moved to Lovo Parish, a country parish, where he remained for over thirty years.

In 1977, he founded the Anders Frost's Foundation with the purpose of "promoting the renewal with hymns and ballads." Anders was a prominent leader in the development and renewal of hymns in Sweden. He loved simple basic melodies and the traditional hymns of Sweden. Anders also studied hymns that derived their message from *Psalms*. In his books, articles and hymns he wanted to convey the energy and power of *Psalms*. His work became so revered that *the Official Swedish 1986 Hymnal* was referred to as the *Frostensonska*. In the World Council of Churches

Hymnal, six of the eight Swedish hymns included in the collected works from Sweden were written by Anders.

In 1981, he was awarded an honorary doctorate in theology at the University of Lund for his scholarly work and for his devotion to hymns and his collection of hymns.

Anders continued to work well into his 90s. He died in 2006, one month shy of his 100th birthday.

(References: *Perspectives on Contemporary Hymns*, 2000, Inger Selandar, translated by translate.com 2014; *Dogma and Poem: About the Hymn Writing Grounds of Anders Frostenson*, 2002, translated by translate.com 2014; *God is One of Us: Ander Frostenson's Works*, 2007, Lectures at Orebro University, translated by translate.com 2014)

Gabarain, Cesareo

Cesareo was born in 1936 in Hernani, Guipuzcoa Province, Spain. He was born in humble surroundings where children were expected to go into military service, workman service, but seldom to the university or service as a minister.

Cesareo showed an unusually keen intellect as a young boy as well as considerable musical talent. His gregarious but thoughtful nature endeared him to friends, relatives and teachers. Cesareo's family and teachers encouraged Cesareo to study and prepare for an academic career. They knew that his education in the small community would not challenge his intellectual gifts, so they worked together to qualify him for the Minor Seminary.

At the age of ten, Cesareo entered the Minor Seminary (a boarding school typically for teenage boys interested in becoming a priest in Roman Catholic institutions) in Zaragoza, Spain. Cesareo was the youngest boy in the Minor Seminary; consequently, he had a difficult time adjusting to the routine, physical rough play, and intellectual expectations of boys at least three years older than him; many of them were between the ages of fourteen and eighteen. However, his optimistic and engaging personality won friendships while his intellect put him in the favor of the teachers and priests. Cesareo enjoyed the academic challenges at the school that expanded his intellectual curiosity. He also enjoyed music. In fact, his love for music developed to the point where he began trying to compose songs, primarily hymns when he was only twelve years old. He did not share those compositions with anyone at that time, but some of them were later rewritten and became notable hymns.

After six years at the Minor Seminary, Cesareo continued his religious and music studies at the Mayor de San Sebastian Seminary. After graduating, he was ordained as a priest at the young age of twenty-three. Soon thereafter, he worked as the Chaplain of the College of the Marist Brothers in Anzuola, Spain. Cesareo endeared himself to the community for his work to support families living in poverty and for his frequent visits to homes for the elderly and disabled. Cesareo found inspiration from those visits, and he transferred those feelings to music. It was during this time that he honed his music composition skills.

Cesareo thought that many of the hymns of that era were too complex and therefore difficult for worshippers to learn and follow. He determined that hymns could and should provide spiritual context and lyrical joy. This view guided his composition of hymns. After several years in San Sebastian, he moved to Madrid, Spain to become the director of Religion at the College of San Fernando and Co-Adjudicator at the Our Lady of the Snows parish.

Cesareo's long-time love of music and hymn composition caught the attention of several people who encouraged him to publish them, and he did to great reception and success. He wrote over 500 hymns and became famous because of them. The hymns were widely sung in Spanish parishes across Spain and in the Hispanic-speaking Christian world. Cesareo made thirty-seven albums of hymns and won the Gold Record award in Spain, a prestigious award, making him the only Roman Catholic composer to receive the award. Pope John Paul II appointed Cesareo the Priest Chaplain Prelate of His Holiness.

Cesareo's most famous hymn is ***The Fisher of Men***, which has been translated into over eighty languages. His hymns have also been used in major motion pictures, such as the pictures ***Alive*** and ***Camino***.

In addition to his legendary hymns, he became world famous for his ministry to cyclists who were on tours, including the Tour de France. In fact, he often rode with them.

Cesareo was in great demand around the world. He frequently conducted workshops on various topics with support from the Oregon Catholic Press, as well as from many other supporters. Each time he scheduled a workshop they were full.

In 1991, while touring several dozen cities in the United States, Cesareo fell ill. Upon his return to Spain, he learned that he had cancer. He became gravely ill, but he did not share the news of his illness with his friends and fans, so his death in 1991 at the age of fifty-five came as a shock of grief to them.

Cesareo's hymns can be found today in almost every Christian hymnal around the world. His hymns have been translated into over sixty languages.

(References: *Priest Bases Hymns On Call to Be Fishers of Men*, 2013, The Methodist Reporter, Michael Haven; *Walk On, O People of God*, Michael Hawn, UMC. Retrieved 2015; *Hymns, Psalms, and Spiritual Songs*, 1990, Westminster John Knox Press)

Gabriel, Charles

Charles was born in 1856 in Wilton, Iowa. His family lived on a farm. They had to work hard but they loved the land and were devoted to each other and their religious beliefs. Charles grew up surrounded by parents and siblings who helped and encouraged each other. After a hard day of work, they found relaxation and enjoyment in music. In that atmosphere, Charles developed a keen interest in music.

As a young boy, he was determined to learn how to play the family's old reed organ even though he had no music training, experience, or music knowledge. However, he had a natural talent and ear for music, which was accompanied by his hard work and determination, led to a mastery of music. Charles' music ability became well known throughout the town of Wilton.

A story is told that the town minister, Reverend N. A. McAulay saw Charles one day in town and asked the young boy if he knew any hymns that might accompany the topic of his sermon the next Sunday. The minister told Charles the theme of the sermon and thought no more of the conversation until Charles just a few days later came to the church to share with the minister a hymn he had composed—words and music. The minister was shocked that Charles composed a hymn and even more surprised when he heard the hymn. He loved it. The hymn was played in church the following Sunday. Applause broke out at the end of the hymn when the minister announced that Charles had composed the hymn.

By age sixteen Charles was teaching music and singing in schools and giving private tutoring sessions. His reputation grew steadily and his musical talents were put on display in many churches and community venues in several states. Charles' extraordinary worship music talent led him to the position of director of music at the Grace Methodist Episcopal Church in San Francisco, California. It was while he was working at Grace that his first hymn was published, ***Send the Light***. After almost three years at Grace, Charles moved to Chicago and went to work for Homer Rodeheaver Publishing Company. He obviously had creative musical talents, but Charles also was a gifted writer and editor. Charles enjoyed receiving manuscripts and original hymns at the publishing house. He edited forty-one Christmas cantatas, thirty-five gospel books, twenty-three choir cantatas, ten children's cantatas, eight Sunday school songbooks, seven books of music for male choruses, six books of music for female choruses, and dozens of books on musical instruction. Even with his heavy workload, he continued to compose music and write.

Charles published several books of gospel music that contained some of his own compositions. His books ***Gospel Songs and Their Writers; The Singers and Their Songs***, and ***Golden Bells*** were top sellers for the publishing house. One of his most popular creations was the ***Dream of Fairyland***, a children's cantata that has remained popular for many years. Charles was well known for his work and the works he edited, but he was also recognized for his military style marches and waltzes for bands. Charles was such a creative and prolific writer he feared that people would not accept the volume of work he produced as his own, so he used almost a dozen pseudonyms.

Due to the quality, creativity and volume of his work, he was inducted into the Gospel Music Hall of Fame.

Charles remained productive his entire life until a brief illness took his life in 1932 at the age of seventy-six in Los Angeles, California. Many of his hymns were played at his memorial service, which included a children's choir, photographs of famous people with Charles, a display of his literary works, and some of his original hymns.

(References: *The Gospel Songs of Charles H. Gabriel*, 2013, La Vista Church of Christ Journal, Wayne Walker; *Charles H. Gabriel—Inductee Biography*, 1982, Gospel Music Hall of Fame; *Charles Gabriel*, 2013, Encyclopedia of American Gospel Music, W.K. McNeil)

Gaither, Gloria

Gloria was born in 1942 in Battle Creek, Michigan where she spent most of her early life. She attended public elementary and high school there and worked part-time at the Kellogg Company.

After high school, Gloria attended Anderson University in Anderson, Indiana, majoring in English, French, and Sociology. Gloria was a very good student with a talent for languages and music. She wanted to be a teacher, so after college, she found a job teaching French at Alexandria Monroe High School. It was at the high school where she met her future husband, Bill Gaither (see the biography for Bill Gaither) who was teaching English. They both enjoyed music, poetry, and writing, so they experimented with writing songs. Soon they married and while teaching during the day they honed their music writing skills at night. Gloria was not certain if their compositions were worthy of professional status, but took so much pleasure in writing gospel songs she wanted to share her joy.

They recorded a few of the gospel songs and shortly thereafter her career along with Bill's grew rapidly nationwide and eventually worldwide. In collaboration with Bill, they have written well over 700 songs. She is also an author, having published over forty books, including twenty children's books. Gloria is also a scriptwriter, a gifted speaker, narrator, editor, and recognized scholar. Her hymns are in hymn books around the world and she continues to be a popular performer of gospel music.

Being a life-long learner, Gloria decided to go back to college. She loved scholarly work as much as creative work, so at the age of forty-nine, she enrolled in college. Her scholarly work was so impressive she was hired by Anderson University as an adjunct professor. Gloria loved teaching and she was a very popular professor. If her music career had not been so successful and time-consuming, Gloria could have become a tenured professor. She has been awarded seven honorary doctorate degrees.

Gloria has won numerous awards for her music, performances, publications, and speeches. She and her husband were named Christian Songwriters of the Century by the American Society of Composers, based on songs written over the last century.

She continues to write songs, publishes other works and performs around the world.

(References: *Gloria Gaither*, gaither.com. Retrieved 2014; *It's More Than Music: Life Lessons on Friends, Faith and What Matters Most*, 2003, Bill Gaither and Ken Abraham; *Homecoming*, 1997, Bill Gaither and Jerry Jerkins)

Gaither, William (Bill)

Bill was born in 1936 in Alexandria, Indiana. He has one brother and one sister.

At a very young age, Bill discovered his love for music. He listened to all types of music on the radio, but he particularly enjoyed gospel music. Bill was a good student in both elementary and high school and he was very active with his music.

After graduating from high school he enrolled at Anderson College. By then Bill recognized his talent for music and realized that he could compose music, so he formed the Bill Gaither Trio with his brother and sister while in college. He tried to balance college with a singing career, which became increasingly difficult. Also, he felt like his personal priorities and values were not in order. It was after a concert in Ohio when Bill realized he had to make a change in his life.

At the age of nineteen, Bill committed his life to God. His commitment to God helped Bill make better decisions and find purpose in his life. It also helped his self-discipline. Bill earned a Bachelor of Arts degree in English and after graduation worked as an English teacher. He met his future wife, Gloria, when she was teaching French at the same high school where Bill taught. He enjoyed teaching but he loved music just as much, if not more. Adding to his dilemma was the fact that he was excellent at both teaching and music. But he finally accepted the reality that he could not manage both effectively, so he committed his attention to the music profession full-time and gave up his teaching position.

Bill's breakout song was ***He Touched Me***, a deeply felt and beautifully composed gospel song that in 1964 launched his music career. Since then Bill has been a prolific composer of gospel music. His wife left her teaching position not long after Bill left the profession and joined him in the music industry. Their marriage has been almost perfect in many ways, including music. Gloria often writes the lyrics and Bill writes the music. This collaborative effort has resulted in over 700 songs and still counting. In addition to concerts which have been held around the world, he also manages the family business—the Gaither Music Company.

Bill has been a supporter and father-figure to many other gospel singers as they try to make it into the world of gospel music. He is known to stop in the middle of a hectic day to counsel and encourage a struggling young musician.

Bill and Gloria have together won eight Grammy Awards and have been nominated for several others, named Songwriter of the Year eight times, and have twenty-six Dove Awards from the Gospel Music Association.

They have remained in Alexandria, Indiana, where they continue to create music, minister to young musicians, and operate the successful family business.

(References: *William Gaither*, gaither.com. Retrieved 2014; *It's More Than Music: Life Lessons on Friends, Faith and What Matters Most*, 2003, Bill Gaither and Ken Abraham; *Homecoming*, 1997, Bill Gaither and Jerry Jerkins)

Gelineau, Joseph

Joseph was born in 1920 in Champ-sur-Layon, Maine-et-Loire, France. This area of France is famous for wine vineyards. In fact, Joseph's family has a legacy in the wine-growing region that extends back 400 years.

As a child, Joseph was small, frail, and often physically ill. When he entered school he contracted tuberculosis which kept him mostly bedridden during much of his childhood. There were times when he seldom left the house for months. Due to his illness, he did not return to school.

Joseph's physical condition was tenuous but he had a keen intellect and he enjoyed music. A relative bought him a horn for his music interests, but Joseph also discovered that blowing the horn improved his respiration, so he played frequently. One good result of his illness is that it disqualified him for military service during World War II. Instead of going into the military, Joseph entered the Jesuit seminary. He studied theology at the seminary in Lyons, France, and later music in Paris. He earned a doctorate in theology; the subject of his thesis was the *Book of Psalms*. Joseph became a French Catholic Jesuit priest who loved music and was a prolific composer of hymns.

Throughout his life, Joseph was enthralled by the *Book of Psalms*. He was also fascinated by Gregorian chants (a form of monophonic sacred songs of the Western Roman Catholic Church that were traditionally sung by choirs of men and boys in churches). Divine inspiration helped him bring the two together, and from that union, he created the ***Gelineau Psalmody***, which is a method of putting Psalms to songs. The ***Gelineau Psalmody***, which was published as ***24 Psalms and a Canticle***, became popular in France and Europe during the 1950s and when translated into English in the early 1960s (known as the ***Grail Psalms***) became part of hymnals around the Christian world, and remain popular today.

Joseph's work was not limited to Psalmody; he wrote many other hymns and canticles for French Catholic churches. Additionally, he was recognized as a liturgical scholar. He published ***Chant et Musique Dans le Culte*** which was translated into English as ***Voices and Instruments in Christian Worship***. This book had a significant influence in the United States and Europe for its focus of resurrecting the long-lost form of responsive *Psalms* that was a traditional part of Catholic Mass centuries ago.

Joseph continued his prolific and influential writing throughout his life. He published several hymns, books, articles, and compositions too numerous to list. It is also important to know that Joseph was a beloved teacher and priest who by everyone's account was brilliant beyond measure but also kind, patient, and courteous to everyone.

Joseph is also remembered for his phenomenal singing voice. People came from miles away to hear the singing priest with the "heavenly voice."

After suffering complications from a fall, Joseph died in 2008 at the age of eighty-seven. He was buried in Grenoble, France. The memorial service included many of his favorite hymns, as well as testimony from many friends and colleagues who told stories about Joseph's generosity and kindness.

(References: *Rest in Peace Fr Joseph Gelineau*, S.J., Obituary in French Jesuit, August 11, 2008; *Psalms: A New Translation Singing Version*, 1963, Joseph Gelineau; *Psalms of David*, GIA Publications, Joseph Gelineau and Richard Proulx. Retrieved 2015)

Gerhardt, Paul

Paul was born in 1607 in the small town of Grafenhainichen, Germany near Wittenberg. His family was middle class and active in the community. It was a close-knit community where families took care of each other as if each person was an extended family member.

After an unremarkable experience in grammar and secondary school, at age fifteen Paul enrolled in Frusten School in Grimma which was known for stern discipline (some said cruel) and intellectual rigor. Paul did not like the school, and he missed his family. He was there for only a few months before the school was temporarily closed because the plague ravaged the small town and the school. Paul and his family survived the plague, and he returned to the school.

Perhaps due to the loss of life and the harshness of the plague, the atmosphere of the school changed. The school remained rigorous with a focus on discipline, but there was also support for and encouragement of the students.

Paul discovered that he was the intellectual equal to any student at the school; thereafter, he excelled in the school. His intelligence and insight greatly impressed the teachers, who encouraged him to attend college and become a teacher or college scholar.

After graduating from secondary school, he attended the University of Wittenberg. It was while attending Wittenberg that he met the legendary Lutheran leaders, Paul Rober and Jacob Martini. Paul learned from them about the value and importance of using hymns to teach spiritual lessons and to motivate spiritual feelings and pastoral care. Paul would become a great hymnist primarily because of the early influences of Paul Rober and Jacob Martini.

Paul expected to become a pastor after graduating but the effects and disasters associated with the Thirty Years War forced him to move to Berlin to find a job. Even in Berlin, he could not find a job. Finally, he found a few students to tutor in order to have at least a meager income. Paul continued to write hymns and when some of them were published his reputation began to soar.

The Cantor of Nicolaikirche (St. Nicholas Church) in Berlin heard one of Paul's hymns and was immediately impressed with the depth of the composition. Because the Cantor was also the organist at St. Nicholas he appreciated Paul's hymns and began to play some of them in the church services. He transformed many of Paul's compositions into hymns that were published in his ***Praxis Pietatis Melica*** (***Practice of Piety in Song***). The hymns were very well received and sealed his reputation. They became very popular throughout Europe.

Even though he was receiving recognition for his hymns, Paul wanted to be a pastor in a church, so he accepted a pastor position in Mittenwalde. Though he and his wife missed Berlin they at the same time enjoyed the small town of Mittenwalde. Most of Paul's hymns were written while he was in Mittenwalde.

Later he accepted an invitation as an associate pastor at Likolaikirche in Berlin. In Berlin, there was growing animosity between the Lutheran and Reformed (Calvinist) clergy. Because the Elector, Friedrich Wilhelm I of Brandenburg, was a member of the Reformed, he purged the Lutherans from pastor appointments and from teaching at the University of Frankfurt. Wilhelm even prohibited Lutherans from serving as tutors in private homes. This was unfortunate for Paul, being an ordained Lutheran, but he continued to meet with members of his church and his sermons continued even as he faced possible exile at any moment.

Although Paul was a leader among the Lutherans, he was known for his diplomacy and patience with others; he was a natural diplomat, which put him in good standing with the Reformed leaders. In fact, many Reformed members attended his services. Friedrich was not one of Paul's admirers, and it is believed that he resented the fact that his wife was respectful of Paul and frequently attended his services. Whether out of jealousy or actual dislike of Paul and/or his Lutheran beliefs, Friedrich removed Paul from his position in 1666. The move backfired and created a small rebellion in Berlin, leading to a widespread petition by numerous citizens of Berlin to have Paul reinstated. However, Paul could not work under the conditions established by Friedrich, so he remained unemployed for several months. During this time, he faced great hardship, including the death of his beloved wife. Finally, Friedrich recanted his edict against Paul. After many months scraping by on support from friends and others, he became the Archdeacon of Lubben in Saxe-Merseburg (The Duchy of Saxe-Merseburg was a territory of the Holy Roman Empire, and existed from 1656 to 1738). Paul served there until his death eight years later in 1676 at the age of sixty-nine.

Although he was a prolific hymn writer most of his life there is no record of him writing any hymns during the last ten years of his life. Some of his friends claim that he drifted into depression after the death of his wife and the turmoil in Berlin. For the rest of his life, Paul regretted leaving Mittenwalde. He felt that his wife would have lived longer, his career would not have been interrupted and his faith would not have been darkened had he remained in Mittenwalde instead of giving into ambition and moving to Berlin.

Even so, Paul wrote hundreds of hymns during his lifetime and is considered one of the greatest German hymnist of all time and one of the most famous hymnists in the world. One of his hymns became legendary and is found in almost every modern day hymnal, ***Give to the Winds Thy Fear***.

(References: *Paul Gerhardt,* Encyclopedia Britannica. Retrieved 2013; *Paul Gerhardt as a Hymn Writer and His Influence on English Hymnody,* 1918, Theodore Brown Hewitt; *Paul Gerhardt,* 1920, Encyclopedia Americana; *Hymns of Paul Gerhardt,* CyberHymnal.org Retrieved 2015; *Biography of Paul Gerhardt 1607-1676,* Stem Publishing; *Hymns and Hymn Makers,* 1908, Duncan Campbell)

.llard, Richard

.ichard was born in 1953 in London, England, but he was raised in New Zealand, beginning at age three, along with six siblings. He has lived there since then.

Richard was raised in a Christian home. His father was Pentecostal and his mother was Anglican. Richard was always interested in music and religion, starting at a very young age, but he aspired to be a teacher.

He taught himself how to play several instruments, beginning at age seven, but he especially enjoyed the ukulele and guitar. Richard became very good at playing both. He has carried that love of music with him throughout his life.

Richard was a good and conscientious student in secondary school, and he participated in school activities and events, including musicals. After secondary school, he attended a teacher's training college. He also explored his skills in music. Richard enjoyed folk music and grew to enjoy folk-gospel music.

After graduating from college he became a teacher and taught in primary level schools for a few years. He then took a job in a commercial warehouse so he could make more money. During that time, he was very active in St. Paul's Anglican Church in Auckland. Richard and others, including his wife, started a folk-gospel group at the church called the St. Paul's Singers. Richard encouraged the children and youth in the church to participate in the singing group. He began writing songs several years earlier but he rewrote and updated some of them for the St. Paul Singers. The group performed in many churches and at several events across New Zealand. The group's reputation grew as did the popularity of Richard's compositions. Many of his songs were published, but perhaps his most famous song is ***The Servant Song***, which Richard described: "It was in the first half of 1976 that I wrote Verse 3, but initially no more than that. It wasn't until one particularly summery Sunday afternoon in December 1976 or January 1977, back in Auckland, that I took that scrap of paper out of my guitar case and began to meditate on that single verse, exploring the possibilities that it suggested. I remember that the other verses came quickly—although not in the order in which we now sing the song." The hymn has been performed across the world by different performers.

Richard remains active with the St. Paul's Singer and he continues to write musical compositions. Many of his musical pieces are included in hymnals and are especially popular with children and youth church programs and activities.

Like his music, Richard is described as a person who carries joy and praise with him every day and shares his joy of life with others.

(References: *Richard Gillard,* Dictionary of North American Hymnology. Retrieved 2014; *Hymns for Today,* 2009, Brian Wren; *Richard Gillard,* The Canterbury Dictionary of Hymnology. Retrieved 2014; *Hear My Song: Meditations on Life Through Favorite Hymns,* 2010, Pam Rhodes)

Gilmore, Joseph

Joseph was born in Boston in 1834. He worked in his family's business and tried to balance school with work. He displayed an early interest in theology and philosophy, but his passion and gift were in literature. Joseph learned to read and write at home and in the small local school. When he worked, he helped some of the older employees learn how to read.

In his twenties, Joseph discovered that he had the ability to combine his knowledge of literature with his interest in theology and his talent for public speaking into a preaching career. At the age of twenty-eight, he became a pastor. Even though he received some teaching from the local pastor, most of what he learned about religion, liturgy, and theology he taught himself.

Joseph was greatly troubled by the American Civil War. He knew that many people were losing their faith in God due to the on-going horrors of the war. He later said that the daily reports of the brutality of the war played a significant role in his decision to focus on his spirituality and the love of God.

ɜeph did not intend to write hymns and was surprised that ɩething he wrote during an incidental gathering with a friend -sulted in a famous hymn. Joseph was invited to give a sermon at the First Baptist Church of Philadelphia. His sermon focused on *Psalm 23,* and particularly on the theme of "He leadeth me ..." At a gathering after his sermon, he wrote on his sermon manuscript the poem, "He leadeth me! O blessed tho't! O words with heavenly comfort fraught! Whatever I do, wherever I am, still it is God's hand that leadeth me!" Sometime later when he picked up a church hymnal to join in singing, he saw his words written into a hymn. He learned that his wife had sent his poem to the literary publication *The Watchman and Reflector,* and they published it. A famous hymn composer of the era, William Bradbury, saw the poem and added music to what would become a beloved hymn, ***He Leadeth Me, O Blessed Thought***.

Joseph continued to combine ministry with literature and soon thereafter was offered a professorship at the University of Rochester in New York, where he worked for almost thirty years.

Joseph died in 1918 at the age of eighty-four. The self-taught minister, poet, hymnist, writer, and professor became famous. His funeral was attended by many famous people of the era.

(Reference: *Joseph Gilmore's Memorable Hymn,* Christianity.com. Retrieved 2015; *J.H. Gilmore,* Hymnary.org. Retrieved 2015; *101 Hymn Stories,* 1982, Kenneth Osbeck; *The Hymns and Hymn Writers of the Church,* 1911, Charles Sumner Nutter and Wilbur Fisk Tillett)

Gladden, Washington

Washington was born in 1836 in Pottsgrove, Pennsylvania. Washington's name was Solomon Washington Gladden but was changed to George Washington Gladden by his parents. Washington dropped George from his name because people kept referring to him as George Washington.

Washington lived in a modest home until age six when his father, who was a school teacher, died unexpectedly. Shortly thereafter he moved in with his uncle on a farm near the New York state town of Owego, a small farming community. Washington worked hard on the farm, as was required of all members of the family. It was the standard for living, for surviving. His uncle was a caring man and deeply religious. He believed in the power and word of the Bible and that farming was doing God's work.

Washington's adopted family encouraged him to read, but other than some old newspapers and catalogs related to farming, the only book he had to read of substance was the Bible. Consequently, he read the Bible through and through, and he took many of the lessons from the Bible to heart.

The region of New York that he lived in saw a constant flow of revivals with various types of ministers and preachers. Washington's uncle took him to several of them, but being wholly familiar with the Bible himself, Washington was not impressed with the sermons he heard at revivals. At times, he thought his understanding of the Bible exceeded that of preachers.

Washington received a minor education in the local school but he worked much of each day on the farm until his sixteenth birthday when he left the farm to take a job at the *Owego Gazette*, which was a weekly community newspaper, in Owego, New York. He started off doing menial jobs but he was exposed to a wide variety of books, newspapers, magazines, and printing presses. Washington took books and newspapers home to his boarding house room every day after work.

Washington attended the local church and joined the Order of the Good Templars, who focused on temperance. Having gained confidence in his self-taught education, he enrolled at Owego Academy. At the academy, he learned quickly and was very successful. His academic success allowed him to gain admission to Williams College. At Williams College, he was popular, involved in many college activities, and he became a scholar with notable literary skills. Washington wrote the alma mater for the college, ***The Mountains***. He graduated with honors.

Washington was ordained at the age of twenty-four and thereafter ministered in churches in Brooklyn, New York;

Morrisania, New York; North Adams, Massachusetts; Springfield, Massachusetts; and finally at the First Congregational Church in Columbus, Ohio, where he remained for thirty-six years.

Washington's reputation as a minister grew nationally, as did his reputation for advancing social justice. For example, he was involved in resolving a coal miners' strike. Washington supported unionization as a way for employees to settle grievances and unsafe working conditions.

Even with a very busy schedule, he maintained an active writing life, including editing the *New York Independent* and the *Sunday Afternoon* journals. In fact, he was a prolific writer. He wrote hundreds of hymns, poems, editorials, books, and articles. His hymn ***O Master Let Me Walk with Thee*** has been published in almost 500 hymnals. Additionally, he was vice president of the American Missionary Association for four years and served as the president for three years. It was during this time that he traveled to Atlanta, Georgia to visit Atlanta University and meet W. E. B. Du Bois. After hearing about and then witnessing the squalid living conditions of southern Black families, he became a spokesman for equality and anti-racism.

Washington received many awards, including an honorary doctorate degree from the University of Notre Dame, for his ministry, his writing, and his social activism.

He remained active with his writing and his social equality work up until a stroke took his life in 1918 at the age of eighty-two.

(References: *Washington Gladden: Prophet of Truth*, 2011, Timothy C. Ahrens; Washington Gladden Society Archives online. Retrieved 2014; *Social Gospel, Dictionary of American History*, 2003. Retrieved 2014; *The Systematic Thought of Washington Gladden*, 1968, Richard Knudten)

Grant, Amy

Amy was born in 1960 in Augusta, Georgia but was raised in Nashville, Tennessee.

She attended Harpeth Hall School where she was a good student. Amy was active in a local church in Nashville and she was greatly influenced and encouraged by her beloved great-grandfather and grandfather who regularly attended church with Amy at Nashville's Ashwood Church of Christ. Her great-grandfather was the founder of Life and Casualty Insurance Company and owner of the Life and Casualty Tower building in Nashville as well as principle owner of WLAC Radio Station in Nashville.

Amy enjoyed different types of music and showed an early talent for singing. She especially loved gospel music and sought a career as a gospel singer. According to her autobiography, Amy wrote her first song, ***Mountain Man,*** and performed in public for the first time at Harpeth Hall School, the all-girls school she attended. She recorded a demonstration tape for her parents with church youth leader Brown Bannister. Soon thereafter when Brown was dubbing a copy of the tape, Chris Christian, the owner of the recording studio, heard the demo and called Word Records. He played it over the phone, and, consequently, Amy was offered a recording contract five weeks before her 16th birthday.

By the time Amy was seventeen years old she had released a gospel album that made her famous in the Christian music world with hits such as ***Father's Eyes***; ***El Shaddai*** (Hebrew for God Almighty); ***Angels*** and others.

Amy enrolled at Vanderbilt University, but her music career became an early success with the release of gospel albums that sold very well, so she dropped out of college to pursue her music career full-time. Amy's first music love was gospel, but she ventured into country music and was an instant hit. Amy became the most successful crossover artist in history, with over 30 million record sales. Her first Billboard hit was a duet with Peter Cetera entitled ***The Next Time I Fall.*** Her recording ***Heart in Motion*** remains one of the top-selling recordings of all-time. Numerous other hits followed and she became known as the "Queen of Country Music".

Amy has won six Grammy Awards and twenty-two Gospel Music Association Dove Awards. She is the only country music singer to have an album go Platinum, which means over one million copies sold.

Amy has and continues to be active in charity work. Her recording, ***She Colors My Day***, was released to coincide with breast cancer awareness month in October 2008. She is also a member of the Red Cross Celebrity Cabinet and supports the Children's Health Fund, Children's Miracle Network Hospitals, Colon Cancer Alliance, Creative Recovery Communities, Special Olympics, and Tuberous Sclerosis Alliance.

Amy remains one of the most popular singers in the world.

(References: *My Life So Far*, 2007, Amy Grant; *Shining Through: Amy Grant*, 2015, Vanderbilt Magazine, Seth Robertson; *In Perfect Harmony: Vince Gill and Amy Grant*, 2013, Ladies Home Journal, Laura Brounstein)

Green, Fred Pratt

Fred was born in Roby, Lancashire, England in 1903. Roby is a small village with a history dating back to the 10th century as a Norse settlement.

Fred was the third child in the family. His father was a leather merchant. Fred attended Huyton High School where he excelled in his school work and was gregarious and very popular among his classmates and teachers. He participated in several school activities and was known for his intelligence and creativity.

Fred was interested in becoming an architect but settled on working with his father in the leather business. However, he moved in an entirely different direction after hearing a sermon by John Masefield entitled *The Everlasting Mercy*. Fred was inspired enough to consider the Anglican priesthood path but felt the pull of the Holy Communion of the Methodist and its open invitation for all to participate.

Fred attended Nazarene Theological College in Manchester, England in 1925. He was ordained as a Methodist minister in 1928 and served churches in northern and southern England for almost forty years. During that time, he also wrote poems and plays, but it was not until his retirement in 1969 that he became a prolific writer.

Fred is credited with writing over 300 hymns, including perennial favorites such as ***God is Here!***; ***O Christ, The Healer***; ***Let Us Praise Creation's Lord***; and ***Rejoice in God's Saints***. He was also a well-known poet. One of his most famous poems was ***The Old Couple*** which was included in *The Oxford Book of 21st Century English Verse*. Fred said that one of the highlights of his life was the selection of one of his hymns in the official Order of Service for the nationwide celebrations of the Jubilee of Queen Elizabeth II in 1977. In 1995, he was honored by the Queen of England with the MBE (Most Excellent Order of the British Empire) for services to hymn writing.

Fred has been described by many as the finest Methodist hymn writer since the legendary Charles Wesley. His works are in the Pratt Green Collection at Durham University in Durham, England, and his fifty-one scrapbooks are in the Pitts Theological Library at Emory University in Atlanta, Georgia. Fred's scrapbooks are an amazing collection of his thoughts, pictures, and words that illustrate the depth of his creative genius and heartfelt faith.

Fred continued to write until his health deteriorated beginning in 1988. He died in 2000 at the age of ninety-seven.

(References: *The Fred Pratt Green Trust Papers - Hymns and Ballads of Fred Pratt Green*, 1982, Bernard Braley; *Fred Pratt Green*, Dictionary of Hymnology, 2000, Retrieved 2013; *Fred Pratt Green*, Hymnary.org. Retrieved 2014)

Gurney, Dorothy

Dorothy was born in 1858 near Finsbury Circus in London, England. She was the eldest daughter of Reverend Blomfield, the Rector of St. Andrew's Undershaft Church in London. Her grandfather was Dr. F. Blomfield who was the Bishop of London.

Dorothy was an energetic, curious, and creative child. Her musical talents were noticed when she was young, so her father and grandfather encouraged Dorothy to pursue her musical interests and gift by involving her in many church musical events, activities, and concerts. She attended the best private schools and colleges in London and participated in numerous school and college music productions.

Dorothy began writing in college and soon found that she had a talent for composing poems, hymns, and other songs. She sent them to publishing companies and they were almost always published, and they received positive public comments.

Dorothy achieved immortality with a hymn she wrote for her sister's wedding in 1883. The hymn ***O Perfect Love*** has arguably been played at more weddings than any other song before or since she wrote it on a Sunday evening at the request of her sister.

She was visiting her sister at Windermere, England. Dorothy joined her sister and several friends to sing hymns a couple of days before the wedding. As they sang the hymn ***O Strength and Stay***, Dorothy's sister said that it was her favorite musical tune, and it was a pity that the words were not fitting for a wedding. She turned to Dorothy and commented almost in jest that since she was musically gifted she should take the tune and write lyrics appropriate for a wedding. Dorothy looked at her sister and said, "I can do that for you." She retreated to a room and in less than thirty minutes Dorothy returned with the words to what would later be called ***O Perfect Love***. The hymn was played at her sister's wedding and word of it spread quickly among young women in London and then throughout Great Britain and into Europe and across the Atlantic to America. The hymn has been included in many hymnals since then.

Dorothy has another claim-to-fame, although many people do not know that she wrote it. The poem is often found in gardens, in the homes of people who love to garden and many other places for garden lovers. Dorothy loved gardening, too, and from that inspiration she wrote ***God's Garden***: "The kiss of the sun for pardon; the songs of the birds for mirth; one is nearer God's heart in a garden than anywhere else on earth."

Dorothy wrote poems and hymns throughout her life and she and her husband traveled extensively around the world. She often said that she would hear her hymn ***O Perfect Love*** almost every time she attended a wedding anywhere in the world. The hymn was translated into several languages.

After a brief illness, she died in London in 1928 at the age of seventy. Several famous people of the day attended her memorial service and many of her favorite hymns were sung.

(References: *Dorothy E. Gurney,* Hymntime.com. Retrieved 2015; *101 More Hymn Stories,* 1985, Kenneth W. Osbeck; *Favorite Wedding Classics for Solo Singers,* 2010, Patrick M. Liebergen; *Lamentations: A Collection of Poetry,* 2015, Kazeem Olalekan)

Hammarskjold, Dag

Dag was born in Uppsala, Sweden in 1905. His father was the governor of the province of Uppland. The family focused on the values of education and community service. Dag's childhood was filled with intellectual exploration and exposure to classical music. He also attended church on a regular basis with his family and participated in numerous church activities.

Dag was an excellent student. He routinely scored at the top of his class in all examinations and intellectual pursuits. After his school work was recognized for excellence, he was accepted at the University of Uppsala. Dag enjoyed his time at the university. He thrived on the intellectual challenges and he developed many friendships that would last a lifetime. Dag's professors encouraged him to pursue graduate work after he completed his undergraduate studies. He earned a Bachelor of Arts degree in only three years. Dag loved the field of economics, so he did graduate work in that field of study for over three years. During his study of economics, he discovered an interest in law. He shifted from economics to law and earned a law degree.

While Dag was in college, his father's role in government expanded. At the Universal Christian Conference one year, Dag's father was one of the organizers and leaders of the conference. He brought Dag with him as a steward. The conference made an impression on Dag and increased his interest in religion. Dag's intellectual curiosity had no end. He had an equal interest in law, economics, religion, and government.

When his father retired and the family moved to Stockholm, Dag enrolled in economic studies at the University of Stockholm. He loved the intellectual challenge, but he also loved hiking the mountains. During his hikes, he discovered and began to appreciate the beauty of the world and God's hand in creating such beauty.

Dag's first government work came when he was appointed Secretary of the Royal Commission on Unemployment. During that time, he also taught classes at the University of Stockholm and he became Permanent Undersecretary in the Ministry of Finance. He performed so well he was elected Chairman of the Board of the Bank of Sweden. Due to his remarkable skills, Dag became Chairman of the Swedish delegation to the United Nations and eventually head of the United Nations Security Council. He became well known and respected around the world for his intellect, integrity, and diplomacy.

After a remarkable career, he was awarded an honorary doctorate degree from Oxford University. It was not until his death in 1961 that the public realized that Dag was also a poet. His masterwork titled ***Waymark*** was published and became a literary sensation. Some of his poems were translated and a few were composed into hymn/prayers.

At the height of his career, Dag became ill and as a shock to the world, he died in 1961 at the age of fifty-six in Stockholm. His friends said he died from a weary and world-worried heart that finally gave out. Dag is remembered in Sweden as one of its greatest intellectuals and diplomats.

(References: *Dag Hammarskjolds Vitbok*, 1970, Gustaf Aulen; *Dag Hammarskjold: Strictly Personal*, 1969, Bo Beskow; *United Nations Notebook: The Relationship of Dag Hammarskjold with the Press*, 1987, Development Dialogue, Kay Rainey Gray)

Hankey, Arabella Katherine

Katherine was born in 1834 in London. She was called Kate all of her life. Her father was a successful and wealthy banker in London. Her family life was one of comfort, influence, and worship. Her family members were all devout Christians. That is probably why at a very young age, Kate became devoted to her religious beliefs and prayed often each day.

She was influenced and inspired by the Methodist revival at that time led by John and Charles Wesley. The depth of her devotion can be seen by her attempts as a preteen to organize a Bible study class for her neighborhood girlfriends. A few years later as a teenager, she organized and taught Sunday school classes for girls in her London neighborhood. When word spread about Kate's Sunday school classes for girls, several girls from all walks of life started attending the classes. It was during this time that Kate discovered a talent to translate her strong beliefs to poems, which she often handed out in class. Also, because her Sunday school lessons were so popular, she acquiesced to requests for copies of those, too.

In addition to her work at the local church and in her community, Kate encouraged her family and the members of her Sunday school classes to support foreign missions. She did missionary work in Africa, along with her brother, who was a medical missionary, but at age thirty-two, Kate became gravely ill and was bedridden for several months. Nevertheless, she continued her daily prayers and kept an active reading and writing routine.

It was during this convalescent period that Kate wrote a lengthy poem about Jesus that included 100 verses. She was fascinated and inspired by Biblical stories, and she wished that the story of Jesus could be expressed in poetry. So, Kate started a daily ritual of writing the story of Jesus in a poem. She decided to write two stories within the poem. The first section of the poem tells the story of the life of Jesus and the second section tells the story of Jesus' influence on the world. The long poem became the basis for two of the most famous hymns in the Christian world, ***Tell Me The Old,***

Old Story and ***I Love To Tell The Story***. These two hymns are in every Christian hymnal around the world and have been translated into over fifty other languages. They have been recorded by famous performers and included in movies and other productions.

Kate eventually recovered from her illness and resumed her missionary work and revisions on her poems and hymns. Kate earned the respect and admiration of a generation of worshipers and missionaries from around the world. She became a spokesperson for missionary work and devotion to improving the lives of others.

Kate enjoyed a productive and rewarding life. She died in 1911 at the age of seventy-seven.

(References: *Arabella K. Haney*, The National and Religious Song Reader, 1996, William Emmett Studwell; *Sisters in Song*, 2013, Leslie Clay; *Arabella Katherine Hankey*, Cyberhymnal.org. Retrieved 2015; *Kate Hankey*, Hymnary.org. Retrieved 2015)

Harkness, Georgia

Georgia was born in 1891 in Harkness, New York, a town in the Adirondacks named after her grandfather who founded the town. The Harkness family was famous in the state of New York for its community work, political influence, and integrity.

Georgia was a thoughtful and intelligent child who could be seen frequently with a book in her hands. Her family was financially stable and thrived in the community; therefore, she was afforded a good education, especially considering the limitations of the era on the type and quality of education available for girls. She had several friends in the local school, and she frequently participated in church activities.

Georgia was raised in a Methodist family, and she devoted her spirit to God during a revival when she was fifteen years old. It was at that time she first recognized and accepted a calling to serve the church.

Georgia aspired to attend college, and she was accepted at every major college for women; many of them recruited her and offered her scholarships. However, Georgia wanted a broader experience, so she sought and gained acceptance at Cornell University. She loved Cornell because it allowed her intellectual prowess to develop. Georgia was fully engaged in the university life, often participating in activities and events at the university. She received a Bachelor of Arts in Philosophy in 1912 at the age of twenty.

Georgia was unclear about her future direction, so she accepted a teaching job in a high school and settled into a routine that did not suit her intellectual curiosity or her need for spiritual development and interest in the work of the church.

She wanted to pursue her interest in theology, so she took the bold step of leaving her secure job and enrolling at Boston University. However, because of her gender, she was denied enrollment in Boston University's School of Theology. Georgia's relentless nature and determination to expand her knowledge of theology kept her going, so she went instead to the university's Department of Religion and earned a Ph.D. in philosophy of religion in 1923, at the age of thirty-two.

She greatly enjoyed the atmosphere of universities, which allowed her to interact with motivated and bright students while pursuing her own professional interests and personal development. This attraction of the university world led her to teach religion and philosophy for fifteen years at Elmira College in Elmira, New York, and thereafter was Regents Professor of Philosophy and Religious Studies at Mount Holyoke College in Massachusetts for almost ten years, before moving to the Garrett Biblical Institute in Illinois where she became the first woman to hold full professor of theology status in a major seminary. She later taught classes at the Pacific School of Religion in Berkeley, California. Also, she was ordained by the Methodist Church (later the United Methodist Church).

Georgia was a prolific writer. She had over thirty books published during her lifetime and one was published after her death in 1974. Georgia's works included three books of poems with hymns. Her most well-known work is the hymn ***Hope of the World,*** written for a contest sponsored by the Hymn Society of America in 1954. Georgia's hymn won despite competition from almost 500 other entries in the contest. This award brought attention to the hymn and to her a measure of fame. In fact, the hymn was sung that year at the opening service of the World Council of Churches, a distinguished honor. The hymn is very important in the United Methodist world of worshipers, and can be found in every version of United Methodist hymnals over the last forty years.

Georgia continued her writings and studies up until her death in 1974 at the age of eighty-three.

(References: *Georgia Harkness: The Remaking of a Liberal Theologian,* 2010, Rebekah Miles; *Hope of the World,* 1981, Marilyn Kay Stulken; *Georgia Harkness: For Such a Time as This,* 1992, Rosemary Skinner Keller)

Harlow, Samuel Ralph

Samuel was born in 1885 in Boston, Massachusetts. His family was wealthy and influential. His paternal grandfather was a prison reformer.

Ralph's mother and father lived near the Charlestown State Prison. Ralph was actually born in the warden's house on the prison campus. He was raised to appreciate education, respect for others, the value of family, and the gift of service to others. Due to his mother's influence, Ralph told his family when he was only twelve years old that he wanted to be a missionary.

After excelling in his school work in secondary school, Ralph enrolled at Harvard University. His best friend at Harvard was William James, who would become the "father of psychology." Even though Ralph graduated with a degree in pre-med, he never really considered a career in medicine. Instead, he attended Union Theological Seminary and upon graduating became an ordained minister. He took a position as assistant minister at Spring Church in New York City.

His interest, however, remained in doing missionary work, so Ralph became a missionary to Turkey where he worked with Christian Armenians and Greek churches. He became the Chaplain of The International College in Turkey. A few years later, the Ottoman Empire government passed a law prohibiting any effort to convert Muslims to Christianity. This forced Ralph and his family to leave the country they loved. They moved back to Boston.

Ralph went on a speaking tour which included criticism of the United States for not protecting Christians in Turkey. He rallied enough support for his protests to motivate the United States Secretary of State to file a formal protest with the ruling government of Turkey. Under pressure from the international community, including harsh and repeated communications from the United States, the Turkish government softened its position toward Christians; consequently, Ralph and his family moved back to Turkey where he took back his position at The International College. Within a few years, however, the instability of the Turkish government became dangerous for foreigners, so again the family moved out of the country and back to Boston.

Ralph became Secretary of Student Volunteers Movement and later Professor of Religion at Smith College in Hampton, Massachusetts, where he worked for thirty years.

Ralph was a talented musician and he loved to write and compose music, especially hymns. He composed thirty hymns, the most famous of which is ***O Young and Fearless Prophet***. Ralph published several biographical, scholarly, and opinion books and articles, too.

His book ***Life After Death*** became a best-seller and went through several reprints. The book focused on the interchange and possible relationship between paranormal and spiritual experiences. The genesis of the book started fifty years before Ralph wrote the book when his sister, Anna, showed a psychic sensitivity that matched many of his own. His book includes the fascinating story of a woman, Patience Worth, who had the words of several poems and three novels come to her during Ouija Board experiences. Ralph's book used these stories and others to illustrate the reality of a forever-after.

Ralph died in 1972 in Hampton at the age of eighty-seven.

(References: *Life After Death*, 1960, S. Ralph Harlow; *S. Ralph Harlow*, Obituary, 1972, Martha's Vineyard Times; *S. Ralph Harlow Papers 1862-1970*, World Catalog. Retrieved 2014)

Hart, Joseph

Joseph was born in 1712 in London, England. In his autobiography, Joseph recounts his childhood by describing his parents as religious and happy, optimistic and enthusiastic. They emphasized the good things in life, especially the necessity and beauty of God's spirit and His work on earth.

Joseph had an excellent education. He learned a lot from respected scholars who taught him literary classics and classical languages of Latin, Hebrew, and Greek. Joseph was a brilliant student; consequently, he supplemented his education with his own additional studies of the classics, in both literature and language. He became so proficient that the scholars determined that he was their intellectual equal and encouraged him to teach.

Joseph stepped into a professor role and became well-respected and popular. Teaching became his beloved vocation, but he continued his research, also. Joseph translated several works from antiquity and classics, such as the writings of Herodian, Phocylides, and Plato.

Being energetic and curious, Joseph also enjoyed music and tried his hand at composing hymns. He excelled at that, too. His hymns became widely known as "Hart's Hymns" and were frequently sung in churches throughout England. Joseph published his collection of hymns in a book aptly named, ***Hart's Hymns***. Little did Joseph imagine that his hymns would remain popular and beloved by tens of thousands of people for more than 100 years.

Joseph's religious life and spiritual faith were not always linked to a lifestyle that befitted those beliefs. There was a time in his youth when he felt that believing in Jesus Christ and God was enough—that one's life did not have to parallel one's faith. He believed that God would understand and forgive anything and everything, so people should live freely with that knowledge. Joseph even publicly challenged John Wesley's beliefs in a widely published treatise on their differences, hoping to influence John Wesley's growing ministry. John Wesley quickly and succinctly labeled Joseph's position and theory as un-Christian and ignored him thereafter.

A few years later, Joseph had a spiritual "reawakening" that changed his life and made him more mindful of his lifestyle and behavior. He began to worry if he was truly saved, based on his beliefs and previous lifestyle. Joseph worried about this for several months. Just a few days before Easter when he was forty-five years old he felt that God gave him a sign that he needed to repent and move back toward God and away from the temptations that clouded his mind and spirit. He openly said that the renewal of his faith and dedication to God changed his life. His teaching, composing, and behavior all improved. His life and faith became more rich and rewarding.

In addition to teaching and composing, he became a talented preacher at Jewin Street Chapel in London. When word spread about his speaking talents, musical talents, and his creative and positive preaching style, his congregation outgrew the modest size chapel. The church had to add additional worship services to accommodate the growing number of worshipers. Joseph also became respected for his devotion to his congregation. He often visited the sick and dying to offer comfort and support.

At the peak of his fame, Joseph became ill and was bedridden for several weeks. It is believed that he had pneumonia. Joseph died in 1768 in London at the age of fifty-six.

His family and friends did not know how to arrange for his funeral because he was beloved by thousands of people who attended his church, heard him speak at different events, and/or sang his famous and spiritually moving hymns frequently. The Jewin Street Chapel was filled to overflowing for his funeral service, but it was what occurred at his gravesite at Bunhill Fields that was unexpected. Tens of thousands of people made the trip to the cemetery to honor Joseph. The crowd was so large and vast that a fully accurate accounting of the number of attendees, according to the *London Times*, was impossible. Regardless, it was obvious to all who were at or near the cemetery on the day that Joseph was laid to rest that his life and work had a positive influence on countless lives. And almost 250 years later, Joseph is still influencing lives through the power of his hymns.

(References: *Hymns Composed on Various Subjects*, 1760, Joseph Hart, 2010 reproduction; *Biography of Joseph Hart*, Stem Publishing. Retrieved 2015; *The Methodist Hymn Book: Illustrated with Biography, History, Incident, and Anecdote*, 1894, George John Stevenson. Retrieved from Library of Congress online archives)

Hatch, Edwin

Edwin was born in 1835 in Derby, England. His parents were deeply religious and raised Edwin as a non-conformist (do not conform to the governance of the Church of England).

From the time he entered grammar school and later as he completed secondary school, Edwin excelled in all academic studies. Edwin attended King Edward's School in Birmingham, England where he was influenced by James Prince Lee, a theology scholar. James would become the Bishop of Manchester. James was one of the first to witness and appreciate Edwin's intelligence and independent mind. He also admired Edwin's almost fanatical study habits.

After King Edward's School, Edwin was accepted into Cambridge University where he graduated near the top of his class at a young age. Edwin then entered Pembroke College at Oxford University. At Oxford, he continued to reveal a high level of intellectual gifts. He was awarded the prestigious Edward Ellerton Theological Essay Prize. Edwin graduated with highest honors at age twenty-two with a degree in theology.

Edwin was ordained as an Anglican priest shortly after graduating from Oxford and soon thereafter accepted a professorship of classics at Trinity College in Toronto, Canada. He worked at Trinity for three years, during which time his lectures and publications became well known and respected.

He moved to Quebec where he became the Rector of Quebec High School and professor of classics at Morrin College. Edwin was appointed University Reader in Ecclesiastical History and Hibbert Lecturer. He became a famous intellectual throughout Canada, the United States, and England.

Edwin loved Canada but he wanted to return to England. Upon his return, he became Vice Principal of St. Mary Hall, Oxford and Rector of Purleigh.

He was a prolific researcher and writer. Edwin's book ***Influence of Greek Ideas and Usages Upon the Christian Church*** became very popular in the academic world. In addition to his intellectual pursuits, Edwin enjoyed music and especially hymns. He was intrigued with Scripture lessons that were taught through hymns. Edwin tried his hand at hymn writing, but he wrote only a few hymns because most of the time he spent studying scholarly work and because he did not think his hymns were worthy of publication. However, he shared a few of his hymns with friends who encouraged him to publish them.

One of his hymns has become a classic and is included in almost every Christian hymnal around the world, ***Breathe on Me, Breath of God***. He wrote the hymn after being inspired *by John 20:21-22*, which is the account of the Resurrection when Jesus said to John "Peace be with you. As the Father has sent me, so send I you." Edwin pictured Jesus breathing these words and inspiration on John. All of Edwin's hymns were published posthumously a few years after his death in ***Towards Fields of Light***.

To the surprise and grief of his friends, family, colleagues, and countless others, Edwin died in 1889 in Oxford, England after a short illness. Edwin was only fifty-four years old at the time of his death.

(References: *Aspects of Edwin Hatch,* 1974, Peter Carlsson; *The Influence of Greek Ideas Upon the Christian Church,* reprinted 2012, Edward Hatch; *Edwin Hatch,* Library of Congress. Retrieved 2013)

Haugen, Marty

Marty was born in 1950 in Wanamingo, Minnesota. His family was devoted Lutherans and he was consequently raised in an American Lutheran Church while growing up in Minnesota.

Marty was a good student in school and participated in activities at the church and the school. He particularly loved music and theater.

After completing secondary school, Marty was accepted at Luther College where he earned a Bachelors in Psychology. At first, he wanted to go into the field of psychology, but he later decided that his heart was in pastoral studies. Consequently, he earned a Master in Pastoral Studies at the University of St. Thomas in St. Paul, Minnesota.

Marty has been involved in hymnal work for several years, and he has had a successful career as a liturgical composer and trainer. His music has wide appeal among all denominations for its messages of understanding, spiritual guidance, faith, hope, grace, and support of others.

Marty has several publications and enjoys an international reputation for his music work. His best-known works are ***Holden Evening Prayer***; ***The Feast and Celebration***, and ***Mass of Creation***. Many of his hymns are sung in worship services around the world, such as ***Gather Us In***; ***Eye Has Not Seen***; ***Canticle of the Sun***; and ***Shepherd Me, O God***. Arguably he is best known for his hymn ***All Are Welcome***, a mainstay in most hymnals.

Marty's hymns can be found in hymnals of the United Methodist Church, Presbyterian Church USA, Mennonite Brethren, United Church of Christ, Church of Jesus Christ of Latter Day Saints, United Church of Canada, Church of England, Church of Scotland, and Roman Catholic groups in Great Britain, Canada, Ireland, and Australia.

He has recorded thirty CDs and is currently the Composer-in-Residence at the Mayflower Community Congregational Church in Minneapolis, Minnesota.

(References: *Marty Haugen Hymns and Songs*, martyhaugen.net. Retrieved 2013; *Marty Haugen*, GIA Publications, Inc. Retrieved 2013; *History of Hymns*, Michael Hawn, UMC. Retrieved 2013)

Havergal, Frances Ridley

Frances was born in 1836 in Astley, Worcestershire, England at her father's rectory.

Her father was a tremendous influence in her life. He was the first to recognize Frances' unusually mature intellect when she was very young, but he was also concerned about her fragile health and was faced with the dilemma of guiding and raising an intellectually mature and energetic but physically frail young girl.

Frances was reading at age three and writing with remarkable skill by age seven - composing poems and writing short stories. By the age of ten, she was not only a mature writer she was also a music prodigy. She learned to play the piano and could read music. She also tried composing hymns from poems.

Frances' poems were first published before she turned sixteen years old in the book ***Good Words***. Also, many of her poems, because of their spiritual and encouraging outlook, were published in religious publications such as newsletters, journals, and periodicals.

Frances often traveled with her father and stepmother. She especially benefitted from a trip and long stay in Germany. There she enjoyed learning the language, culture, literature and music. In Germany, she studied for a year in the Louisenschule at Düsseldorf and in the family of a German pastor at Obercassel until the family returned to England in 1853.

Upon their return home, Frances and her father began working together on a revised edition of his book ***Psalmody,*** a publication that was well-known in the religious publication world during that era. However, her father died suddenly from an apparent heart attack before the work was finished. Frances took the work on herself and the revised book was published.

When her mother died Frances moved to South Wales where she lived and worked for the rest of her short life. In addition to writing, she was also involved in philanthropic work. In tribute to her charity work, which helped hundreds of girls complete college, a private girls' college in Toronto was named for Frances, the Havergal College.

Her lifelong health issues became too much for her frail body to cope with and she died in 1879 at the age of forty-two of peritonitis at Caswell Bay in Wales.

During her short life, Frances was a prolific writer, but most of her poems and hymns were published after her death. Her sisters were instrumental in organizing Frances' work for publication, which included ***The Ministry of Song***; ***Under the Surface***; ***Loyal Responses***; ***Life Chords***; ***Life Echoes***; ***Coming to the King***; ***Poetical Works*** and many others. These were extremely popular in religious worship circles.

Frances' autobiography, ***Memorials of Frances Ridley Havergal***, was also published by her sisters and became a very popular book.

(References: *Frances Ridley Havergal*, 1979, Janet Grierson, The Havergal Society; *Memorials of Frances Ridley Havergal*, 1880, M.V.G. Havergal, Havergal College Archives. Retrieved 2014; *Take My Life: a Portrait of Frances Havergal*, 2000, N.J. Collingswood, The Bible for Today; *In Trouble and in Joy: Four Women Who Lived for God*, 2004, Sharon James)

Hawks, Annie Sherwood

Annie was born in 1836 (some references say 1835) in Hoosick, New York.

At a very young age, possibly as young as three, she started reading and by the age of six, she was writing long passages of verse. She was an avid reader, enjoying literature of all types, but she especially enjoyed poetry. Annie wrote several poems before her tenth birthday, but she kept most of them to herself. When she was twelve years old, she shared a few of her poems with her parents who were surprised at the maturity and quality of her writing. They encouraged her to continue writing.

Annie excelled in school and it was obvious to her teachers that she possessed an unusual gift for writing. With the encouragement of her parents and teachers, Annie submitted one of her poems to a Troy, New York newspaper and it was accepted for publication. Her poem and her age became an overnight sensation, and from that time on and for many years Annie frequently contributed poems to newspapers and magazines.

She graduated from college at age twenty-one. After college, she married Charles Hawks and they moved to Brooklyn, New York. They began attending Hanson Place Baptist Church, and it did not take long for the congregation and its pastor, Robert Lowry, to recognize Annie, the well-known and respected poet. Annie and her husband became close friends with Robert, who was always fascinated with poems and hymns. He had a talent for composing poems into hymns, having created hymns himself for years. That was the beginning of a prolific teamwork of production.

Annie would write over 400 poems that Robert composed into hymns. By far, the most famous of which is ***I Need Thee Every Hour***. About the famous poem and hymn, Annie recalled (to a reporter at the *New York Herald*): "I remember well the circumstances under which I wrote the hymn. It was a bright June day, and I became so filled with the sense of the nearness of my Master that I began to wonder how anyone could live without Him, in either joy or pain. Suddenly, the words "I need Thee every hour" flashed into my mind, and very quickly the thought had full possession of me. Seating myself by the open windows, I caught up my pencil and committed the words to paper - almost as they are today. A few months later Dr. Robert Lowry composed the tune for my hymn and also added the refrain. To me, the hymn, at its writing, was prophetic rather than expressive of my own experiences, for it was wafted out to the world on the wings of love and joy, instead of under the stress of great personal sorrow, with which it has often been associated. At first, I did not understand why the hymn so greatly touched the throbbing heart of humanity. Years later, however, under the shadow of a great loss, I came to understand something of the comforting power of the words I had been permitted to give out to others in my hours of sweet serenity and peace."

That hymn would have a different and even more powerful meaning to Annie after her husband of thirty years, Charles, passed away in 1888. Her grief was almost overwhelming. Annie's only relief was her writing and a daily reading of ***I Need Thee Every Hour***.

Annie went to live with her daughter in Bennington, Vermont after Charles' death and continued to write poems and hymns until her death in 1918 at the age of eighty-two.

(References: *A Woman of the Century*, Google Books. Retrieved 2014; *Annie Sherwood Hawks*, Great Christian Hymns. Retrieved 2014; *101 More Hymn Stories*, 1985, Kenneth Osbeck)

Herklots, Rosamond Eleanor

Rosamond was born in 1905 in Masuri, India, which is in Northern India. Her parents were British government employees assigned to India. Rosamond enjoyed the culture, literature, and artwork of India and its people.

She learned to read at a very young age and tried writing poetry before she was an adolescent. Rosamond continued writing, as her education expanded into new intellectual challenges. She was an excellent student and very popular with her peers and teachers.

After several years in India, Rosamond returned to England to attend Leeds University where she was trained as a teacher. After graduation, she took a position as a teacher but did not find it satisfactory to her interests. She left that position to become a medical administrative assistant to an eminent and internationally known neurologist. Rosamond viewed the job as a temporary position until she could decide what she wanted to do. However, as with everything she did, she worked very diligently. Her efficiency and competence were the pride of the neurologist, who often bragged about Rosamond. It was her work reputation that led to an offer to be the lead medical administrative assistant in the main office of the Association for Spina Bifida and Hydrocephalus in London.

Even though Rosamond wrote poetry in her spare time, she did not think anyone would take her work seriously. She also enjoyed music and recognized that many hymns were like poems. Late in her life, she started writing and composing hymns. Rosamond reluctantly shared them with some friends who encouraged her to publish them. However, it was not until members of the Hymn Society of Great Britain and Ireland supported her did she submit hymns to Oxford University Press. Oxford published them and asked Rosamond for more. Eventually, she would write over 100 hymns that were published in several British hymnals across the country and in parts of Europe.

Rosamond's most famous hymn is ***Forgive Our Sins***. She was inspired to write the hymn after working one long, hot day in her garden trying to remove all of the weeds. She thought that many of the negative thoughts and feelings of people such as jealousy, bitterness, anger, hatred are like the weeds in the garden—forever seeking to take over and crowd out the good growth, to cover what is good in life. Rosamond wrote in her hymn that God is forever taking care of his garden on earth, caring for our souls and weeding out the sin that tries to poison our lives.

Several of Rosamond's hymns became popular throughout the Christian world and many of her hymns can be found in hymnals today.

She continued to write poems and hymns until she died in Bromley, Kent, England in 1987 at the age of eighty-two.

(References: *Rosamond E. Herklots,* Presbyterian Hymnal Companion, 1970; *Hymns by Rosamond E. Herklots*, 1966, Preston Lee Ventures; *Rosamond Herklots,* eHymnBook.org—Oxford Dictionary of Hymns. Retrieved 2014)

Hermanus Kaan, Frederik

Frederik (Fred) was born in 1929 in Haarlem the Netherlands.

Fred had a very difficult and traumatic youth. When he was a young teenager, the German Nazis occupied the town and eventually the country. The townspeople were not allowed the basics of life, causing many of them to starve or die from the elements or when trying to escape the occupation of the Nazi regime. Fred witnessed the death of three grandparents who died from malnutrition. Fred also lived with the intense and daily pressure of knowing that his parents were harboring resistance fighters. His parents were active participants in the Dutch resistance for several years.

These early experiences influenced Fred deeply. He was not anti-religion but he did not attend a church until he was almost twenty years old, because he could not understand how God would allow such atrocities to occur. His grandparents were religious and the thought of entering a church brought the horror of their gruesome deaths to his mind. Fred sought the life of a pacifist and in doing so he felt the need to connect with his spiritual side, so he started attending a church and was confirmed.

After his confirmation, he entered Utrecht University to study psychology, but while attending the university he developed an interest in theology. A pen-pal who was a devoted English Congregationalist convinced Fred to pursue his theology degree and ordination, so Fred enrolled in Western College in Bristol, England and upon graduation was ordained as a Congregational minister.

His first ministry was at Windsor Road Congregational Church in Barry, Wales. It was during this time that Fred became interested in and active with the church's music program. He loved hymns and began to try his hand at composing hymns, some of them from poems. Fred also tried translating poems into hymns and translating hymns from other languages. He also wrote stories.

Later he moved to Plymouth, England to become the minister at the Pilgrim Church. His writing blossomed there, and he developed a kinship with his congregation. Fred's fellow clergyman saw considerable talent in him and they admired his gentle ways with people. For that reason, he was sent to the International Congregational Council in Geneva to help resolve the growing split in the Congregational Church. Fred was instrumental in the formation of the World Alliance of Reformed Churches where he worked for over ten years. The Alliance focused on human rights and Congregational communications and relationships between and among the churches in the Alliance. Fred wrote many articles and served as the editor for the Alliance's journal. Also, he co-produced the Alliance's radio program, *Intervox*.

Serving for the Alliance and serving as chair of the Council for World Mission gave Fred the opportunity to travel around the world. He visited over eighty countries, but he grew tired of traveling and accepted a position as Moderator of the West Midlands Province of the United Reformed Church where he worked for seven years. During this busy time, Fred always managed to find time to write and compose hymns and translate poems for hymns.

He published six collections of hymns that have been translated into twenty languages and are used in churches throughout the world. His book, ***Pilgrim Praise,*** a book of hymns, has been through several editions and is still widely referred to, as is his modern day classic, ***For the Healing of the Nations***.

Fred's hymnology work led to him being named a Fellow of the Hymn Society of both Canada and the United States. Further illustration of his success was the awarding of honorary doctorate degrees from Debrecen Theological Academy in Hungary and Geneva Theological College in Switzerland.

Toward the end of his life, Fred suffered from Alzheimer's disease and cancer. He died in Penrith, England in 2009 at the age of eighty.

(References: *Fred Kaan: Minister and Celebrated Hymn Writer*, 2009, Keith Forecast; *Fred Kaan*, Obituary, January 6, 2013, Paul Oestreicher; *My Hymn Writing Journey*, 2013, Fred Kaan)

Hewitt, Eliza Edmunds

Eliza was born in 1851 in Philadelphia, Pennsylvania. Eliza was one of five children. All of them were born and raised in Philadelphia.

Her mother, Zeruiah, was well educated and interested in the education of girls and women. Eliza's father, James, was a captain of a large merchant ship. His ship traveled the trade routes that covered the Atlantic, North Atlantic, and the Caribbean Islands; consequently, Captain Hewitt was frequently away from home. Her father was away many days each year but his income from his work and his financial investments were successful, so the family had a nice home, furnishings, standing in the community, and each child received a good education.

The family's fortunes changed during the aftermath of the Civil War when many of Captain Hewitt's holdings lost considerable value. Still the family could have sent the children to private schools, but Eliza's parents wanted them to attend public school in order to be prepared for the world.

Eliza enjoyed school and excelled in all subjects in elementary school and secondary school. Her intellect and music abilities matured considerably in secondary school. Eliza was such an excellent student she graduated valedictorian at the Girl's Normal School of Philadelphia.

After graduation, she became a teacher in Philadelphia. Eliza greatly enjoyed teaching even though she sometimes struggled with the behavior of the students. The school principal was a stern man who believed in strict discipline and quick and severe punishment for misbehavior. Most of the time Eliza's students were well-behaved, but there were times when she had to be strict about their behavior; otherwise, she would be in trouble with the principal. One day when she was still quite young, she had a student who continued to be unruly for much of the day. She disciplined him and eventually threatened to send him to the principal. With the principal's reputation for meting out brutal paddling in their minds, the students feared being sent to his office. On this day Eliza finally had enough of the student's disruptive behavior and sent him to the principal where he was severely punished—some said he was severely beaten. At the end of the school day as Eliza was leaving her classroom the unruly student took out his anger on her. He slammed a heavy piece of slate into her back. The blow was so hard it damaged her spine. Consequently, Eliza was in a heavy body cast for over six months.

Due to the severe injury, her teaching career was over because she was essentially bed-ridden. Even after the cast was removed she endured terrible pain for several additional months and seldom left her house. While she was recovering, Eliza occupied her mind and time by writing, with much of her writing including poems related to the Scriptures. She became deeply religious and felt like her contribution to God's word could be through her poems. Eliza wrote several dozen poems.

During her recovery period, members of her church, the Tabernacle Presbyterian Church of West Philadelphia, were regular visitors to her house. She was deeply moved by the care and concern of her church members and its pastor who also frequently visited her. Eliza wrote a poem for the pastor entitled ***Winning Souls for Jesus***. He treasured the poem and its spiritual depth that it was placed in the cornerstone of the church. Later Eliza gave the Sunday school teachers her Scripture-based poems to use in the classes. They were very popular among the children and teachers. One of the teachers shared Eliza's poems with Dr. W. J. Kirkpatrick, a professor at Temple University. He immediately wrote Eliza and asked if he could put her poems to music to create hymns. Eliza agreed and there began a long professional relationship.

As her spinal condition gradually and slowly improved, Eliza wrote even more. Realizing that she would not be a chronic invalid, as she feared, she became even more determined to regain her health and life. She began leaving her house for short walks, and as her condition improved she started visiting a nearby park to walk and feel the sun on her face. One day upon her return home from the park she penned the poem ***There is Sunshine in My Soul Today***.

When Eliza regained her strength she did not return to teaching; instead, she worked with the church, guided camps for children, and helped with church projects and programs. Eliza also served as a Sunday School Superintendent for several years. She continued to write poems but primarily for children. The poems became regular Scripture teaching materials in Sunday schools.

Eliza remained active with her poetry and church work until her death in 1920 in Philadelphia at the age of sixty-eight. Over eighty of her poems became hymns, and many of them are in hymnals.

(References: *101 Hymn Stories*, 1985, Kenneth W. Osbeck; *Biography of Gospel Song and Hymn Writers*, 1914, Jacob Henry Hall; *Eliza Edmunds Hewitt: Songs from a Bed of Pain*, 2010, Dan Graves, Christianity)

Hine, Stuart

Stuart was born in 1899 in Hammersmith Grove, London, England. His family was very dedicated to Christianity and spent a considerable amount of their time supporting and worshipping with the Salvation Army.

Stuart enjoyed his family, his church, and he was an excellent student in school. At the age of fourteen, he dedicated his life to Christ while attending a worship service at the local Salvation Army near London.

From an early age, Stuart wanted to work in Christian ministry, but he also discovered a love for music. Stuart was dedicated to his beliefs and he wanted to pursue his study of music, but he felt an obligation to serve his country, so he joined the British Armed Forces and served for four years.

Upon his return home from military service, he felt a call to do missionary work. Following that call, he did missionary work in Czechoslovakia and Poland. After he married, his wife joined him in missionary work in Western Ukraine, which was part of Russia at the time. Stuart and his wife returned to London to share their missionary experiences and the gospel not only in London but throughout Great Britain. They received a lukewarm response at first, but the power of Stuart's message and the growing influence of his hymns and gospel songs spread rapidly through the Christian communities. Many worship services began using his hymns. Stuart became a prolific writer and composer, and the success of his music allowed him to retire.

During his retirement from ministry, Stuart continued to publish songbooks and music. He was so grateful for his life that he donated much of his income to support missionary work around the world. Stuart's name will live forever because of one hymn that transcends time, for he is the author of the number one hymn in the United States and in other parts of the world, ***How Great Thou Art***. The hymn was inspired during a trip to the Carpathian Mountains when he heard Ivan Prokhanoff's Russian hymn *Mighty God* which was based on a poem by a Swedish poet, Carl Boberg. Carl's poem *O Store God* was rearranged by Ivan and became a popular hymn. Stuart took the inspiration and worked various versions of the concept for several years before he was finally satisfied with his version of ***How Great Thou Art,*** which was not only inspired by Ivan's hymn but was also influenced by the beautiful vistas that Stuart observed in his travels across the majestic mountains of Russia and the Western Ukraine. Shortly after the powerful hymn was published, it became a sensation in the Christian world and its popularity has endured ever since.

Stuart wrote many other hymns and songs, published many song and hymn books, wrote poetry and was dedicated to missionary work, but he felt that his hymn ***How Great Thou Art*** was a divine inspiration that served God's purpose of messaging the power and grace of faith.

Stuart died in London in 1989 at the age of ninety. ***How Great Thou Art*** was sung during his funeral service.

(References: *Biography of Stuart K. Hine,* 2012, Hope Publishing Company. Retrieved 2013; *Stuart K. Hine,* Gospel Music Hall of Fame Biography Inductee Archives. Retrieved 2013; *Not You, but God: A Testimony to God's Faithfulness,* 1973, Stuart K. Hine; *The Sound of Light: A History of Gospel Music,* 1990, Don Cusic)

Hoffman, Elisha

Elisha was born in 1839 in Orwigsburg, Pennsylvania. His parents immigrated to the United States from Germany. Elisha's father was a minister in Evangelical churches for over sixty years, and Elisha's mother was also very active in the work of churches, as she was often seen working with other women and their children to help them cope with the disappointments and tragedies of life.

Elisha was an inquisitive child who grew up surrounded by music and ministry. He loved the active life of a minister's work and cherished church music, as well as the music in his home, for both of his parents loved to sing hymns and other songs at home. Consequently, he showed an early interest in how hymns and other songs were written. Elisha also enjoyed poetry and often commented that hymns were poems put to music.

He attended public schools in Philadelphia, Pennsylvania, where he excelled in most subjects, but he especially enjoyed science. Elisha graduated from Central High School, where he took every science course the school had to offer. At one point, he considered a science career, but the strong influence of his family and his own developing spirituality led him to attend Union Seminary, an Evangelical seminary. After graduating, he was ordained as a Presbyterian minister.

Even though he had been surrounded by hymns growing up in his father's church, he did not have many opportunities to actually study music. However, he never lost interest in music and his love of music eventually moved to the forefront in his life. He wrote his first hymn when he was only fifteen years old, but he kept it to himself and as far as anyone can guess, he did not share it publicly with anyone until later in his life. At age eighteen, Elisha wrote a hymn that was shared with his parents and his church. The accolades he received from this work, although he later admitted that it was not very good, spurred him on to write more.

Elisha followed his love of music and ministry and took a position with the Evangelical Association of Publishing in Cleveland, Ohio, where he specialized in writing and editing hymns. He worked there for almost eleven years.

After growing tired of the publishing business, and wanting to serve a ministry, he started a career as a minister. He served in several churches in the Midwest, including churches in Cleveland and Grafton, Ohio, Benton Harbor, Michigan and Cabery, Illinois.

Elisha found the balance in the life that he sought. He ministered to the needs of others, shared the message of God, and brought music to both. Even after he retired, Elisha continued to do volunteer work at churches and was emeritus minister for a while. He continued to compose hymns until his death in 1929 in Chicago at the age ninety.

Elisha is credited with composing well over 2,000 hymns. Perhaps his most famous hymns are ***What a Wonderful Savior*** and ***Leaning on the Everlasting Arms***. He also edited fifty-two hymnals and song books.

(References: *Some German Contributions to American Hymnody,* 1940, Clifford Homaday; *Elisha Albright Hoffman,* Journal of Congregational Song, 1984, Robert Wilson and Melvin Wilhoit; *Biography of Gospel Song and Hymn Writers,* 1914, Jacob Henry Hall)

Hopper, Edward

Edward was born in 1818 in New York City, New York. His father worked as a successful merchant with influence in city management and politics. Edward's mother was descended from the persecuted French Protestants.

Edward received his education at local elementary and secondary schools before studying in the local church to become a minister. He was ordained and served as a minister at various small churches in the New York City area. However, his career and life changed significantly when he accepted a position as minister at a church in the New York City harbor known as the Church of Sea and Land.

Many of the Church of Sea and Land attendees were sailors living temporarily in ships anchored in the New York harbor. It was through them that he learned about the hardships of a sailor's life and the difficulties faced by their families. Edward met sailors from around the world at his church. He spent time with them and ministered to them. Edward boarded ships to minister to sailors and crew members on the ship. He was always welcomed and his ministry to sailors became legendary. It was this insight, experience and inspiration that led him to write the world-famous hymn, ***Jesus, Savior, Pilot Me***. The hymn, which finds its inspiration from *Matthew 8: 23-27*, when Jesus calmed the raging sea, became and remains one of the most popular hymns ever written. These first three lines have taken on the fame of immortality: "Jesus, Savior, pilot me over life's tempestuous sea; Unknown waves before me roll, hiding rock and treacherous shoal; Chart and compass come from Thee—Jesus, Savior, pilot me."

It seems difficult to believe now that Edward published the majestic hymn anonymously. It was not until several years later that he was identified as the author of the famous hymn. On the occasion of the Special Friend of the Sea Society festival, Edward was asked to write a new hymn for the event. Instead, he brought ***Jesus, Savior, Pilot Me***. Then for the first time, it was revealed that he wrote the hymn.

Edward's enduring fame is based primarily on the hymn, but during his time as minister, he was equally famous for the power of his sermons and other poems and hymns that he composed. It was rumored at one time that sea captains purposely sought anchor privileges at the New York harbor so that their sailors could hear Edward's sermons.

He remained active in ministry and music for his entire life. Edward continued to write poetry and hymns up until his death in 1888, at the age of seventy, when he was found sitting in his favorite chair with his writing pen in hand and a pad of paper in his lap with the beginnings of a poem about heaven written on the paper. It was if the last line of his famous hymn was on his mind: "Fear not—I will pilot thee."

(References: *The Story Behind "Jesus, Savior, Pilot Me,"* plymouthbrethren.org. Retrieved 2013; *Story of Our Hymns*, 1999, Christian Classics Ethereal Library. Retrieved 2013; *Edward Hopper*, Hymnary.org. Retrieved 2013; *This Day in Presbyterian History*, 2012. Retrieved 2013)

Hosmer, Frederick Lucian

Frederick was born in 1840 in Framingham, Massachusetts. His family focused on spirituality and education, and his parents emphasized the value of education. His father, Charles Hosmer, was a community leader and businessman.

At a young age, Frederick tried his hand at writing poetry. His parents, especially his mother, encouraged him to keep writing poetry, which he did for the rest of his life. Frederick's interest in composing hymns would come much later in his life.

After he excelled in all school work in elementary and secondary schools, his intellect, and academic prowess earned him admission into Harvard College (later changed to Harvard University). At Harvard College, he was known for his intellect and creative genius with poetry. During his undergraduate education, Frederick developed a strong interest in theology and his experience attending the college chapel sparked that interest even further.

After receiving a Bachelor of Arts degree he entered the Harvard Divinity School where he earned a Master of Divinity degree. Shortly thereafter Frederick was ordained as a minister of the First Congregational Church of Northborough, Massachusetts. He ministered there until he accepted a position as minister at the Quincy Unitarian Church in Quincy, Illinois.

Frederick's sermons and work in the community, as well as his enlightened work with children, brought him recognition across several states. Consequently, he was offered several minister positions throughout the United States and Canada. Frederick accepted an offer to become the minister of the First Unitarian Church of Cleveland, Ohio. The church had been a powerhouse of community influence in its earlier days, but its influence had waned, so had the size of the congregation. Under Frederick's ministry and leadership the church flourished and membership and attendance grew rapidly, so that every Sunday the church was overflowing. His influence in the community's efforts to assist its citizens and fund programs for children across the city was widely recognized as an example for other community leaders. He remained there for over fourteen years before relocating to St. Louis, Missouri at the Church of the Unity for five years.

Frederick was persuaded to expand his message to the growing western section of the United States; consequently, he started the First Unitarian Church of Berkeley, California in 1900. He remained there after retirement as an emeritus minister.

Interestingly, even though Frederick remained a poet his entire life, he did not show any interest in composing hymns until he was almost fifty years old. Thereafter, he wrote or co-wrote over fifty-six hymns. His most productive work was with his college roommate William Gannett, who he worked with to publish ***Singing the Living Tradition***, a book of hymns, and ***Unity Hymns and Chorales for the Congregation and the Home*** which had popular appeal and was reprinted several times and updated twice. Frederick and William also published ***The Thought of God in Hymns and Poems***, a book that contained over fifty of Frederick's poems and hymns.

Frederick's most famous hymn is ***Forward Through the Ages*** which would later become a social gospel anthem. He wrote that hymn while living in Berkeley, California, and shortly before his death. Other hymns that can be found in most hymnals include ***Now While the Day in Trailing Splendor***; ***I Walk the Unfrequented Road***, and ***From Age to Age***. Frederick also wrote a hymn for one of the commencement events of the Meadville Theological School. The hymn ***Thy Kingdom Come*** was considered by many at the time as one the most beautiful poem/hymns ever written. Hymnologist Percy Dearmer said the hymn was "one of the noblest hymns in the [English] language."

Frederick was frequently asked to write hymns or poems for special occasions. Other long-time popular hymns that can be found in hymnals are ***Father, to Thee We Look in All Our Sorrow*** and ***O Day Light and Gladness***.

He continued to write and was an emeritus minister in Berkeley until his death in 1929 at the age of eighty-nine. Many of his hymns were sung at his memorial service.

(References: *Historical Dictionary of Unitarian Universalism*, 2003, Scarecrow Press, Mark Harris; *Between the Lines: Sources for Singing the Living Tradition*, 1995, Jacqui James; *American Hymns Old and New*, 1980, Charles William Hughes)

How, William Walsham

William was born in 1823 in Shrewsbury, England. His father was Shrewsbury's well-known and respected solicitor for several years. The children were expected to get a good education and work hard around the house. Self-discipline and duty to family and community were highly valued.

William's father was determined that his son was going to follow in his footsteps as a solicitor, so he put great emphasis on William's education and self-discipline.

William attended Shrewsbury School where he enjoyed studying all subjects, but he mostly enjoyed music, literature, and Bible study. Because of his excellent academic performance and the position of his father, William received an appointment to Wadham College, Oxford and later attended University College, Durham to complete his advanced studies.

At the university, William drifted away from the study of law to his preference for theology. He earned a Bachelor of Theology degree. He was ordained at the age of twenty-three and became the Curate at Kidderminster. Later he was Curate of Abbey Church in

Shrewsbury; Rector of Whittington; Rural Dean of Oswestry, and Bishop of Bedford in London.

William's most prolific writing and composing years were while he worked at Whittington. His publication ***Commentary on the Four Gospels*** became popular in the English world of theological studies. William believed that Holy Communion was the most sacred of all moments during church services, second only to prayer, but as he visited other churches, he saw a wide variety of methods of Holy Communion, most of which were bland, uninspired and at worst close to disrespectful. What he saw greatly disturbed him. Consequently, he published a manual for Holy Communion, ***Holy Communion, Preparation, and Companion,*** that he thought would focus on the sanctity of it and create a ritual of consistency and respect. The manual was published by the Society for Promoting Christian Knowledge and distributed across the country. It became the standard text and method for Holy Communion for decades. In fact, many churches in the Christian world still have copies of the manual and for its standards.

William founded the East London Church Fund, as a means to help impoverished families and children. He was very successful in creating a large band of volunteer citizens to provide community services and help spread the word of God. His charismatic personality made him a favorite among children, and he stopped everywhere he went to speak to and brighten the day of children.

William's aid to the communities and children as well as his powerful sermons and organizational ability brought him an appointment as the Bishop of Wakefield in northern England.

He continued throughout his life to minister to the poor and rally volunteer support for the needy. He also found time to write and compose hymns. William's hymn ***For All the Saints*** became very popular and well-known and was often sung in the local churches. Soon thereafter it could be heard in churches across England. He was so admired for his community work, his sermons, his hymns, and his gregarious personality, William was asked to consecrate several churches.

When he died in 1897 at the age of seventy-four, thousands attended the service and many of his hymns were sung. William was buried in Whittington where he spent almost thirty years of his life and where he composed most his fifty hymns. He was so beloved that a memorial plaque was placed inside the Church of St. Helen's in London that says, "Sweet is the calm of Paradise the blest," which is a line from his hymn ***For All the Saints***.

(References: *Hymns Ancient and Modern*, 1950, G.H. Knight and J. Dykes; *William How*, Encyclopedia Britannica. Retrieved 2014; *William Walsham How*, hymntime.com. Retrieved 2014)

Howe, Julia Ward

Julia was born in 1819 in New York City into a wealthy, well-educated and influential family with a famous history. Her father, Samuel, was a successful banker on Wall Street; she was descended from two governors of Rhode Island, and she was the great-grandniece of the legendary Revolutionary War hero Francis Marion, better known as the Swamp Fox. Julia's mother was an accomplished poet, but she died shortly after giving birth to her seventh child.

Julia was very pretty, bright, energetic, and creative, but her life decidedly changed after her mother died. Her mother ran the household and nurtured all of the children and provided for them in every way. She was extremely close with her children, so her loss devastated the family and the children mourned for her for several years. Julia's father tried to compensate for the loss, but he was busy with his career.

Julia educated herself and became a powerful intellect during an era when women were very limited in their educational opportunities. Julia benefited from the excellent library of books her brother, Sam, shipped from Europe during his travels there. The books included writers such as Balzac and Sand; writers that her father disapproved of because of his Calvinistic beliefs. Julia was torn between her devotion to her father and respect for his beliefs and her own growing intellectual curiosity and social issues awareness. Julia wanted to expand her knowledge but her father was afraid of the negative influences on her intellectual and spiritual development.

Like her mother, Julia was by nature a happy person, but she was quick to point out an injustice or undisciplined intellect. Julia's brother, Sam, was a world traveler and her equal intellectually, and he, too, was intolerant of prejudice and cruelty and shared her interest in the world of literature. He introduced Julia to famous people such as Charles Dickens, Senator Charles Sumner, Henry Longfellow, Margaret Fuller, and many others.

Sam married into the famous Astor family, of John Jacob Astor fame, the millionaire industrialist. Sam's wife, Emily, became close friends with Julia and introduced her to the New York society world. Julia met even more famous and creative people within that high society world. Her world was filled with creative, charming, intelligent, and wealthy people. As Julia developed her thoughts and creativity combined with her observations of life and politics, she became an even more formidable intellect. Her world and that of her brother, Sam, suffered a devastating shock by the sudden and unexpected death of Emily and her son.

Perhaps due to her grief over the loss of her best friend and her brother's wife and child and the need for comfort and stability, Julia rushed into a marriage with Samuel Howe. Their marriage turned sour almost immediately, and their relationship was filled with many turbulent episodes. She went from living in luxury to a home inside the Perkins Institute for the Blind in Massachusetts, as her husband used her inherited wealth to support his social justice issues and efforts. He took full control of her estate and forbid her from spending any money or supporting any cause that he did not support. Since he was twenty years older he thought he was wiser and smarter.

As it turned out, Samuel's bad investments and clumsy use of Julia's inheritance caused them to lose almost everything. When he died in 1876 he left Julia almost penniless. So at age fifty-seven, she had to start over and fend for herself.

During her marriage to Samuel, she wrote stories and composed music, but he would not allow her to seek publication of her works. Nevertheless, she anonymously published a collection of poems in her book titled ***Passion Flowers***. The ill-disguised author was betrayed by Boston society's deduction that the poems about deceit, dishonor, and infidelity were about Samuel and their troubled marriage. While Samuel was devastated and humiliated, Julia found a new form of release. She became involved in many social conscientious issues like abolition, education, women's rights, civil rights, and prison reform.

She continued to write and publish poems, and even though she was already well-known throughout Boston and other parts of Massachusetts, her poem ***The Battle Hymn of the Republic*** made her an instant sensation across the nation and around the world. The idea for the famous hymn came to her while she was in Washington during the American Civil War. On the way to the Willard Hotel, she saw a review of Union troops at Bailey's Crossroads. In the crowd, someone started singing the Union soldiers' song, *John Brown's Body*. Julia's good friend, Reverend James Freeman Clarke, told her that the words needed to be improved because they were too crude for common use by women and children. He suggested that she rewrite the song. The next morning, at a time when she was still partially asleep in the dim light of the morning, the words came rushing to her. She quickly wrote them down for fear that she would lose them when fully awake.

Julia, mostly because of the legendary hymn, became one of the most famous people of the 19th century. Julia would have seven children (one died in infancy) who prospered under her nurturing. She was such an inspiring and supportive mother, her children together wrote a biography of her that won the 1917 Pulitzer Prize in literature (*Julia Ward Howe,* written by Laura Richards, Maude Howe Elliott, and Florence Howe Hall).

It is also important to note that Julia became an ordained minister and a reformer, in addition to being a writer, poet, and mother. She also edited the *Woman's Journal* and was instrumental in the creation of Mother's Day.

Julia's full life ended in 1910 when she died in Portsmouth, Rhode Island at the age of ninety-one. ***The Battle Hymn of the Republic*** was sung at her funeral.

(References: *Hungry Heart -The Literary Emergence of Julia Ward Howe,* 1999, Gary Williams; *Diva Julia: The Public Romance and Private Agony of Julia Ward Howe,* 2003, Valarie Ziegler; *Private Women, Public Person: An Account of the Life of Julia Ward Howe,* 1994, Mary Grant; *Mine Eyes Have Seen the Glory: A Biography of Julia Ward Howe,* 1979, Deborah Pickman Clifford)

Huber, Jane Parker

Jane was born in 1926 in Tsinan, China to Presbyterian missionaries stationed there. When Jane was two years old her parents, Albert and Katharine moved back to the United States and settled in Hanover, Indiana because her father was selected as president of Hanover College, a Presbyterian Church-affiliated liberal arts college.

Jane was a smart, energetic, and precocious child. She enjoyed school and events at the local church and at the college where her father worked. Jane was a good student, excelling in academics and music. She attended public schools in Hanover until the tenth grade when she transferred to the Northfield School for Girls in Massachusetts, where she graduated with honors. She played music and enjoyed participating in musical productions and events both at school and at church.

Jane enrolled at Wellesley College but completed her bachelor's degree work at Hanover College after her marriage. She moved with her husband to Chicago so he could attend the McCormick Presbyterian Theological Seminary and later to Kansas, Illinois when he accepted a position as pastor. They moved to other cities, as well, as their ministry expanded.

In addition to supporting the efforts of her husband, Jane was actively involved in church activities, including music programs and community events. She served on several Presbyterian committees such as the Council on Women and the Church; General Assembly Mission Council; Advisory Council on Discipleship and Worship; Joint Committee on Women, and the General Assembly Council. Jane was not a passive member of the committees; she was an ardent supporter and leader on each of them. In fact, her work, innovative ideas, and leadership led to several awards for her service. She was most proud of being named a Valiant Woman by the Church Women United.

During her free time, Jane enjoyed listening to a wide variety of musical tunes. She liked to write hymns that could be sung using familiar tunes. She found that her friends and congregations loved the idea and consequently many of her hymns became popular. Inspired by the reception of her hymns, she wrote two books of hymns with over 120 hymns that were published by John Knox Press, and eleven of those hymns were published in the *Presbyterian Hymnal*.

Among the many hymns she wrote include the popular ***Creator God, Creating Still***; ***When in Awe of God's Creation***, and ***Wonder of Wonders Here Revealed***. She wrote articles for *These Days* and *Horizons* magazines.

Jane continued to write hymns well into the later years of her life. She never tired of listening to music, and she loved the companionship of friends and family

She died in 2008 in Hanover, Indiana at the age of eighty-two while listening to music on the radio. Her hymns were sung at her memorial service.

(References: *A Singing Faith*, 1987, Jane Parker Huber; *Singing in Celebration*, 1996, Jane Parker Huber; *Remembering Jane Parker Huber*, in The Hymnist Master, May 31, 2013; *Jane Parker Huber*, humanbeingsanon.org. Retrieved 2014; *The Works of Jane Parker Huber*, hymntime.com. Retrieved 2014)

Hughes, Donald

Donald was born in 1911 in Cambridge, England. His father was a Methodist minister who was very popular with his congregation, and he was well-respected within the academic community. All of the children felt the strong influence of their father, but none more than Donald.

He encouraged Donald to pursue and tone his early-recognized writing and music skills. Donald loved to write verse, poems, music, and stories and his father saw that Donald's gift was extraordinary.

Donald was a vociferous reader and loved school work, but mostly he loved learning. He found the school less than challenging than he expected, but he enjoyed the activities of the school and the fast pace of his life with school, extracurricular activities, and the very active church that his father ministered.

Donald found being in his father's presence was always a learning experience, whether learning more about faith, theology, or watching him interact with other people. This influenced how Donald interacted with people and how he approached life.

After secondary school, Donald enrolled in Emmanuel College at Cambridge. His literary skills blossomed while at Emmanuel. He won several writing awards and graduated from Emmanuel with First Class Honors in English. He also excelled in competitive athletics, especially in the sport of cricket.

After graduating with a Bachelor of Arts degree, he took a position as a teacher at a Methodist school, Leys School. He was a gifted teacher and popular with the students. During his time at Leys School, he continued to write poems and other works. At age twenty-six, Donald contributed chapters in the book ***The Assistant Master Speaks*** and two years later chapters in ***Under Thirty Speaks for Christ***.

Donald reluctantly left Leys School after almost eleven years to become Headmaster of Rydal School, also affiliated with the Methodist foundation. He continued to be a prolific writer, publishing several books. The most popular book was ***The Apostles' Creed***. Other well-known books included ***Public Schools and the Future***; ***Some Educational Foundations***, and ***Reason and Imagination***. He also wrote numerous articles, poems, and hymns. His most famous hymn is ***Creator of Earth and Skies*** which can be found in almost every hymnal throughout the Christian world. It was published and began receiving popular appeal just shortly before Donald was seriously injured in a car accident.

At the time of the accident, he was working on several writing projects, but the seriousness of his injuries halted all of his work. Tragically, Donald died from his injuries in 1967 when he was only fifty-six years old. Reportedly, he told his friends just before he died that he was about to begin a journey "to see the creator of earth and skies."

(References: *Five New Hymns for Youth by Youth*, 1955, Donald Hughes; *Twelve New World Order Hymns*, 1958, Donald Hughes; *One Nation Under God: Religious Symbols, Quotes, and Images*, 2001, Eugene Hemrick)

Imakoma, Yasushige

Yasushige was born in 1926 in Japan. His family valued education and each child was expected to obtain an education that would lead to a career.

Yasushige was a good student at each grade level. He was extremely intelligent and very creative. He completed school and then earned a college degree.

After attending college, he was ordained in the United Church of Christ of Japan. Yasushige ministered to several churches and he also wrote and composed music for worship services. He composed two well-known hymns, ***Make a Gift of Your Holy Word*** and ***Send Your Word, O Lord, Like the Rain***. Both were published in 1965 and they were translated into English by Nobusi Hanaoka in 1983. ***Send Your Word*** became a world-famous hymn and is many hymnals and in many languages.

In an interview with the *Christian Hymns Today,* Yasushige said this about the hymn: "The hidden case of confusion and the slaughter in the contemporary world seems to lie in the judgment by God on the Tower of Babel, resulting in the babble of the language or the inability to understand the words of others. The way out of such a situation is gaining or regaining, by the grace of God, of understanding of the language of others. Therefore, we must pray saying, 'Just give me a word,' as the Roman centurion asked for in Mathew 8:8."

The hymn ***Send Your Word*** was originally copyrighted by the Hymnal Committee of the United Church of Christ in Japan, but apparently the copyright is now shared with Yasushige. Regardless of the copyright, the hymn is sung somewhere in the world every Sunday during worship services.

Yasushige continues his ministry in Japan as a voice for Christian love, tolerance and understanding.

(References: *Yasushige Imakoma,* December 23, 2012, Tsukuba Gakuen Church–United Church of Christ Japan. Retrieved 2015; *Yasushige Imakoma,* Christian Hymns Today, September 2000)

In Lim, Ok

Ok was born in Korea in 1915. Her family was of humble origins. Her parents instilled confidence and self-discipline in Ok from the time she was a young child.

Ok took her school studies seriously and excelled academically at every grade level. She was expected to attend college and she prepared herself for college by taking academically challenging courses. She also used a tutor to advance her studies and her preparation for college.

Ok attended Nora Teacher's College in Japan. She wanted to be a teacher because teachers are one of the most respected careers in Japan and Korea. Ok was at the top of her class in every subject area. She graduated with honors with a Bachelor of Arts degree.

During college, Ok shifted her career goal from being a public school teacher to becoming a college professor. Her college professors encouraged her to remain in higher education, so she became a college professor of literature and economics at Konkook University in Seoul, Korea. After teaching for several years, she was promoted to Dean of Economics at the university.

Ok published nine scholarly books and received numerous awards for her work, including the prestigious Korean Women's Literature award.

In addition to her scholarly work, Ok had a gift for music and she especially enjoyed hymns. She thought hymns were important to worship. Ok wrote and composed hymns. Many of her hymns were inspired by her surroundings. She wrote the beautiful hymn ***Mountains Are All Aglow*** at a time when she was inspired by the beauty of nature that endured even during her difficult times. The hymn was written in 1966 and was published in 1967 in the *Korean Hymnal* and later in the *United Korean Hymnal*. When the hymn was translated by the first Korean United Methodist Bishop, Hae Jong Kim, to English in 1988 it became immediately popular in the English-speaking churches around the world.

Ok continued her scholarly career until her retirement in 1980 from the university. She continued as professor emeritus until her death in 2000 at the age of eighty-five.

(Reference: *The Mountains are Aglow*, 1989, Hope Omachi-Kawashima, The United Methodist Publishing House; *A New Hymnal for Colleges and Schools*, 1992, Jeffery Rowthorn and Russell Schulz-Widmar; *Famous People from South Korea*, Library of Congress, Retrieved 2015)

Iverson, Daniel

Daniel was born in 1890 in Brunswick, Georgia. His family members were pillars of the community. Daniel was expected to attend college and have a professional career.

At a young age, Daniel developed an interest in reading, literature, math, and music that led to successful elementary and secondary school experiences. Daniel excelled in all academic areas, participated in school activities, and was very active in his local church.

After graduating from high school, he attended the University of Georgia where he majored in philosophy. It was during college that he decided to become a minister. He entered Moody Bible Institute, after graduating from the University of Georgia. He also attended the Columbia Theological Seminary and the University of South Carolina.

When he received a Master of Divinity degree, Daniel was ordained in the Presbyterian Church in 1914. He ministered at several churches in Georgia, South Carolina, North Carolina and Florida. He founded the Shenandoah Presbyterian Church in Miami, Florida where he ministered for over twenty-five years.

Daniel is well known and remembered as an excellent minister but also for a hymn that became famous, ***The Spirit of the Living God***. Daniel wrote the hymn after hearing an inspirational sermon by George Stephens during a revival in Orlando, Florida. He shared the hymn with others and it was printed and passed out at a revival for everyone to sing. The printed leaflets failed to include his name. A member of the choir that night kept a copy of the hymn and sent it to a publisher. It was published in the popular hymnal *Revival Songs* in 1929 without crediting Daniel. After decades of claiming authorship of the hymn, in 1960 Daniel was finally credited as the writer of the popular and famous hymn.

Daniel wrote a few more hymns and remained active in community work after his retirement in 1951. He died in Asheville, North Carolina in 1977 at the age of eighty-seven.

(References: *Companion to the United Methodist Hymnal,* 1993, Carlton Raymond Young; *Daniel Iverson,* Hymnary.org. Retrieved 2015; *Contending with the Culture,* 2002, Rob Shearer, Frances Schaeffer Study Center. Retrieved 2014)

Janus, Martin

Martin was born in 1620 in Merseburg, Saxony-Anhalt, Germany. He was raised with modest means in a small town. His family was strict but supportive of each other.

The town took pride in its small but academically strict school. Martin received a good education at the school that prepared him for university studies. He showed a keen intellect and unusual insight for someone of his age. Martin was a conscientious student because he wanted to attend college.

He was accepted at the University of Konigsberg (known as the Albertus-Universität Königsberg in East Prussia founded in 1544) where he studied theology and philosophy. Martin considered an academic career in philosophy but he did not want to spend his career tied to the university life. He was also gaining notoriety locally for his excellent poems (none has survived through the centuries).

After he received a degree in theology, he was ordained a cantor in Steinau, Germany. He served there for several years before fleeing to Lower Lusatia (in the German state of Brandenburg) to avoid the human devastation of the Thirty-Years War. There he became the music director at Sorau Evangelical Church. While working there he met Baron Sigismund von Promnitz Seifried who helped advance Martin's standing in the community as well as his career. During Martin's time at Sorau, he wrote and composed many of the hymns that were performed by the church choir. It was his ability to convey spiritual messages through his hymns that first attracted the attention and favor of the Baron.

After the Baron died, Martin was anxious to expand his experiences so he accepted a position as rector and cantor at the town school in Sagan, Germany. He was also the pastor at the Village of Ecker near the town's small school which allowed him time to work at the school tutoring and advising students. Martin greatly enjoyed his work at the school and in the church, but once again turmoil disrupted his life and forced him to move. Protestant preachers were expelled from Germany which forced him to leave his beloved town of Sagan. It was a difficult decision to leave his friends, colleagues and the students who so greatly admired him, but with so much turmoil in the region he had to leave to find work.

Martin had a difficult time finding a position in a school or church because of his Protestant background. Finally, after several weeks, he became the cantor in Ohlau, Germany. He continued to write poems and hymns, but only one hymn survived through the ages, ***Jesus, Meiner Seelen Wonne*** (***Jesus, My Soul Delights***). The only larger work that was not lost was his collection of Protestant passion lyrics, perhaps the first of its kind, titled ***Passionale Melicum***.

Martin died in 1682 in Silesia (a region of Central Europe now located mostly in Poland, with small parts in the Czech Republic and Germany) at the age of sixty-two after a brief illness. Many of his former students and colleagues mourned his passing, but most did not learn of his death until several months later. Some of them traveled to Silesia to offer prayers at his gravesite.

(References: *Martin Jahn (Janus),* Bach Cantatas Website. Retrieved 2015; *Martin Janus,* 1907, Dictionary of Hymnology, John Julian)

Janzen, Jean

Jean was born in 1933 in Dalmeny, Saskatchewan, Canada. Jean was the seventh of eight children. Their parents were Mennonites.

Her family relocated to Mountain Lake, Minnesota because her father was offered a pastor position at the local church. He was also a well-respected and gifted teacher and very well-liked in the community. However, the family only resided in Mountain Lake for one year, and then they moved to Kansas to look for more income and a more stable life.

Jean was a very creative child who loved to write, beginning at a young age. She tried her hand at writing poetry when she was in the third grade, and she showed unusual insight and talent for her age. The poems, fortunately, were saved by her mother, so we have insight into the quality of her first five poems. The poems showed unusually mature observations of the world and spirituality. Jean was also a reader, and she particularly liked Bible stories; they fascinated and enthralled her. Additionally, she learned to play the piano when she was young, and her love of music remained with her throughout her life.

Jean excelled in high school, especially in literature and writing. Her talent in writing was admired by her teachers for the quality and depth of her subjects and the creativity of her style. Jean's intellectual curiosity extended to her study of the Bible. Her intellectual and spiritual interest in the Bible never diminished, so she attended Meade Bible Academy and then Tabor College and Grace College where she learned to love all types of literature. She decided to major in world literature. Her focus was on the works of female writers, especially Emily Dickinson. Professors encouraged Jean because she was a talented poet in her own right, but she lacked the self-confidence to believe she had the talent to be a professional writer.

Jean's life turned when she met Louis Janzen. Louis was a brilliant medical student whose work took him to Chicago. Before leaving for Chicago, the couple married. While he completed his internship, Jean worked and took classes at Northwestern University. When Louis became a pediatrician, they moved to Fresno, California. They had four children, two daughters, and two sons. During this time, Jean maintained her interest in poetry and music, and when her youngest child entered school she joined a writers' group where each person shared their own compositions. The group was greatly impressed with Jean's poetry.

Jean later went back to college and earned a Bachelor of Arts in English at Fresno Pacific College and a Master of Arts and English at California State University. Even though several people including college professors were convinced Jean had a potential career as a writer, she was still not convinced herself. It was not until she received a grant from the National Endowment for the Arts that she realized her potential.

Her poetry took on more maturity and depth and was never far away from her strong spiritual beliefs and her devotion to the Mennonite Church. She wrote hymns for the College Community Mennonite Brethren Church in California, many of which are in several hymnals across the United States and other parts of the world. ***Mothering God, You Gave Me Birth*** is her most popular and famous hymn.

Jean teaches poetry at Fresno Pacific University and still writes poetry and hymns. She has published seven books of poems. Several of her recent poems were published in ***The Christian Century***.

(References: *The Birth of a Hymn*, 2015, CMW Journal. Retrieved 2015; *Jean Janzen - Mothering God, You Gave Me Birth*, Dictionary of Hymnology, Retrieved 2014)

Johnson, James Weldon

James was born in 1871 in Jacksonville, Florida. His parents moved to Jacksonville two years before James was born in order to find work.

His father became the headwaiter at a Jacksonville resort hotel that catered to the rich and famous and his mother was a school teacher. James' mother also earned money as a part-time musician. He said he gained his love of music and his talent from his mother. More importantly, he learned self-confidence from both of his parents who also taught him not to fear any man of any race.

James' mother and the school he attended in his youth gave him an excellent education. His mother wanted him to study English, including English literature, and traditional music of the European influence. James loved school and he loved to learn. He read and studied with much enthusiasm and dedication, and he excelled in elementary and secondary school. After graduation from secondary school, he enrolled at Atlanta University. Upon receiving his Bachelor of Arts degree he became the principal at Stanton High

School in Jacksonville. While serving as principal he studied law on his own time. On his first attempt at taking the Florida Bar exam, he passed.

He started a law practice but James maintained his interest in music, poems, and composing songs. He also found time and inspiration to write a song in memory of Abraham Lincoln's life on Lincoln's birthday that led to one of the most famous songs and hymns ever written, ***Lift Every Voice and Sing***.

In 1901, he gave up his law practice and then moved to New York to work with his brother on Broadway musical arrangements. The work was not steady so he took a job with the United States Consul to Venezuela. He enjoyed the work and during his free time he wrote poetry and music.

Many of his poems were published and some of his songs were used in Off-Broadway plays. He also published the ***Autobiography of an Ex-Colored Man***. The book created controversy because it told the story of a man who rejected his heritage.

James continued his career with the government's Foreign Service and after several years, he became the Consul to Venezuela and later to Nicaragua. After retiring from a successful career in the United States Foreign Service he became a writer for a newspaper and a leader in social justice issues.

James was one of the founding fathers of the NAACP, where he worked for several years. He was a leading and steady influence on the rapid growth and moral strength of the NAACP. He participated in many events to promote social equity and the demise of segregation.

No matter how busy he was in his career promoting social justice, he always found time to write poems, hymns, and other types of music. James enjoyed sharing his talents with family and friends. He also enjoyed the intellectual stimulation of the college campus, so he accepted an offer to teach at Fisk University in Nashville, Tennessee.

At the time of his death in 1938, as the result of an automobile accident, he was a professor of creative literature and writing at Fisk University. He died at the age of sixty-seven.

During his lifetime, James received numerous awards, including the Spingarn Medal from the NAACP; Harmon Gold Award for his hymn ***God's Trombones***; Julius Rosenwald Fund grant award for his creative works; W. E. B. Du Bois Prize for Literature, and many others. Also, James appeared on the United States postal stamp as part of the "Black Heritage USA" series of the 1970s.

Many of James' songs and hymns can be found in modern day books and hymnals, especially the classic ***Lift Every Voice and Sing*** which was sung at his memorial service.

(References: *James Weldon Johnson*, 1987, Robert E. Fleming; *James Weldon Johnson*, 2004, Elizabeth Hester; *James Weldon Johnson: Black Leader, Black Voice*, 1973, Eugene Levy; *James Weldon Johnson's Modern Soundscapes*, 2013, Noelle Morrissette)

Johnston, Julia Harriette

Julia was born in 1849 in Salineville, Ohio. Her family moved to Peoria, Illinois when Julia was six years old because her father, Robert Johnston, accepted a position as minister at the First Presbyterian Church there. Julia lived in Peoria for the rest of her life.

She was a lively and precocious child who loved music and enjoyed activities at her father's church. Julia attended Peoria High School where she was an outstanding student in the classroom and in musical productions.

Julia was devastated when her father died unexpectedly when she was fifteen years old. Her grief lasted a lifetime, but she often found comfort in her work at the church. Even at a young age, she was very involved in the church's Sunday school, not just as a student, but also as a teacher's aide and later as a teacher. In fact, she would be a Sunday school teacher at the same church for over forty-one years.

Julia was a long-standing member of the Presbyterian Missionary Society of Peoria, serving in several leadership roles, including serving as president. She was very proud of the fact that her mother was a founding member of the Society and its humanitarian work.

She began her writing career by crafting Sunday school study material for children. Julia became a full-time writer when many of her Sunday school lessons and supporting materials were published by the David C. Cook Publishing Company in Chicago, which at that time was one of the country's leading publishers of educational material. Julia became a prolific writer. Her book ***School of the Master***, published when she was thirty-one years old, became a best-seller within the Sunday school community. Her books ***Bright Threads*** and ***Fifty Missionary Heroes*** made her well-known throughout the United States.

Despite her writing, teaching, and very busy schedule, Julia never lost her love of music. Julia is credited with writing over 500 hymns accompanied by several different music composers. Her most famous hymn is ***Grace Greater Than Our Sin***.

Julia continued to write up until her death in 1919 at the age of seventy in Peoria, Illinois, where she remains a legendary figure.

(References: *Then Sing My Soul Book 3: The Story of Our Songs*, 2012, Robert J. Morgan; *The Magazine of Poetry—Julia Harriette Johnston*, 1892, Charles Wells Moulton, Library of Congress archives. Retrieved 2013)

Joncas, Michael

Michael was born in 1951 in Minneapolis, Minnesota. He attended the University of Notre Dame, where he received a Master of Arts degree in liturgy. Michael later studied liturgy in Rome, Italy at the famous Pontifical Liturgical Institute. He was a brilliant student at the institute. Many of his professors encouraged him to become a scholar and professor of liturgy. After graduating, he was ordained in 1980.

Michael was always precocious and gregarious, generating goodwill and support to the community and to his friends. His growing circle of friends and admirers encouraged his many talents. Michael's composing talents produced many popular and widely played hymns, but his most famous and enduring hymn is ***On Eagle's Wings***, which has been performed at many memorial services, as well as in churches across the world. Michael's concerts often carry the theme and title from the hymn. He loves to intersperse his concert music with stories and anecdotes.

In 2003, he became suddenly ill with painful arms and legs accompanied by respiratory distress. He was later diagnosed with Guillain-Barre Syndrome (a disorder in which the body's immune system attacks part of the peripheral nervous system). He spent several months in a hospital and in rehabilitation suffering from terrible pain. Michael said that his physical and mental suffering during those difficult months impacted his musical compositions. He made a slow but painful recovery.

It is the opinion of experts that Michael's musical compositions are representative of the popular style of music that has appeared in American Catholic parishes in the wake of the Second Vatican Council. His music has enjoyed widespread success throughout the English-speaking world.

Michael is a professor at St. Thomas University and also teaches classes at the University of Notre Dame.

(References: *Michael Joncas,* Online Liturgy Resources. Retrieved 2015; *Michael Joncas,* GIA Publications. Retrieved 2014; *Guillain-Barre Journey Transformed Priest's Life,* Vision, Volume 20, No. 3, 2010, Laurie Hansen Cardona)

Kaiser, Kurt

Kurt was born in 1934 in Chicago, Illinois. Kurt developed an interest in music at a very young age, and his parents encouraged him to pursue music.

After successfully navigating his adolescent years, Kurt enrolled in the American Conservatory of Music and Northwestern

University. He earned both Bachelor and Master of Arts degrees in music. After college, he took the position as director of artists and repertoire at Joined Word, Inc. Kurt remained there for several years. He rose through the ranks to become Vice President and eventually President of the corporation.

Kurt's work with many recording artists has made him famous throughout the world. He is revered in the music industry. In addition to composing and arranging music for recording artists he also finds time to write lyrics, including over seventy hymns. His most famous hymn is ***Pass It On***, which has for many years been a favorite of youth groups both in and out of the church. Hearing the first line evokes rich memories for countless people across generations: "It only takes a spark to get a fire going ..." His recording ***Psalms, Hymns, and Spiritual Songs*** won the Dove Award. Kurt's book ***Baptist Hymnal*** is one of the most successful hymnals in the history of the Baptist church.

Kurt has received too many awards and honors to list, but it is important to note that he received a Lifetime Achievement Award from the American Society of Composers, Authors, and Publishers; an honorary Doctor of Sacred Music degree from Trinity College; an honorary Doctor of Humane Letters degree from Baylor University; a Faithfulness in Service Award, and he was inducted into the Gospel Music Hall of Fame as well as the Hall of Honor by the Christian Booksellers Association.

After thirty years in the professional music world at Joined Word, Inc., Kurt left the company and started his own music business.

He maintains a busy life in Waco, Texas. He still performs, typically with a piano, and he enjoys writing music as well as playing with his many grandchildren and serving as Deacon at the Seventh and James Baptist Church in Waco.

(References: *Kurt Kaiser,* The Canterbury Dictionary of Hymnology. Retrieved 2014; *Kurt Kaiser,* Encyclopedia of American Gospel Music. Retrieved 2014; *Kurt Kaiser,* Baptist Standard. Retrieved 2015; www.kurtkaiser.com. Retrieved 2014)

Kennedy, Gerald

Gerald was born in 1907 in Benzonia, Michigan but he was raised in California after his family moved there when he was young. Gerald was an active child who participated in school and church activities as well as community activities and events. He was constantly in motion and inquisitive about most everything.

Gerald enjoyed school but was easily bored because of his keen intellect and natural curiosity. After completing secondary school with moderate success, he attended the College of the Pacific where he received a bachelor's degree. In college, he excelled academically and he was involved in musical programs and events. He also developed an interest in religion. Gerald decided to study religion, so after he graduated from the College of the Pacific he enrolled in the Pacific School of Religion. He embraced the challenge and promise of religious studies and sought even more education; therefore, he also attended the Hartford Theological Seminary in Hartford, Connecticut where he received a Master of Divinity degree.

After being ordained into the Methodist church, he served as pastor to some of the largest Methodist churches in Connecticut, California, and Nebraska. When he was in Nebraska he also taught religion at Nebraska Wesleyan University.

Gerald was only forty years old when he was elected to the Episcopacy as a Bishop and assigned to the Portland, Oregon region. Four years later he was assigned to the very large Los Angeles Area Episcopacy. There he served Arizona, Hawaii, and Southern California. Gerald remained in the Los Angeles Area Episcopacy for over twenty years. He also served as President of the Council of Bishops of the Methodist Church.

Despite his busy schedule, Gerald was a prolific writer. He published many books. Several of his books are well known and are frequently cited by other authors. His book ***The Character of a Methodist*** is considered one the finest works about the beliefs, values, and lessons of John Wesley, the founder of the Methodist church. Another book of Gerald's, ***The Marks of a Methodist***, is a classic within the denomination. Gerald's scholarly work was recognized around the world; consequently, he received invitations to provide guest lectures at Yale University.

In addition to publishing an incredible seventeen books, he also wrote hymns and published a book of hymns, ***The Methodist Hymnal***. His most famous hymn is ***God of Love, God of Power*** that he wrote when he was serving at his first church in San Jose, California. Gerald wrote about the hymn: "At my first church after seminary which was the Calvary Methodist Church in San Jose, California, I became acquainted with a man who was head of one of the music departments in one of the junior high schools. He said to me one day that he would like to write a hymn tune if I would write the words ... I was a young preacher just starting out and tried to express my feeling of the main Christian theme of that particular period. The young people here and there began to get hold of it and it became a fairly popular hymn in California. Then it spread here and there and I was quite thrilled when they sang it one night in Australia at a youth rally where I spoke a couple of years ago."

He remained active in his role as a bishop and it was his efforts to remain actively involved in church activities that led to a decision that became controversial—he assigned himself to the First United Methodist Church of Pasadena, California as pastor. He remains the only person to serve in both capacities at the same time. Gerald remained bishop and pastor at the Pasadena church until his death in Laguna Hills, California in 1980 at the age of seventy-two.

(References: *The Methodist Church-A Concern for Religious Relevance,* Time Magazine, May 8, 1964—Bishop Gerald Kennedy Cover Story; *The Preacher's Commentary—Gerald H. Kennedy,* 1999, Stuart Briscoe)

Kerr, Hugh

Hugh was born in 1872 in Elora, Canada. His family valued education and hard work.

Hugh attended a small school in the town, and he excelled in all subjects. Upon completing secondary school, he attended the University of Toronto, where he discovered a love of theology and developed his own spiritual interests. He pursued those interests by enrolling in the Western Theological Seminary in Pittsburgh, Pennsylvania. Hugh was an eager and conscientious student who had a gregarious but studious nature.

After seminary, he was ordained a Presbyterian minister, but due to the high level of his academic work, Hugh had several job opportunities as a scholar. He turned the job offers down because he wanted to participate in the world of spirituality and share God's word, so he accepted a pastoral position in Kansas. Later, he moved to Illinois, but he found his home at Shadyside Presbyterian Church in Pittsburgh. He had fallen in love with Pittsburgh during his time growing up and attending seminary there and he very much wanted to return. He became the pastor at Shadyside Presbyterian Church in 1913 and remained there for over thirty years.

In 1917, as the United States prepared to enter the First World War, Hugh became a chaplain to several U.S. Army training camps in upstate New York. After the war, Hugh considered the best and most effective ways to reach people. He turned his attention to radio. It is not commonly known now that Hugh was a true pioneer of religious broadcasting. In his era, radio ruled the entertainment and news world, and he envisioned the power of the radio as a medium for extending the gospel all around the country. He made history with a Christmas Day sermon in 1922, which was broadcast to the North and South Poles by radio station KDKA, and some of his broadcasts were picked up by radios at U.S. Army military camps and in some large cities and small towns across the nation.

In addition to being a gifted pastor, Hugh was a prolific writer, including sermons, children's story-sermons, and hymns. He is legendary in the Presbyterian Church for his compilation of the ***Presbyterian Hymnal*** that was published in 1931, and for his ***Book of Common Worship*** which became well-known around the

Christian world. His most famous hymn is ***God of Our Life,*** which he wrote for the 50th anniversary of Shadyside Presbyterian Church in Pittsburgh.

The concept of and later wide-spread participation in the Worldwide Communion Sunday was Hugh's idea. Even today, almost seventy-five years after he conceived the idea, the Worldwide Communion Sunday is recognized and practiced around the world.

Hugh was a unique pastor who combined creative ways to teach and deliver sermons without losing any of his respect for the holiness of God's word and support of the spirit of mankind.

After an amazingly productive life, Hugh died in Pittsburgh in 1950 at age seventy-eight.

(References: *The Highway of Life and Other Sermons,* September 1918, Hugh T. Kerr; *Our Life in God's Light,* 1979; *Hugh Kerr - Author and Theologian,* March 31, 1992, New York Times obituary)

Kethe, William

William was born in Scotland. The date of his birth is not documented, but some have speculated that he was born around 1530 in a small Scotland village.

At various times in his life, he moved back and forth between Frankfurt, Germany and Geneva, Switzerland. He is most well-known for his production of the ***Geneva Bible,*** a translation of the Scriptures, and for the hymn ***All People That on Earth Do Dwell,*** which is taken from *Psalm 100* and remains one of the most popular and oldest hymns in the Methodist Hymn Book.

Twenty-four of his hymns can be found in the old versions of the Anglo-Genevan Psalter (dated 1560). William was influenced by John Calvin who did not support hymns in church because he thought they defiled the meaning of Scripture, so the only hymns he would allow were those that came directly from *Psalms.*

After spending many years in Germany and Switzerland, William went back to England and served as Vicar of Childe

Okeford in Dorsetshire for several years. Queen Elizabeth the First appointed William to twice serve as a Rector of Dorset, and he also served as a military chaplain.

While the date of William's birth remains uncertain, his death was well documented. He died in 1594 in Dorsetshire, England when he was approximately sixty years old. William's funeral was attended by members of the Royal Family.

(References: *William Kethe,* Hymnary.org. Retrieved 2015; *William Kethe,* hymntime.com. Retrieved 2015; *Hymns Based on Psalms,* Bartleby.com. Retrieved 2015; *Favorite Hymns,* 2006, Marjorie Reeves and Jenyth Worsley)

Kierkegaard, Soren

Soren was born in 1813 in Copenhagen, Sweden to an affluent family. He was the youngest of seven children. His father, Michael, was a wealthy hosier, having made his fortune at a young age after learning about the clothing business from his uncle. Soren inherited his father's wealth, keen intellect, and melancholy tendencies. Soren's mother was the intellectual equal of her husband. She was devoted to Soren and was very protective of him. She and Soren's father valued education and the qualities of life, including respect for others and an intellectual curiosity, which they instilled in Soren.

Soren excelled in school and was also a creative genius who loved to experience the good and ugly aspects of life on the streets of Copenhagen. His mother would pull him back from those adventures and counsel him. With her encouragement, he attended the School of Civic Virtue where he studied Latin, classics literature, and history.

Soren appeared to others as a natural philosopher because of his interest in the larger questions about life. He often told his friends that he wanted to know "what am I to do" and "what must I know". As he matured, his intellectual curiosity blossomed and he wanted to attend college so he enrolled at the University of Copenhagen where he studied theology. Soren was a brilliant student. He became a theology scholar before he completed his degree. After completing his studies at the University of Copenhagen he attended pastoral seminary. Shortly before enrolling in seminary, he became engaged to Regina Olsen who became the subject and inspiration of a literary love story as described in both his personal and public journals.

His master's thesis in seminary was so finely developed that it would later become his doctoral thesis. Soren completed his doctorate in 1854. He then worked on his long-term ambition to be a writer. His book ***Either/Or*** made him famous. The book was the literary sensation in Copenhagen and eventually throughout Europe. His future as a significant and influential writer and philosopher was set. However, Soren's free and uncensored writings were not always well received, such as ***Fear and Trembling*** and ***Sickness Unto Death***. He took on controversial subjects, such as the church and religion, and he was often condemned for his points of view. The criticism became so personal that he published several books under pseudonyms.

Soren became a chronic critic of the Church of Denmark through his journals and newspaper articles. Nevertheless, he was a respected philosopher whose published works remain popular today and are often studied and quoted.

He also enjoyed music and wrote several hymns. At first, he considered his hymns as a hobby not to be taken too seriously, but over time he discovered the power of hymns; consequently, he took hymn composition seriously. Several of his hymns survived, but his hymn ***Breathe Deeply in Faith*** continues to be his most popular hymn.

In 1855, Soren collapsed on a street in Copenhagen and was hospitalized for well over a month before dying at the age of forty-two. He was buried in the Assistens Kierkegaard in the Norrebro Section of Copenhagen.

(References: *Encyclopedia of Philosophy,* 2005, W. McDonald; *Soren Kierkegaard,* Stanford Encyclopedia of Philosophy, 1996. Retrieved 2014; *Soren Kierkegaard,* Britannica.com. Retrieved 2014)

Kim, Helen

Helen was born near Seoul, Korea in 1899 to a humble family that valued education, hard work, and dedication to the family.

Helen attended local schools where she excelled in all subjects and courses. She was dedicated to every task she undertook and her determination was admired and rewarded by her teachers and parents.

After completing her local education, she attended Ewha College (Ewha means peach blossom) for women in Seoul where she earned a Bachelor of Arts degree at age nineteen.

In college and after she graduated, Helen volunteered to work with the local children and youth. She became concerned about the lack of activities available for girls, so she organized an association of volunteers that provide activities and events for girls. Helen is credited with starting the campaign that led to the national Korean YWCA in 1922.

Helen wanted to continue her studies, and she was advised by several people to seek a graduate program in the United States. She received information about several colleges and universities, but she was most impressed and influenced by Ohio Wesleyan University. She moved to the United States and took classes at Ohio Wesleyan University before transferring to Boston University to complete work for her Master of Arts degree. Her professors and colleagues urged her to pursue a doctoral degree. Helen enrolled at Columbia University Teacher's College and earned a Ph.D.

Soon after graduating, she returned to Korea to work at Ewha College. She held several positions at the college, including professor, department chair, and dean. In 1939, much to the delight her colleagues, the board of directors, and students, Helen was named the president of Ewha College. At the time, there were 900 students attending the college, which would later become Ewha Womans University ("Womans" does not include an apostrophe, according to the university website).

Soon after she took the position of president, World War II erupted. Korea was occupied by the Japanese Army and took control of the college. Because of Helen's strength of character, protective nature toward her students, her gift of leadership, and her faith she managed to keep the college open and relatively free of interference by the Japanese. There were changes to some courses and the Japanese tried to completely change the curriculum, but Helen was successful in keeping those changes under control and within reason.

After the war, Helen led the rebuilding and expansion of the college and it grew to over 8,000 students in a short period of time, as it transitioned from a college to a major university. She served as president of the university for twenty-two years. During her presidency, the university continued to grow, and today it is the largest all women's university in the world with well over 20,000 students. Helen brought not only more students into the university, she worked hard to expand the departments, degrees, student services, and she improved and expanded the dorms and extracurricular activities.

In addition to serving as president of the university, Helen was also the founder and editor of *The Korean Times*, the only English-language newspaper in Korea at the time. She also served in numerous roles for the Korean government, including Ambassador-at-Large to the United Nations.

Helen was so influential and respected that a scholarship was named in her honor—the Helen Kim Memorial Scholarship. The scholarship is sponsored by The World Federation of Methodist and the Uniting Church Women.

Helen is also well known for her famous and beloved hymn ***Lonely the Boat*** which was crafted from her love of *Matthew 8:23-27*.

Helen continued to work on community and university projects for several years after her retirement. She died in Seoul, Korea in 1970 at the age of seventy-one. Her memorial service was attended by thousands of people. She is a revered figure in South Korean history.

(References: *Helen Kim,* Korea Times, August 2013; *Sisters in Song,* Women Hymn Writers. Retrieved 2015; *Helen Kim,* Hymnary.org. Retrieved 2015)

Kimbrough, Jr. Steven

Steven was born in 1936 in Alabama. He was a child prodigy who soared through his childhood by excelling in virtually everything he attempted. School work came easy to him and his talent in music, especially his singing, was obvious to everyone when he was just a young boy. He cultivated his writing and singing skills in school and in the church as well as in community activities and events. Steven showed the rare combination of extraordinary intellect, musical gifts, charismatic personality, a kind nature, ambition, and a spiritual seeker.

After secondary school, he attended Birmingham Southern College where he honed his academic and musical skills while working to earn a Bachelor of Arts degree. His highly honored work led him to a full scholarship at Duke University Divinity School. Steven received a Master of Divinity degree at Duke. He later was accepted at Princeton University Theological Seminary, where he earned a doctorate in Old Testament and Semitic languages.

Through his study, research, and publications, Steven became an internationally well-known scholar and an expert on Charles Wesley, who with his brother founded the Methodist movement.

After being ordained, Steven served churches in Alabama, North Carolina, New Jersey, and Germany, and for several years, he served as Associate General Secretary for Mission Evangelism of the General Board of Global Ministries of the United Methodist Church.

Steven has published numerous books of a scholarly nature that are recognized around the world as classics such as ***A Heart to Praise My God*; *Charles Wesley: Poet and Theologian*; *Methodism***

in Russia and the Baltic States: History and Renewal; Orthodox and Wesleyan Spirituality and many others.

Steven is also known for his beautiful singing voice. He has performed in many events and as a one-person show on the international stage. For over a decade he was the lead baritone for the Bonn Opera Company. Steven wrote and performed the famous one-person musical drama ***Sweet Singer*** that portrayed the dramatic and inspiring life of Charles Wesley. ***Sweet Singer*** debuted at Carnegie Hall in New York City and then went on a worldwide tour.

In addition to performances, Steven also continues his scholarly work by teaching at Princeton Theological Seminary; Friedrich Wilhelm University of Bonn, Germany; New Brunswick Theological Seminary, New Jersey; Illiricus Theological Seminary of Zagreb (formerly Yugoslavia), Wesley Theological Seminary, Washington, D.C. (as Distinguished Scholar), and Theological School of Drew University where he is the Bell Scholar.

For thirty years Steven has served as a member of the Center for Theological Inquiry at Princeton University. He has also written several hymns, and he has served as a consultant to the Hymnal Revision Committee of the United Methodist Church. His performance recordings include the CD, ***Songs of Freedom, Justice and Peace***.

(References: *The Hymns and works of Steven T. Kimbrough*, www.stkimbrough.com. Retrieved 2014; *The Lyrical Theology of Charles Wesley: A Reader*, 2014 edition, Steven T. Kimbrough; *CharlesWesleySociety.org*. Retrieved 2014; *S.T. Kimbrough,* The Canterbury Dictionary of Hymnology. Retrieved 2012 and 2013 and updated 2014)

Lafferty, Karen

Karen was born in 1948 in Alamogordo, New Mexico. Karen showed her musical talents at a young age. By the time she was fourteen it was obvious that her musical talents were going to develop into a professional career.

During her teenage years, she was busy almost every week performing with various musical groups, including rock music, folk music, musical productions, bands, orchestras, as part of choirs and performing solo. Karen also participated in church activities at her local Baptist church, with the encouragement of her parents.

After secondary school, Karen enrolled in Eastern New Mexico University where she earned a Bachelor of Music Education degree with honors. The following year she found her first professional musical career job in southern California as a nightclub entertainer. She enjoyed the work but she was troubled by the lifestyle and lack of morals she saw in nightclub workers and patrons. So in her own subtle, gentle way she began talking to them and witnessing to them about the love, support, and grace of God.

Karen found her own spiritual needs met at the Calvary Chapel near Costa Mesa, California, where she became very active in the church as an administrative, worship, and music leader. Karen also taught Bible study classes. During a Bible study class on *Matthew 6:33* she was inspired to write ***Seek Ye First the Kingdom of God,*** a hymn that became well known throughout the Christian world. Karen joined *Maranatha! Music,* which is a Christian recording company. She recorded four albums that became successful in the United States, Canada, and Europe. The success and popularity of her albums led to invitations from other countries to perform on tours. It was during those tours that she discovered the importance of missionary work in spreading the word of God.

Karen was invited to participate in missionary training in Amsterdam, Holland with *Youth With A Mission* (YWAM). She was so inspired by the power of missionary work that she founded the *Musicians for Missions International* (MFMI) in 1981 when she was thirty-two years old. Karen facilitated an agreement that led to MFMI working with YWAM, using the influence and powerful message of music to share the grace of God to all people. The work of both organizations has influenced people for over thirty years.

Karen has toured and taken the work of MFMI to almost sixty countries in her tireless effort to reach out to others through what she called the "Music in Missions." She came back to the United States full-time to care for her elderly parents. Karen lives in Santa Fe, New Mexico where MFMI is also located. She remains active in church work, performs at concerts, and shares her missionary influence.

(References: *Encyclopedia of Contemporary Christian Music*, 2002, Mark Powell; *Seek Ye First: Interview with Karen Lafferty*, Reformed Worship. Retrieved 2014; *Karen Lafferty*, www.karenlafferty.net Retrieved 2014)

Lanier, H. Glen

Glen was born in 1925 in Statesboro, North Carolina to a family that was deeply religious and hardworking. Glen was raised to work, take care of the family first, and attend the small local church whenever the doors were open for worship. Glen had eight siblings, and he played an essential role in taking care of them.

Although he lived in a rural town with a small local school and only a few resources, Glen showed an early aptitude for schoolwork. He was a prodigious reader with a photographic memory. Glen amazed his teachers with his understanding of literature, his memory of details, and his early efforts at writing poetry. The quality and maturity of his poems were unexpected from such a young boy. Glen also showed an uncommon insight into nature and people. Glen's teachers encouraged him to write poetry. At home, his parents doubted that writing poetry would offer Glen a livelihood, but they did not want to discourage him.

After excelling in secondary school and winning some local awards for his poetry he enrolled in High Point College in High Point, North Carolina to study literature. He earned a Bachelor of Arts degree. While at High Point he developed a keen interest in theology and religion and some of his poems were composed into hymns. His academic success at High Point led to his admission to the Duke University Divinity School where he received a Master of Divinity degree. After being ordained in the United Methodist church he became the pastor of the First United Methodist Church of Thomasville, North Carolina. He also served United Methodist churches in Wilkesboro and Statesville, North Carolina.

Glen wrote over 1,000 poems and numerous hymns. Seventeen of his hymn texts were published and widely distributed in the United States and Canada. Many of them are in hymnals, such as ***America, My Homeland Fair***; ***Father, God, We Come Before Thee***; and ***For All the Joys of Living***.

Glen was a beloved pastor and a well-respected hymnist and poet. He had more hymns and poems to write, but after a brief illness, he died in 1978 in Statesville, North Carolina when he was only fifty-two years old.

(References: *Glen Lanier,* Dictionary of North America Hymnology. Retrieved 2014; *The Seasons of Life,* 1960, Glen Lanier; *Composers in the Classroom,* 2011, James Michael Floyd)

Lathbury, Mary Artemesia

Mary was born in 1841 in Manchester, New York. Her father was the preacher at the Manchester Methodist Episcopal Church and her mother was also a devout Christian. Mary and her two brothers were raised in a family that valued God, family, and hard work. Both of her brothers would become Methodist ministers.

Most of Mary's education was in the local school, but she also received training at home and learned much about music, literature, and art from her mother and father. Mary showed a talent for both music and art when she was very young. She composed poems and lyrics before she reached adolescence. Mary also had a gift for sketching and painting. Frequently, she painted or sketched images to accompany her poems. She was devoted to developing her talents.

As she grew older, her talents developed quickly. Mary became a regular contributor to journals, magazines, and periodicals that were geared toward children and parents. Her work caught the attention of the Secretary of the Methodist Church's *Sunday Union Periodical,* Dr. John Vincent. He met with Mary and was impressed with her talents, her maturity, her kindness, and her devotion to

Christian beliefs. He offered her a job in the editorial department which she gladly accepted.

The periodical benefitted from Mary's talents and Mary benefitted from the exposure to world events and various types of writing. It was during this time that Mary learned of the Chautauqua Movement. Chautauqua is an Iroquois (Native American Indian) word that describes a lake in southwest New York. The "movement" was aimed at formalizing and professionalizing the teaching profession. It was not affiliated with any Christian denomination but instead was devoted to encouraging the teaching of science and other subjects for all children and adults. Once Mary learned more about the movement, she volunteered and became a staunch supporter. The leaders of the movement, John Vincent and Lewis Miller, greatly appreciated Mary's interest and support and they also admired her vast artistic and musical talents. She became such an integral part of the movement that she became known as the "Laureate of Chautauqua."

Mary also became an accomplished and well-respected national writer. She published the magazine ***Woman and Temperance*** and was a frequent contributor to *Harper's Young People* magazine. Many of Mary's poems became popular hymns, and she also had a keen ability to compose hymns for special occasions. Mary published several hymns. Many of them are in hymnals today, such as ***Break Thou the Bread of Life***; ***Day is Dying in the West***, and many others.

Mary remained active in the movement and with her writing and artwork until her health declined in 1910. She was often ill over the next three years and died in 1913 in East Orange, New Jersey at the age of seventy-two.

(References: *Mary Artemesia Lathbury,* Cyberhymnal. Retrieved 2015; *Mary A. Lathbury*, 1907, Dictionary of Hymnology, John Julian; *Biography of Mary Lathbury,* Stem Publishing. Retrieved 2015)

Lincoln, Eric

Eric was born in Athens, Alabama in 1924 to a family ravaged by poverty in a segregated community. Shortly after his birth, Eric's father left the family to look for work, but he never returned and left no communication of his whereabouts. Eric's family lived day to day, as his mother tried to raise a family of several children while also helping other families in the community in similar circumstances. His mother was often physically and spiritually weakened by the stress.

Eric woke one morning to find that his mother had left. His only choice was to live with his grandmother, who took him in and cared for him, even though she lived in abject poverty, also. At a very young age, when he was twelve or thirteen years old, Eric went to work to help his grandmother. He would forego school most days to work in cotton fields with adults and other children to make a few cents. Eric realized that education was his only way out of poverty, so he studied hard when he entered the local segregated high school. After school, he worked in the fields in the afternoon and stayed up late at night studying. Eric found learning was stimulating and interesting. He also discovered that he was intelligent and had the gift of insight.

Eric graduated with honors from high school; in fact, he was the valedictorian. He migrated to Chicago looking for work and a way to continue his education, but he found that difficult so he joined the Navy, serving from 1943 to 1945. After an honorable discharge from the Navy, Eric heard about an opportunity for veterans to attend college in Memphis, Tennessee. There he enrolled in LeMoyne-Owen College and earned his Bachelor of Arts degree in both sociology and philosophy in just two years. Eric taught, played music, preached and continued his education for the next few years. Then he attended Fisk University in Nashville, Tennessee, where he received a Master of Arts degree.

His growing interest in philosophy and religion led him back to college, and at the University of Chicago, he earned a Bachelor of Divinity degree. Soon thereafter, he was ordained as a Methodist minister. Eric would later earn another master's degree and a Ph.D. in social ethics from Boston University.

Eric had various jobs, but his academic prowess took him to Clark Atlanta University where he taught for over eleven years. During his time there, Eric served as a visiting professor at Portland State University; Union Theological Seminary in New York; Fordham University; Brown University; New York State University, and the University of Ghana.

Adding to his busy life, Eric became an author, president of the Black Academy of Letters, and played and wrote music. He always had a great love of spiritual hymns, so he studied hymn music and wrote hymns.

Eric's growing academic reputation took him to Fisk University where he became a full professor of Religion and Sociology and chairman of the department. A few years later Duke University recruited Eric, and for seventeen years Eric was a professor of religion and culture at Duke University.

He became well known because of his bestselling book, ***The Avenue, Clayton City***, a portrayal of a fictional southern town that highlighted the plight of black families. It was published while he was at Duke University and it became a bestseller and winner of several awards, including the Lillian Smith Book Award and the International Alice Browning Award. Eric also wrote ***The Black Muslims in America*** and ***The Black Church in the African-American Experience***, both of which won several awards for academic excellence. Eric wrote, co-wrote or edited over twenty books.

Eric composed several hymns. His hymn ***How Like a Gently Spirit*** is in most Christian hymnals. In 1990, he was elected to the Fellowship of Southern Writers, and in the same year, he was honored by Pope John Paul II for his scholarly service to church and mankind. Famous leaders including Dr. Martin Luther King and Malcolm X were Eric's friends. They frequently sought his advice. Writers such as Alex Haley, the author of ***Roots***, also admired Eric's observations about life, religion, history, and philosophy.

Eric died from diabetes complications at the age of seventy-five in 2000 while living in Durham, North Carolina.

(References: *C. Eric Lincoln,* May 17, 2000, New York Times Obituary; *Black Hymnody: A Hymnological History,* 1992, Jon Michael Spencer; *Tribute to Dr. C. Eric Lincoln,* September 30, 1994, Congressional Record)

Longfellow, Samuel

Sam was born in 1819 in Portland, Maine. He was the youngest of eight children. One of his brothers was the famous poet Henry Wadsworth Longfellow, who Sam adored and admired.

Sam was described as the most serious-minded of the children; yet, he was creative and gregarious. Sam was a serious student of the classics, and he greatly enjoyed reading and writing. He enrolled in Harvard University and excelled in all academic areas. Sam was considered a scholar even when he was still a student. The quality of his work was noted and highly respected by his professors. He graduated with honors and eighth in his class when he was only twenty years old.

Sam developed a strong interest in theology and philosophy, so he entered the Harvard Divinity School. He continued with his academic success and he also met several influential people, including Samuel Johnson. Together they collaborated on several hymns, which were published in ***A Book of Hymns for Public and Private Devotion***. The book became popular and was later expanded to include more hymns. Sam also published ***Vespers*** and ***Hymns of the Spirit,*** as well as many other works.

After graduating from Harvard Divinity School, Sam was ordained and took a pastoral position at Fall River Church in Massachusetts as a Unitarian minister. Later he worked at churches in Brooklyn, New York and Germantown, Pennsylvania. After the death of this famous brother Henry, Sam retreated to Henry's home in Cambridge, Massachusetts to work on a biography of his beloved brother. Sam's biography of Henry titled ***Life*** is a two volume masterpiece and became a bestselling book.

Sam never approached the level of fame his poet brother enjoyed; nevertheless, during his lifetime, he was highly regarded and widely respected. Also, many of his hymns are still found in hymnals, including ***Holy Spirit, Truth Divine***; ***Bless Thou the Gifts***; and ***Now on Land and Sea Descending***. Sam died in 1892 at the age of seventy-three in Cape Elizabeth, Maine.

(References: *The Quiet Radical: The Biography of Samuel Longfellow*, 2008, Joseph Abdo; *The Presbyterian Hymnal Companion*, 1993, LindaJo McKim; *American Transcendentalism: A History*, 2007, Philip Gura)

Longstaff, William D.

William was born in 1822 in Sunderland, Durham, England into a wealthy family. His father was a ship owner who made a fortune in trading and shipping goods around the world.

William was a precocious child and a good student who quickly moved through elementary and secondary school. He did not distinguish himself academically, but he was gregarious, curious, made friends easily and was much admired for his loyalty to friends and his good character.

William learned a lot about the business world from his father, and when he completed college he went into the trade business, also. He became a very successful businessman. William was a leader in his community and contributed considerable amounts of money to philanthropic work and to his church. For several years, he was the treasurer of the Bethesda Free Chapel in Sunderland, and an active member of the church in several other ways. With his wealth, William could have traveled the world or lived a life of secluded leisure, but he wanted no part of either. He did travel some, primarily in Europe, but he never stayed away from Sunderland for very long.

William enjoyed reading and writing poetry, and it was one of his poems that made him forever famous because it became one of the most revered hymns in the Christian world and has remained so for over 150 years.

William was attending a conference to hear the famous missionary, Dr. Griffith John, speak about his missionary trips to China. William was thrilled to hear Dr. John and he made note of almost everything he said. But there was one comment Dr. John made that struck William like a thunderbolt. Dr. John said even in the darkest times, God is with us and that's when we should remember to "take the time to be holy." William wrote that down and at home that night he wrote a poem with that theme and titled it ***Take Time to Be Holy***. While some of his other poems were composed into hymns, most of them have been forgotten over time, but his hymn ***Take Time to Be Holy*** can be found in virtually every Christian hymn book.

William made another endearing and infinitely important contribution when he befriended two struggling evangelists, D. L. Moody, and Ira Sankey, who had come to England seeking a sponsor for their evangelical revivals. The person they were counting on to support their work had died prior to their arrival in England. On their own and with virtually no money they began taking their message of God's good grace to anyone who would listen. In town hall spaces or back rooms of stores or restaurants, they gathered with a few people to share the Holy Spirit. After several months and many hungry days, they managed to have a steady worship group of about fifty people. William heard about the two and was curious to hear their message. He was impressed with their message of hope, charity, and God's work through people to help others. With his wealth, he offered financial resources including advice and guidance on how to manage money and invest money. With William's support of resources, the size of the congregation grew rapidly as word spread about the work of the worship leaders. Soon the number of worshippers grew to 20,000 in London and even larger groups met in Scotland. This was the beginning of the Salvation Army. It is possible and actually very likely that there would be no Salvation Army without the support and contributions from William.

William continued writing poetry throughout his life, but other than those that were composed into hymns in a Salvation Army hymnal published in 1880, only a few of William's poems survived. William was active until his death in 1894 at the age of seventy-two. He was buried in his beloved Sunderland, Durham, England. Several members of the Salvation Army attended his memorial service and his hymn ***Take Time to Be Holy*** was sung.

(References: *Forty Stories of Famous Gospel Songs,* 1977, Ernest K Emurian; *My Favorite Hymn Stories,* 2010, Warren Shiver; *Take Time to Be What?* 2007, Gordon MacDonald; *Companion to Baptist Hymnal,* 1976, William J. Reynolds; *William Dunn Longstaff,* The Canterbury Dictionary of Hymnology. Retrieved 2014)

Lowry, Robert

Robert was born in 1826 in Philadelphia, Pennsylvania. He was a very active young boy who developed an early interest in music because many relatives and friends who frequently visited the house brought musical instruments and filled the house with music and singing. Consequently, Robert was exposed to a wide array of musical instruments and he was fascinated with all of them.

As he grew older his interest in music turned into a love of music. Robert also became interested in learning more about the spiritual side of life, so he took a more serious interest in church. He attended the First Baptist Church of Philadelphia where he sought a better understanding of his beliefs. When he turned seventeen years old he joined the church and thereafter became a very active member of the church. He became a Sunday school teacher and a member of the choir. The minister and elders of the church were impressed with Robert's devotion to the church and its activities, and they saw in him an intellectual talent as well as wonderful human relations skills. They encouraged him to consider going into ministry work, and Robert did.

At age twenty-two he enrolled at the University of Lewisburg (now Bucknell University). He worked at the church and attended classes when he could. After laboring with work and college, he graduated at age twenty-eight with honors. Robert then entered the ministry after being ordained as a Baptist minister.

He served as minister of Baptist churches in Lewisburg, Pennsylvania; New York City; Brooklyn, New York, and in Plainfield, New Jersey. While in Pennsylvania, Robert taught at the University of Lewisburg in addition to being a minister.

Robert became famous for his sermons and his music. He used vivid language and illustrative verbal images to convey his sermon messages. The music he selected and sometimes composed augmented the sermons. Robert's music was filled with allegory and almost visceral messages.

Robert was also a writer. He edited books, wrote articles, and published books of music. His Sunday school songbook ***Pure Gold*** became a bestseller in the United States, selling over one million copies. That successful songbook was followed by several other popular ones, including ***Welcome Tidings***; ***Brightest and Best***; ***Glad Refrain***; ***Good as Gold***; ***Joyful Lays***; ***Fountain of Song***; ***Bright Array***, and many others. A ***New York Times*** reporter once asked Robert, "Do you write the words to fit the music or the music to fit the words?" Robert answered, "I have no method. Sometimes the music comes and the words follow, fitted insensibly to the melody. I watch my moods, and when anything good strikes me, whether words or music and no matter where I am, at home or on the street, I jot it down. Often the margin of a newspaper or the back of an envelope serves as a notebook. My brain is a sort of spinning machine, I think, for there is music running through it all the time. I do not pick out my music on the keys of an instrument. The tunes of nearly all the hymns I have written have been completed on paper before I tried them on the organ. Frequently the words of the hymn and the music have been written at the same time."

Of the hundreds of hymns and other songs he composed, Robert often said that his best was ***Weeping Will Not Save Me***. Many people would argue that point, for his ***Shall We Gather at the River*** is considered one of the most popular and most often sung hymns ever written.

Robert received numerous awards and Lewisburg University awarded him with an honorary doctor of divinity degree. Even in retirement, Robert continued to compose music, sing and play several instruments.

After a short illness, Robert died in 1899 in Plainfield, New Jersey at the age of seventy-three. A bronze plaque was installed in Plainfield, New Jersey in 1911 to commemorate his dedication and service. Robert remains one of the most popular hymnists of all time.

(References: *American Hymns Old and New,* 1980, Charles William Hughes; *The Harvard Biographical Dictionary of Music,* 1996, Don Michael Randel; *Robert Lowry,* STEM Publishing. Retrieved 2013)

Luther, Martin

Martin was born in 1483 in Saxony, which at the time was part of the Holy Roman Empire. His family was part of the aristocracy. His father was a member of the local council and a community leader. Martin had several siblings, but he was considered by his father to be the most talented and gifted of his children; therefore, he determined that Martin would be a lawyer.

Martin was sent to the finest schools possible, including the Latin schools in Magdeburg. Martin later in life described his time in the Latin schools as "purgatory and hell at the same time." When he was nineteen years old, he enrolled at the University of Erfurt where he was subjected to daily routines of rote learning and self-discipline. He disliked the routine and the style of teaching, but he endured long enough to receive a Bachelor and Master of Arts degree.

Against his own wishes, but to follow his father's advice, Martin entered law school at the University of Erfurt. He was immediately unimpressed and uninspired by his law school experience. His broad-based and expanding intellect moved him away from law and toward philosophy and theology. Martin was drawn to Aristotle, Gabriel Biel, and William of Ockham, but it was his two tutors that influenced him to the most. Bartholomaeus Arnoldi von Usingen and Jodocus Trutfetter convinced Martin to question virtually everything he was taught, even the works of the most famous philosophers, such as Aristotle. They argued that accepting the philosophical works and beliefs of others without question was contradictory to the nature and purpose of thought and self-development. Martin became almost obsessed with these types of questions, to the point that he abandoned law school over the howling opposition of his father.

Martin chose to enter the closed friary of Augustinian in Erfurt to become a monk at the age of twenty-two. He found comfort and deep solace during his first years in the monastery, but he entered into "deep spiritual despair" and felt like he had lost touch with Christ. He continued his pursuit of true belief and spirituality and was ordained to the priesthood in 1507. At the invitation of the dean of the University of Wittenburg, Martin went to the college to teach theology. He continued his own studies at the college, earning two more degrees. In 1512, at the age of twenty-seven, Martin was awarded a Doctorate of Theology, and a short time later was elected by the university senate to become a theology faculty member at the university.

The genesis of the Reformation grew from Martin's disdain for "indulgence." His concerns were ignored by the leadership, so Martin nailed his "Ninety-Five Theses" to the door of All Saints' Church in Wittenburg on October 31, 1517. His friends made print copies of the theses. The copies were passed out and quickly spread across England, France, and Italy. The leaders of the Magdeburg Church sent the ninety-five theses to Rome to determine if they were heresy. There were accusations, hearings, and many leaders called Martin an enemy of the Pope. Finally, he was excommunicated by Pope Leo X in 1521. With a chance for redemption in the eyes of the religious leaders, he renounced any efforts to make him change his mind. He refused to recant his writings, often saying, "Here I stand, I can do no other." In 1526, Martin organized a new church, Lutheran, a church based on personal faith and he became its spiritual and administrative leader. This was the beginning of the great Lutheran Movement that spread around the world.

Martin became a prodigious writer. He wrote academic treatises, opinion articles, and hymns in the first Lutheran hymnal. Of his many writings, Martin's ***On Christian Liberty*** and ***Faith Alone*** remain popular today. Also, several of his hymns remain popular, such as ***A Mighty Fortress Is Our God; Savior of the Nations, Come***; and ***Come Christ Lay in Death's Strong Hands***.

By age forty-eight his health began to deteriorate, but he continued to lead his church and write. During the next several years, Martin had bouts of severe illness that weakened his body but not his spirit and determination. Martin died in 1546 at the age of sixty-two. It was reported that soon after his death, a piece of paper was found in his handwriting that said, "We are beggars." The significance of the finding illustrated his belief that mankind held all things in the hope that God will always be present and will surely provide the path to fulfillment.

(References: *Martin Luther's Basic Theological Writings,* 2012, Timothy Lull and William Russell; *On Being a Theologian of the Cross,* 1997, Gerhard Forde; *Martin Luther,* Biography Online, Liberty University. Retrieved 2014)

Lynch, Thomas

Thomas was born in 1818 in Dunmow, Essex, England to a wealthy family. His father Michael was a well-known physician. Thomas was raised by his father and mother to appreciate the value of an education and understand the importance of a full spiritual life.

At an early age, Thomas showed little that would foretell his great influence later in life. He was disinterested in most things and at times sickly and inactive. Thomas had few friends and no hobbies. He attended the Islington School and finally graduated after several years of lackluster effort and performance.

At the insistence of his parents, Thomas enrolled in Highbury Independent College but soon withdrew due to his claim of ill health. There is much speculation that he left college primarily because he lacked the discipline for study and did not like rising early for classes and following a daily routine. However, as Thomas matured he resumed his studies and changed his lifestyle to that of a more responsible student. As he began to take college more seriously, he discovered that he enjoyed learning. Thomas also found that his intellect was at least equivalent if not superior to his classmates' abilities. He graduated from college with excellent grades.

After completing his college studies, he became a minister of a small church for a few years until he took over a larger church at Fitzroy Square. Thomas was happy and dedicated to his church and the congregation. However, he became gravely ill and disabled for almost three years due to several medical complications. As he slowly recovered, he resumed part-time duties at the church until he could rejoin the church as the full-time minister. A few years later he became the minister of a new church, Mornington Church in Hampstead Road, London.

None of his churches were large, but his influence over time stretched far and wide. Thomas' sermons became legendary as did his hymns, and he had a great influence on a large number of theology students at the Theological College of London. His sermons and writings were purposely inspirational, as were his many hymns. He composed over 200 hymns; many of them were published in ***The Rivulet: A Contribution to Sacred Song***, including ***All Faded is the Glowing Light***. Several of his sermons and hymns were also published in a book by William White.

Thomas remained at Mornington Church until his death in 1871 at the age of fifty-three in Camden Town, Middlesex, England. Reportedly, his last words were, "Now I am going to begin to live." His memorial service was attended by hundreds of worshipers and friends.

(References: *Thomas T. Lynch*, Cyberhymnal.org. Retrieved 2014; *The World's Most Controversial Hymn Book*, 2011, Brenda T. Wed;

Memoirs of Thomas T. Lynch, 1874, William White, Retrieved note from Library of Congress 2014)

Lyte, Henry Francis

Henry was born in 1793 in Ednam, Scotland. His family life was very difficult because his father refused to work, even when neighbors and friends offered him work. Instead, he was often seen fishing and hunting while Henry and his brothers and mother struggled to survive. Henry's father was, nevertheless, a gregarious and persuasive personality. He arranged for Henry and his older brother to attend the Portora Royal School at Enniskillen, County Fermanagh. Soon thereafter, his father abandoned the family and within a year, Henry's mother and the youngest son both died of tuberculosis that was in part related to the family's squalid living conditions.

Henry was seen by his teachers as a very intelligent student. He showed remarkable intellectual gifts. His teachers played a key role in Henry being accepted to attend Trinity College in Dublin, Ireland. Henry thrived in the college environment. He excelled in all of the academic areas but he showed an exceptional talent in English poetry. Henry also developed an interest in theology. Having witnessed his father's behavior and the death of his mother and youngest brother from neglect and poverty, Henry was determined to find a career where he could have an income without sacrificing his intellectual curiosity.

Upon completing his theology studies at Trinity College, Henry was ordained in 1815 at the young age of twenty-two. He was offered the position of Curate of Marazion near Cornwell, England. Two years later he met and married Anne Maxwell, the daughter of a well-known and respected Scott-Irish family. They were oddly mismatched, as many often noted, with Henry being strikingly handsome and beguiling while Anne was plain and shy. Nevertheless, they were a happy couple that produced five children, who distinguished themselves in their own right.

Henry preached in several Ireland parishes and even a few English ones. For most of his career, however, he was pastor at All Saints Church in Lower Brixham, Devonshire, England. It was there that he wrote, preached, and started a children's Sunday school and a Sailor's School to teach Biblical studies. These two schools provided the only education many children and seamen ever experienced because of the availability of education was otherwise non-existent for them. Henry was one of the few preachers that would board a ship to deliver a sermon. The seamen, whose lives were terribly difficult and, consequently, made them a rough and rowdy group were beholden to Henry and admired him for showing his concern by entering their ships to pray with them.

Henry loved his community and often provided special events, especially for the children. His Annual Treat Festival brought over 1,000 children to the festival that included a religious service followed by food, tea, sports events and brief theatrical plays. Henry became so well-known for his sermons and his community service that church attendance overflowed the small structure, to the point that it had to be enlarged. Henry also enjoyed the music of his church, and he often wrote hymns for his services. One of his hymns is the legendary ***Abide with Me***, which has maintained its popularity in hymnals around the world for almost 200 years.

Henry tutored pupils in his home. Probably the most famous of his pupils was the blind brother of Robert Gascoyne-Cecil. Robert would later become the Prime Minister of Great Britain. Many of his pupils went to college and later became ministers, doctors, lawyers, and artists.

The depth of Henry's universal talents seemed to have no end. It was commonly known that Henry was an expert flute player; he seldom ventured anywhere without his flute. Also, Henry spoke, at least, four languages, was an amateur botanist, and collector of books. He had so many books that he turned an abandoned military hospital into a spectacular library filled with books about nature, theology, poems, old English stories, and many other volumes. Henry was remarkable in another way, too. He did all of these things while suffering chronic asthma and other related respiratory illnesses like bronchitis.

Eventually, due in part to his illness and the gradual decline of his congregation due to an exodus to other congregations as nearby towns developed, he began to spend more time in the warmer climates of France and Italy. In 1847, he died in Nice, France, at the age of fifty-four. His famous hymn ***Abide with Me*** was sung at his funeral.

(References: *Henry Frances Lyte and the Story of Abide with Me,* 1957, Henry James Garland; *Henry Francis Lyte,* Oxford Dictionary of National Biography, online edition. Retrieved 2015; *Our Hymn Writers and Their Hymns*, 2005, Faith Cook)

Marshall, Jane

Jane was born in 1924 in Dallas, Texas, where she has lived her entire life. She was a star student with a gift for writing and music that was manifest at an early age. She was a brilliant student in elementary and high school, and she was involved in many musical programs and events.

After high school, Jane attended Southern Methodist University where she received a Bachelor of Arts degree in music. Her professors encouraged her to pursue a master's degree in music and she did, earning her graduate degree a couple of years later.

After receiving her college degrees, she worked in several United Methodist churches in Texas. Jane also taught music in public schools and at the university level. In addition to being a gifted teacher, Jane also became a composer of choral music, a hymnist, and poet.

She has been a member of the Meadows School of the Arts theory faculty and the Sacred Music graduate faculty at Perkins School of Theology at Southern Methodist University for several years. She has written several hymns and has served on numerous editorial committees that reviewed and edited hymnbooks. Jane has been honored twice by the Southern Baptist Musicians Conference and more recently by the Fellowship of United Methodist

Musicians for her contributions to church music. She is the author of ***Grace, Noted,*** which is a collection of homilies, essays, and hymns. Jane's hymn ***Sometimes a Light*** has been sung by several recording artists.

She became interested in *Psalms* and began composing hymns based on *Psalms*. Jane published a book titled ***Psalms Together*** that included hymns such as ***A Psalm of Peace; Shout to the Lord,*** and others. She has written over 200 hymns and choral works, but arguably her most famous are ***Awake, My Heart; He Comes to Us*** and ***My Eternal King.***

Jane continues to write from her home in Dallas, Texas.

(References: *The Works of Jane Marshall,* Hymnary.org. Retrieved 2014; *Jane Marshall,* UMCdiscipleship.org. Retrieved 2014; *Writer Biographies,* St. Francis de Sales Parish, 2012; *I Remember Tom Landry,* Denne Freeman and Jaime Aron, 2001)

Martin, Civilla Durfee

Civilla was born in Nova Scotia, Canada in 1866. Civilla's childhood was filled with family activities, and she was always considered to be a very intelligent and happy young girl who wanted to be a teacher.

After attending college, she taught for several years in nearby schools. At a young age, she married John F. Geddes, who was a minister in Jordan Falls Methodist Church in Nova Scotia. That marriage ended and she later met and married an American evangelist and Bible scholar, Walter Martin. Walter was a traveling evangelist, frequently in demand. Civilla traveled with him until her poor health required her to limit her travel. While at home, she enjoyed reading and writing. She especially liked poetry, and she found that she had a talent for writing poems. Her interest in music and her talent for poetry combined to create hymns. Civilla produced several hundred poems and hymns.

Her first published hymn was in 1904, ***God Will Take Care of You.*** It became widely used in churches, but people did not know that it was her work, because she used "C. D." rather than her full name and instead of using her husband's name. The hymn became so famous and well known that soon it was revealed that Civilla was the author. Even though that hymn was widely popular, her hymn ***His Eye is on the Sparrow*** made her famous around the world. Civilla said that the hymn was inspired by the 10th chapter of *Matthew*. When describing how she wrote the most famous hymn, Civilla said, "Early in the spring of 1905, my husband and I were sojourning in Elmira, New York. We contracted a deep friendship for a couple by the name of Mr. and Mrs. Doolittle—true saints of God. Mrs. Doolittle had been bedridden for nigh twenty years. Her husband was an incurable cripple who had to propel himself to and from his business in a wheelchair. Despite their afflictions, they lived happy Christian lives, bringing inspiration and comfort to all who knew them. One day while we were visiting with the Doolittle family my husband commented on their bright hopefulness and asked them for the secret of it. Mrs. Doolittle's reply was simple: 'His eye is on the sparrow, and I know He watches me.' The beauty of this simple expression of boundless faith gripped the hearts and fired the imagination of Dr. Martin and me. The hymn 'His Eye Is on the Sparrow' was the outcome of that experience." Today, the hymn remains a staple of worship services.

After her husband died in 1935, Civilla moved to Atlanta, Georgia and lived a quiet and uneventful life. Many of her friends and church members at the First Christian Church of Atlanta, where she attended for over twenty-nine years, did not know that she wrote ***His Eye is on the Sparrow***. She remained humble and grateful for God's gifts and the spiritual insight that led to the creation of the beloved hymn.

Civilla died in Atlanta in 1948 at the age of eighty-two. She is buried in one of Atlanta's most famous cemeteries, Westview Cemetery, and is for the most part largely forgotten as the creator of one of the most famous hymns ever written.

(References: *Great Christian Hymn Writers*, 1997, Jane Smith and Betty Carlson; *Civilla Durfee. Martin*, CyberHymnal.org. Retrieved 2015; Civilla D. Martin, Hymnary.org. Retrieved 2015)

Martin, George Currie

George was born in 1865 in Portobello, Scotland (Portobello is a coastal suburb of Edinburgh that was once a famous beach resort; it is located three miles to the east of the city facing the Firth of Forth, in eastern central Scotland.). Portobello was a resort town during most of the 19th century, primarily for residents of Edinburgh, Scotland. George's father was a merchant and his siblings worked at various jobs in the store.

His father wanted him to become a solicitor, so he emphasized education all through George's youth. George worked hard and was a diligent student. His interests ranged from archaeology to music. After secondary school, George enrolled in George Watson's College in Edinburgh. He was an excellent student who made friends easily and his academic work was stellar. George was such a creative and perceptive thinker his professors encouraged him to pursue philosophy instead of law. Although George considered a philosophy degree he also knew he had to earn a living and philosophy teaching positions were difficult to find. He turned to theology because of his spiritual strength, the possibility of a career, and because of the philosophical side of theology. George determined that he would enjoy being a minister.

He entered the University of Edinburgh to study theology and received a bachelor's degree and later he earned a Master of Divinity degree at Marburg University. George also attended New College in London, England. After he completed his education, he was ordained to the Congregational ministry in Nairn, Scotland. He became the pastor there and a few years later accepted a position as co-pastor at Reigate, Surrey, Scotland, and within eighteen months became the full-time pastor.

George enjoyed the church life but he also missed the university life and the intellectual stimulation. After six years at Reigate, George excitedly accepted a position as Professor of New Testament Language and Patristics (the study of early Christian writers) at United College in Bradford, England and at Lancashire College in Manchester, England. His scholarly work and publications became well-known and respected and led to his appointment as Foreign Secretary of the London Missionary Society (a non-denominational missionary society formed by Evangelical Anglicans and Congregationalist with missions primarily in Africa and the South Pacific islands—it became the Council for World Mission) for over three years. After leaving the London Missionary Society he was a lecturer at the National Adult School Union for over eighteen years. Even in retirement he kept writing, teaching and traveling. He was on a trip to Morlaix, Brittany, France when he died in 1937 at the age of eighty-two.

George was a prolific writer of poems, hymns, and scholarly work. Arguably his most enduring publication is his book ***Hymns, Tunes, and Carols,*** which is still in print, and his hymns, such as ***Your Words to Me are Life and Health,*** are still being sung in churches across the world.

(References: *George Currie Martin,* The Canterbury Dictionary of Hymnology. Retrieved 2013; *George Currie Martin,* Catalogue of the General Theological Library. Retrieved 2013; *George C. Martin,* The New Schaff-Herzog Encyclopedia of Religious-Hymns, 1910, Johann Jakob Herzog, Albert Hauck, and Samuel Macauley Jackson)

Martinez, Nicolas

Nicolas was born in 1925 in Argentina. His family worked hard and supported each other through difficult times. They were strongly religious and devoted to worship.

Nicolas was raised as a Roman Catholic throughout his childhood and into his adolescent years. However, another family in his community invited Nicolas to attend Evangelical worship services. He enjoyed the sermons and the Sunday school classes, but he especially liked the music. Nicolas converted to Evangelical Christianity at age sixteen. It was during this time that he considered being a minister. He loved attending church, and the ministers were role models for him. With the assistance of the ministers, Nicolas studied for the ministry after school each day. He impressed everyone with his dedication to his studies and spiritual development.

In 1948, he was ordained as a minister in the Disciples of Christ and served churches in Argentina and Paraguay. Nicolas enjoyed music in his churches, where he often augmented the message of his sermon with hymn selections, some of which he wrote. His hymn ***Christ is Risen*** is one of the most frequently sung hymns at Easter services across the Christian world. It has been translated into over fifty languages. Nicolas wrote several versions of the hymn, as he struggled to find the right message of the resurrection. Finally, he decided that Christ would enjoy the simple message that life is everlasting for those who worship God through Jesus Christ, and not even death can break that bond and promise.

Nicolas continued his ministry work for several years, even after he officially retired. His messages and sermons were positive and supportive, and they always carried a tone of hope and resurrection. Nicolas died in 1999 at the age of seventy-four.

(References: *Nicolas Martinez,* Ancestry.com. Retrieved 2015; *Nicolas Martinez,* hymntime.com. Retrieved 2015)

Mason North, Frank

Frank was born in 1850 in New York City into a middle-class family that valued education and devotion to family.

He was an active young boy who was often too busy playing outside to take studying seriously. However, when he entered high school he discovered his intellect matched or exceeded his classmates. Frank's teachers encouraged him to be a more conscientious student because they all recognized his intellectual and academic potential. With fresh confidence, he took school seriously and became a good student.

After secondary school, Frank entered Wesleyan University where he struggled during his freshman year, especially as he tried to balance academic rigor with being away from home. However, each year he grew more confident and began to excel academically; plus, he became more comfortable socially. Frank developed an interest in theology during his junior and senior years in college. He graduated from Wesleyan University at the age of twenty-two and immediately entered the ministry of the Methodist Episcopal Church the same year.

Over the course of the next twenty years, he ministered at churches located in Connecticut, Florida, and New York. While serving as a minister in New York, he was also the Secretary of the Church Extension and Missionary Society of New York City. It was during that time that he edited *The Christian City* magazine. Also, for four years Frank was the President of the Federal Council of Churches of Christ. In this capacity, he supervised a number of urban parishes, immigrant congregations, and inter-racial centers, including the Church of All Nations. Frank also directed the National City Evangelical Union and became the corresponding secretary of the Board of Foreign Missions for twelve years. Frank was a delegate to several General Conferences (1908, 1916, 1920, 1924, 1928), the World Missionary Conference (1910), the Methodist Committee on Unification (1920-1928) and the International Mission Council (1921-1928). In his capacity with the International Mission Council, he contributed significantly to relief work during World War I and for his efforts he was decorated by the French and Greek governments.

Frank was not a prolific writer of hymns; he wrote about two dozen, but he will be forever known for his hymn ***Where Cross the Crowded Ways of Life*** which he wrote to convey the message that no matter how difficult or busy life becomes, Christ is always there.

Frank continued his ministry even into retirement. He was a beloved member of his community and greatly admired by his colleagues. After a brief illness, he died in 1935 at the age of eighty-five while living in Madison, New Jersey.

(References: *Guide to the Frank Mason North Papers*, The General Commission on Archives and History, 2012, Drew University; *Frank Mason North*, Hymnology.org. Retrieved 2015)

Matheson, George

George was born in 1842 in Glasgow, Scotland. He was the oldest of eight children. His father was a successful merchant. George wanted to be a merchant like his father, but his father had a different goal for him. He recognized George's intellect and keen insight. He also thought that George's weak eyesight might cause him problems in the merchant world, so he encouraged him to pursue academic studies.

George's academic gifts became apparent when he attended Glasgow Academy where he amazed his teachers with his incredible intellect and insight. After completing the academy, he enrolled in the University of Glasgow. Even though his vision grew weaker he still excelled in all academic work and wrote many excellent papers and research works. George graduated first in the classics, philosophy, and logic. He also mastered Greek, Latin, and Hebrew.

Despite his academic successes and the attention that he was earning for his work, George knew that his time was running out because he was losing his eyesight. By the time he turned twenty years old, George was blind. However, with encouragement from his family and friends, he was determined to become a minister. His sisters encouraged him and helped him when they could.

In that era, it was unusual for a major university to accept a blind person into graduate studies, but George was accepted into the University of Edinburgh where he majored in theology. George had to make many adjustments and learn and recite a lot of material, but not only did he successfully complete his work at Edinburgh, he was conferred the degree of Doctor of Divinity. He received a standing ovation at the graduation ceremony.

George was ordained a minister in the Church of Scotland. His first ministry was on the Argyll Coast at Innellan. George loved his time there, and the congregation adored him. He was very active in the community and was always available to assist individuals and families. Frequently visitors to the church failed to recognize that George was blind because he would memorize his sermons and when he came to a part of the sermon that required reference to the Bible he would quote the Bible verbatim. He remained at Innellan for eighteen years, before leaving to take the ministry at St. Bernard Parish Church in Edinburgh. George ministered at St. Bernard for thirteen years. It was during those years at St. Bernard that his reputation as a minister and writer spread across the country and then into France and other parts of Europe. George was offered several positions as a minister and even more as a professor. He was a Baird lecturer and a St. Giles lecturer, and was invited to lecture at Gifford University, but his health did not allow him to accept that offer.

George, because of his gift as a minister and due to his scholarly work, was elected a Fellow of the Royal Society of Edinburgh. Queen Victoria heard about George and sent people to listen to his sermons. They gave her such glowing reports she invited him to preach at Balmoral Castle (a vacation site of Queen Victoria). Queen Victoria was so impressed with George's sermon on Job she had it published.

George wrote several books that were well received by the public and praised by scholars. The most prominent were ***Aids to the Study of German Theology***; ***Can the Old Faith Live with the New***, and ***The Growth of the Spirit of Christianity from the First Century to the Dawn of the Lutheran Era***. George did not compose many hymns, but one that he did create has remained popular in hymnals, ***O Love That Wilt Not Let Me Go***. George always said that it was the divine inspiration that delivered that hymn. He said, "My hymn was composed in the manse [a house occupied by a Presbyterian minister] of Innellan [Argyllshire, Scotland] on the evening of the 6th of June, 1882, when I was forty years of age. I was alone in the manse at that time. It was the night of my sister's marriage, and the rest of the family were staying overnight in Glasgow. Something happened to me, which was known only to myself, and which caused me the most severe mental suffering. The hymn was the fruit of that suffering. It was the quickest bit of work I ever did in my life. I had the impression of having it dictated to me by some inward voice rather than of working it out myself. I am quite sure that the whole work was completed in five minutes and equally sure that it never received at my hands any retouching or correction. I have no natural gift of rhythm. All the other verses I have ever written are manufactured articles; this came like a dayspring from on high."

George continued to be active even though his health was uneven. In Edinburgh, he died unexpectedly of a stroke in 1906 when he was sixty-four years old. Thousands attended the funeral and many speakers noted George's intellect, his strong beliefs and spirit, his love of mankind, and his unfailing joyfulness.

(References: *The Gospel in Hymns*, 1950, Albert Bailey; *Hymnal Companion to the Lutheran Book of Worship*, 1981, Marilyn Kay Stulken; *The Blind Seer: George Matheson*, 1959, John Crew Tyler)

McAfee, Cleland Boyd

Cleland was born in 1866 in Ashley, Missouri. He was one of five children of John McAfee who was the founder of Park College in Parkville, Maryland, where he served as president for fifteen years.

Cleland was greatly influenced by his father's love of education and learning. Cleland aspired at a very young age to learn music and the classics. He excelled in his academic work and when he completed secondary school he followed his dream and the family's expectation and enrolled in Park College. At Park, he was a serious student and he participated in several activities and events, including most music programs. Cleland was interested in theology and music.

He entered the Union Theological Seminary in New York after graduating from Park College with honors. Upon completing seminary and being ordained he served as a professor of philosophy, choir director, pastor and dean of Park College until 1901. Thereafter, Cleland was a minister in Chicago and later in Brooklyn. While in Chicago, he was a professor of theology at the McCormick Theological Seminary for eighteen years. Cleland was also a strong supporter of missionary work and often recruited people to serve as missionaries. He served as director of the Presbyterian Board of Foreign Missions for six years.

Throughout his career as a minister, he also wrote hymns. He is world famous for the stirring hymn ***Near to the Heart of God,*** a powerful hymn that is a mainstay in all Christian hymnals and is considered one of the most popular hymns of all time. Cleland wrote the hymn after the death of two infant nieces who died close together of diphtheria. His daughter wrote a book about her father, and in the book, she wrote about the circumstances of the deaths and Cleland's subsequent composition of the famous hymn: "The family and town were stricken with grief. My father often told us how he sat long and late thinking of what could be said in word and song on the coming Sunday. So he wrote the little song. The choir learned it at the regular Saturday night rehearsal, and afterward they went to Howard McAfee's home and sang it as they stood under the sky outside the darkened, quarantined house. It was sung again on Sunday morning at the communion service. The hymn was first included in ***The Choir Leader,*** in October 1903."

Cleland also composed several other hymns and published ***The Greatest English Classic: A Study of the King James Version of the Bible.*** One of his three daughters, Mildred, became the president of Wellesley College and the first director of the Women Accepted for Volunteer Emergency Service (the famous Navy WAVES of World War II).

Cleland died in 1944 at the age of seventy-eight in Asheville, North Carolina.

(References: *The Presbyterian Hymnal Companion,* 1993, LindaJo McKim; *Cleland Boyd McAfee,* Liberty University. Retrieved 2014; *Hymns of the Spirit,* 2009, Jimi Hall)

Merrick, Daniel

Daniel was born in Bloomington, Illinois in 1926. His family noticed Daniel's intellectual capabilities when he was very young. He also had a good sense of humor and was charming to adults and admired by his friends.

Daniel thrived in elementary and secondary school, displaying a keen intellect and an equally engaging personality and creativity. After secondary school, Daniel attended Phillips University in Oklahoma where he earned a Bachelor of Arts degree. Daniel was interested in philosophy and theology so he enrolled at the Phillips Theological Seminary where he received a Bachelor of Divinity degree. After his ordination, he was a minister in several churches, including churches in Illinois, Milwaukee, and the Panama Canal Zone.

Daniel quickly developed a widespread reputation for powerfully emotional sermons. Daniel often used his famous story-telling abilities during sermons to help people more easily understand the lessons and points of his sermons.

Daniel also had a talent for writing poems and hymns. He used his love of reading and travel and his study of theology and the Bible to find inspiration for his hymns. He won many awards for his hymns. He received his first award when he was a young minister. In 1967 his famous hymn ***O God Whose Love Compels Us*** was the winning entry at the American Baptist Convention. Daniel's hymns have been and are still included in almost every hymnal in the Christian world. He composed over 1,100 hymns during his fifty plus years of writing. He also wrote numerous poems.

Daniel received numerous awards. Phillips University named him a Distinguished Alumni for his contributions to society. He remained active until his death in 2004 in Illinois at the age of seventy-eight. His obituary noted: "Dan possessed a sense of curiosity, loving to explore ideas as well as places; he loved to read and travel. His great interest in genealogy resulted in entertaining celebrations of his Welsh heritage. Dan enjoyed family visits, especially the time spent with his grandchildren and great-grandchildren, telling them stories and encouraging their interests. His sense of humor and special proclamations and celebrations made family events very special."

(References: *Daniel B. Merrick,* The Dictionary of North American Hymnology. Retrieved 2013; *Daniel Merrick,* Phillips University Alumni Association Archives. Retrieved 2013; *New Honors for His Name,* 2002, Daniel B. Merrick)

Merrill, William

William was born in 1867 in Orange, New Jersey but he was raised in Newburyport, Massachusetts for many years before the family settled in New Brunswick, New Jersey. William's parents were of English descent, were well educated and expected the same for their children.

William was a gifted student in every elementary grade and throughout secondary school. William was groomed by his parents to enter the ministry, and that suited him because of his strong interest in theology and humanitarian causes. He was raised in the era after the Civil War and he grew up hearing about slavery, emancipation, reconciliation, reconstruction, and injured and missing veterans of the war. He was a young witness to a country trying to reunite and heal war wounds. This was a time of spiritual recovery for individuals, families, and churches.

William enrolled in Rutgers University at age seventeen and by the age of twenty-three he had earned both a Bachelor of Divinity and a Master of Divinity degree. He also received a Bachelor of Divinity degree from the Union Theological Seminary in New York City. Later, William earned a Doctor of Divinity degree from Rutgers University. After his ordination, he became the pastor of the Trinity Presbyterian Church in Chestnut Hill, Pennsylvania.

William's sermons and his gift for writing hymns evolved over time, but he was especially productive while at Trinity Presbyterian Church. He left there to accept a position as pastor of the Sixth Presbyterian Church in Chicago for a short period of time before becoming the pastor of the Brick Presbyterian Church in New York City. William served as pastor there for over twenty-five years, until the church merged with the Park Avenue Church; thereafter he was pastor emeritus for several years.

During his career, William was considered one of the most well-known and influential church leaders in the United States. He was a strong advocate of the pacifist philosophy and beliefs. William was named the first President of Church Peace Union that advocated pacifism. Its members included the clergy, politicians, and academics.

William's sermons were captivating and soothing to a nation that was trying to heal. Famous people frequently attended his church to hear his powerful sermons and to hear the hymns he wrote. He was a prolific writer, but he is probably most remembered for his hymn ***Rise Up, O Men of God*** and for his legendary sermon on peace called ***The Making of Peace***—widely held as one of the greatest sermons in American history. William's writings, hymns, and sermons were widely printed and quoted. His most frequently noted quote is, "There is nothing in the world so much like prayer as music." William lived until 1954 when he died at the age of eighty-seven while living in New York City.

(Reference: *William P. Merrill,* Cyberhymnal.org. Retrieved 2014; *William P. Merrill,* hymntime.com. Retrieved 2015; *William P. Merrill,* www.carnegiecouncil.org. Retrieved 2015; *The Rev. William P. Merrill,* The New York Times Archive. Retrieved 2014)

Miles, Charles Austin

Charles was born in 1868 in Lakehurst, New Jersey.

At an early age, Charles loved music and showed a talent for playing and writing music. He participated in all musical activities in his church and local school. Charles was fascinated with the organ and began learning to play it when he was only six years old, and he learned very quickly. By the time he was ten years old he occasionally played the organ during church services, and he had his first music-related job at age twelve when he played the organ at a funeral. Even though he contemplated a life as a musician, a well-meaning aunt convinced Charles that a career in music would not lead to a steady career and income, so she convinced him to become a pharmacist after he completed high school. Convinced that his aunt was right, Charles enrolled at the Philadelphia College of Pharmacy and was a model student. He worked hard and excelled in the academically challenging courses, but he spent his spare time writing music.

Charles graduated at age twenty-one and became a pharmacist in Camden, New Jersey. However, during his career as a pharmacist, he longed for the music world, so he kept writing music and played music at every opportunity—in churches and at community events. Charles wanted to learn more about music, so he enrolled in music classes at the University of Pennsylvania. His wife, Bertha, encouraged Charles to write and play music since that was his beloved pastime, but she also encouraged him to consider selling his music to publishers.

Even though he was hesitant to do so, Charles offered four hymns to the Hall-Mack Publishing Company. To his surprise, the company offered to purchase them for $2.50 each. After working as a pharmacist for ten years, Charles walked away from his job and started a career as a song and hymn writer. He sold more hymns to Hall-Mack Publishing Company, and so impressed the leadership of the company that they hired him. Soon thereafter and for the next thirty-seven years, Charles served as editor and general manager of the company. He also served as his church's music director.

Charles was a prolific writer of songs and hymns. Some people estimate that he wrote an incredibly large number of hymns, believed to be as many as 30,000. Without a doubt, his most famous hymn, a hymn with everlasting popularity was ***In the Garden***. One verse of the hymn has arguably been sung and quoted as often as any hymn ever written: "And He walks with me, and He talks with me, And He tells me I am His own."

Charles tells the story of how ***In the Garden*** was created. He was an amateur photographer who developed his own film in a makeshift darkroom he created in his home's dark and damp basement. Charles had several pictures that he was developing one day and he was somewhat annoyed because the development process was taking a long time and there was a church function that he wanted to attend. As he sat somewhat impatiently in the dark room waiting for the developing process to finish, he had a profoundly inspiring and incredibly clear vision of Mary Magdalene looking in the tomb for Jesus, and not finding him there she walked into a garden and heard him clearly call her name. From that point, the words to ***In the Garden*** flowed in his mind so quickly and clearly he feared he would not be fast enough writing them down to capture this inspiration. Fortunately for all of us, Charles remembered the words and composed the famous hymn. Later that same year, 1912, the hymn was published. It soon became well-known; the popularity of the hymn soared far beyond Charles' wildest dreams. The famous evangelist, Billy Sunday, adopted the hymn as his theme song in the 1950s. Pop singer Perry Como added to the hymn's popularity when he recorded it in 1951. Roy Rogers and Dale Evans, Tennessee Ernie Ford, Doris Day, Elvis Presley, Willie Nelson and many others performed the hymn on albums and in concerts. It is estimated that the hymn has been printed over 3 million times; however, Charles never made money from the hymn. He sold the hymn rights to Halls-Mack Publishing Company for four dollars.

Charles' incredibly creative mind and spiritual heart continued to produce hymns until he died in 1946 in Philadelphia at the age of seventy-eight. His hymn ***In the Garden*** was performed during his funeral service.

(References: *I Have Been Brought to This Place,* 2012, Gary A. Rath; *The Cambridge Companion to Evangelical Theology,* 2007, Timothy Larsen; *The National and Religious Song Reader,* 1996, William Emmett Studwell; *Separate and Strong,* 2012, Shawn McCammon)

Miller, Sy and Jackson, Jill

Sy was born in 1908 in New York. He was a gifted musician at a young age and played in many church events, community events, and school events. After secondary school, he traveled to California to work in the movie business. His talent was recognized and he became a Hollywood writer and composer.

Jill was born in 1913 in Lawrence, Missouri and endured a tragic and traumatic childhood. Her mother died when Jill was only three years old; additionally, Jill was abused and neglected, as were her three older siblings. She faced more traumatic events when one of her brothers died from a fireworks accident when he was young. Eventually, Jill and her sister became wards of the state and lived as foster children for several years.

Jill attended Northeast High School in Kansas City and then a community college. She made good grades and was active in the college's drama club activities. This led to a desire to become an actress, so she moved to Hollywood on her own without any resources or an agent. Fortunately, in those days, young aspiring actresses could live at the Studio Club, a safe and secure home for young ladies trying to land jobs in the entertainment industry. She starred in a few westerns and a serial but gave up her career to marry Felix Jackson, a writer, and director. Jill was happy in the marriage and was shocked and broken-hearted when Felix suddenly left her and later divorced her without ever telling her why. She was so depressed that she attempted suicide.

Still suffering a deep depression from the breakup, she went back to work acting. She met and married Sy, who encouraged Jill to develop her writing talent because he saw that ability in her. She wrote articles for magazines and children's stories. When she shared the story of her suicide attempt with Sy and her discovery of God's forgiveness he encouraged her to write about it. He worked with her and together they produced a song that for decades was one of the most performed songs in the world, ***Let There Be Peace on Earth.*** Almost every major recording artist recorded it. It won several awards, including the George Washington Honor Medal by the Freedom Foundation at Valley Forge for "Outstanding achievement in helping to bring about a better understanding of the American Way of Life."

Sy and Jill lived and worked together with great respect and love for each other for many years. Jill survived and recovered from many tragic events and heartbreaks in her life, but she suffered another heartbreak when Sy passed away after a brief illness on August 17, 1971, at the age of sixty-three. However, with the support of prayer, faith, and friends, Jill continued her work until her death in Hawaii in 1995 at the age of eighty-two.

(References: Jill Jackson *Janleemusic.com*. 2015; *Lettherebepeace.com*. Retrieved 2015; *Let There Be Peace*, 2009, Michael Hawn, UMC. Retrieved 2015)

Monsell, John Samuel Bewley

John was born in 1811 in St. Columb's, Londonderry, England. John's family was well-known throughout England because his father, Thomas, was the Archdeacon of Derry. John and his siblings were raised in a disciplined household where faith and family ruled everything, and where daily worship was required and expected.

John was a quiet and studious child who enjoyed reading and music. It was expected that he would follow his father's path into theology and a career as a priest. John seldom questioned the expectation. His education from childhood through elementary and secondary school was aimed to that end.

John entered Trinity College in Dublin where he received a Bachelor of Arts degree at age twenty-one. Shortly after graduating from Trinity he was ordained a deacon and a few months later ordained as a priest. His first assignment was as chaplain for the famous Bishop Mant in the combined dioceses of Down, Connor, and Dromore. There his reputation grew. He became known as a gifted theologian and priest whose sermons were of the highest organization and spirit.

John found both joy and sorrow in his private life. He was joyfully married but his eldest son died during the Crimean War in a shipwreck off the coast of Italy, and his eldest daughter died from an infection when she was only in her twenties. Despite his personal losses, John's professional life continued to expand. He became the Curacy of Templemore for two years and then the Chaplain of Chapel of Ease at St. Augustine for almost three years. John then moved to Belfast for the position as Chaplain of Magdalene College. He left Magdalene College to become the Rector of Donaghy for one year before becoming Rector of Ramoan in the Diocese of Connor. There he met and started an on-going correspondence with the legendary William Gladstone (served as Prime Minister of England four times). After six years at Ramoan, he accepted a position as Vicar of Egham in Windsor and remained there for over seventeen years before becoming the Rector of St. Nicolas Church of Guildford. John's professional reputation and his dedication to meet the needs of his community advanced his name all the way to the Royal family. After meeting with her, he became the Chaplain to Queen Victoria.

John wrote tirelessly even while he was extraordinarily busy with his responsibilities. He published over 300 poems with many of them becoming hymns. His works included ***Hymns and Miscellaneous Poems****;* ***Parish Musings or Devotional Poems****;* ***Spiritual Songs for the Sundays and Holy Days throughout the Year****;* ***His Presence, Not His Memory****;* ***Hymns of Love and Praise for the Church's Year*** and many others.

John's influence extended beyond his sermons and his legacy is more than his service and hymns. He was also responsible for building the Ballycastle Church, the Englefield Green Church, and the St. Nicolas Church. In fact, it was his dedication to these efforts that cost him his life, for while inspecting the St. Nicolas Church he lost his balance and fell from the roof. He sustained serious injuries that led to his death in 1875 at the age of sixty-four. John was buried in the Guilford Cemetery in Surrey, England.

Of his many hymns, John is most remembered for ***God is Love****;* ***God of That Glorious Gift of Grace****,* and ***Holy Offerings, Rich and Rare****.*

(References: *John Samuel Bewley Monsell,* Dictionary of National Biography. Retrieved 2014; *John S.B. Monsell,* Dictionary of

Hymnology, 1907, John Julian; *The Biography of J.S.B. Monsell*, Stem Publishing Company. Retrieved 2014)

Moody, Dwight

Dwight was born to a large family in Northfield, Massachusetts, in 1837. He had six siblings, five brothers, and one sister. His father died at age forty-one, leaving Dwight's mother to raise the seven children on her own. She tried in vain to support the family, but she often could not find work and when she did the work was temporary and offered minimal wages. Finally, in desperation, the children were sent out to find other places to live. Dwight was determined to keep the children together, so he looked for work and housing for all of the children. Dwight and his siblings found room and board at a factory where they had to work. They received no money for a full day of work; their compensation for working was cornmeal, porridge, and milk three times a day. Even during those difficult times, Dwight made sure that his siblings attended church with him.

When Dwight turned seventeen, he moved to Boston to work in his uncle's shoe store. He did not want to leave his siblings behind, but this opportunity could turn his life around and offer some support for his siblings. Dwight's uncle insisted that in return for providing him a place to live and work, Dwight would attend the Congregational Church of Mount Vernon where Dr. Edward Norris Kirk served as the pastor. Dwight was captivated by Dr. Kirk's sermons, and he felt a connection to him. Dwight's uncle introduced him to Dr. Kirk and a mentor relationship began that influenced Dwight's life. Dwight's interaction with Dr. Kirk sparked the start of his career as an evangelist.

After studying under Dr. Kirk's supervision, Dwight started a career as a revival minister. He became well-known for his sermons that attracted hundreds of people. Dwight traveled the country spreading the inspiration of the word of God. By his own admission to friends, during the quiet moments of self-reflection, he began to question if his faith was as strong as it once felt. At the height of his self-doubt, he was at an evangelistic meeting in Boston sharing the word of God while coping with those troubling thoughts in the back of his mind. He did not think he was at his best that evening, but during the meeting, a young man stood up and said, "I am not quite sure that God will save me and forgive my sins, but I'm going to trust, and I'm going to obey." A spark of inspiration was ignited inside Dwight by a young man's proclamation to trust and obey. Dwight asked the music leader, Daniel Towner, if he heard what the young man said. Daniel acknowledged that he did and he noted that it was such a powerful moment that he wrote down what the young man said verbatim. On the way home that evening, Dwight kept repeating "trust and obey" to himself. It was a spiritual reawakening for Dwight at a time in his life when it was sorely needed. In the meantime, Daniel wrote a letter to his friend, John Sammis, recounting that evening and including the words the young man spoke about trusting and obeying. He asked John to put the words to music. John transformed those words into a hymn chorus: "Trust and obey, for there's no other way to be happy in Jesus, but to trust and obey." John added five stanzas to go with the chorus, and he sent them to Daniel, who composed the tune that we still sing today, ***Trust and Obey***. The heartfelt words of that anonymous young man inspired an evangelist to renew his commitment to God and with his friend, John, to write powerful lyrics and music that for almost 150 years have influenced millions of people.

Dwight's influence extended far beyond hymns and sermons. He was keenly interested in educating children in a Christian environment, and he noted the lack of educational opportunities for girls. In response to those concerns, he founded a school for girls, the Moody Bible Institute, and he founded Moody Publishers as a means to fund the school and at the same time publish noteworthy Christian books for educational purposes. Both were very successful and remain well-known and respected institutions. The Moody Bible Institute has campuses in Spokane, Washington, and Chicago, Illinois.

After an extremely full and productive life that included world travel and giving sermons to as many as 15,000 people in venues such as the Botanic Gardens Palace in England, he returned to America and found audiences with as many as 20,000 anxiously waiting to hear his sermons. Dwight never seemed to slow down and relax; he felt like there was too much to do to take time for himself. Perhaps that is why his health declined—he worked himself to death out of dedication to helping others find their way to Christ. Dwight died of congestive heart failure at the relatively young age of sixty-two in Northfield, Massachusetts in 1899. It's also important to note that Dwight never forgot his siblings; they joined in his success.

(References: *The Shorter Life of D.L. Moody*, 1900, Paul D. Moody; *A Passion for Souls: The Life of D.L. Moody*, 1997, L.W. Dorsett; *Dwight L. Moody: American Evangelist 1837-1899*, 1969, J.F. Findlay)

Moore, Thomas

Thomas was born in 1779 in Dublin, Ireland. His father owned a grocery store and the family lived above it on busy Aungier Street. Thomas was the oldest of three children. He had two younger sisters that he adored, and they, in turn, adored him.

At an early age and throughout his childhood Thomas had the opportunity to meet a lot of people coming and going in the grocery store. He loved to entertain them with music, stories, and plays that he created on his own. Thomas showed musical and creative talent at a very young age and he enjoyed all types of music and plays. He and his friends participated in several plays in the school and in the city; almost all were musical plays. The response from the audiences gave him the inspiration to become an actor. However, his parents insisted on Thomas receiving a good education because his mother aimed for Thomas to become a lawyer.

Thomas attended English Grammar School and later a secondary school where he excelled academically. He enrolled in Trinity College to prepare for a career in law. He did not excel in college, however, primarily because of so many distractions, both inside the college and in the turbulent world outside the college. The French Revolution had broken out and there was growing sentiment of a possible revolution in Ireland, too. Thomas found all of this a distraction to studying, especially since many of his friends at the college were trying to ferment revolution. Despite the distractions, Thomas earned a Bachelor of Arts degree at Trinity College, but the revolutionary friends he made at the college influenced him, such as Edward Hudson.

At age twenty, Thomas moved to London, England to study law at Middle Temple College. There he enjoyed the busy city but he barely had enough money to survive. Were it not for his sister's friend, Barbara Chichester, who helped with food and clothes, Thomas may have been forced to return home. He completed his legal studies and accepted an appointment as registrar to the Admiralty in Bermuda. However, he only stayed a few months because he became quickly and completely bored with the monotonous duties he performed each day. Although he was unhappy there, he loved the beauty of the island which did inspire him to write poetry about Bermuda, such as his poem ***Ode to Nea,*** which became well-known.

Within three months after moving to Bermuda, he relocated to Norfolk, Virginia. From there he traveled throughout the United States and even into parts of Canada. Thomas did not like what he saw. He thought the politicians he met, including Andrew Jackson, were primitive of mind and philosophy and unaware of the value of all kinds of different people. He hated everything related to slavery. While visiting Canada he wrote the famous ***Canadian Boat Song*** while staying at Sainte-Anne-de-Bellevue.

After a couple of years of traveling, he returned home to Ireland. Shortly after returning home, Thomas published his book ***Epistles, Odes, and Other Poems***. Thomas soon thereafter abandoned legal work and became a poet, balladeer, singer, writer, and critic. He became famous for publications such as ***The Harp That Once Through Tara's Halls***; ***Believe Me***; ***If All Those Endearing Young Charms***, and many others. ***His Irish Melodies*** became an international hit and made him wildly popular. It contained songs such as ***The Minstrel Boy; The Last Rose of Summer; Oft in the Stilly Night; Farewell! But Whenever You Welcome the Hours The Minstrel Boy***.

Thomas' operatic creations with Michael Kelly and Charles Edward Horn became enormously popular throughout Great Britain and Europe. Thomas starred in musicals and even in comedies that were well-received by audiences from around the world. He had a natural talent for acting and his comedic roles in plays such as ***The Rivals*** and ***The Castle of Andalusia*** broadened his already considerable reputation. Despite his success, Thomas' lavish lifestyle and a debt attributed to a mistake he made while working in Bermuda left him penniless. Many friends offered him financial assistance but he refused to accept any money or loans. He was forced to leave Great Britain due to mounting debts.

Thomas toured Europe and his performances were very successful and lucrative. He lived in Paris for three years. In 1822, after he finally paid off all of his debts, he returned to England. In his travels, he met Lord Byron. They developed a close friendship. In fact, Thomas was asked by Byron to publish his biography after his death, but Lord Byron also had a special request for Thomas; he wanted him to destroy all of his records and diaries because they were potentially scandalous. Thomas fulfilled his friend's request and published the ***Letters and Journals of Lord Byron with Notices of His Life*** six years after Lord Byron's death. The book caused a sensation and the international reaction was unanimously positive.

As he grew older, Thomas' productivity waned and he basically lived on a state pension after suffering a stroke. His beloved wife cared for him until his death in 1852 at the age of seventy-three in Wiltshire, England. It is important to note that Thomas faced numerous personal tragedies including the loss of all five children at different times during his lifetime. Because of his tragedies, prose, international fame, charming personality, and extraordinary talent and productivity, Thomas remains one of Ireland's most favorite sons. He is considered Ireland's National Bard.

(References: *Field Day Anthology of Irish Writing*, 1991, W.W. Norton; *Thomas Moore*, 1967, Miriam DeFord; *The Harp That Once: A Chronicle of the Life of Thomas Moore*, 1937, Howard Mumford Jones; *The Bard of Erin: A Study of Thomas Moore's Irish Melodies*, 1981, Theresa Tessier)

Mote, Edward

Edward was born in 1797 in London, England to parents who made a living by managing a British-style pub and who spent very little time with their children. Edward was so active and curious that he was always getting into trouble in the pub which was too much of a distraction for his parents to manage. At those times, they told him to return to the small family living quarters above the pub. Going unsupervised, Edward spent most days on the streets of London learning about the seedy side of life.

Some of his friends would later become criminals of the streets, but he also made friends with young boys who were interested in various trades. One friend introduced Edward to cabinetry. Edward was immediately fascinated with how wood could be fashioned into beautiful pieces of furniture. He was trained as a cabinet maker and worked at the trade for several years in London.

It was through his trade that he met various types of people, mostly citizens with money and influence. One of the customers invited Edward to attend church. He found the experience inspirational. Edward was fascinated with the ministers and how they could speak with such intelligence and authority - so much so that he attended different churches to hear various ministers. It was during this time he decided that he would like to be a minister. Edward thought he was good at teaching and telling stories and he determined that the most excellent and effective ministers were those that had those same skills. He was especially inspired by Reverend J. Hyatt, the minister at Tottenham Court Road Chapel. Edward became a regular attendee of the church where he took notes of Reverend Hyatt's sermon delivery style.

Edward studied for the ministry by working with several ministers. They tutored Edward and encouraged him. When Edward became a minister he tried to emulate Reverend Hyatt before his own delivery style evolved. Edward was offered a minister position at the Rehoboth Baptist Church in Horsham, West Sussex. He found his vocation, his love, and his life at the church. Edward loved all aspects of his ministry. He enjoyed doing the research and writing in preparation for his weekly sermon; he enjoyed the inspiration each week of the church services, and he greatly enjoyed the church music. His congregation loved him so much they offered him the church building as a gift, to which he said: "I do not want the chapel; I only want the pulpit and when I cease to preach Christ then turn me out of that."

Edward composed several hymns, including the books of hymns, ***Hymns of Praise*** and ***A New Selection of Gospel Hymns***. Also, he wrote over a hundred pamphlets containing inspirational messages. Some of the inspirational messages in his pamphlets and hymns came from his experiences. For example, a member of his congregation became seriously ill and Edward was asked to visit and pray for her as she lay dying. That visit inspired Edward to finish a hymn, ***Jesus All in All***, that Edward had had trouble completing. He wrote about the experience: "He [the husband] said that it was his usual custom to sing a hymn, read a portion, and engage in prayer with his wife. He looked for his hymnbook but could find it nowhere. I said, 'I have some verses in my pocket; if he liked, we would sing them.' We did; and his wife enjoyed them so much that he asked me, as a favor, to leave a copy of them for his wife. I went home, and by the fireside composed the final verses to the hymn I had been struggling to finish."

Edward lived his life as a minister with pride and service, and in doing so was beloved by his congregation and the community of worshippers around the country.

He died in Horsham, Sussex, England in 1874 at the age of seventy-seven. The memorial service was attended by thousands of people.

(References: *The Day the Cabinet Shop was Closed,* 1990, Terry Lindsay; *Towards Singing with the Understanding,* 1992, Frances Mosher; *Edward Mote,* 1992, Handbook to the Baptist Hymnal, Milburn Price)

Murray, Shirley Erena

Shirley was born in 1931 in Invercargill, New Zealand. She is married to Reverend John Stewart Murray and they have three sons and six grandchildren. Reverend Murray was a Moderator of the Presbyterian Church in Aotearoa, New Zealand and the founder of the New Zealand Hymnbook Trust.

Shirley grew up in the Methodist tradition. At an early age, she loved music of all types and enjoyed going to church, and Shirley was a very good student. After secondary school, she attended the University of Otago, New Zealand. She earned Bachelor and Master of Arts degrees with honors in French, Latin, and the Classics.

Shirley wanted to be a teacher but she also enjoyed other intellectual endeavors such as research. She worked as a teacher, and after marrying, John moved with her to Wellington. It was while living in Wellington that she began writing hymns. Some of the hymns were tried in the church services and were well liked by the congregation. So much so that John and her friends encouraged Shirley to compose and publish them, which she did. She was surprised that every hymn she sent to publishers were accepted and published. She had found her talent, love, and a career—hymn compositions.

Shirley has written over 150 hymns that are found in hymnals around the world and have been translated into numerous languages. In addition to publishing hymns and books of music, such as ***In Every Corner Sing***; ***Every Day in Your Spirit***; ***Faith Makes the Song' Touch the Earth Lightly***; ***Sing for Peace*** and others, Shirley has produced radio hymn programs and performed as an organist and pianist. She has written more than twenty Christmas carols that are traditional in New Zealand and the United Kingdom.

Shirley is the recipient of many awards for her hymns and books. She continues to work and lives with her husband at Raumati Beach near Wellington. Regarding her work and the importance of appreciating God's gifts, she said, "I have a sad feeling that we've never got past 'all things bright and beautiful'. We need to take on what it means to care for Creation rather than admire it."

(References: *Shirley Erena Murray*, The Canterbury Dictionary of Hymnology. Retrieved 2015; *Shirley Erena Murray*, Hope Publishing Company. Retrieved 2015; *Hymn Writer Stresses the Power of Words*, 2009, Presbyterian Church of Aotearoa New Zealand. Retrieved 2015)

Neander, Joachim

Joachim was born at Breman, Germany in 1650. He was the eldest son of the family. His father was a teacher of considerable reputation, as was Joachim's grandfather.

Joachim was an intellectually precocious child who was described as possessed of high energy, enthusiasm, and curiosity. He entered the Gymnasium of Bremen (an academic academy) at age sixteen. He followed his intellectual interests during that time, as well as his social interests. He developed an affinity for philosophy and theology, as well as literature and debate. Joachim found satisfaction in questioning the established thought and philosophy of the day, but he was not rabid about or interested in revolution.

The year 1670 marked a critical time in Joachim's life. That was the year that Theodore Undereych came to Bremen to take the leadership role in St. Martin's Church. With the new minister, Joachim and some other members of the congregation thought they had a good opportunity to air their complaints about the church. One Sunday, Joachim with a few others went to the church to complain to the minister about various aspects of the church and how it functioned. Joachim was mesmerized and influenced by the powerful words of Theodore. Joachim very much wanted to understand Theodore and learn more about how Theodore could take complex concepts and ideas and fashion them into a message that offered both clarity and inspiration. They met again and Theodore became Joachim's tutor. Joachim's friends were so impressed by the change in him and by the intellectual and personal charm of Theodore that several of Joachim's friends joined Theodore's tutorship.

In 1674, after studying under Theodore for four years, Joachim became the Rector of a Latin school at Dusseldorf. At Dusseldorf, Joachim was inspired by the music of the choir which motivated him to write hymns. He wrote several hymns. However, this productive time was marred by controversy at the school. The headmaster and minister of the school were jealous of Joachim's talent and successes and they became particularly envious of Joachim's obvious talent for poetry, music, and intellectual thought. Joachim was forced to sign a document that alluded to accusations questioning his piety and beliefs. He was confused and devastated by the episode. He felt forced to leave, so he returned to Bremen as an assistant to Theodore at St. Martin's. Joachim became ill shortly after his return to Bremen, and he suffered from health problems for over two years, during which time he was barely able to work. It is believed that he had tuberculosis, but that was not confirmed.

Joachim died in 1680; he was only thirty years old.

Even though he died at a very young age, Joachim had a significant influence in many ways. His hymns were considered the beginning of the German Reformation and today many of his hymns are found in every Lutheran hymnbook, as well as in many other hymnals around the Christian world. His hymns are especially popular in praise sermons and Thanksgiving sermons.

(References: *Joachim Neander,* Berean Bible Heritage, 2009; *Joachim Neander Biography,* The Oxford Dictionary of the Christian Church, 3rd edition revised, 2005, F.L. Cross and Elizabeth Livingstone; *101 Hymn Stories*, 1982, Kenneth Osbeck; *The Christian Book of Records*, 2002, Mark Walter)

Neumark, Georg

Georg was born in 1621 in Langensalz, Thuringia, Germany. His parents were deeply involved in community work. His father was a lawyer who inspired Georg to study law, also. Both of his parents enjoyed music and they encouraged Georg to learn to read music and play an instrument.

Georg learned to love all types of music, and at a young age attempted to compose music. Georg attended Schleusingen Gymnasium (school) for a few years before transferring to the more academically rigorous Gotha School. When Georg completed his academic work there he enrolled at the University of Konigsberg to study law. During his time at the university, he continued to write music, as he did throughout his life no matter where he lived or worked. He also studied and wrote poetry.

The collateral effects of the Thirty Year's War spilled into parts of Germany and forced Georg to flee Konigsberg. He went to Keil, Germany, to live temporarily with friends, but with the uncertainty and unsettled conditions in Germany work was difficult to find even with his friends trying to help him find employment. After several weeks, Georg was about to give up and move to another city when he heard that a tutor of children of an aristocratic family had abruptly quit. With references from his friends he was offered and accepted a position as a tutor. The children he tutored loved him and he enjoyed teaching. Georg worked there for three years.

When Konigsberg was safe again, Georg moved back there and began working as a tutor to raise money to return to the university to complete his law studies. He continued his music work, and in fact increased the amount of time he spent on his musical compositions.

After completing law school, Georg started a modest law practice in Danzig, Germany. A few years later he moved to Thorn, Germany for two years and practiced law there, but he was not happy, so, he returned to Thuringia. Georg lived with his uncle, who was a government official and friends with Duke Wilhelm IV of Saxe-Weimar. The Duke was so impressed with Georg's intellect, work ethic, gregarious nature, musical abilities, and charming personality that he appointed him Librarian, which was an honored position in the city. Later Georg would be elevated to Guardian of the Shrine. The Duke encouraged Georg to continue his music compositions and to publish them. When one of his hymns was published it became an immediate success. It was titled ***Wer nur den Lieben Gott läßt walten*** (***Who Only the Good Lord Can Exercise***). The Duke so favored Georg and his talents that he was instrumental in Georg becoming a member of the prestigious Fruchtbringende Gesellschaft (otherwise known as the Fruitbearing Society or Academy), an academy of exclusive membership that became the first academy of German arts and letters that would come to include many princes, officials, poets, scholars, and influential noblemen. The academy supported efforts to enhance Germany's culture through literature, conversation, philology, religion, and scientific writing. Georg became a favorite among the members of the academy.

His poetry became increasingly popular in Germany, but at the height of his success and for unrecorded reasons, Georg went blind suddenly and could not work. He would have been reduced to begging but his many friends and the public that loved and admired his work supported him; consequently, he was able to maintain an active life until his health declined rapidly in 1680, probably related to whatever caused his blindness.

Georg died in 1681 in Weimar, Germany at the age of sixty. Out of respect and reverence to his memory and body of work, the Evangelical Church annually marks the memorial on his life and death each July 9th.

(References: *Desperate Georg Neumark Let God Guide Him*, 2007, Dan Grave; *Georg Neumark*, Christian Classics Ethereal Library. Retrieved 2013; *Georg Neumark—Hymn Writer and Composer*, Bach Cantatas Website. Retrieved 2015; *Georg Neumark Biography*, 2015, Michael Ludscheit)

Newman, John Henry

John was born in 1801 in London, England as the oldest of six children—three boys and three girls. John's mother was descended from the famous Huguenot family. His father was a banker with the international banking firm of Ramsbottom, Newman and Company—a bank with interests in Europe and other parts of the world.

From the time John was a small boy, he heard about his mother's family of noble heritage and intriguing family stories, as well as his father's stories about the economies and trading ventures in international markets. The family was financially well-standing with a fine home on Southhampton Street in Bloomsbury and a country home near Richmond, England.

John was raised with an expectation of a prominent career and scholarly education. Therefore, at age seven he was sent to the prestigious Great Ealing School administered by George Nicholas and where prominent teachers such as Thomas Huxley and Walter Mayers taught. John was an excellent student but did not have any interest in extracurricular activities, or "games" as he called them. He preferred to spend his spare time reading; he especially enjoyed Walter Scott novels, but he read a variety of books. Before he turned fifteen years of age he had read the works of Thomas Paine, Voltaire, David Hume, Plato, Aristotle, and others. John became interested in theology and began a self-evaluation of his spiritual life, which led to his conversion to Christianity. This became a difficult time for John because of his conversion. This was not so much a time of joy as a time of self-discovery and led him to question many aspects of life.

During this introspective time, his father's company collapsed under the weight of too much speculative debt. John's proud father and the proud family took this news very hard. In desperate need of money, John's father took a job running a brewery. The family survived, but for a time, John's education was at stake and doubtful. As the family recovered from the financial losses and began adjusting to a different lifestyle, John continued in school.

John was influenced by his teachers and he became an Evangelical Calvinist, which was anti-Catholic.

After graduating from Ealing School, John attended Trinity College at Oxford. He graduated from Trinity College with highest honors, and because of his brilliant academic work, he became a Fellow of Oriel (the oldest foundation at Oxford). At the age of twenty-three and recently ordained he became the Vice Principal of St. Alban Hall and later as a teacher at Oriel College of Oxford. Later he was a Public Examiner and a Select University Preacher.

After being involved in a controversial religious movement, his life settled down and he converted to the Catholic faith. He became Father Superior of the Oratory of St. Philip Neri in Birmingham, England. John's theological reputation grew, as did his literary reputation. He had written poetry for several years, but his poems and lyrical pieces gained rapid popularity as he became well-known for his sermons. He had poems published in the ***British Magazine***. As his academic, literary, and theological fame grew, John was named Rector of the Roman Catholic University in Dublin, which became the University College of Dublin - the largest university in Ireland. He is credited with being a major influence in the growth of the university.

In 1879, the Pope named John a Cardinal. Cardinal Newman's reputation grew far and wide, with more attention paid to the quality and character of his poems and prose than ever before. Some of his poems were composed into hymns by Fredrick Faber, who was a famous hymnist in his own right. Probably the most well-known hymn is ***Lead, Kindly Light***.

Cardinal Newman translated several Latin hymns into English - many of them are in modern day hymnals. Cardinal Newman's major literary works include ***Tracts for the Times***; ***Apologia Pro Vita Sua*** (***A Defense of His Life***); ***Grammar of Assent***; ***The Dream of Gerontius*** (Gerontius was a 4th century Roman Army commander), and many others.

He died in 1890 at the age of eighty-nine in Birmingham, England.

(References: *John Henry Newman,* 2010, Ian Ker; *John Henry Newman,* Catholic Encyclopedia. Retrieved 2013; *Blessed John Henry Newman,* Britannica.com. Retrieved 2013)

Newton, John

John was born in 1725 in Wapping, East London, England. His father was a shipmaster and his mother was considered a "non-conformist," a term used to characterize people who did not conform to the English government's allegiance to the Church of England.

John was devoted to his mother and was in his early years greatly influenced by her beliefs and her fearlessness in speaking about her faith. To John's shock, his mother died when he was only seven years old. Four years later, at the very young age of eleven, John went to sea with his father for six voyages. He greatly enjoyed the sea, the adventure of being on a large ship, and the banter and stories of the sailors. He would gladly have ventured on more voyages but his father retired.

John did not know that his father had plans for him. John was to sail to Jamaica and learn the sugar plantation business. His father did not want John to follow in his footsteps as a seaman or shipmaster; he did not think that life was suited for John and he did not think John could handle the physical and mental demands of the seafaring lifestyle. John had other plans; he signed on a merchant ship scheduled to traverse the Mediterranean Sea, but while visiting friends, he was kidnapped ("pressed into service," according to the Royal Navy) and served aboard the *HMS Harwich* as a midshipman. In one of the ports, he tried to escape but was captured and tortured in front of the crew. Later he was transferred to a slave ship that sailed from England to West Africa. He was forced to work for the notorious slave trader, Amos Clowe, who saw John as a "gift" for his wife, Princess Peye, an African Duchess. She abused John as much as she abused the slaves.

Word reached John's father about his son's dire situation, and he commissioned a rescue mission. John was rescued and stole away to England on the merchant ship *Greyhound.* It was during that voyage home that John experienced what he later called a gift from God that led to his spiritual conversion. A storm near hurricane strength pounded the ship; the ship was in peril of sinking. It was driven deep into towering waves and howling winds spun the ship out of control. The damaged ship began to take on water but the heavy load of cargo shifted and plugged up the hole that would have sunk the ship and killed all on board. The ship drifted to safety after surviving the storm because of what John called a miracle. His previous lifestyle of drinking, swearing, and gambling shifted to one of self-reflection and spiritual development. This marked a change in his life and conversion to evangelical Christianity.

Upon his return to England, he accepted a position as tax collector in Liverpool. During this time his spiritual awakening convinced him to be a minister, so he studied the Bible, theology, and learned Greek, Hebrew, and Syrian. He became a lay minister. After seven years of applying to the Church of England for ordination, he was finally ordained as a priest in the Church of England. He was eventually accepted into the evangelical order as a Curate of Olney.

John worked hard and was dedicated to helping people in the community. He became very popular and well-known for his work and the power of his sermons. The congregation attendance grew so large that the church added a gallery to accommodate the increasing attendance.

John's interests included music, poetry, and hymns. With assistance from other priests, John composed several hymns, which resulted in the publication of the legendary ***Olney Hymns*** in 1779. He remained at Olney for several years before accepting a position as Rector of St. Mary Woolnoth in London. John's fame grew each year of his life. He would become world famous for his sermons, writings, and hymns. He was presented with an honorary Doctor of Divinity by Princeton University (known at the time as the College of New Jersey).

John is probably most famously and endearingly known as the composer of ***Amazing Grace.*** He wrote the hymn to share the important messages of forgiveness, reconciliation, and redemption. He pulled the words of the hymn from his own experiences of pain, suffering, and disappointment and how no matter how desperate his own life became he was amazed by God's grace. It has been estimated that the hymn is played millions of times each year.

John was devoted to his wife, who died at the age of forty. He wrote about his grief over her death in ***Letters to a Wife***. He lived until 1807 when he died after several months of poor health. John was eighty-two years old. He was buried with his wife in Olney, England.

(References: *John Newton: From Disgrace to Amazing Grace,* 2007, Jonathan Aitken; *Finding God in the Story of Amazing Grace,* 2007, Kurt Bruner and Jim Ware; A *Biography of John Newton,* 1994, John Dunn; *John Newton,* Oxford Dictionary of National Biography, Retrieved 2014)

Nichol, Henry Ernest

Henry was born in 1862 in Hull, Yorkshire, England. His family was well educated and well known in the community for being a close-knit family that worshiped every Sunday and participated in community activities and events.

Ernest was a studious child who was a keen observer of the world around him. He was not shy, but he preferred reading to socializing. He was provided with music lessons when he was young. He did not enjoy the lessons at the beginning but as it became apparent that he had natural music skills his interest increased. However, he loved mathematics and when it became apparent to his parents and teachers that Ernest was brilliant at mathematics, he was encouraged to become an engineer.

When he completed secondary school, he took exams to qualify for Oxford University. Ernest excelled on the exams, especially on the math exam; consequently, he was admitted at Oxford. He enjoyed university life but he did not enjoy the civil engineering classes even though he liked the mathematical challenges. It was not too long before Ernest drifted toward music studies. He attended some music classes on his own and found that he greatly enjoyed them. So he switched his major to music, against the advice and wishes of his parents. He received a Bachelor of Arts degree from Oxford University and began a career writing music.

Ernest composed over 130 hymns, many of which were first sung at Sunday school programs under the pseudonym of "Colin Sterne." There has been much speculation as to why he used a pseudonym—some experts believe he wanted to see if the hymns would be well received and properly used before taking credit for them. Ernest published fourteen sets of ***Sunday School Anniversary Hymns***. Many of his hymns were also published in the Pratt Green Hymnology Collection at the University of Durham. Some of his most enduring hymns are ***Life is Opening Out Before You*** and ***Rest, O Rest!,*** but his most famous hymn is ***We Have a Story to Tell to the Nations***.

Ernest lived until 1926 when he died at the age of sixty-four in Skirlaugh, Yorkshire, England, after a brief illness.

(References: *H. Ernest Nichol,* Psalter Hymnal Handbook. Retrieved 2015; *Henry Ernest Nichol,* Cyberhymnal.org. Retrieved 2015; *Henry E. Nichol,* The Canterbury Dictionary of Hymnology. Retrieved 2015)

Nicolai, Philipp

Philipp was born in 1556 in Mengeringhausen, Hessen, Germany. His father was a Lutheran clergyman who was strict but loving. Philipp's mother enjoyed literature and music and spent a lot of time with the children encouraging them to read and learn to play a musical instrument.

Philipp was schooled at home until he was old enough to attend a private school that focused on language and the classics. It was during those years that he discovered a life-long love of learning and writing. Philipp enjoyed poetry; he tried his hand at writing poetry during his teen years.

He followed in his father's footsteps and attended the University of Erfurt and later the University of Wittenberg to study theology. Philipp continued to write poetry while he was in college and he experimented with composing hymns. Upon completing his university studies, he became the pastor in Herdecke an der Ruhr for a short period of time.

The violence of the Spanish Counter-Reformation drove him and many of the town's people away from the town and the region, because mercenary troops terrified and slaughtered people during the religious war. Philipp was not certain what to do or where to go. A friend convinced him to move to Cologne, France. Philipp followed his friend's advice and moved to Cologne, where he quickly found an opportunity to preach to Lutheran congregations. However, he soon found out that the city was a predominantly Catholic city that had little tolerance for other denominations. So much of his preaching took place in small rooms with small congregations. At one point, the intolerance toward the Lutherans grew so strong that they were forced to meet secretly. Eventually, Philipp decided he could not live under those conditions. He moved back to Hessen. There he became Court Preacher and tutor to the young Count of Waldeck.

Despite the turmoil and frequent moves, he continued to write poetry and compose hymns, many of which were sung in the church services. Philipp would have likely spent the rest of his life in Hessen, but he was persuaded to accept the pastor position in Unna, Westphalia, Germany.

These were tragic years for Philipp, primarily because of a plague swept through Germany and over 1,300 of his parishioners died. His normally positive nature and personality turned gloomy and dispirited because of daily burials; one day he presided over thirty funerals. It was during this time that Philipp found solace in writing. He wrote a book of hymns, ***Joyous Mirror of Eternal Life***, which contained several hymns, including his most famous hymns, ***Wake, Awake for Night is Flying*** and ***O Morning Star, How Fair and Bright***, as well as several meditations about life and eternal life.

The inspiration for his writing came from his faith and also from St. Augustine's book the *City of God*.

After Philipp led his congregation through the tragedy of the plague and the unbelievable loss of life, Philipp became the pastor at St. Katherine's Church in Hamburg, Germany when he was forty-five years old. He served that congregation until his death at age fifty-two when he tragically died after becoming ill while traveling a great distance to ordain a close friend.

Philipp was buried at the famous church in Katharinenkirche, Hamburg, Germany. The church was destroyed during World War II. Fortunately, the church was restored in 1954.

Although Philipp was famous throughout Europe as a masterful preacher, he was even better known for the hymns he wrote.

(References: *Philipp Nicolai Society,* Wittenberg Trial. Retrieved 2013; *Philippi Nicolai,* Hymnwriter.org. Retrieved 2013; *Philippi Nicolai,* Hymnary.org. Retrieved; *Philipp Nicolai,* hymntime.com. Retrieved 2013)

O'Driscoll, Herbert

Herbert was born in 1928 in Cork, Ireland. His family resided in Cork for generations, and the children were raised in the Irish tradition of farming and raising livestock.

Herbert was an intelligent, inquisitive, active, and loving child. In elementary and secondary school, it was obvious to Herbert's teachers that he possessed a keen intellect and talented insight. That plus his inquisitive and gregarious nature made him an extraordinarily popular and gifted student. After secondary school, he attended Trinity College in Dublin, Ireland. He greatly enjoyed the college life and participated in many college activities, including activities at the chapel. After graduating from Trinity College, Herbert was ordained a pastor at age twenty-three. He served in the Pastorate at Monkstown, Ireland for two years. He was hesitant about leaving Ireland, but he accepted a position in the Pastorate at Ottawa, Ontario for several years. After working in Ontario,

Herbert served in the Naval Chaplaincy in Dartmouth, Nova Scotia for three years. Herbert also became the Rector of Carp back in Ontario for six years before being appointed Cathedral Dean in Vancouver, British Columbia. In 1982, Herbert moved to Washington, D.C. to work at the College of Preachers at Washington Cathedral, but stayed there only one year. He preferred living in Canada, so he moved back there.

Herbert is known worldwide as a brilliant scholar, but he is also known for his Irish storytelling skills born from the Irish tradition. Some of his fondest memories were listening to men in his community telling stories in homes, around campfires, in pubs, at church activities - at virtually every place where people gathered. Being exposed to storytelling and witnessing all types of stories and deliveries of stories, Herbert became one of Ireland's best and most treasured storytellers.

Herbert is also a prolific writer. He has published over thirty books. His book on Celtic spirituality, ***Doorway in Time***, includes his own spiritual journey and has been popular with the general public and with scholars. Some of his other books include ***For All the Saints; City Priest, City People; Conversations in Time with Men and Women of the Bible; Eucharist; The Unshakable Kingdom; The world Today Reflections on the Readings of the Revised Common Lectionary; Emmanuel; Heritage; Year of the Lord,*** and many others. Herbert has also composed several hymns that can be found in hymnals throughout the world. Many of his hymns are in his book, ***Praise My Soul***. In the introduction to the book, Herbert wrote: "Just like human beings, hymns come into the world at every conceivable hour and in every conceivable place. For curiosity, I began to recall where and when some of the hymns in this collection came into being. First of all, I know that every hour of day and night is somewhere on my list—including a number of occasions that involved rising from bed as the world slept and furiously scribbling some lines before they vanished with morning light."

Approaching the age of ninety, Herbert remains active and continues to compose hymns and tell Irish stories

(References: *Herbert O'Driscoll,* Dictionary of North American Hymnology. Retrieved 2013; *Sermon by The Rev. Canon Herbert O'Driscoll,* November 25, 2013, Christ Church Cathedral; *The Leap of the Deer: Memories of a Celtic Childhood,* 1994, Herbert O'Driscoll; *A Feast with Herb O'Driscoll,* WordPress.com. Retrieved 2013)

Oatman, Johnson

Johnson was born in 1856 in a small community near Medford, New Jersey. Johnson was raised in a family that was deeply religious, and a family that enjoyed worship, prayer, and the music of the church. His father, who was well known as a gifted singer with a powerful voice, often sang in the local church choir, and he was known to sing frequently around the house. Johnson adored his father, and they always sat together in church. When he was too young and small to read the hymnal as his father and the congregation rose to sing, Johnson would stand in the pew and sing the hymns with his father. He also occasionally joined his father in the choir loft. Johnson's father took the time to teach him at a very young age the hymns of worship and from that Johnson learned to love music. With encouragement from his father, Johnson learned to read music and play the piano and organ. When he tried his hand at composing hymns somewhat reluctantly Johnson's father was delighted and strongly urged him to keep working at it.

Johnson attended the local public schools, but his intellect was not challenged or nurtured there so he went to Herbert's Academy in Princeton, New Jersey. It was there that Johnson developed his considerable skills for composing music. It was also at Herbert's Academy and later at the New Jersey Collegiate Institute in Bordentown, New Jersey where he developed the self-confidence he would need to pursue his interests. Johnson decided that he not only wanted to compose music; he also wanted to become a minister. So he joined the local Methodist church and studied theology under the tutelage of Bishop Merrill for several years.

Johnson also continued to write hymns while he studied for the ministry.

During the week and on Saturday's he worked with his father at their company, Johnson Oatman, and Son, a successful mercantile business. With his incredibly busy life, Johnson managed his religious studies well enough to be ordained by the Methodist church, with the approval of Bishop Merrill. He became a visiting preacher to local churches because of his business success; it took much of his time. When Johnson's father died, he left the mercantile business and went into insurance, where he was also successful.

It's remarkable how prolific a hymn writer Johnson was considering his professional business life and his part-time preaching duties. During his lifetime, Johnson wrote over 5,000 hymns. He calculated that he wrote anywhere from 150 to 200 hymns each year. There is probably not one hymnal in print today that does not contain at least two or more of his hymns. Johnson's favorite hymn was ***No Not One***, but his most famous hymn is arguably ***Higher Ground***.

Johnson had no interest in publishing rights or royalties from the sale of his hymns, but his publisher insisted so he set the price of one dollar for each of his hymns. It is estimated that the royalties from his hymns would have made him a millionaire, or close to it. However, Johnson's reward came from knowing that his hymns were enjoyed by people around the world and that his very own words were being sung in churches each Sunday.

Johnson continued to write until his health declined in 1920, and even then he wrote on days when he was physically able to. He died in 1922 in Norman, Oklahoma at the age of sixty-six. He was buried in New Jersey. Johnson is considered by many as one of the most influential and successful hymn composers of all time.

(References: *Biography of Gospel Songs and Hymns*, 1914, Jacob Henry Hall; *Then Sings My Soul*, 2003, Robert Morgan; *101 Hymn Stories*, 1985, Kenneth Osbeck; *The Complete Book of Hymns*, 2006, William J. Petersen and Ardyth Petersen)

Olearius, Johannes

Johannes was born in 1611 in Halle (in some places it is referred to as Salle), a city in the southern part of the German state of Saxony-Anhalt. His father was Johann Olearius, the pastor of St. Mary's Church and city superintendent, which was the equivalent of being city manager.

Johannes lived a strictly obedient life and was told repeatedly that his father's reputation demanded good, righteous behavior and hard work and effort at all times from his children. Johannes gladly lived up to these expectations. He greatly admired his father and wanted to follow in his footsteps as a leader and influencer in the community.

Johannes discovered that he inherited his father's intellectual acumen and curiosity. He was a vociferous reader and seemed to retain everything he read. He enrolled in the University of Wittenberg where he earned Bachelor, Master, and Doctor of Divinity degrees. Between degrees he served as a lecturer at the university and later became an adjunct professor of philosophy there.

Johannes was a prolific writer and researcher and he was greatly admired as a scholar and lecturer. He was offered the position of superintendent of Querfurt and soon thereafter was appointed by Duke August of Sachsen-Weissenfels as chief court preacher and private Chaplain of Halle. Johannes performed extraordinarily well in everything he did and he worked exceedingly hard, too. In 1664, he was named general superintendent which means he was responsible for the administration of the city. He held similar positions at Magdeburg and Weissenfels.

Johannes became well known for his publications, particularly for his ***Commentary on the Bible***. He also compiled the largest German hymn book of his era, the ***Geistliche Singe-Kunst***, which contained 1,218 hymns, of which 302 were penned by him but noted as written by "D.J.O." His second volume of hymns included 1,340 hymns. Several of his hymns are still found over 350 years later in hymnals around the world with perhaps his most popular hymn being ***Come Thou Precious Ransom***.

Johannes continued to write and compile hymns until his death in 1684 in Weissenfels, Germany at the age of seventy-three.

(References: *Hymnal Companion to the Lutheran Book of Worship*, 1981, Marilyn Kay Stulken; *Johannes Olearius*, Umfassende Genealogische Darstellung und Biographie. Retrieved and translated by translate.com 2015)

Olejar, Peter

Peter was born in 1937 in North Carolina.

He was a precocious and gregarious child who loved to be around people and who was energetic and inquisitive about many things. He loved to read beginning at a very young age and has maintained his love of reading throughout his life. Peter excelled in all academic areas in elementary and secondary school, which led to an academic scholarship at Yale University where he earned Bachelor of Arts and Master of Arts degrees in music. Peter then earned another master's degree from Duke University. He was also in doctoral studies at the University of Toronto.

Peter has been writing and composing music for several years and he is an accomplished arranger of music and composer. His publications include the widely used ***Chalice Anthems***. He published several carillon pieces that have been played around the world in churches, music productions, and at public events. The major motion picture, ***Once Around***, starring Richard Dreyfuss, included Peter's arrangement of ***Fly Me to the Moon***. His hymn ***Now We Come Before God's Presence*** can be found in almost every Christian hymnal in the world.

Peter studied conducting with Epic label recording artist Gustav Meier and trombone with Robert Nagel of the New York Brass Ensemble. He has written music for chamber orchestra, brass ensemble, string quartet, theater orchestra, symphony orchestra, big bands, chorus, children's plays, children's chorus, musicals, children and adult solo vocal music, carillon, piano, and organ. Peter's song ***Et Inspiravit*** (***He Breathed***) won an award at the 2014 Festival of the Arts in Perpignan, France. His song ***Panegyrikos*** was played as the opening theme for the World Carillon Federation Congress and at the inauguration of a Duke University president.

Peter continues to be commissioned to write music pieces for various events and occasions throughout the United States. Currently, Peter is the director of Music at St. Paul's Christian Church in Raleigh, North Carolina.

(References: *Peter Olejar*, St. Paul's Christian Church, Biography online. Retrieved 2015; *Chalice Anthems*, 1999, Peter Olejar)

Olivar, Jose Antonio and Manzano, Miguel work together composing music that is well-known around the world, especially for a hymn they composed together—***When the Poor Ones (Cuando el Pobre)***. The hymn has been translated into several languages, but it skyrocketed to popularity when it was translated by George Lockwood into English in 1976. Jose was born in Spain in 1939 to a seafaring family that endured many difficult times and several family tragedies. He and his four brothers lost both parents during the Spanish Revolution. Thereafter, he and his brothers were raised by their maternal grandmother. She had strong beliefs about religion and education. Her strength of character, her strong faith, and her devotion to her grandchildren instilled purpose and responsibility in each of the grandchildren. She raised them to be a Christian.

She recognized Jose's intelligence and good nature, so she decided he should attend seminary. She sent him to the Seminary of Covadonga and Oviedo. He learned the classics, theology, and he studied music. Jose showed intellectual depth and a serious-minded study of theology, but he discovered that he had a gift for writing, especially poetry. His teachers encouraged him to write poetry, and he has been writing poems ever since then. Jose has won several awards for his poetry.

After completing his education, he worked as a journalist in national newspapers and popular magazines, such as *Hello*. For a short period of time, Jose was the deputy director of the magazine. His work with the magazine allowed him to travel the world to meet famous people for interviews. In 2012, he was awarded the prestigious ***Honor Manin***—2012 (Man of the Year).

Miguel Manzano was born in 1930 in Aillamor de Cardozo, Spain, which is near Portugal. He was raised in a religiously devoted family. His family was very spiritual and believed deeply in their religious rituals. Miguel's family also enjoyed music, and it was his mother who first noticed Miguel's gift for music.

His musical career began when he was only eight years old and thereafter his formal education included music education. He studied under the famous teacher, Gaspar Arabaolaza, who taught him piano, harmony, and organ. Gaspar saw Miguel's music talent and encouraged him to attend the internationally recognized Higher School of Sacred Music in Madrid, Spain. The Higher School was difficult to get into, but it is believed that Gaspar helped Miguel gain admission. Miguel thrived in the Higher School where he studied harmony, polyphony, rhythm, and Gregorian Modality. He continued his studies at the Catholic Institute of Paris. Miguel's music has been chosen to complete the repertoire of the *National Liturgical Hymnal* of the Episcopal Committee of Spanish Liturgy. At present, he is a professor of ethnic music at the Higher Conservatory of Music in Salamanca, Spain.

Jose and Miguel met many times over the years and they shared a love of music and worship. They decided to work together on a few projects and events and soon developed a mutual love and respect for each other. They have composed many songs and hymns, but experts say that their ***When the Poor Ones (Cuando el Pobre)*** is one of the most powerful lyrics in contemporary hymnology: "When the poor ones who have nothing share with strangers; when the thirsty water give unto us all; when the crippled in their weakness strengthen others; then we know that

God still goes that road with us." Jose and Miguel remain active and extremely popular and well known around the world.

(References: *Jose Olivar and Miguel Manzano - When the Poor Ones,* Hymnary.org. Retrieved 2013; *Glory to God,* 1971, Jose Antonio Olivar and Miguel Manzano; *Hymns for Today,* 2009, Brian Wren)

Osler, Edward

Edward was born in 1798 in Falmouth, Cornwall, England. Edward's father was a merchant who worked long hours to support the family. He wanted his four children to receive an education and become either a teacher or minister, so they would have a steady income and not be exposed to the difficult and unpredictable life of a merchant.

Edward's parents observed that he was unusually intelligent and precocious. Edward had a photographic memory and mature insight and creativity. Consequently, his parents decided that Edward should study to be a doctor. Edward attended the small local school but at age fifteen began to apprentice under a surgeon in his hometown. He also attended medical lectures at the Brookes Blenheim School of Anatomy in London and he attended classes at the Guy's Hospital Medical School. Surgeons were rare in that era and yet very much in demand; consequently, Edward became a resident surgeon at Swansea Infirmary in Wales at the age of twenty-one. He remained there for six years until he joined the Royal British Navy as a ship's surgeon.

Edward's ship was assigned to the West Indies. Onboard the ship and in the islands Edward learned a lot about all aspects of the field of medicine, including various viruses, diseases, and emergency surgery situations such as impromptu surgical procedures under difficult and primitive circumstances. He also became fascinated by the customs and history of the Royal British Navy. There were many months when Edward had long stretches of time with little to do, so he took an interest in writing. He wrote books about medicine, nature, science and nature, and the history of the Royal British Navy. Edward also began to write hymns that were sung on the ship and in churches on the islands. His book ***The Biography of Admiral Viscount Exmouth*** was very well received when it was published in England. Also, the scientific community praised his books on medicine and science.

When he returned to England after years at sea, he turned his attention to writing and spent less time as a surgeon. Eventually, he gave up surgery for a full-time career in writing. He used his experience in the West Indies and other places to write books such as ***Burrowing Marine Animals***; ***Poems Written at Sea and in the West Indies***; ***The*** Voyage, and ***Illustrated Natural History***. He authored several more books and became the editor of the *Royal Cornwall Gazette* when he lived in Truro, Cornwall, England. He was the editor for several years. Edward began to write more poetry when he moved to Cornwall. Edward also wrote numerous hymns, many of them were published in his books ***Mitre Hymn Book*** and ***Psalms and Hymns Adapted to the Services of the Church of England***. Many of his hymns can be found in modern hymnals, including ***O God, Unseen, Yet Ever Near*** and ***Worship, Honor, Glory, Blessing***.

Edward continued to write poems and hymns until his death in 1863 in Cornwall at the age of sixty-five. At his memorial service, he was honored by the British Royal Navy, the Hymn Society, and was attended by other dignitaries.

(References: *Edward Osler,* Dictionary of Hymnology, John Julian, 1907. Retrieved 2014; *Hymnal Companion to the Lutheran Book of Worship,* 1981, Marilyn Kay Stulken; *The Methodist Hymn-Book Illustrated,* 1924, John Telford; *Edward Osler,* The Canterbury Dictionary of Hymnology. Retrieved 2014)

Ostergaard, Kristian

Kristian was born in 1855 in Hjerm Parish, Jutland, Denmark. His father owned a farm in rural Denmark and struggled to make the farm a success. Kristian along with several siblings helped on the farm working long hours, but he also was a vociferous reader, often reading by candlelight late into the night.

As Kristian read more and varied works he decided that he wanted to pursue an education, so he wrote a short paper arguing that people from all segments of society should have the opportunity to receive an education—even the children of farmers. After receiving approval from his father, Kristian took the article to the local newspaper. The newspaper editor met with Kristian and read the article. He asked Kristian a few questions and expressed his surprise that Kristian could by himself craft such a finely written article. The article was published with no editing. The community read the article and it became a point of conversation for several weeks. Kristian's father saw the article in the newspaper and it convinced him that Kristian should be offered an education, so Kristian was allowed to leave the farm to attend a boarding school, Askov Folk School, where he received a classic education.

The headmaster of the school, Ludvig Schroeder, made an impression on Kristian by his daily devotionals, his intellect, and his worldview of life and sense of individual responsibility. Ludvig often spoke of the importance of and need for a spiritual life. While at the school it became obvious to the teachers that Kristian was a talented writer and a potential scholar. He loved the school and all of the activities of the school almost as much as he enjoyed talking to Ludvig. To illustrate his devotion to the school, one year he remained at the school during the Christmas holidays to complete a comedic play that he wrote for the student body to perform. The act of selflessness impressed his classmates and his teachers immensely.

Kristian completed his studies at the school and became a teacher. Kristian's job took him to several schools in Denmark. He was a very popular teacher wherever he went. He was also invited to write for a Danish newspaper that was marketed in Denmark and in the United States. It was called the *Dannevirke.* He provided articles for the newspaper for many years. Copies of the weekly were printed in Cedar Falls, Iowa for the Danish community where it was published by the Hoist Company.

Kristian immigrated to America and taught at the Elkhorn Folk School in Elkhorn, Iowa where many Danish immigrants lived. Four years later he helped found the Ashland Folk School in Grant, Michigan where he worked until 1885 when he and his wife moved to Stovring, Jutland, Denmark to found the famous Stovring Folk School. The school still operates today, over 130 years later. However, there were times during the first years of the school that challenged its existence. One setback occurred shortly after the school opened.

At the dedication of Stovring Folk School, Kristian made an impassioned and uncomplimentary remark about Denmark's tyrannical Prime Minister. A local newspaper writer took the remark and published it in a small article about the school's opening. The Prime Minister was outraged by the comment and cut off the state's subsidy to the school (each school in Denmark at the time was subsidized by funds from the central government). This would have been a death sentence to most any other school in Denmark, but Kristian raised enough local funds and received other donated funds to keep the school running. During less tyrannical times, the newly elected Prime Minister's office reinstated the school subsidies. In the meantime, however, the work to keep the school operating was more than Kristian and his wife could cope with. She died from exhaustion and left Kristian with six children.

Kristian and his children moved to America to find relief from the stress of running the school. He decided that he would enter the ministry instead of returning to teaching, so he took local courses in religion in classes offered at a Lutheran school in Luck, Wisconsin. Kristian met his future wife there and he remarried and fathered six more children. After being ordained in the Lutheran church he ministered at churches in Iowa, South Dakota, Illinois, and Nebraska, each time taking his wife and twelve children with him. The family finally settled in Tyler, Minnesota.

Kristian always enjoyed writing and despite the turbulence and heartbreak in his life, he seldom stopped writing. He wrote several songs, hymns, and novels. Most of his novels told the story of how immigrants struggled to carve out a life in the prairie. Kristian also published an anthology of songs about the mid-west and west entitled ***Songs of the Prairie***. His hymns were spiritual with references to the Bible. Kristian's most widely popular hymn was ***That Cause Can Never Be Lost Nor Stayed***. His hymns were included in Christian hymnals and many of them are in hymnals around the world.

Kristian continued to write stories, newspaper articles, poems, and hymns even after he retired. He died in 1931 at the age of seventy-six surrounded by his family and friends. Hundreds of admirers attended his funeral in Tyler, Minnesota.

(References: *The Danish Folk High School and its Reception in the United States*, 1994, Harold Stubblefield and Patrick Keane; *The Scandinavian Immigrant Writer in America*, Dorothy Burton Skardal, Volume 21, 2005, Norwegian-American Historical Association; *Kristian Ostergaard*, hymntime.com. Retrieved 2015)

Oxenham, John

(Born as William Arthur Dunkerley)

John was born in 1852 in Manchester, England. His family was of modest means, running a small family business.

John had the basic exposure to public education but did not excel or show any particular talent as a student. He had a gift for business, however, and so he was determined to operate his own business someday. He learned about the wholesale grocery business, and he loved the hectic and risky nature of the fast-paced business. John had a talent for speculating on which grocery products were top sellers, and he did the work to find out which distributors were reliable and honest. Consequently, he made a small fortune in the wholesale grocery business.

There was a side of John that most of his business partners and even some of his friends did not know about. He was a prolific writer. John, known to his friends as Bill Dunkerley, used the pen name of John Oxenham (taken from a character in the novel *Westward Ho!*, written by Charles Kingsley) and sometimes as Julian Ross.

He greatly enjoyed writing, but he was also interested in the publication business. His interest in publishing started when his publisher refused to publish his small book of poems. His publisher had no interest in it and refused to finance it, so John published it himself as ***Bees in Amber***. The book became widely popular, selling over 300,000 copies. John determined then that he could be a publisher. With the help of several investment partners, he started a publishing business. He started two weekly publications, ***The Idler*** and ***To-Day***. His poem ***Greatheart*** was famous throughout the English-speaking world, and it was later translated into several languages. During World War I, he published many poems that he dedicated to the soldiers fighting along the Western Front in France. He also composed a hymn for the soldiers, ***Hymn for the Men at the Front***, with sales from the hymn going to aid wounded soldiers. Incredibly, over eight million copies of the song were sold worldwide.

As a well-known writer and publisher, he was commissioned to write a script for an international missionary display that was to be shown in London. The script became a hymn - a hymn that has been in almost every hymnal since then, the famous ***In Christ There is No East or West***.

During his lifetime, he wrote over forty books, hundreds of poems, numerous magazine articles, and dozens of hymns. John's daughter, Elsie Jeanette, became a famous children's book writer with her Abbey Series for girls.

John served as a deacon and teacher at the Ealing Congregational Church before moving to Sussex when he was seventy years old. There he became a leader in the community, rising to become mayor, and was charitable with his wealth. John continued to write until the time of his death in 1941 in Worthing, Sussex, England. He was eighty-nine years old.

(References: *Works of John Oxenham,* 1925, John Oxenham; *John Oxenham—WWI Poet,* 2014, WordPress.com. Retrieved 2015; *John Oxenham Biography,* IMDb.com. Retrieved 2015; *John Oxenham,* allpoetry.com. Retrieved 2015; *Lives of War Poets,* warpoetry.co.uk. Retrieved 2015; *Selected Poems of John Oxenham,* World Catalog.com. Retrieved 2015)

Palmer, Ray

Ray was born in 1808 in Little Compton, Rhode Island. His father was a prominent judge who cherished his small family and who was also a pillar of the community. Judge Palmer insisted that his children receive a good education, he was adamant about Ray's education because he wanted his son to be an attorney and follow in his footsteps as a judge.

Ray was eager to please his father, who he greatly admired, and although he was obviously very intelligent he was not the most ambitious student in school. He made good grades but he did nothing to distinguish himself as a gifted student, much to the disappointment of his father. When it appeared that Ray was not going to be an academic scholar, he was sent to visit with relatives in Boston, Massachusetts.

When Ray was only thirteen years old he took an opportunity to work as a clerk in a dry goods store in Boston. While working there he became involved community activities and attended Park Street Congregational Church. At the church, he met the minister, Dr. S. E. Dwight. Dr. Dwight saw the unusual intellect of Ray and he took an interest in him. It was Dr. Dwight's influence that convinced Ray to expand his intellectual potential, which led to a decision that would change his life.

With Dr. Dwight's assistance and encouragement, Ray applied for and was accepted at the prestigious and academically challenging Phillips Andover Academy in Andover, Maryland. The intellectual challenges at the school, plus the self-discipline and the sense of responsibility prepared Ray for the rigors he would face when he was accepted at Yale University. He also improved his social skills and he made several friends. One of his friends at Phillips was Oliver Wendell Holmes.

Ray was very successful at Yale. He met all intellectual challenges and he participated in many social activities at the university. After graduating from Yale, Ray moved to New York City where he studied theology on his own while teaching at the Institute for Women, a college for women. His private study of theology prepared him to enter the ministry, which he did at the age twenty-seven when he became pastor of the First Congregational Church of Bath, New York and later at the Congregational Church in Albany, New York. He remained at each church for over fifteen years. Ray then moved back to New York City to take a job as the Corresponding Secretary of the American Congregational Union, a job he held for thirteen years. He retired from that job and returned to private life in Newark, New Jersey, where he lived until his death in 1887 at the age of seventy-nine.

During the combined years of service and into his retirement years, Ray was a prolific writer. He published eleven books and numerous hymns, papers and sermons. Ray's most famous works were his books ***Hymns and Sacred Pieces*** and ***Hymns of My Holy Hours and Other Pieces***. Altogether he composed seventy hymns, but some of them he never published. Over forty of his hymns are still used in hymnals in various denominations.

Many experts name Ray as one of America's greatest hymnist. One of the most beloved hymns written in America by an American was his hymn ***My Faith Looks Up to Thee***. Less known but equally powerful is Ray's poem ***The Spirit's Life***, written when he was twenty-nine years old. The poem captures the depth of his spiritual beliefs, the importance of hope, renewal, and one's spiritual life. The lengthy poem conveys hope: "O come the better day when every gale that sweeps from heaving hill or sunny vale shall sweetly breathe of purity and peace." It is a long-forgotten poem that should be remembered and cherished.

Ray's last publication before his death was ***Voices of Hope and Gladness***, written in 1881 when he was seventy-three years old. He was always fascinated by the concept of hope and the role of hope in one's spiritual life. He wanted to leave a legacy of hope and he desperately wanted others to find hope even during the most challenging and traumatic times. Ray was especially troubled by the tragedy and unbelievable loss of life during the American Civil War.

Ray's was a life of service to others, and although he died almost 140 years ago, his influence lives on through his hymns and poems.

(References: *The Gospel in Hymns*, 1950, Albert Bailey; *American Hymns Old and New*, 1980, Charles Hughes; *Dictionary Handbook to Hymns for the Living Church*, 1978, Donald Hustad)

Paton, Alan

Alan was born in 1903 in Pietermaritzburg, Natal Province in South Africa. His father was a low-level civil servant who made just enough money to provide for the family of several children. Alan's family had a comfortable lifestyle, but it was basic.

Alan was a good student in school but he showed no particular talents or strong interests in his studies. He enjoyed music and he had several friends, but he was unclear about his future. When Alan entered secondary school he was slow to mature, but by the time he reached his 17th birthday he decided that he needed to attend college. Gaining admission to a college, however, was not certain, so he gathered up his best effort and made good grades and did well on his exams and was admitted to college.

Alan understanding of the value of education and the awakening of his social consciousness that would be a mainstay of his life reached full development when he went to Maritzburg College and later to the University of Natal where he earned a Bachelor of Science degree and a certificate to teach.

Alan took a teaching position at Ixopo High School and later he taught at Maritzburg College. During this time in his life, he spoke out about social issues, especially how the Black citizens were being mistreated and ignored. He was especially concerned about the plight of young Black children and the lack of education and hope in their lives. Alan began writing articles about apartheid (a form of segregation, discrimination, and neglect) as he tried to open other people's awareness of and consciousness about the inequity that he knew would eventually harm everyone, including all races.

Due primarily to his social commitment that he took on a very difficult job as the principal of Diepkloof Reformatory, a juvenile detention and education center for young Black delinquents. Alan implemented many reforms while at the center. Many of the reforms were intended to prepare the youth for work when they left the reformatory. He also made certain that all of them received an education and he tried to teach them about trust and loyalty.

When Alan arrived at Diepkloof, each juvenile inmate had to prove he was worthy of walking the campus without first being in confinement. Alan conveyed a sense of trust in the inmates when he opened up the detention center campus for the young men to walk freely inside the compound. He even allowed some of them to work outside of the compound grounds. A few of them left and some dismissed his trust in them and tried to take advantage of his kindness and enlightenment. However, the vast majority appreciated and admired Alan's enlightened view of them and his trust of them.

When World War II broke out, Alan tried to volunteer for the Armed Services, but he was refused because his social ideas were viewed as radical and perhaps even contagious. During the war, he remained at the Reformatory and his progressive ideas caught the attention of other reformers.

After the war ended Alan went on a tour to visit correction facilities. He visited the United States and Canada, as well as Scandinavia and Europe. While he journeyed the world, he made use of the travel time to begin a novel, the novel that would make him famous and his voice heard around the world. It was ***Cry, The Beloved Country***. Alan actually completed the novel while in San Francisco which was fortuitous because his friends there knew the famous editor of Ernest Hemingway novels, Maxwell Perkins. With

Alan's permission, they shared a copy of the manuscript with Maxwell. He loved the novel and his company, Scribner, published it. Literary critics loved the novel as did the general public. It became a worldwide bestselling novel.

When Alan returned to South Africa, he founded the Liberal Party of South Africa (LPSA) to represent organized opposition to apartheid which was being introduced into law by the National Party. Supporters of apartheid laws broke up Alan's LPSA. His opposition to apartheid and the violent behavior of some former members of the LPSA brought controversy to Alan's life. His passport was revoked and remained so for over ten years. Ironically but intentionally, his passport was revoked upon his return from the United States where he was awarded the Freedom Foundation Award.

Alan retired to his beloved Botha's Hill home but his legend lived on in the bright light of recognition. A Hollywood movie was made from his novel ***Cry, The Beloved Country*** in 1951 (and a remake was made in 1995). Alan became a prolific writer. He wrote several novels, articles, short stories, poems, and hymns, and he won several awards for his humanitarian and literary work.

Alan died in 1988 at the age of eighty-five in Durban, Natal, South Africa. In honor of his work the Alan Paton Literary Award was created to recognize a non-fiction book annually.

(References: *Cry, The Beloved Country*, 1948, Alan Paton; *Some Sort of a Job: My Life with Alan Paton*, 1992, Anne Paton; *Alan Paton Speaking*, 2008, Roy Holland)

Peacey, John

John was born in 1896 in Brighton, Sussex, England to a family dedicated to worship and education. His large family of siblings became educated and successful adults due to the influence of the parents and each other.

John showed an early talent for music and he had a creative mind and energetic spirit. While attending St. Edmund's School in Canterbury, John excelled in all subjects and in athletics. His teachers said he was fearless both in his studies and in his participation in athletic games.

This fearlessness would prove valuable and noble during his World War I experiences. When he was eighteen years old, he entered the war as a lieutenant in the Sussex Royal Garrison Artillery. During the war, he showed remarkable courage and calm under attacks and assaults by the Germans. He steadied his men and never retreated from his artillery positions, even when faced with the likelihood of a German frontal assault. For his courage under fire, John was awarded the highly prestigious Military Cross for Bravery. The soldiers under his command were fearlessly loyal to him, and many of them credit John with saving the lives of several soldiers.

After the war, he attended Selwyn College, Cambridge to study theology. He graduated with First Class Honors and received his Bachelor and Master of Arts degrees. Soon thereafter he was ordained a deacon and one year later as a priest. He accepted a teaching post at Wellington College but then he received an offer to return to his alma mater, Selwyn College. He went to Selwyn as dean and Fellow.

John's interests varied widely and his curiosity about the influence of religion and education led him to accept the job as Headmaster of Bishop Cotton School in Simla, India. He loved living there and remained at the school for eight years. Then he became Principal of Bishop's College in Calcutta, India for over ten years. John was in India when World War II broke out. It was during this time that his courage again held steadfast against difficult times and threats from many sources. He stood up to various bands of invaders who tried to threaten the students and staff at the school and intimidate John. John made them back down as he stood tall, showed no fear, and ridiculed their bullying tactics.

After the war, he returned to England and served as Canon at Bristol Cathedral and as director of Ordinands for the Diocese. He also wrote a book about his time in India, ***The Flute of Jesus***, which became a bestselling book.

After he retired, John remained involved in service as acting Rural Dean of Hurst and as a writer of several hymns, including ***Filled with the Spirit's Power,*** which is found in many hymnals. Many of his hymns were published in ***Go Forth for God***—a widely used hymnal.

John died in 1971 in Sussex, England at the age of seventy-five. He remains a cherished figure in England and India.

(References: *Christian Hymnody in 21st Britain and America,* 2001, David W. Music; *Filled with the Spirit's Power,* 2015, Jenee Woodard; *A New Hymnal for Colleges and Schools,* 1992, Jeffery Rowthorn; *Christ's Time for the Church,* 2011, Laurence Stookey)

Perry, Michael

Michael was born in 1942 in Beckenham, Kent, England.

Michael was a literary and musical prodigy. At a very young age, he wrote prose and sang a variety of songs. Before he was sixteen years old he composed music and wrote lyrics for hymns. He was a very thoughtful, caring child who loved church and church music. Michael was also a good student in elementary and secondary school. He often told his parents and friends that he wanted to write and compose music for his career. That was his goal.

After secondary school, he attended Dulwich College, a school for boys in Dulwich, southeast of London, England. After receiving an undergraduate degree he attended the University College of London; Oak Hill Theological College; Ridley Hall at Cambridge University, and the University of Southampton. Michael received several degrees.

He greatly enjoyed the universities and during his time there that he wrote several hymns, including arguably his most famous hymn ***Calypso Carol***. Michael said that he wrote the hymn for a college concert and it was very well received; in fact, it was recorded. However, other than people at the concert and those around the university, the hymn was not well known until odd circumstances occurred. In 1964, Cliff Richard, a radio host, was looking for a recording to play on his radio show and in his haste and failure to find what he was looking for he turned to the closest recording he had on hand which turned out to be Michael's ***Calypso Carol***, so he played it on the radio. Public reaction was immediate and overwhelmingly favorable for the hymn. It became an almost instant classic and has remained popular ever since.

When Michael was ordained in the Church of England Diocese of Liverpool he became the minister at St. Helens Church in Merseyside for a few years before accepting a ministry at Bitterne, Southampton, England. While there he served on the Hymnal Committee that produced the hymnals ***Psalm Praise*** and ***Hymns for Today's Church*** that were popular then and can still be found in church hymnals. Michael left Bitterne to become Rector of Eversley, Hampshire for almost eight years. During that time, he continued to write hymns.

Michael began suffering from headaches during this time, but they were only occasionally severe enough to hamper his daily routine. His hymns were becoming nationally known and he was offered the job of Secretary of Jubilate Hymns as editor of books and other publications. While working for Jubilate he was also a part-time chaplain and adjunct professor at the National Police Staff College in Bramshill. In recognition of his work and devotion to his God-given grace and talent, he was elected to the Church of England's General Synod (it considers and approves legislation affecting the Church of England). In 1989, he was named Vicar of Tonbridge in Kent, and remained in that position until 1996 when he became gravely ill from severe chronic headaches. He learned that he had an inoperable brain tumor.

Michael fought bravely and courageously for several months thereafter, but he died at his home in Kent in December 1996 at the age of fifty-four. Many of his hymns were sung at his memorial service which was attended by hundreds of admirers and friends.

During his legendary career, Michael wrote over 300 hymns. Many of them can be found in hymnals across the world and in many different languages. Michael is considered one of England's greatest hymn composers.

(References: *Michael Perry—Church Hymnals,* Hope Publishing Company. Retrieved 2015; *Christian Hymnody in 20th Century Britain and the United States,* 2001, David Music; *Michael Perry - Hymnwriter,* 2011, Nuadha Trev)

Phelps, Sylvanus Dryden

Sylvanus was born in 1816 in Suffield, Connecticut. The family struggled, as did most other families in the community during that era. Nevertheless, Sylvanus' mother insisted that all seven children have an education, so they attended a small church-affiliated school near the town.

Sylvanus was a gregarious child who loved to be around people and who loved the activities of the local church. He enjoyed reading, writing, and music. When he turned sixteen, he enrolled in the Connecticut Literary Institute. There he excelled in all academic areas, especially in the classics. Because of his academic success and considerable talents, he was accepted into Brown University where he received a bachelor's degree. He was very interested in literature but he had a growing interest in theology, so he applied for and was accepted to Yale University Divinity School. He earned a Master of Divinity degree there and soon after graduation was ordained as a Baptist pastor.

Sylvanus became the pastor of the First Baptist Church in New Haven, Connecticut, where he remained for almost thirty years. He also became a writer. Sylvanus wrote articles, poems, and hymns, and he published several books, including well-known books: ***Eloquence of Nature and other Poems; Sunlight and Hearthlight Poems; The Holy Land*** *(later published as* ***Bible Land****);* ***The Poet's Song for the Heart and House,*** and ***Sermons in the Four Quarters of the Globe.***

Sylvanus was commissioned by his church to visit Europe, Egypt and the Holy Land with the only condition being that he had to keep a journal of his travels to share with the congregation when he returned home. His journal turned into a 400-page book titled ***The Holy Land with Glimpses of Europe and Egypt.*** He also served as the editor of *The Christian Secretary* magazine and as the president of the Connecticut Baptist State Convention. Even with a very busy schedule and with several responsibilities and activities including several children and a wife, he still managed to find time to write poems and hymns, including hymns that remain popular, such as ***Once I Heard a Sound at My Heart's Dark Door; Savior, Thy Dying Love; Sweet is Hour of Prayer; This Rite Our Blest Redeemer Gave,*** and others.

Sylvanus died in 1895 in New Haven, Connecticut at the age of seventy-nine. Due to his widespread popularity and gregarious nature, hundreds of people attended his funeral; in fact, one witness estimated that over 1,000 people attended.

(References: *S. Dryden Phelps,* Dictionary of Hymnology, Part II, 1907, John Julian; *Appleton's Cyclopedia of American Biography,* 1999, edited by James Grant Wilson; *The Gospel in Hymns,* 1950, Albert Edward Bailey)

Pierpoint, Folliot Sandford

Folliot was born in 1835 in Spa Villa, Bath, England. His family was a well-educated and religious family.

Folliot's father expected him and encouraged him to excel in his academic work and to learn classical music. He was exposed to classical literature and learned classical music composition. After he completed secondary school under the watchful eye of his father, Folliot enrolled at Queen's College, Cambridge University where he matured into an intellectual and academic star student. He graduated with highest honors in the classics. Folliot became a gifted scholar. He also became an expert in many other areas of study, including music and poetry.

He loved to write music and poetry that were inspired by nature. Folliot had a great appreciation of nature's beauty and God's hand in that beauty. He published ***The Chalice of Nature and***

Other Poems*; *Songs of Love*,** and ***Lyra Jesu, each dedicated to the beautiful confluence of nature, poetry, and music.

After graduating from Queen's College, he became a professor of classics at Somersetshire College. He continued to write and compose music, including several hymns. He contributed hymns to one of the era's most popular book of hymns, ***The Churchman's Companion***.

Folliot's most memorable work has withstood the test of time. His famous hymn ***For the Beauty of the Earth*** has been sung in churches for almost 150 years. Folliot wrote the hymn when he was twenty-nine years old while he walked through the countryside near his home. He always admired nature and unlike so many of his contemporaries (and even today) who fail to take notice of the miracle of nature, he basked in the glory and majesty of nature. On the day that inspired his classic hymn, he felt connected to the flowers, trees, warm breeze, clouds, and the sounds of nature. Foliot was always very proud of ***For the Beauty of the Earth***; it was his favorite work.

Folliot continued to write until his health declined in 1915. He died in 1917 in Newport, Monmouthshire, England at the age of eighty-two.

(References: *The Sacred Poets of the 19th Century*, 2011, Alfred H. Miles; *For the Beauty of the Earth*, sharefaith.com. Retrieved 2013; *For the Beauty of the Earth—Folliott Pierpoin*t, songsandhymns.org. Retrieved 2013; *For the Beauty of the Earth*, 2015)

Plumptre, Edward Hayes

Edward was born in 1821 in London, England as the eldest son of Edward Hallows Plumptre, a well-known solicitor in London. Edward's father wanted him to follow in his career path and study law, but Edward had other interests and talents. His brother, Charles John Plumptre, did become a barrister and also an expert in elocution.

Edward and his brother attended private schools before entering King's College. It was in college that Edward became passionate about the study of theology. He was a gifted student and showed an extraordinary intellect in many areas of study. Upon completion of his studies at King's College, he entered University College, Oxford, where his intellect became almost legendary. All of the various Oxford dons wanted him for their college. He took a rare double First Class in mathematics and classics under the internationally known and notoriously stern Sir George Bowen, Dean Bradley, and Edward Poste. Due to his intellectual gifts, Edward received a Fellowship at Brasenose College, which he held for three years.

At the age of twenty-six, Edward was ordained in Holy Orders and joined the staff of King's College, where he remained for almost twenty-one years. He was very innovative on the behalf of the students. He wanted learning to be inspirational for the students. Edward was influential in efforts to elevate the education of women and he introduced evening classes at the college. He held a series of important positions: Assistant Preacher at Lincoln's Inn; Select Preacher at Oxford; Professor of Pastoral Theology at King's College; Dean of Queen's, Oxford; Prebendary in St. Paul's Cathedral; Professor of Exegesis (study of Scripture) of the New Testament in King's College; Boyle Lecturer; Grinfield Lecturer on the Septuagint, Oxford; examiner in the Theological schools at Oxford; member of the Old Testament Company for the Revision of the A.V. of the Holy Scriptures; Rector of Pluckley; and Vicar of Bickley.

Edward became the Dean of Wells University and was a great positive influence on the university and the community of Wells. He was often seen nurturing the unfortunate patrons of what was referred to as the "almshouse", or public support housing for citizens with no income, typically the elderly in England. Edward was also respected and much loved by his colleagues and students, often speaking up on behalf of students and staff.

Edward's works are far too numerous to list because he was a prodigious writer who wrote about history, divinity, and the Bible. He also wrote biographies, poems, and hymns. Some of his most popular works were his books of poems, ***Lazarus and Other Poems***; ***Master and Scholar***, and ***Things New and Old***. The subject of his poems included the life of the church, the spiritual life of students in schools and colleges, the work in hospitals and almshouses, and the spiritual support offered by prayer and belief.

Edward continued to teach up until the time his health declined. After a brief illness, he died in 1891 in Wells, England at the age of seventy.

(References: *The Gospel in Hymns*, 1950, Albert Edward Bailey; *Edward Hayes Plumptre*, 2004, Oxford Dictionary of National Biography, R.C. Browne; *Sacred Poets of the 19th Century*, 1907, Chronicled in Bartleby by William Garrett Horder, 2012; *Edward Plumptre*, The Cambridge Bibliography of English Literature, Volume 2, 1969, F.W. Bateson)

Pollard, Adelaide (Sarah)

Adelaide was born in 1862 in Bloomfield, Iowa.

Beginning at a very young age, Adelaide was very creative and interested in reading and music. She took her school work seriously and decided she wanted to become a teacher. Adelaide's birth name was Sarah but she did not like that name so she took the name Adelaide as her own.

Adelaide received her education in Denmark, Iowa; Valparaiso, Indiana; the Boston School of Oratory; and the Moody Institute in Chicago, Illinois. When she finished school, Adelaide followed her dream to be a teacher. She found a teaching job in Chicago where she also discovered an interest in and talent for physical culture, cultural anthropology, and elocution. Adelaide loved teaching and her students greatly admired her as both a teacher and mentor. She also became well-respected for her abilities as a Bible study teacher in several churches in Chicago.

Adelaide's spiritual development continued and she became interested in the work of evangelists who have a "healing" ministry. She firmly believed in the healing power of prayer and divine intervention. In fact, she said prayer healed her own diabetes. Adelaide met another evangelist who preached wholly on the imminent return of Jesus to the world. Both evangelists helped form and firm Adelaide's beliefs in the power of God and the calling to expand the gospel across the world. She tried several ways to join in overseas missionary work, but she was not successful. To partially satisfy her missionary zeal, she became a teacher at the Missionary Training School in Nyack-on-the-Hudson. Nevertheless, she continued her efforts to raise money for a missionary trip to Africa, but with little success. Her failure led to a success because one evening as she was sharing her frustration and disappointment with a friend at a prayer meeting she heard a lady praying: "Lord, it doesn't matter what you bring into our lives, just have your way with us." This inspired Adelaide who went home and composed her most famous hymn ***Have Thine Own Way, Lord.*** In the hymn she describes God as a potter.

Adelaide, after several years finally made a missionary journey to Africa for a short period of time. Her trip was cut short because of the war storm clouds building over Europe that would eventually erupt into World War I. Adelaide spent most of the War years in Scotland teaching the Gospel and writing hymns.

When she returned to the United States shortly after the end of World War I, she became ill and remained in poor health for several years. Despite her ill health, she continued to teach, preach, and compose hymns. Over her lifetime Adelaide wrote over 100 hymns, or at least that is the best guess; it could be more than that because she seldom signed them.

Adelaide died in 1934 at the age of seventy-two from a ruptured appendix. She was traveling from her home in New York City to New Jersey to visit family and friends during Christmas when her appendix ruptured while she waited to catch a train in the New York City railroad station. Adelaide was buried in Fort Madison, Iowa.

(References: *Crusader Hymns and Hymn Stories,* 1967, Cliff Barrows and Don Husted; *Adelaide A. Pollard,* cyberhymnal.com.

Retrieved 2014; *Stories Behind the Hymns*, January 11, 2013, Warren Shiver)

Rankin, Jeremiah Eames

Jeremiah was born in 1828 in Thornton, New Hampshire. His family was a long-standing family of historical recognition dating back to 1780. His father was a farmer and merchant and a very religious man. Jeremiah and his many siblings were raised to honor God, family, and a strong work ethic.

His parents noticed Jeremiah's unusual intellect when he was a young boy. He learned to read at a very young age and was curious about many subjects. Jeremiah was seldom challenged in school because of his intellect and voracious reading habits. He was easily bored, so he began reading the Bible and studying music and history on his own.

After secondary school, he attended Middlebury College where he graduated at age nineteen with a Bachelor of Arts degree. Jeremiah had for years been interested in becoming a pastor and he enjoyed the study of theology, so upon his graduation from Middlebury College he entered into seminary studies at Andover Theological Seminary. A few years later, after returning to Middlebury College, was awarded a doctorate degree.

Jeremiah was ordained as a pastor in the Presbyterian Church and the Congregational Church. He served several churches in New York, Massachusetts, Vermont, New Jersey, and Washington, D.C. He created controversy in D.C. because he attempted to integrate the church and frequently corresponded with Frederick Douglas. His sermons became so well-known that people traveled for miles to hear him. Jeremiah's sermons were popular with the Vice President of the United States, Woodrow Wilson, and to many members of Congress. At the urging of many people, two of his sermons, ***The Bible and the Security of American Institutions*** and ***The Divinity of the Ballot***, were published and quickly circulated around the country with much attention and comment.

While serving at the Washington First Congregational Church he also supported Howard University, serving as Professor of Homiletics and Pastoral Theology. In 1889, he became President of Howard University. During his presidency, the university grew in student enrollment and expanded its degree offerings. Howard University's Andrew Rankin Memorial Chapel was named for Jeremiah's brother.

Jeremiah published many poems and hymns, but he is probably most remembered for his hymns ***Seeking Christ***; ***God Be With You Till We Meet Again,*** and ***Tell It to Jesus***. He also edited the books ***Gospel Temperance Hymnal*** and ***Gospel Bells*** which included some of his hymns. Jeremiah's favorite poem and the one that became very popular was ***The Babie*** which experts said was written in the style of Robert Burns, the Scottish poet.

In addition to his creative work, he served as Delegate to the General Conferences of the Methodist Episcopal Church and to the Congregational Union of England and Wales.

Jeremiah remained influential up until the last few years of his life. His gentle soul, kindness to others and creative genius endeared him to many people throughout his life. Jeremiah died in 1904 in Cleveland, Ohio, at the age of seventy-six.

(References: *Eames Rankin Jeremiah,* 1902, Dictionary of Hymnology, John Julian; *Sing it Again,* 1985, John Irving Erickson; *Eames Rankin Jeremiah,* Wordwise Hymns. Retrieved 2015; *Gospel Bells, 1880,* updated by nethymnal.org. Retrieved 2013)

Reid, Jr., William

William was born in 1923 in New York City. His father was a hymnist, so William grew up with music almost every day in his life, beginning at a very young age. He took piano lessons when he was only six years old and quickly learned complicated pieces. He loved school and music, and he greatly enjoyed the hymns that his father composed. William was very proud of his father's work, and he wanted to follow in his footsteps as a hymnist.

After a stellar academic record in both elementary and secondary schools, William was offered a scholarship at Oberlin College. He completed his Bachelor of Arts degree in only three years and was then accepted into Yale Divinity School, where he received a Bachelor of Divinity degree.

World War II broke out and William went into the Army. He was trained as a medic and served proudly and bravely in the European Theatre. William was courageously loyal to the soldiers he treated on the battlefield; he often put his life in danger. While tending to a wounded United States Army soldier he was captured by the Germans because William refused to abandon his patient. For over eight months William was a prisoner of war (POW) in Germany. In the prison, he often treated the wounds and illnesses of soldiers who were maltreated by the German soldiers. He survived the POW camp and returned to the United States at the end of the war. As the result of his military service, he was awarded three Battle Stars.

Upon his return, he was offered the pastor's position at a Methodist church in North Dakota. Over the course of several years, William was the pastor of other churches in North Dakota and later in Wilkes-Barre, Pennsylvania where he also served on the Wilkes-Barre City Council for four years and helped considerably in the community's recovery efforts in the aftermath of the catastrophic flooding in 1972. He offered more public service when he served as a Wyoming County Commissioner for eight years.

Due to his father's influence, William started writing hymns when he was a young man, and he continued composing hymns until his health declined. William is the author of several published hymns, including many published in the Hymn Society books ***Fourteen New Rural Hymns*** and ***Twelve New World Order Hymn.*** His hymn ***O God of Every Nation*** is in hymnals throughout the world and is his most famous hymn. The hymn won first place in a contest co-sponsored by the Hymn Society of America (now the Hymn Society in the United States and Canada) and the National Council of Churches.

William died in 2007 at the age of eighty-four.

(References: *William Reid, Jr*. 1989, Michael Hawn, UMC. Retrieved 2014; *William Reid, Jr.*, Dictionary of Hymnology. Retrieved 2015; *Still Dews of Quietness*, 2009, E. Jane Seeman)

Rinkart, Martin

Martin was born in 1586 in Germany. He was the son of a poor coppersmith, who struggled to find work to support his family. Nevertheless, his parents did the best they could for the children.

His parents observed early in his life that Martin was exceedingly talented in music. They noticed this when they attended the local church and participated in the music program. He developed a gift for playing and reading music, and he began writing music at a young age. A young minister at the church encouraged Martin to study music and work hard in the local small school to prepare for college.

Through sheer will, hard work, perseverance, and his gregarious nature, young Martin worked his way into the University of Leipzig. The admission counselor was not convinced that Martin could handle the academic rigor of the university, so he offered to tutor him. However, Martin's intelligence allowed him to adjust to the university setting and also thrive in it. Against all odds, Martin earned a Bachelor of Arts degree.

After graduation, he became the Precentor (helps facilitate worship services) of the Church of Eisleben, where he would devote his life to the community until his death in 1649. He became known for his steadfast and untiring work during the horrible plague of 1637. The entire town council and a devastatingly large number of children, as well as almost all of the neighboring clergymen, died from the plague. At times, Martin seemed to be the only adult taking care of hundreds of people in Eilenburg. Even after the plague subsided, the community and country faced gruesome famine that resulted in people fighting and killing over any food or living or dead animal. Martin almost single-handedly kept the community from falling apart and descending into complete chaos. Later, scholars estimated that Martin presided over the burial of over 4,000 men, women, and children and saved the lives of as many as a thousand. But the worst was not over for Martin or the community.

The Swedes invaded after the plague and famine, and once again Martin had to draw on his spiritual strength and determination to save the lives of people, as he negotiated all of his future meager earnings to ensure that the children in the town would receive food and shelter during the Swedes invasion and takeover of the community.

Martin continued through all of the tragedies and threats to hold his faith and to offer sermons, prayers and care for others while writing and composing hymns. His faith had to be strong to help him endure one tragedy after another. He often found comfort in composing hymns. Composing hymns helped Martin cope with the almost constant tragedies. He is most famous for writing the brilliant and eternal ***Now Thank We All Our God***, which was set to music by Johann Cruger.

Martin kept the faith and served his community until his death in 1649 at the age of sixty-three in Saxony, Germany. He is a model for everyone on how the strength of faith and service to others are divine and serve God. His life should be studied and revered by everyone.

(References: *Martin Rinkart,* Cyberhymnal.org. Retrieved 2014; *Martin Rinkart,* Bach Cantatas Website. Retrieved 2013; *A Church of Ireland Rector in Rural Leinster,* 2011, Ian Poulton; *Annotations Upon Popular Hymns,* 1893, Charles Seymour Robinson; *Favorite Hymns,* 2001, Marjorie Reeves and Jenyth Worsley)

Rippon, John

John was born in 1751 in Tiverton, Devonshire, England. He was the son of a Baptist minister. His family valued their religious beliefs, family, and education above all else.

John attended public school and was an excellent student. He also participated in all school, church, and community activities. He especially enjoyed music and musical productions.

After attending the small school in Tiverton, he enrolled at Bristol Baptist College, where he developed an interest in theology and philosophy, as well as church music. After graduating he was ordained and took a position as minister at what was referred to as the "meeting-house" on Carter Lane at Tooley Street. It was not a church per se, but worship services were held there. The meeting-house gatherings had to move to a building on New Park Street due to the remodeling of London Bridge. There it became the New Park Street Chapel. John was only twenty years old when he became the minister, and he never left. His devotion to his church and congregation was unshakeable. He remained at New Park Street Chapel until his death sixty-three years later.

John's reputation as a minister and writer was widespread. He edited the *Baptist Annual Register* for several years. The periodical contained information about the important events in the history of the Baptist denomination in both Great Britain and America. It was also during that period when John composed several hymns, although he actually began composing a few hymns when he was a young minister. He studied the history of hymns and in doing so became interested in the hymnist, Isaac Watts. John wrote a book about Isaac Watts. John also created a book of hymns for his church, a book that many churches used. Due to the popularity of his hymn selections, he composed a hymnal, ***A Selection of Hymns from the Best Authors***. The hymnal became so popular that it was reprinted thirty times over the course of ten editions. Each time a new edition was published, people would find even more hymns, some of which were composed by John. The book became so large that it was renamed ***The Comprehensive Edition***. It is estimated that over 200,000 copies were sold. For that era, that was a remarkable number.

John was a conscious spiritual leader who followed the plight of his congregation and others, including the impact on them from the escalation of the American Revolutionary War. He carried on a correspondence with fellow Baptist ministers across the Atlantic, offering encouragement for them to provide spiritual guidance to the citizens bravely fighting and enduring the war. His continuous and heartfelt support of the Baptist ministers in the United States led to the Baptist College of Providence, Rhode Island, giving him the Doctor of Divinity degree.

John continued to compose hymns, edit his hymnal, and preach up until the time he died in 1836 at the age of eighty-five. On Christmas Eve, he was buried in Bunhill Fields, in London Borough of Islington. Several other famous people were buried at the famous cemetery.

(References: *John Rippon,* Dictionary of Hymnology, 1907, John Julian; *John Rippon,* Cathcart's Baptista Encyclopedia - reformedreader.org. Retrieved 2014; *Three Hymnals That Shaped Today's Worship,* Christian History Institute, William Reynolds)

Roberts, Daniel

Daniel was born in 1841 in Bridgehampton, Long Island, New York. He had a humble but steady upbringing in a modest household with a family that kept to itself and in its own way firmly valued family and God.

He was a shy child, adolescent, and adult. Daniel was a good student in the local schools but he did not excel academically. However, he was successful enough to qualify for college. After completing secondary school Daniel enrolled at Kenyon College in Ohio where he graduated with a bachelor's degree.

He worked at various jobs until the outbreak of the American Civil War led to his enlistment in the 84th Ohio Volunteers of the Northern Union Army. He served with distinction, often putting the safety of his companions before his own. At the end of the war, he studied to be a minister and was ordained in the Episcopal Church as a priest. Daniel served as a priest at the Christ Church in Montpelier, Vermont; St. John's Church in Lowell, Massachusetts; St. Thomas Episcopal Church in Brandon, Vermont, and at St.

Paul's Church in Concord, New Hampshire. He served at St. Paul's for several years. He was also the President of the New Hampshire State Historical Society; President of the Normal School of Vermont, and Chaplain for the National Guard of New Hampshire.

Daniel was a well-respected clergyman and citizen, but his fame came from bursts of creativity and inspiration—he wrote the legendary hymn ***God of Our Fathers***. He was inspired to write the famous hymn out of respect for the many generations of believers who shared their unwavering faith in God and the spirit of Jesus to ensure that the messages created an unbroken chain of faith from one generation to another. He wrote the original hymn for the 1876 Centennial Fourth of July Celebration in Brandon, Vermont. Several years later he sent the hymn anonymously to the General Convention of the Episcopal Church for possible inclusion in the hymnal for churches. Daniel was not certain that it would be accepted and he thought he would face embarrassment if the hymn was ridiculed or neglected by the Convention. The hymn was accepted and published. It was not immediately noticed, but over time people began to notice and enjoy the hymn and with growing momentum it became increasingly popular throughout the United States. With the mounting popularity of the hymn came much interest in the author of the hymn. Daniel declined almost all opportunities to cash in on his fame or became a source of newspaper or journal or magazine articles. He told a reporter one time, "I remain a country parson, known only within my own small church and community." Daniel's hymn received many awards, as did he, including an honorary Doctor of Divinity degree from Norwich University.

After a short illness, Daniel died in 1907 in Concord, New Hampshire at the age of sixty-six.

(References: *Daniel Crane Roberts,* Cyberhymnal.org. Retrieved 2013; *Hymns of the United Church,* 1921, Herbert Lockwood Willett and Charles Clayton Morrison; *Daniel C. Roberts,* 1907, Dictionary of Hymnology, John Julian)

Robinson, Robert

Robert was born in 1735 in Swaffham, Norfolk, England. Robert was only eight years old when his father died, which left the family to struggle for survival. His family moved in with other family members to share resources and to support each other.

Robert was a very bright and active child, who was stubborn and often disrespected even to his father. After his father's death, he became increasingly more difficult for his mother to handle. When Robert was fourteen years old, his mother sent him to London for an apprenticeship with an uncle who was a barber. The change did not help, for Robert proceeded to get into even more trouble, taking on a life of drinking, gambling, and fighting. His uncle tried in vain to change Robert's life. He even extended Robert's work hours to lessen his free time. Robert never complained and his behavior did not change. He was a creature of the night. Somehow he could work fourteen hours and stay out most of the night and maintain his energy, work ethic, and sunny disposition. That would change, however.

One night when he was seventeen years old, Robert and some of his drinking buddies decided to attend an evangelistic meeting, with a plan to make fun of the proceedings. They laughed and connived all the way to the service. Robert did not like the idea of disrupting a worship service, but by the time the gang reached the worship service, Robert was all in, even adding that he would fake a religious conversion and then pull a bottle of whiskey out and drink in front of everyone. George Whitfield was the minister, a well-known theologian and powerful speaker with a commanding presence. He immediately sensed why the young ruffians were there. Whitfield bore in on the unruly gang with his most profound voice, but he focused on Robert and delivered a powerful message without taking his eyes off of Robert during most of the sermon. Robert felt as if the sermon's message was just for him. He later admitted that he was stunned by the presence of a spirit that he could not understand.

Robert did not respond to the altar call that night, but the words of the evangelist haunted him for the next three years. For three years, Robert frequently harkened back to that evening with Whitfield, and gradually, ever so slowly his behavior and attitude changed. He became more serious at work and time with his unruly friends became shorter and more controlled. The change was subtle but certain.

On Dec. 10, 1755, at age twenty, Robert finally yielded his life to Christ, and very soon thereafter he answered a call to the ministry. A few years later, as he was preparing to preach his first sermon at the Calvinist Methodist Chapel in Norfolk, England, Robert relived that fateful night when Whitfield touched his heart and soul. In response to that memory and that inspiration, he wrote the hymn ***Come Thou Fount of Every Blessing*** to complement his sermon. The hymn has since been included in most hymnals in England and the United States and has been recorded by several professional artists.

Robert became a leading theologian of his day. He published several works, including the very influential ***History of Baptism and Baptists*** and ***Ecclesiastical Researches***.

Robert died in his sleep in 1790 at the age of fifty-five while staying with a friend in Birmingham, England.

(References: *Robert Robinson 1735-1790*, Dictionary of National Biography. Retrieved 2013; *Annotations of the Hymnal*, 1872, Charles Hutchins; *Robert Robinson*, Dictionary of Hymnology, 1907, John Julian)

Rossetti, Christina

Christina was born in London, England in 1830 to well-known parents. Her father, Gabriele Rossetti, was a poet and teacher and being a political exile from Vasto, Abruzzo (Italy) made him exotic to the citizens of London. Christina's mother, Frances Polidori, was the sister of the famous Lord Byron's friend and distinguished physician, John William Polidori.

Christina was the youngest of four children, two girls, and two boys. One brother, Dante, became a popular artist and poet while her other brother, William, and her sister, Maria also became writers. Christina, however, was the most prolific writer of the children.

She was extremely energetic, creative and gregarious. Even as a very young child, Christina loved to make up stories and she took turns dedicating her stories to her mother and father. She would say, "Mother, this story is especially for you." "Father, I wrote a story just for you." With creative and educated parents, Christina took her schooling at home, which included religious study, classics, fairy tales, eclectic writing from around the world, poetry, and popular novels of the day. She was an energetic reader, reading everything that was brought into the house, but she favored Scott, Keats, Radcliffe, Lewis, Alighieri, and Petrarch. She especially enjoyed Italian literature. Her enjoyment of Italian writing may have been related to her family's open door to Italian revolutionaries, scholars, artists, and poets, whom they welcomed and entertained on a regular basis.

Christina's happy world began to fade away as her father's physical and mental health deteriorated, finally to the point that he was unable to work. Christina suffered greatly as she watched her father's decline and her way of life change. She began experiencing long episodes of depression. The only joy in her life at this time was her brother, Dante, who had become a popular and successful artist. He often asked Christina to set for many of his paintings. In fact, Dante Rossetti's most famous paintings are of Christina. His masterpiece, ***The Girlhood of Mary Virgin***, was modeled by Christina. Her brother encouraged her to try writing stories, since at one time she loved to write for their parents. Christina took his advice to heart. She found her voice in poems; poetry became her temporary salvation from episodes of depression.

When she was seventeen years old, she tried her hand at sonnets, hymns, and ballads. Her public career and the popular discovery of her talents started when she was eighteen years old with the publication of two poems, ***Death's Chill Between*** and ***Heart's Chill Between***. She also contributed to the widely read magazine, *The Germ*. Christina's masterwork appeared in 1862 when she was thirty-one years old. The famous collection of poems entitled ***Goblin Market and Other Poems*** was a sensation across Great Britain and Europe. Many even spoke of her as the natural successor to the world-famous poet Elizabeth Barrett Browning. Christina's fame, however, never reached that level, even though she was widely read and respected. She fought to cope with chronic depression which drained her energy and probably kept her from achieving the level of fame so many people thought she would achieve. Even so, she published many works and remained well-known for many years. Two of her hymns remain popular, ***In the Bleak Midwinter*** and ***Love Come Down at Christmas***.

After a series of illnesses, Christina passed away in 1894 at the age of sixty-four.

(References: *Christina Rossetti—English Poet,* Encyclopedia Britannica. Retrieved 2014; *Christina Rossetti: A Literary Biography,* 2012, Jan Marsh; *Christina Rossetti: A Biographical and Critical Study,* 2010, MacKenzie Bell)

Routley, Erik Reginald

Erik was born in Brighton, England in 1917. He was an only child to John and Eleanor. Erik's father was the Mayor of Brighton.

As a child, Erik showed unusual intellectual understanding of everything he read, and he was a voracious reader. Erik excelled in his school work and enjoyed writing and music. He began composing music at a very young age with the encouragement of his mother, who taught music. Erik attended Fonthill Preparatory School where he was extraordinarily successful. After secondary school, he attended Lancing College, where he showed a gift for writing, music, and composing. Erik then attended Magdalen and Mansfield Colleges in Oxford. He graduated with honors. Erik earned a Bachelor of Arts and a Doctor of Philosophy degree.

Erik served as Chaplain of Mansfield College for over ten years and also at Edinburgh College and Newcastle College. He became Professor of Church Music at Westminster Choir College in

Princeton, New Jersey in 1975. Prior to his move to New Jersey, Erik was well known for his music compositions. His hymns became popular in churches and blended well with the spirit of worship. He was credited with starting what was called "The Hymn Explosion" in Great Britain in the early 1970s. When he relocated to New Jersey he brought that enthusiasm for hymns to the United States.

Erik was much more than a hymnist. He published several respected scholarly books on worship, music, and other works. His book ***Congregational Praise*** received praise throughout the world. He followed that with an equally popular book, ***The University Carol Book***. However, he became even more famous for his hymns. Erik's hymn ***Sharpthorne*** is still considered a classic. Several of his books are viewed by experts as standard texts for hymns and tunes, such as ***All Who Love and Serve Your City***, ***A Panorama of Christian Hymnody***, and ***New Songs of Celebration***.

Erik passed away in 1982 in Nashville, Tennessee at the age of sixty-five after a brief illness.

(References: *Erik Routley*, The Times obituary, Wednesday, October 20, 1982; *Erik Routley and the 1970s Hymn Explosion*, 1974, Hope Publishing Company; *Erik Routley*, The Canterbury Dictionary of Hymnology. Retrieved 2014)

Saint Irenaeus

Irenaeus was born sometime during the 2nd century, between 115 and 142. The wide range of birth years has been a source of debate for centuries.

Apparently, Irenaeus was born in or near Smyrna in the area now known as Turkey. He was a Greek Christian having been raised as a Christian by his parents and extended family. Irenaeus' education was provided through the town's church. His religious training was from the local church, also, and led to him becoming a priest at the Church of Lyon. It was during this time that the Roman Emperor, Marcus Aurelius, began a reign of terror in Lyon aimed at persecuting Christians. Christians were not even allowed to visit the town's marketplace, and some of the religious leaders in the Christian community were imprisoned.

Irenaeus was a young priest, compared to the others, and strong in his faith and very articulate and skilled in writing. For those reasons, the senior clergy of Lyon asked him to take a letter to Pope Eleuterus explaining the plight of Lyon and the persecution from the emperor. While he was in Rome, a massacre of Christian leaders and other citizens took place in Lyon. Pothinus the Second Bishop of Lyon was one of the casualties (Pothinus would later be declared a saint). Irenaeus took his place as the Second Bishop of Lyon after delivering the message to the Pope. The Pope and Marcus Aurelius were troubled by the massacre, especially after Irenaeus had appealed to Rome for peace; consequently, an uneasy peace settled over the town and the persecution of Christians abated. During this time of peace, Irenaeus served his duty as Bishop, but he also encouraged and led missionary work outside of the city and he also began writing. His reputation grew, especially after the publication of his work, ***Against Heresies***, which includes five books that justify and document the word of Jesus through his disciples. In fact, in Book IV, he includes Jesus' sayings and focuses on the unity of the Old Testament and the Gospel. Irenaeus' publication aimed to debase the followers of Magus the Magician whose pagan worship was based on the illusion of magic.

Irenaeus remained in Lyons for the rest of his life, but it is believed that his influence extended to Pope Victor I and included support of the celebration of Easter. He also wrote hymns, the most famous being ***You Are the Work of God***, which was played in the local church as well as other churches throughout Europe and remains popular in hymnals over 400 years after his death.

Toward the end of the century, he died, but there is no record of how he died or the exact date of his death. He was buried beneath the Church of Saint John in Lyon which was later renamed the Church of Saint Irenaeus to honor him when he was granted sainthood; however, his tomb and the church were damaged in 1562 by the Huguenots.

(References: *St. Irenaeus of Lyons: Against the Heresies Book 1* (Ancient Christian writers), 1991, Dominic J. Unger; *Irenaeus on the Christian Faith*, 2011, James Payton; *Irenaeus of Lyons on Baptism and Eucharist*, 1991, David N. Power)

Sammis, John

John was born in 1846 in Brooklyn, New York to hardworking parents. John grew up with several siblings.

John was a bright young man but restless. When John was old enough to venture away from his Brooklyn neighborhood he liked to walk around to the side of town that included homes of the wealthy. He was fascinated with the large homes in other neighborhoods and the large polished carriages of the rich. He decided then that he wanted to become a businessman.

He completed his education in Brooklyn and took jobs in various stores in the area. When he was twenty-three years old he heard about a job training program in Logansport, Indiana that promised a career in business, so he took a chance and moved there. John applied what he learned and became a very successful businessman and a community leader. He was also interested in the work of the local church as well as the YMCA that used the church and other venues in the town. John became a part-time volunteer and later a part-time worker at the YMCA. It was this work that awakened his spiritual side.

To the shock and surprise of his family and friends, he gave up his business career so he could study for the ministry. John studied at the McCormick and Lane Seminary. After graduation, he became an ordained Presbyterian minister. He served as a minister in Iowa, Indiana, and Minnesota. Because of his widely popular sermons and his devoted work in the community, he was offered several jobs. One of them was a job to teach at the newly founded Los Angeles Bible Institute. John accepted the job because he wanted to expand his experiences and knowledge. He greatly enjoyed teaching and remained at the institute for the remainder of his career.

John is best known for writing the lyrics to one of the most popular and long-lasting hymns in history - ***Trust and Obey***. The composer of the music to the hymn, Daniel Towner, was the music director for the legendary revivalist, Dwight Moody. During one of the revivals, a young man rose during the sermon and said he was going to trust and obey God. Daniel wrote those words down and sent them to John. John was immediately inspired by these simple but profound words and he spent the next several days working on lyrics to a hymn based on those words—a hymn that would become the legendary ***Trust and Obey***.

John wrote over 100 hymns during his life, some of them after he retired from the institute. He died in 1919 in Los Angeles at the age of seventy-three.

(References: *Story Behind the Song—Trust and Obey*, Sharefaith.com. Retrieved 2014; *John Henry Sammis Biography*, Nethymnal.org. Retrieved 2014; *John H. Sammis*, Ancestry.com. Retrieved 2014; *Trust and Obey*, April 16, 2015, The Courier-Tribune, Warren Shiver)

Sandell-Berg, Caroline

Caroline was born in 1832 in Froderyd, Smaland, Sweden.

Biographers argue over her name. In some books, she is listed as Karolina Wilhelmina Sandell and other biographers refer to her as Caroline Sandell. Regardless, she was referred to by family and friends as Lina. Her father was a Lutheran minister.

Lina was a precocious child who loved music and poetry. She tried writing poems when she was only about ten years old, and with the encouragement of her father, mother, and her teachers she continued to write poems. As she learned more about music, she became enamored with the process of writing and reading music, so she learned both. With the combination of poems and music coupled with the considerable amount of time she spent in her father's church, Lina learned how to turn poems into hymns.

By the age of seventeen, she was writing and composing hymns on a regular basis, and some of the hymns were played in her father's church. Her first publication was at age twenty-one with a book of poems. Another book of poems was published two years later. Lina's work began to receive positive acclaim across Sweden, and she developed a modest degree of recognition.

Lina's life took an unexpected turn because of a personal tragedy. While on a boating trip with her father across Lake Vattern in Sweden, a sudden lurch of the boat caused her father to stumble and fall overboard. He was drowned before he could be rescued. Lina was a witness to her father's death, and it deeply disturbed her for the rest of her life. Many of her poems and hymns following his death were in response to her loss. Though some biographers dispute the claim, most agree that her most famous hymns, ***Children of the Heavenly Father*** and ***Day by Day*** were inspired by her father's death.

Over time, Lina became world famous and legendary in Sweden. Her fame grew when the famous performer Oscar Ahnfelt put many of her poems to music and played for audiences throughout Scandinavia and Europe. But there is much more to the Lina and Oscar story. During this time in Scandinavia, a revolution was taking place. It was called the Rosenius Movement which was intended to persecute evangelical messengers. Oscar was not only a performer, he was also a preacher. Members of the Rosenius Movement wanted evangelicals silenced, so they petitioned King Karl XV, who ruled over a united Sweden and Norway, to ban evangelicals from the kingdom. The King refused to make a declaration without first hearing Oscar, by then known as the "spiritual troubadour" of evangelicals. An arrangement was made for the King to hear Oscar. Oscar went to Lina and requested a special hymn just for this occasion, and Lina's composition was brilliant. Oscar went to the Royal Palace with his guitar and sang Lina's hymn and other selections. The King was visibly moved by Oscar and his message. Many witnesses said that the King had tears in his eyes when he told Oscar he could sing anywhere in both kingdoms and as often as he would like.

Other performers, like the extremely popular Jenny Lind, also performed Lina's hymns and helped her publish many of her hymns and poems. In her lifetime, Lina wrote over 2,000 poems and over 600 hymns. She became and remains Sweden's most famous and prolific poet and hymnist.

Lina worked on poems and hymns up until the time of her death in 1903 at the age of seventy. She was buried at Solna Church in Stockholm.

(References: *Twice Born Hymns,* 1976, J. Irving Erickson; *Lina Sandell Berg: Songs out of Tragedy,* Christianity.com. Retrieved 2015; *Dictionary Handbook to Hymns of the Living Church,* 1978, Donald Hustad)

Schutte, Daniel

Daniel was born in 1947 in Neehah, Wisconsin and grew up in Elm Grove, Wisconsin.

He was raised in a caring family and as a young boy, it was obvious to his family, relatives, and friends that Daniel had a kind, caring, and loving nature. He loved being around people and he enjoyed reading and music. Daniel was a very good student in elementary school and in secondary school. His reputation as a musician grew while he attended Marquette University High School, but he also had an interest in becoming a religious leader. After high school, Daniel earned two master's degrees from the Jesuit School of Theology at Berkeley.

Daniel became one of the founding members of the St. Louis Jesuits who are well-known for their contemporary style of worship music. This was at the time of the reforms of Vatican II when the use of English was encouraged. Therefore, the St. Louis Jesuits had permission to take sacred texts and write them in English and sing them in worship services in English. The talent and spirituality of the St. Louis Jesuits created a widespread reputation and popular demand for access to their music. In fact, their second collection of hymns, ***Earthen Vessels,*** sold over one million albums. Altogether,

Daniel and the St. Louis Jesuits recorded nine collections of their music including a thirty-year anniversary collection in 2005.

For over thirty years their music has been a standard in Catholic parishes throughout the United States and Canada. Daniel and the St. Louis Jesuits' hymn ***Mass of the Savior,*** which was published in 2012, has become the most widely used Mass Settings in the English-speaking world. Daniel's most famous hymns are the ***City of God***; ***Only This I Want***; ***Blest Be the Lord***; ***You Are Near***; ***Though the Mountains May Fall***; ***Sing a New Song***; ***Glory and Praise to Our God***; and ***These Alone Are Enough***.

Over time, many of Daniel's hymns began appearing in Protestant hymnals. Also, many famous recording artists have recorded Daniel's compositions, including Amy Grant and John Michael Talbot. Daniel's book ***Walking the Sacred Path—Spiritual Exercises for Today*** became a recent bestseller.

He left the Jesuits several years ago but he continues to compose music and perform around the world and is presently the Composer-in-Residence at the University of San Francisco.

(References: *The St. Louis Jesuit*, Oregon Catholic Press Archives, 2006. Retrieved 2014 and 2015; *Daniel Schutte*, www.DanSchutte.com. Retrieved 2015)

Scott, Clara

Clara was born in 1841 in Elk Grove, Illinois. Her parents, Sarah, and Abel were hardworking Midwesterners and were devoted parents and citizens.

Clara showed musical interests and talent when she was very young but she did not take music seriously until she was an adolescent. Thereafter she enjoyed all types of music. Clara was especially drawn to church hymns. She loved the poetry of hymns and she was fascinated by the process of writing music.

After completing her local education, Clara looked for opportunities to learn more about music. Her timing was fortuitous because at that time the first Music Institute was held in Chicago, Illinois by C. M. Cady, a remarkably talented woman who wanted to advance the study of music. When she attended the Music Institute, Clara wrote several poems and hymns. After receiving music training at the Music Institute, Clara taught music at the Ladies Seminary in Lyons, Iowa. It was there that she met and married Henry Clay Scott. Her husband strongly encouraged her to continue her work and he was instrumental in convincing Clara to seek a publisher for her poems and hymns. His encouragement led to a historical moment in music because Clara became the first woman to publish a volume of anthems. Horatio Palmer, who was a well-known and respected musician, helped Clara get her book published. The book was titled ***The Royal Anthem Book*** and it was a publishing sensation for the fact it was written by a woman and because the hymns revealed her remarkable talent. The book and the hymns became very popular—some of them are in modern day hymnals. Perhaps the most famous of her hymns is ***Open My Eyes That I May See***. Clara was inspired to write the hymn after hearing a sermon that focused primarily on *Psalm 119*.

At the height of her career and popularity tragedy struck. She was invited to Dubuque, Iowa to visit with friends and share her music with the community. She was riding through the town in a carriage with friends when the horse was startled by a loud noise. The horse bolted out of control which caused the carriage to shift radically from side to side. Clara and other passengers were thrown from the carriage. Clara was gravely injured and did not recover. She died from her injuries in 1897 at the age of fifty-six.

(References: *Clara Scott,* Ancestry.com. Retrieved 2015; *Clara H. Scott,* The Canterbury Dictionary of Hymnology. Retrieved 2015; *Clara H. Scott,* Library of Congress. Retrieved 2015)

Scott, Robert Balgarnie Young

Robert was born in 1899 in Toronto, Ontario. His father was a Presbyterian minister in the Presbyterian Church of Canada. Robert had a childhood filled with intellectual curiosity and exposure to religious events and church music.

He attended a secondary school where he excelled academically. After secondary school, he attended Knox College and the University of Toronto where he earned a Bachelor of Arts degree and two years later he received a Master of Arts degree. Robert was a brilliant student and scholar; consequently, his professors encouraged him to enter the doctoral program which he did immediately after receiving his master's degree. Four years later he was awarded a Ph.D. when he was only twenty-six years old. While working on his doctoral degree he became an ordained minister in the United Church of Canada.

After the receipt of his doctoral degree, Robert taught at Vancouver Union College for three years. His reputation as a scholar began there, as his writings and teaching gained attention from the academic world. Robert was offered a full professorship of Old Testament Language and Literature at the United Theological College of Montreal. He taught there for several years, during which time he became widely known as a brilliant scholar and theologian.

McGill University recruited Robert to teach Old Testament there as a regent's professor. He taught seven years at the university and then became the Dean of Faculty for the College of Divinity at McGill University. Also, he was a member of the World Council of Churches for over six years, where he showed a keen intellect as was the voice of reason and creativity. In 1955, Robert was appointed to the very prestigious position of Danforth Professor of Religion at Princeton University. He became the Chairman of the Department.

Throughout his career, Robert wrote extensively about the Old Testament, became a recognized internationally known scholar of the Dead Sea Scrolls, and wrote numerous hymns. His publications included popular and scholarly books such as ***The Relevance of the Prophets***; ***The Way of Wisdom***; ***Treasures from Judean Caves***; ***The Psalms as Christian Praise***; ***The Anchor Bible Series*** and ***Proverbs and Ecclesiastes***. He wrote twenty-four hymns, with the most famous being ***O Day of God Draw Nigh*** which can be found in most hymnals in Canada and several in the United States and the Anglican Churches in England and Australia. It was sung at Westminster Abbey at the memorial service for John Smith, the former leader of the British Labor Party.

Robert was ill for several years before his death in 1987 at the age of eighty-seven in Toronto, Canada. He is remembered for his intelligence, creativity, wisdom, influence, and strong faith.

(References: *Hymns of Robert Balgarnie Young Scott,* The Canadian Encyclopedia. Retrieved 2015; *The Way of Wisdom,* 1971, R.B.Y. Scott; *Robert B.Y. Scott,* The Presbyterian Hymnal Companion, 1993, Lindajo H. McKim; *Sing It Again,* 1985, John Irving Erickson)

Sears, Edmund

Edmund was born in 1810 on a farm in Sandisfield, Massachusetts. The family farm was near Berkshire Hills. Ed was the youngest of three sons.

Because of the duties of the farm that the family depended on for its livelihood, Ed did not receive much education. However, he was exposed to literature because of his father's love of reading and especially his love of poetry. Ed's father frequently read poetry to the family and talked about the beauty of the written word. His father and mother were very traditional and religious in their ideas about morality and hard work. These beliefs were embedded in Ed and he was true to them throughout his life.

Even though he did not have a formal education in his youth, he applied to and was accepted at Union College in Schenectady, New York when he was twenty-one years old. Primarily because of his age, he started as a sophomore. Almost immediately, his professors grew very fond of Ed's engaging and charismatic nature. Also, his talent in verse and poetry became well known at the college. He won a prize for his poetry. He earned a Bachelor of Arts degree.

After graduation, Ed studied law for almost a year under a lawyer in Sandisfield. He then moved to Vermont and taught at

Brattleboro Academy. Not content with the idea of being a lawyer or a teacher, Ed soon began to study for the ministry under Addison Brown, minister of the Unitarian Church in Brattleboro. It was when he read several books about theology while studying under Addison that his interests swung completely that way. He enrolled in Harvard Divinity School and graduated in 1837.

Ed was still uncertain about his career choice, but he wanted to experience the ministry so he preached in Toledo, Ohio for a short time before moving to larger churches in the Boston area. Ed distinguished himself through his sermons and writings. Many experts claim that Ed's theological reasoning and clarity of writing influenced many 19th century ministers. Although his reputation as a theologian was widespread, Ed is known today for another reason—a legacy that has lasted over 160 years.

In 1849, when he was in a melancholy mood about his life and career, Ed wrote a sentence, "It was upon a clear midnight." From that moment of divine inspiration, he wrote one of the most endearing Christmas hymns in history, ***It Came Upon the Midnight Clear.*** Ed showed the hymn to a friend who immediately saw the beauty of the hymn. He urged Ed to send the hymn to a publisher. It was published and from that day on it has been a classic and legendary hymn born from a brilliant man who later looked out of the window in his study and saw the moon's glow on a clear night.

Ed would continue his distinguished career for many years, including writing several popular books and serving as the associate editor of the *Monthly Religious Magazine.*

Ed died in Weston, Massachusetts in 1876 at the age of sixty-six.

(References: *The Hymns and Hymn Writers of the Church,* 1911, Wilbur Tillett; *Edmund H. Sears,* 1907, Dictionary of Hymnology, John Julian; *Edmund Sears - American Hymns Old and New,* 1980, Albert Christ-Janer; *American Unitarianism,* 1989, Charles Edick Wright)

Shurtleff, Ernest Warburton

Ernest was born in 1862 in Boston, Massachusetts to a wealthy family that insisted that all of their children receive the finest education possible.

Ernest attended a private school in Boston, the Boston Latin School, where he excelled in all subjects including creative writing and music. He showed an early talent for poetry and a keen interest in music and languages. After he completed the Boston Latin School he was granted admission at Harvard University where he graduated with honors with a Bachelor of Arts degree. Ernest then attended the Andover Theological Seminary in Maryland and received a Master of Divinity degree. He was ordained in the Congregational Ministry and became the pastor at Palmer Congregational Church in Massachusetts. Soon thereafter he moved to the Plymouth Congregational Church. Later Ernest became the minister at the First Church in Minneapolis, Minnesota where he remained for several years. He continued his education at Ripon College where he earned a Doctor of Divinity degree.

Word of his sermons, poems, hymns and scholarly work spread and he received several offers of positions across the United States and Europe. Ernest visited Europe and became interested in working there to carry his messages and to broaden his own experiences and knowledge. He founded the American Church in Frankfurt, Germany, and after getting the church on a firm foundation financially and spiritually he moved to Paris, France to work at the Academy Vitti. Vitti was founded to provide assistance to poverty-stricken people by providing spiritual, financial, and vocational support.

Despite a busy life and many commitments, Ernest always found time to continue his writing and hymn compositions. One of his most famous hymns is ***Lead On, O King Eternal*** which he wrote while attending Andover Theological Seminary. His classmates knew of Ernest's poetic abilities and talents since he had already by then published two volumes of verse, so they asked him to write a hymn that they could all sing at their graduation commencement.

Consequently, he wrote ***Lead On, O King Eternal*** which has since then been a standard in most hymnals. His many publications include ***Poems***; ***Easter Gleams***; ***New Year's Peace***; ***Hymns of the Faith***; ***Songs of Hope***; and ***Shadow of the Angel***. Ernest worked to help others with their spiritual needs up until the time of his sudden death in 1917 in Paris when he was only fifty-five years old. At his memorial service, many of his friends gave testimony to how Ernest had influenced and inspired their lives.

(References: *Ernest Warburton Shurtleff*, Appletons Encyclopedia, 2001. Retrieved 2015; *Ernest Warburton Shurtleff*, The Canterbury Dictionary of Hymnology. Retrieved 2015; *Poems of Ernest Warburton Shurtleff*, University of Westminster Library. Retrieved 2015)

Singh, Sundar

Sundar was born in India in 1889.

Sundar was raised as a Sikh but at age sixteen he became a Christian Sadhu (Holy Man) and from then on through ridicule and physical cruelty and social isolation continued to spread the gospel.

With no money and painfully few resources, Sundar crossed the Himalayas from India to Tibet several times so that he could share the gospel with Sikhs, Buddhists, Hindus, Untouchables, and many others. His endurance and faith became legendary, and he was considered by some to be a saint.

The story of his bold and heroic trip into Nepal to preach to its citizens drew attention from around the world. Word of his physical torture was revealed several months later. While preaching in the town of Ilam, Nepal in the marketplace a large crowd gathered to hear him. He encouraged questions from the people and as the crowd grew larger and more interested in his words, the Nepalese political leaders took notice and panicked. Led by a high-ranking government official, soldiers were sent to arrest Sundar. They asked him for his permit to speak in public, and under whose authority did he come to the town. When Sundar said the spirit of Jesus Christ compelled him to visit Nepal he was immediately arrested. As they carried him away he told the soldiers and the listening crowd that "I am not afraid of this imprisonment. If I had been afraid I would never have come here in the first place. Though you can nail my feet to a log so that I cannot walk, I will still be free in my soul." When he was told by the high-ranking officer to quit talking, Sundar said, "As long as I have life in me and a tongue to speak, I shall not stop talking about Christ. I am ready to give my life that many hear the good news." He was locked in a damp, dark cell. In jail, they pulled his robe off and he was made to lie face down on the filthy cell floor while his feet and hands were chained. Sundar could see soldiers entering the cell with a large clay pot. He felt the contents of the jar being emptied on his bare back, followed shortly by excruciating, unbearable pain. The soldiers had emptied a pot full of leeches onto his back. They bored into his skin deeply to suck his blood. The gathered crowd could see the jail and what was happening to Sundar, and instead of protesting his treatment, they began to throw trash, rotten fruit and other vile things at Sundar to increase his torment. Incredibly, Sundar endured the unbelievable pain and public humiliation and somehow despite his torment started preaching the gospel from the jail cell. His love of Christ and his devotion stunned the crowd and a strange calmness spread throughout the jail and crowd. He used the moment to explain to them that they were witnessing the power of Christ right before their eyes as he was still able and willing to preach. The crowd grew restless and rebellion against the soldiers seemed to be forming, so they released him and sent him away in his physically appalling condition. Upon his painful return to Dehra Dun, word of his torment and courage spread throughout the region.

As he preached, Sundar wrote sermons and an occasional hymn. His most famous hymn is ***I Have Decided to Follow Jesus***. Sundar wrote the hymn, not from his many experiences, but instead from the inspiration he felt from another person's experience. The title of his hymn came from the last words of a man in Assam (northeast India) who along with his family converted to Christianity in the 19th century because of Welsh missionary work. The village faith leader instructed him to renounce his Christian faith under penalty of death if he refused. Instead of renouncing his faith in Christ, the man said, "I have decided to follow Jesus." The village chief was outraged and threatened to kill the man. Undaunted, the man refused to abandon his faith. The chief said he would kill the man's two young children. Again the man refused to abandon his faith, saying "I have decided to follow Jesus." His children were put to death by arrows. The man's wife then was threatened and once again the man said he loved Christ, even as he witnessed his wife's death. He was next. As he lay dying from arrow wounds, the man's last words were, "I have decided to follow Jesus." Sundar was motivated to write a hymn in honor of the man's steadfast faith and belief in Christ. The hymn became immediately popular in Indian churches. Some United States missionaries returning from India told the story of Sundar and the family's plight captured in Sundar's powerful hymn. When the legendary gospel singer, George Beverly Shea, learned of the story about the hymn he sang it at all Billy Graham crusades. The hymn and the story behind the hymn became legendary.

Stories of Sundar's roving ministry, his unending faith, his influence, and his endurance of pain and suffering continued up until his death in India in 1929 at the age of forty.

(References: *The Riddle of Sadhu Sundar Singh*, 2004, Mrs. Arthur Parker; *The Story of Sadhu Sundar Singh*, 1963, Cyril Davey; *The Saffron Robe*, 1975, Janet Lynn Watson)

Sleeth, Natalie

Natalie was born in 1934 in Evanston, Illinois. Her family worshiped at the local church and participated in many community activities.

Natalie attended the local public school where she showed an early interest in and aptitude for music. Her parents observed this and arranged for Natalie to have piano lessons. They also wanted her to learn not just music for piano, but to learn about all aspects of music. Natalie showed an unusual talent for music, so her lessons became a broad study of all aspects of music. She became involved in school and church music programs and activities and was frequently one of the stars of the events.

After an excellent high school experience with music and other studies, she decided to major in music in college. She studied music, piano, organ, and music theory at Wellesley College in Massachusetts where she earned a Bachelor of Arts degree in music theory. During her college years, she composed music and arrangements. This fulfilled her love of music and drew upon her musical talents, so she decided that writing and composing music would be her vocation.

Natalie wrote and published over 200 songs and hymns for churches and schools. Her first anthem, ***Canon of Praise***, became a bestseller for the publishing company and remains the company's top-selling anthem. She wrote numerous other anthems and hymns that became famous. They were and still are frequently sung and performed in churches and schools across the country and the world. Several of her hymns and anthems have been translated into many languages. One of her well-known anthems is ***Joy in the Morning***. At the request of her husband, she wrote the anthem for his inauguration as President of West Virginia Wesleyan College. Another hymn became a Christmas season standard—***Were You There on That Christmas Night***.

Arguably, Natalie's most famous hymn is ***In the Bulb There is a Flower***. It was written for the Pasadena Community Church in St. Petersburg, Florida. The hymn can be found in almost every Christian hymnal in the world, regardless of denomination. Natalie's inspiration for the hymn came when she was grieving over the death of a friend. She thought of the seasons of life as the four seasons of nature and from that she found comfort in spring following winter and resurrection following death.

For her accomplishments, Natalie received honorary doctorates from West Virginia Wesleyan College and Nebraska Wesleyan College. Natalie also received many other awards for her music and musical compositions.

Even though she was famous and very busy composing music, Natalie was devoted to her husband and helped him in his battle with cancer until his death in 1985. A few years later she would enter into her own fight with cancer. She lost her courageous battle in 1992 when she was only sixty-two years old. Many of her songs, anthems, and hymns were played at her funeral in Denver, Colorado.

(References: *Natalie Sheen*, 1985, Hope Publishing Company Biographies. Retrieved 2015; *Companion to the Worshipping Church*, 1993, Donald Hustad; *There's Nothing Like a Song*, 1980, Natalie Sheen)

Smith, Samuel

Samuel was born in 1808 in Boston, Massachusetts. His family was influential in the Boston community, being involved in the mercantile business and politics.

Sam attended private schools that focused on preparing students for college. He became an excellent student at the Latin School of Boston after getting off to a difficult start. Sam's initial lack of self-confidence made school challenging for him, but once he adapted to the school's rigorous routines he thrived. After winning academic honors at the Latin School, Sam was accepted at Harvard College (Harvard University). He was a model student who loved the college atmosphere and the friendships he developed there. Sam also rose to meet the academic rigor and excelled in all areas of study. While at Harvard, Sam developed an interest in philosophy and theology.

After graduating from Harvard, he attended Andover Theological Academy where he received a Master of Divinity degree. Due to his literary talents and scholarly intellect in theology, he was offered the position of editor of the *Baptist Missionary Magazine*. Sam worked there for a few months before being ordained as a Baptist minister in Waterville, Maine, where he also became a minister and professor of modern languages at Waterville College.

A few years later Sam was recruited to move to Newton, Massachusetts to become editor of the *Christian Review* of the Baptist Missionary Union, but he did not want to give up his ministry so he was also the pastor of the First Baptist Church in Newton. During his time in Newton, he wrote poems and hymns as well as scholarly works.

After twelve years at Newton, he left to become the full-time editor of the *Baptist Missionary Union Periodical* and remained in that position for almost fifteen years. On behalf of the Baptist Missionary Union, he traveled extensively throughout Europe, the Middle East, and India. He wrote about his travels in stories about the history and cultures of the regions. One of his greatest pleasures, however, was in composing music. Sam is best known for his song ***My Country 'Tis of Thee*** (more commonly titled ***America***). This magnificent song to his surprise became legendary. ***My Country 'Tis of Thee*** was written initially for a children's Independence Day celebration, but when it was published in the bestselling book *The Choir*, written by Lowell Mason, it became famous. Sam added another stanza to the hymn in honor of the Washington Centennial Celebration. Sam most frequently referred to the song as ***America***.

Among his other popular publications, although at a much lesser level of popularity, were ***The Psalmist***; ***Lyric Gems***, and ***History of Newton***. During his life, Sam wrote over 150 hymns.

Periodically, Sam was asked to preach at churches throughout the United States. He could not accept many of the invitations because of his busy schedule, but he kept his ministry spirit alive as often as he could. Sam remained active even as he grew older and less mobile. He died in 1895 on a train as he was traveling to Readsville to deliver a sermon. Sam was eighty-seven years old.

Although Sam was a legendary song and hymn writer, he was not inducted into the Songwriters Hall of Fame until 1970. One other historical note is the house that Sam lived in is now the Phillips Academy dormitory called America House in his honor.

(References: *Samuel F. Smith,* American National Biography, 1999, John A. Garraty; *Dr. Samuel F. Smith Obituary,* New York Times, November 16, 1895; *The America of Samuel F. Smith, American Thinker,* February 2011, Michael Fraley)

Spafford, Horatio

Horatio was born in 1828 in Troy, New York. The family house was often filled with friends and relatives, so he learned at an early age how to socialize and feel comfortable around all types of people.

Horatio was a very good student in school. He wanted to be a lawyer, so he worked hard and studied law with a lawyer who also understood investments and real estate. When Horatio started his own law firm, it did not take long for him to build up his list of clientele. He was smart, insightful, and gracious with his clients and other attorneys and judges. He became a famous and successful Chicago lawyer with a beautiful home, a lovely wife, Anna, four vivacious and loving daughters and a precocious little boy. He was also a devout Christian and a devout family man.

Horatio was also a pillar of the community, often providing assistance to many poor tenants struggling to find the basic essentials of life. He was often seen working with community leaders to gather food, clothes, water, and shelter for individuals and families that were in desperate need of support.

At the apex of his financial and professional success, Horatio and his wife Anna suffered the tragic loss of their young son, who died unexpectedly after a short illness, believed to be tuberculosis. Horatio grieved deeply for his son, but he still managed his business and charity work.

In that era, Chicago was growing very rapidly; it was the fastest growing city in the United States, so Horatio invested heavily in real estate. However, the Great Chicago Fire destroyed almost every real estate investment that Horatio had. He was not bankrupt but he was close to it. The family had to change its way of life at a time when they were still grieving over the loss of the son. In 1873, Horatio scheduled a trip to Europe aboard a ship across the Atlantic in order to give his wife, daughters and himself a much-needed vacation and time to recover from the tragedies. As they were all about to board the ship, Horatio was called back to his office because of an important last minute change in a legal matter that demanded his attention. He did not know how to resolve the work issue and still on the vacation. Instead of holding up the trip for his wife and daughters, he sent them on the ship while he remained in Chicago. As he hugged them on the ship, he reassured them that he would catch the next ship in a few days and join them. He then went back to his office. A few days later he received the devastating news that the ship carrying his wife and daughters had a collision with another ship and sank. All four of his daughters drowned; only his wife had survived, but she was seriously ill and inconsolable about the loss of their four daughters. With almost unbearable grief, he boarded a ship that would take him to his sick and grieving wife in England.

It is impossible to imagine how Horatio found the strength to make that long trip across the open sea alone with thoughts of a once beautiful family. It was on this trip across the Atlantic, alone in his cabin and alone with God, that he found the inspiration to pen the famous hymn ***It is Well with My Soul.***

He and his wife survived the tragedies and later had three more children—one died of typhoid fever. Incredibly, after all they had been through and with the support of their faith and many hours of prayer, Horatio and Anna were emotionally and spiritually devastated when the minister of their Presbyterian church told their two daughters that the family tragedies were divine punishment, implying that the family was not worthy of God's grace and that God was a punishing instead of a comforting God. The family immediately left the church. They also left Chicago and America, after feeling like they had been abandoned by their church, city, and country. They settled in Jerusalem.

Many of their friends were stunned when they heard how the church had treated them, so several other adults traveled with them to Jerusalem. They established the "American Colony" where they provided education for children and adults of all faiths. The family enjoyed living in the historic city and the community embraced them. They remained there for several years.

Horatio died in 1888 in Jerusalem at the age of sixty. Despite the dreadful tragedies and being abandoned by his church, Horatio never lost his love of God and his faith in Christ. His hymn ***It is Well with My Soul*** has been a source of strength for many individuals and families for over 100 years.

(References: *Our Jerusalem: An American Family in the Holy City*, 1988, Bertha Spafford Vester; *The American Colony in Jerusalem*, Library of Congress exhibition. Retrieved 2014; *The Stafford Children's Center*, Jerusalem, Old City. Retrieved 2014)

St. Francis of Assisi

Born as Giovanni di Pietro di Bernardone was born in Italy in 1181. He is one of Christendom's most beloved figures. He was an intelligent, kind, gentle and compassionate man who observed and loved nature and animals. However, as a youth, he was undisciplined and a drunkard.

Francis' epiphany occurred upon his release from prison after being a prisoner in the war between Assisi and Perugia. He began an immediate change in his life, devoting his life to God and giving up his material wealth.

Francis began to notice the beauty of the world around him and God's love of man and nature. Francis told his friends and followers that God's love for man was matched by His love of nature and animals. After all, Francis said, "God created all things out of his love." Francis joined a monastery and became a monk.

The humble, devout monk was often seen praying in the forests, fields, near rivers and streams, under clear skies and even in the rain. He often stopped to observe animals and he prayed at those times, also. He believed that to love God was to love all His creatures: "If you have men who will exclude any of God's creatures from the shelter of compassion and pity, you will have men who will deal likewise with their fellow men."

One morning when he was walking alone in an open field lined with trees on each side, he was overwhelmed with a sense of God's presence, as if the field and trees were God's sanctuary, a holy place for man, animals, and nature. The sun shone on everything as if God's hands were warming a cold world and God's reassuring touch was in the sun's rays. Francis saw animals in the field and at the edge of the forest as if they too had been called to feel the warmth of God. Francis had never felt so keenly the message that all creatures were God's. After leaving the forest border on his way back to the monastery he walked along a small path lined with wildflowers and the words to the hymn ***All Creatures of Our God and King*** formed in his mind and heart. Francis stopped along the side of the path and knelt to pray a prayer of gratitude to God for his inspiration and guidance. He retreated to his garden and composed the words to the hymn "...with God guiding my hand."

Francis loved music and he encouraged singing in his monastery. He wrote more than sixty hymns for just that purpose. He believed the words of *Psalms 19:1-4*, "The heavens declare the glory of God; and the firmament sheweth his handiwork. Day unto day uttereth speech, and night unto night sheweth knowledge. There is no speech nor language, where their voice is not heard. Their line is gone out through all the earth and their words to the end of the world. In them hath he set a tabernacle for the sun."

Written in 1225, the words of ***All Creatures of Our God and King*** have been a powerful reminder of God's inspiration, and they have remained in the hearts of people around the world for over 750 years. Seven centuries later, the hymn is sung every week in a worship service somewhere in the world.

One day Francis had a vision that he was praying on the mountain of Verna, and a six-winged angel appeared and gave him the "gift" of the five wounds of Christ. In suffering bliss, Francis became ill and no treatment helped him and he did not seek treatment. During his last few days, he dictated many spiritual testaments.

Francis died on October 3, 1226, while softly singing *Psalm 142,* with a small group of his friends gathered around him.

Pope Gregory IX canonized Francis on July 16, 1228. He was designated as Patron Saint of Italy. St. Francis has become a symbol of charity, understanding, forgiveness, and the power of the love of God and Christ.

(References: *St. Francis of Assisi,* Encyclopedia Britannica, Charles Ignatius. Retrieved 2013; *St. Francis of Assisi,* 2009, The Catholic Encyclopedia, P. Robinson; *The Life of St. Francis of Assisi,* 1988 ed., Cardinal Manning Bonaventure)

Stockton, John Hart

John was born in New Hope, Pennsylvania in 1813. His large family was headed by parents who were strongly religious and faithful to the Presbyterian Church.

John's childhood was filled with church activities and a rich experience with music and friends. He developed a love of music at an early age and maintained that love throughout his life. His education came from a combination of home schooling, local public school, and classes at the local church.

Shortly after he finished secondary school or the equivalent of high school in that era, John was converted to the Methodist Church while attending a Methodist camp meeting in Paulsboro, Pennsylvania for teenagers and adults. From that experience of spiritual awakening, John wanted to become a minister. He studied locally for the ministry and soon was ordained as a Methodist minister. He served as minister to several Methodist churches in New Jersey. In many of the churches he also served as the music director or music minister, often out of necessity but always with enthusiasm and joy. John was a minister, a musician, and a composer of hymns. He published two books of hymns, ***The Salvation Melodies*** and ***Hymn Writers of the Church***. Also, several of his hymns were published in other books by prominent authors of music publications. John's most popular hymn is ***Only Trust Him,*** which has been in hymnals for over 150 years.

After several years as a full-time minister and part-time hymn composer, John retired from the ministry due primarily to poor health when he was sixty years old; however, he remained interested in music and actively maintained his vocation of composing music, especially hymns. John was well-known throughout Pennsylvania, New Jersey, and other places due to his robust sermons and lovely and spiritually rich hymns.

After a period of illness, John began to recover but unexpectedly died shortly after attending a church service. His sudden death was captured in an obituary that ran in the Philadelphia Inquiry newspaper on March 27, 1877, two days after John's death: "Sudden Death of a Clergyman: Rev. John H. Stockton, a member of the New Jersey Annual Conference, M. E. Church, who had been in feeble health all winter, thought himself so far improved that he left his home in Camden, N. J., on Saturday last, and crossed the river to visit some friends in this city. He attended church at Arch Street M. E. Church yesterday morning and returned to the house of his brother-in-law, N. Rowland after the service has ended. He was then very cheerful and hopeful of recovery. Soon after his arrival he was attacked with hemorrhage of the lungs and expired almost immediately. Mr. Stockton was highly esteemed as a Christian man and as a preacher of high abilities. His death will be deeply regretted."

(References: *Reverend John H. Stockton,* Philadelphia Inquiry obituary, March 27, 1877; *John Hart Stockton,* 1911, Hymn Writers of the Church, Charles Nutter)

Stone, Lloyd

Lloyd was born in 1912 in California. His father worked for the Associated Oil Company of Coalinga, California. Lloyd's parents were from Tennessee, and maternal grandparents were from Missouri.

Beginning at an early age, Lloyd enjoyed reading and writing. He was an average student, but he had a gift for writing and he loved poetry. He wrote a lot about nature, but he included many other subjects in his poetry, including stories. Lloyd and his parents often visited relatives in Missouri, and it was during those visits that Lloyd became fascinated by the stories of the Ozark Mountains and the early life in that area of the United States. In fact, Lloyd began to take notes of stories he heard from his grandmother. After several years of collecting the stories, he compiled them into a book that was published as ***The Story of an Ozark Grandmother***.

After secondary school, Lloyd enrolled in the University of Southern California where he majored in music. All along he kept writing poetry. Some of his poems were published in local magazines and his writing talent also caught the attention of his professors at the university who encouraged him to become a professional writer. His plan, however, was to teach music in high school, but he had a change of heart. He didn't think he could make a living as a poet, but he was worried about being locked into a teaching position, which might prevent him from visiting other places around the world. So after earning a Bachelor of Arts degree he shocked his family when he decided to join a circus that toured California and Hawaii. At the time, he joined the circus it was headed for Honolulu. He fell in love with Hawaii and decided to remain there when the circus moved on. Lloyd took a job as a jewelry designer in a tourist shop.

While in Hawaii, he continued to write poetry and enjoy music while working. Lloyd participated in several local musical productions, and eventually joined the staff of the Kulamanu Studios as a pianist-composer. Lloyd's poetry subject turned to Hawaii. His love for the beauty of Hawaii captured his imagination and passion. Hawaii's *Islander Magazine* stated that "Mr. Stone is probably among the most versatile contributors to the arts of whom Hawaii can boast. His poetry reflects Hawaii. He does not sing of the palms and the surf, but of the human beauty which is the heritage of the islands. He finds his niche as an interpreter of that which lies beneath the lovely outward shell of Hawaii. He has made Hawaii his home. And Hawaii is fortunate."

His poems began to gain attention throughout the United States. He wrote poems, music, books, and articles. Lloyd also illustrated books, with his most popular being the illustrations for the book ***Eight Children's Songs from Hawaii,*** written by Carol Roes.

Lloyd is probably most remembered for writing the first two stanzas of the famous hymn ***This is My Song*** using the Finlandia Hymn melody (Georgia Harkness wrote the third stanza). The hymn became famous and has been performed by several recording artists.

Lloyd died in 1993 at the age of eighty-one while living in California.

(References: *Lloyd Stone,* Your Daily Poem. Retrieved 2015; *5 Poems of Lloyd Stone,* Poetry Explorer. Retrieved 2015; *Poems to Be Served with Poi Cocktail,* 1940, Lloyd Stone)

Stone, Samuel John

Sam was born in 1839 in Whitmore, Staffordshire, England. His father was a minister, the well-known Rev. William Stone. Sam grew up wanting to follow in his father's footsteps as a man of God and to minister to the people about grace and giving.

Sam was a loving, gentle, and intelligent boy who enjoyed being around his father's church and who enjoyed the company of friends and family. He excelled in all academic work and learned about music out of curiosity more than any great talent. When Sam completed his schooling at Charterhouse School he enrolled at Pembroke College, Oxford. He enjoyed his love of learning while at Pembroke. He participated in many college and community activities and was very popular with and among his classmates. Sam earned a Bachelor of Arts degree at Pembroke and after being ordained he served as Curate of Windsor, Berkshire for eight years before moving to a similar position at St. Paul's Church in Haggerston, England where his father was the Vicar. Four years later he became the Vicar of St. Paul's, following in his father's footsteps at the church.

Sam was a writer, poet, and hymnist. He is famous for his book ***Lyra Fidelium*** (which consists of 12 hymns); ***The Knights of Intercession and Other Poems***; ***Sonnets of the Christian Year***, and other works. During his lifetime, he published several books of poems, and he wrote poems for magazines and newspapers. His hymn ***Lord of Our Souls' Salvation*** was sung at the National Thanksgiving event in 1872. The event brought attention to Sam's talent. He also translated several hymns from around the world into ***Hymns Original and Translated*** that introduced new hymns to the English-speaking world.

Sam wrote hundreds of hymns and many of them are found in hymnals of many denominations. One of his most famous hymns is ***The Church's One Foundation*** which he wrote to help his congregation understand the *Article Nine of the Apostles' Creed*. He thought that the lyrics and music would clarify the meaning of the *Creed*, which affirms the Holy Catholic Church and the Communion of Saints. Sam remained Vicar of St. Paul's for eighteen years.

In 1890, he became Rector of All Hallows-on-the-Wall in London. He remained active in the church and continued to write hymns and poems until his death in London in 1900 at the age of Sixty-one after a short-term illness.

(References: *The Sacred Poets of the 19th Century*, 1907, Alfred H. Miles; *Hymn Stories: The Church's One Foundation*, 2013, Tim Challies; *Samuel Stone*, songsandhymns.org. Retrieved 2015; *Author: Samuel John Stone*, wikisource.org. Retrieved 2015)

Strathdee, Jim

Jim was born in 1941 in Sacramento, California. Jim's father was a minister who believed in the power and messages of gospel music during church services. Jim loved attending church and was deeply involved in many church activities, especially the music activities and programs.

Jim showed an early interest and talent in music. He learned to play the guitar at a very young age and possessed a mature voice, too. He was a good student in all academic areas and participated in several school activities. Jim was so gifted as a musician he was leading the church choir at the age of fourteen.

After graduating from college, Jim married Jean and they both worked as music teachers at Mid-Pacific High School in Honolulu, Hawaii. They moved to Ridgecrest, California and later to Sacramento, California where they became involved in the music program at St. Mark's United Methodist Church. Eventually, they became the co-directors of music at the church. Soon they were performing around the state and eventually around the country. Jim wrote several songs, including hymns. His beautiful and inspiring hymn ***I Am the Light of the World*** is found in Christian hymnals around the world. The hymn was inspired by a Christmas poem written by Howard Thurman that moved Jim spiritually.

Jean and Jim have collaborated on several songs, and they have recorded twenty popular CDs. Jim and Jean speak fluent Spanish and have recorded many of their songs in Spanish. Their music ministry extends into Central America where they have performed and continue to perform in many churches there. Additionally, they have performed in India, New Zealand, and Cuba. Their music is published in many songbooks and religious education curricula. They remain active in their "road ministry."

(References: *Jim Strathdee,* website access strathdeemusic.com. Retrieved 2015; *Jim Strathdee,* Hymnary.org. Retrieved 2015; *Jim Strathdee,* Ancestry.com. Retrieved 2015)

Thomerson, Kathleen

Kathleen was born in 1934 in Jackson, Tennessee, but she had many homes because her family moved several times. She lived in Mississippi, California, and Texas. Kathleen developed a love of music at a very young age, and she showed an early talent for music and lyrics. She was a thoughtful child, who had a kind heart, spirit, and a love of learning.

Even though she attended different schools growing up, she always adapted and excelled academically. After completing secondary school, Kathleen attended the University of Texas where she received Bachelor of Arts and Master of Arts degrees in music. Her love of music led Kathleen to attend Syracuse University to continue her studies. While there she accepted an opportunity to study music at the Flemish Royal Conservatory in Antwerp, Belgium. While in Belgium her talent and compelling intellect drew the attention of people who recognized her ability and capacity to learn. She was introduced to the famous Jean Langlais, who was a world-renowned French composer of modern classical music and a world-class organist. After studying with Jean, Kathleen became a talented organist. She later worked as the director of music at the University United Methodist Church in St. Louis, Missouri. Kathleen also taught organ at the St. Louis Conservatory.

Kathleen's best-known hymn is the beloved ***I Want to Walk as a Child of the Light***, which is in several hymnals. About her famous hymn, Kathleen wrote: "It was written as a scriptural meditation and prayer inspired by many Bible verses—*(Genesis. 1:17, Isaiah 60:19, Psalm 139:12,* and *Hebrews 1:3* - to mention a few). As I wrote the words for the first stanza, I heard the melody to which they were to be sung. The harmonization was worked out later."

Kathleen is currently the music director and organist at Mt. Olive Lutheran Church in Austin, Texas.

(References: *I Want to Walk as a Child of the Light,* 2008, Southwood Lutheran Church online biography. Retrieved 2013; *Kathleen Thomerson,* hymntime.org. Retrieved 2013; *Kathleen Thomerson,* Hymnary.org. Retrieved 2014; *Kathleen Thomerson,* Classical Archives. Retrieved 2014)

Thompson, Will Lamartine

Will was born in 1847 in Smith's Ferry, Pennsylvania. Shortly after his birth, the family moved a few miles down the Ohio River to East Liverpool, Ohio. Will was the youngest of seven children of Josiah Thompson. Will's father was a successful businessman, with considerable influence in the community, and some said control of the community. He worked in the mercantile business, ran a bank, started manufacturing businesses, speculated in the stock market, ran local politics and served in the Ohio legislature.

Will's father had a strong influence on the children, insisting that they pursue their education studies with vigor and seriousness. He also exposed his sons to the business works of the community by taking them with him to work.

Will was destined for a business career. However, his mother's interests in community work to support suffering families and individuals also influenced Will. He often saw his mother take food and clothing to families, and he heard at the family dinner table talk about the needs of the community. This made an impression on Will.

He received his education locally and at home, particularly from his mother who encouraged all of the children to read. At a young age Will showed a strong interest in music; he learned to read music before he was ten years old. By the time he was thirteen years old he had composed music and played at community events.

After completing the equivalent of high school, Will attended Mount Union College in Alliance, Ohio. Due to his love of music, which blossomed full flower while he attended Mount Union College, Will continued his music studies at the New England Conservatory of Music (NECM) and later in Leipzig, Germany, where his music professors encouraged him to study classical music. Will returned to East Liverpool and helped his father with some of the family's business interests, but he was never far removed from his music and he followed the influence of his mother by supporting community activities and needs. For example, Will was concerned about the lack of space for families in the community to gather for picnics, family reunions, etc., so he donated over 100 acres to be used for public parks. Will also built a mansion near the town on the highest point of the hill. There he hosted several community events that were open to the public. The mansion still stands today as a point of pride for the community.

Will continued to write hymns and other types of songs, but he had no success with publishers. Many times the publishers did not bother to respond to him. Will was not one to accept that type of treatment, so he started his own publishing company, the W. L. Thompson Music Company in East Liverpool. Within a few years the business was making a profit, and by the 1880s it was the largest business of its type in the United States, selling sheet music, song books, musical instruments and supplies, and musical gifts. He later opened another store in Chicago, which was also successful. Will's first commercially successful song was ***Gathering up Seashells at the Seashore***, which sold over 246,000 copies. The song became popular enough to broaden his reputation across the nation and drew considerable attention to his music publishing company as well as his own musical abilities.

Will was a prolific composer, and he found inspiration all around him. He once said, "No matter where I am, at home or hotel, at the store or traveling, if an idea or theme comes to me I jot it down in verse and later develop the inspiration." He wrote other popular songs, including patriotic songs, but his enduring legacy centers on his hymns. Will's hymn ***Softly and Tenderly Jesus is Calling*** is one of the most famous and popular hymns of all time. It has been translated into more languages than any other hymn, and it has been used in several movies. It is not an exaggeration to claim that the song has been sung somewhere in a church every Sunday of each year since 1880.

While Will was touring Europe with his family, he became seriously ill, prompting the family to cancel the trip. He remained ill for over a month and sought medical treatment in New York. However, Will succumbed to the illness, believed to be pneumonia, and died in New York in 1909 at the age of sixty-two. He was buried in his beloved hometown of East Liverpool, Ohio, where he remains a legend.

Some of the most famous hymnists in the world say that Will's ***Softly and Tenderly Jesus is Calling*** is one of the best hymns ever written.

(References: *Spiritual Moments with the Great Hymns*, 1997, Evelyn Benca; *A Book of Biography of Song Writers of the Church of*

Christ, 1980, Gene Finley; *Will Lamartine Thompson*, Wikipedia.org. Retrieved 2015; *Will L. Thompson*, Hymnary.org. Retrieved 2014; *Will Lamartine Thompson*, Cyberhymnal.org. Retrieved 2014)

Tindley, Charles Albert

Charles was born in 1851 in Berlin, Maryland. His father was a slave but his mother was not. This made Charles feel like he was free even though he lived among slaves and grew up with slaves. His mother died when he was four years old, and he was separated from his father a year later. Charles was raised by his Aunt Caroline.

Even as a young child it was obvious to all that he was very smart and had a gift for music and conversation. Charles also had an insatiable curiosity. There were no schools to attend where he lived, so he looked for tattered pieces of newspaper, torn out of book pages and desiccated posters so he could learn to read. At night by the light of only wood and pine cone fires he tried to read what he had found. Through sheer determination and will power Charles taught himself how to read, and he never stopped reading throughout his long life. He also taught himself how to write. He had no pencils or paper, so he used charcoal pieces to write on whatever he could find. Charles started by learning how to form letters, then words, and finally sentences. He wrote sentences based on his life and then he compared them with the structure of sentences and spelling of words in magazines that he found in trash cans in the nearby town. He eventually learned the rules of writing, and once he mastered it he was a prolific writer until his death.

Shortly after the end of the American Civil War, he moved to Philadelphia looking for work. His first job was as a brick carrier. He had to carry a small but very heavy pallet of bricks to construction sites. It was grueling work. He found out about a local night school and his dream of an education was close by, but he knew he could not continue with the brick carrier job because he was too tired and exhausted at the end of the ten and sometimes twelve hour days to attend night school. So, he looked for another job. Charles found a job at a church.

Charles was so determined to be an educated man that he attended night school while working as a janitor at the church during the day. When he finished the courses of study in the night school the minister in the church where he worked told Charles about a correspondence school, the Boston Theological School. Charles completed a divinity degree through the school. His goal was to become a preacher, but he was told that without a degree from a college he might not be able to fulfill his dream. However, Charles' work and determination and drive so impressed elders at the local church that they helped him set for the ordination examination by the Methodist Episcopal Church. Charles had the highest score among those taking the exams. Consequently, he was ordained a pastor in the Delaware Conference at the age of thirty-six and as an elder and pastor two years later.

As was the custom during that era, newly ordained pastors had to serve as itinerant pastors before being qualified to be a full-time pastor. Charles served as an itinerant pastor at several locations, including Cape May, New Jersey; South Wilmington, Delaware; Odessa, Delaware; Pocomoke, Maryland; Fairmont, Maryland, and Wilmington, Delaware. After his itinerant experiences, Charles became the pastor of Calvary Methodist Episcopal Church in Philadelphia, Pennsylvania. This was the same church where he had earlier worked as the janitor.

From his first sermon to his last, Charles was one of the leading preachers of his era. His reputation and the size of his congregation continued to grow. At one time the church membership reached almost 13,000. Charles was in constant demand for revivals across the United States, but his talent was not limited to remarkably powerful sermons. Charles' interest in music matched his talent for oratory. He weaved music into his sermons and the inspirational hymns were sung before, during, and after his sermons. The hymns added more inspiration to his messages. In one revival he so impressed the participants that he was referred to as "The Prince of Pastors."

But Charles was much more than a gifted pastor. He raised money to support families and he helped people find jobs, clothes, food, and spiritual support. Charles lived what he preached—God's work on earth was to help others with their lives and with their faith. He was also active in the civil rights efforts, working strongly against prejudice and what he referred to as the masquerading of stereotypes. For example, he organized a march to protest the showing of the movie "Birth of a Nation."

While no one can forget the American Civil Rights anthem ***We Shall Overcome***, many probably have forgotten that the inspiration for the anthem came from Charles' hymn ***I'll Overcome Some Day***. Charles' version was brought to the Highlander Folk School in 1930 and was on the curriculum of songs taught to all students. The song was later altered by students at the school to become ***We Shall Overcome***.

Charles loved gospel music. He composed several other hymns that remain popular today and can be found in Christian hymn books around the world, such as the legendary ***Stand By Me*** and ***Nothing Between***. Charles is considered one of the founding fathers of American gospel music. In 1901, he became the first African-American to publish an original collection of songs.

Charles died in Philadelphia in 1933 at the age of eighty-two. He was mourned by several thousand people who crowded into the church while several more thousand remained outside. During the service, Charles was referred to as "Lincoln in Ebony," because everyone knew that he was a disciple of Christ, a leader of people and a voice for freedom.

(References: *Charles Albert Tindley*, Christian Broadcast Network.com. Retrieved 2013; *Charles Albert Tindley, Prince of Preachers*, 1982, Ralph H. Jones; *Beams of Heaven: Hymns of Charles Albert Tindley (1851-1933)*, 2006, S.T. Kimbrough, Jr.)

Toplady, Augustus

Augustus was born in 1740 in Farnham, Surrey, England to a family with origins in Ireland. After his father was killed in the Battle of

Cartagena de India as an officer in the Royal Marines, Augustus, and his mother moved to Westminster, England. There she encouraged Augustus to advance his intellectual development by enrolling him in Westminster School. During his five years at Westminster School, Augustus excelled academically.

His interest in religion and spirituality increased significantly during a summer visit to Ireland. He was sixteen years old that summer when he was touched by the Spirit of God during a worship service that was being held in a farmer's barn. Augustus thought that the lay minister's message went straight to his heart and soul, unlike the sermons he heard in grand cathedrals and large churches in England. The humbleness of the barn and the lay minister's simple message struck Augustus with the full meaning of belief and salvation. The message derived from *Ephesians* and spoke of the blood of Christ. He felt as though God wanted and planned for him to hear this message in the most basic of surroundings, with no pretentious structure to distract from the true meaning of the message.

After completing his studies at Westminster School in London, Augustus decided to return to Ireland and attend Trinity College in Dublin. He studied religion and philosophy and graduated with honors.

In 1759, he published his first book, ***Poems on Sacred Subjects***. He was ordained an Anglican priest in 1762 at the young age of twenty-two. Augustus was Curate of Blagdon, Ireland and later at Farleigh, Ireland. His reputation for thoughtful and inspiring sermons spread across Ireland. At age twenty-six, Augustus became the Vicar of Broadhembury in Devonshire. He worked there for almost ten years, but he was frequently granted leave to visit and preach at other places across Great Britain.

During his years in Devonshire, Augustus began to question the Anglican Church orthodoxy. In a bold move, and much to the surprise of many, he left the Anglican Church and returned to London. In his search for work and fulfillment, and to guide his spiritual upheaval, he found a sanctuary he liked in a Calvinist

Church in Leicester Fields, England, even though he was still considered the Vicar of Broadhembury in Devonshire. Historical records reveal Augustus' famous feud with John Wesley and the upheaval their religious debate caused throughout England and other parts of Great Britain.

Augustus wrote frequently, including scholarly books, poems, argumentative treatises, essays, letters of correspondence and hymns. Augustus also wrote about the natural world, where he found interest in the animal kingdom and botany. His book ***Sketch of Natural History, with a few particulars on Birds, Meteors, Sagacity of Brutes, and the Solar System*** was considered a masterwork when it was published. Augustus was considered an intellectual giant in his era, but he is most remembered for the hymn he wrote on a road as he walked from one small village to another and got caught in a thunderstorm. It was during this time when he was only twenty-two years old that he wrote the famous hymn ***Rock of Ages***, perhaps the most frequently sung hymn in the history of the Christian church. The legend holds that Augustus was inspired to write the hymn when he was huddled under a large rock overhang while taking cover from a thunderstorm. He never confirmed or denied the story.

Augustus died of tuberculosis in 1778 in Kensington, England. Considering his influence and the quality and quantity of his work, it is difficult to believe that he was only thirty-eight years old at the time of his death.

(References: *Augustus Toplady,* Oxford Dictionary of National Biography, Arthur Pollard. Retrieved 2015; *A Debtor to Mercy Alone,* 2000, Ella George; *Hymn Writer Augustus Toplady*, Christianity.com. Retrieved 2014)

Troeger, Thomas

Thomas was born in 1945 in Suffern, New York.

Thomas was exposed to the Bible at a very early age by his mother, who read the Bible to him every day as he was growing up. His father introduced him to music, mostly the classical music of composers such as Bach and Haydn. Thomas' mother also taught him how to pray, and they often prayed together. Even though his father did not participate in the prayers he was very influential in his belief in God as the Father of the Universe and the One who ordered all things in the universe. Also, while listening to classical music his father would silence the room and say that a particular part of a movement was inspired by God. In an interview, Thomas said, "These [experiences with his parents] are unbelievably powerful experiences because I had two fabulous parents, both strong personalities and exceedingly loving. So over time, anyone who is raised like that is going to be sensitive to God."

Thomas was an extraordinarily gifted student in elementary and secondary schools. His intellectual prowess was obvious to his parents and all of this teachers and friends. Thomas' musical talents were just as conspicuous. In fact, he was an accomplished flutist at a young age. He hoped to improve enough as a flutist to attend the Julliard School of Music. However, he was greatly influenced by a preacher who came to his community. His powerful sermons about the glory of God and God's gifts to mankind stirred Thomas' soul. The preacher's wife taught Thomas in Sunday school and she also deepened his beliefs and spirituality. Their collective influence persuaded Thomas to enroll at Yale University to study religion. He earned a Bachelor of Arts degree cum laude at the age of twenty-two. He then attended Rochester Divinity School for a Bachelor of Divinity degree and Dickinson College to further study religion. He later received a Doctor of Divinity degree at Virginia Theological Seminary.

Thomas has the unusual distinction of being ordained in both Presbyterian (1970) and Episcopal (1999) denominations. After being ordained, he served as a pastor for almost eight years and then accepted a professorship at Colgate Rochester School of Divinity where he taught homiletics (the art of preparing and delivering sermons) for over fourteen years before moving in 1991 to his current position as the Ralph E. and Norma E. Peck Professor of Preaching and Communications at Iliff School of Theology in

Denver, Colorado where he is also the director of the doctor of ministry programs.

In addition to his duties at the college, Thomas writes hymns, books, articles, poetry and collaborate with composers working on setting his poetry to hymns and other songs. His most popular hymns include ***Source and Sovereign Rock and Cloud*** and ***Silent, Frenzied, Unclean Spirit***. He is also the author of over twenty books and is a professional flutist. His books include the popular ***Preaching While the Church is Under Reconstruction***; ***Wrestling with the Patriarchs***, and many others that are frequently referenced.

Thomas is in great demand to speak, conduct workshops, preach, perform his music, read his poetry, and organize conferences.

(References: *Thomas H. Troeger*, Yale Divinity School. Retrieved 2014; *Borrowed Light: Hymns, Prayers, and Poems*, 1994, Thomas H. Troeger; *If You Get the Congregation to God, Sit Down—an interview with Thomas Troeger*, 2011, Homiletics. Retrieved 2014)

Tweedy, Henry Hallam

Henry was born in 1868 in Binghamton, New York.

His family lived in comfortable conditions and supported his efforts to excel in all of his academic studies. Henry was a precocious child whose level of intelligence set him apart from his classmates. His unusually keen intellect and curiosity led to his success at the prestigious Phillips Andover Academy. Henry's work there was recognized by the distinguished teachers as extraordinary. He applied for and was accepted at Yale University after graduating from Phillips Andover Academy with honors. At Yale, Henry continued his intellectual development. He explored many areas of interest, but he became most interested in theology. He decided he wanted to be a teacher or professor of theology or become a minister.

Henry earned a Bachelor and Master degree at Yale and then entered the seminary at Union Theological Seminary. He also attended the University of Berlin where he continued his study of theology. Henry was ordained a Congregationalist minister. He was the minister at Plymouth Church in Utica, New York for ten years and then at South Church in Bridgeport, Connecticut for seven years.

After seventeen years as a minister, he became a professor of homiletics at Yale Divinity School for almost thirty years. He was a legendary professor with many publications about theology, homiletics, and hymns, including the famous ***The Minister and His Hymnal*** and ***Christian Worship and Praise***. Of his many hymns, the most popular and long enduring is ***O Spirit of the Living God,*** which is one of the most popular hymns in history.

Henry is also credited with the famous and often quoted line: "Fear is the father of courage and the mother of safety."

Henry worked and remained very active until his death in 1953 at the age of eighty-five in Brattleboro, Vermont. In his honor, the Henry Hallam Tweedy Scholarship was established in 1991.

(References: *Training the Devotional Life,* 1919, Henry Tweedy; *Henry Tweedy,* hymntime.com. Retrieved 2014; *Henry Tweedy,* Ancestry.com. Retrieved 2014; *Henry Hallam Tweedy,* Yale University Scholarships. Retrieved 2014)

Valerius, Adrianus

Adrianus, also known as Adriaen, was born in 1575 (an estimated date of birth by experts) in Middelburg, Netherlands. His family was considered prosperous because his father was a French notary and customs official with ties to the wholesalers of the trading business as well as connections with the city's political and legal officials.

Adriaen was raised in a family that enjoyed the fine arts, education, philosophy, and was dedicated to community activities and public service. His father's influence increased when he was given the position of Court Scribe to Pier van Reigersbergh, the Mayor of the City of Veere in the province of Zeeland in the Netherlands.

Adriaen received an excellent private education with a focus on the classics. Adriaen worked with his father on a number of projects and often observed how his father interacted with people and resolved conflicts. From this, he learned about the business world and the intricacies of running government offices. At a young age, Adriaen was named Toll and Customs Controller for the City of Veere. He became even more influential after marrying the Mayor's daughter. Adriaen was named the head of tax collections and received an appointment to the city council.

Adriaen was also a poet and composer of songs and hymns. He worked with other writers on the book ***Zeeusche Nachtegael*** which became immediately popular when it was published in 1623. His lasting reputation comes from his great work entitled ***Nederlandtsche gedenck-clanck*** (***Dutch Songs of Commemoration***) which is a book of poems that includes common themes from everyday living and the tragedies of the Dutch War of Independence. He worked on the book for over thirty years, until his death. He did not live to see the book gain international fame. It was published in 1631 by his son, Francois, about seven or eight years after Adriaen's death. The book became an international bestseller and it has remained well-known for over 200 years. The book includes seventy-six songs and hundreds of poems. The themes are religious, spiritual, humanistic, and range from inspiring to introspectively thoughtful and philosophic. The book remains one of the most revered works in Dutch history and its popularity surges during difficult or tragic times.

One hymn within the great work remains extremely popular today and is included in most hymnals around the world—the translation of ***Wilt Heden Nu Treden*** known as ***We Gather Together***. The hymn has become a mainstay during many holiday events and religious services, especially during Thanksgiving.

Adriaen continued to be a civil servant and creative genius until the time of his death believed to be in 1625 when he was only in his fifties.

(References: *A. Valerius,* literatuurgeschiedenis.nl. Retrieved 2014—translated by translate.com 2014; *Adriaen Valerius,* musicksmonument.nl. Retrieved 2014; *Adriaen Valerius Nederlandtsche Gedenck-clanck,* ingeb.org. Retrieved 2013 and 2014—translated by translate.com 2014)

Van Dyke, Henry

Henry was born in 1852 in Germantown, Pennsylvania.

He was a very intelligent and precocious child who enjoyed attending the local school and church. Henry had several friends and he interacted well with adults. Henry excelled in all academic areas in elementary and secondary school. He enjoyed playing with his friends and participating in school activities and he relished the opportunity to receive extra tutoring from the teachers.

Due to his academic success, intellectual development and support of his teachers, he was accepted to Princeton University. He graduated in 1873 with a Bachelor of Arts degree and in 1877 he earned a Master of Arts degree in theology. Henry was popular with the students and staff at Princeton, and he was a gifted intellectual with musical interests and talent. However, Henry's primary love at that time was English Literature. He became an expert on all matters and knowledge of English Literature. His college work was so brilliant Princeton offered him a professorship. He served as a professor of English Literature at Princeton for over twenty-four years. During his tenure, Henry was recognized as an international expert on English Literature. His public lectures were brilliant and well-attended. Henry was a master at reading excerpts from famous works of literature and he was able to help the audiences understand the stories behind the literary works and also to understand the importance of the works he reviewed.

Henry was also a prolific writer but he was very cautious about publishing his works. Despite his reticence about publishing (primarily because he was a perfectionist), he became an accomplished author. He wrote two very unique books, ***The Other Wise Man*** and ***The First Christmas Tree***. Both books enjoyed widespread popularity. His essays ***Little Rivers*** and ***Fisherman's Luck*** were works on religious themes and philosophy. Henry also wrote several hymns, including the legendary ***Joyful, Joyful, We Adore Thee.***

When Henry attended Princeton one of his dear friends was Woodrow Wilson, who became the 28th President of the United States. They remained friends for a lifetime and frequently visited each other. When Woodrow Wilson became president he named Henry as Minister to the Netherlands and Luxembourg.

Henry remained active with writing, poetry, hymns, and politics until his death in 1933 at the age of eighty-one.

(References: *Henry Van Dyke - The International Who's Who in the World,* p. 1043, 1912; *PoemHunter.org*. Retrieved 2014; *Portraits in Song,* Jay Althouse, Patti Drennan, Mark Hayes, Lloyd Larson, Anna Page, Jean Shafferman, and Douglas Wagner, 2006; *The Great Hymns,* June Montgomery and Kenon Renfrow, 2002)

Walford, William

William was born in 1772 in Bath, Somersetshire, England.

Little is known about his early life or his parents, but apparently he received a good education. William attended Homerton Academy and soon after graduation was ordained a Congregational Church minister. He served churches in Stowmarket, Suffolk, England; Great Yarmouth, Norfolk, England and Uxbridge, Middlesex, England. His first ministry was in Stowmarket, Suffolk, England where he served for three years. William then went back to Homerton Academy to teach for eleven years. He planned to spend his entire career at Homerton Academy, but after several years there he missed being a minister and his failing vision made preparations for teaching classes very difficult. So, he left the academy and went to Great Yarmouth, Norfolk, England and later to Uxbridge, Middlesex, England to serve as the minister. His ministry in those churches continued collectively for over thirty years.

During many of the years serving as minister he was almost blind, but with assistance from his staff and his own strong will and determination he was a successful and popular minister. William gradually lost all of his vision but he still managed to preach part-time. He also opened a small gift shop to help his income. He crafted many of the items he sold in his shop—wood and bone carvings, for example. William had many visitors to his shop including tourists, and there are many stories about visitors.

An American clergyman, Tom Salmon, was visiting the city when he heard about William. He was anxious to meet William, known as "the wise blind man of the city." William and Tom immediately liked each other and shared many ideas about prayer and worship. Tom was impressed with Williams' ability to quote verses from the Bible very easily and accurately. During the course of a conversation, William said he had a poem in mind about prayer that he thought might be useful in a hymn. Tom offered to write the words down. With Williams' amazing knowledge and memory of the Bible, he shared his thoughts with Tom who carefully and diligently wrote them into a small notebook. When William finished dictating his poem, Tom was touched to the core of his heart by the beauty of the words, for William, a blind life-long minister, had just given Tom the words to what would become one of the most beloved hymns of all time—***Sweet Hour of Prayer***. The hymn was published and first appeared in the *New York Observer* as a poem. It was soon thereafter sung as a hymn and remains in hymnals around the world.

William maintained his small shop, preached occasionally, and willingly offered advice until his health declined in 1848. William died in 1850 in Uxbridge, Middlesex, England at the age of seventy-eight. Shortly before he died, William said to his gathered friends, "it's time for the sweet hour of prayer."

(References: *Today in 1850—William Walford Died,* Wordwise Hymns, June 2010; *The Hymns and Hymn Writers of the Church: An Annotated Edition of The Methodist Hymnal,* 1911, W.F. Tillett and C.S.

Nutter; *Hymn Story—Sweet Hour of Prayer*, Lectionary.org. Retrieved 2013)

Walter, Howard Arnold

Howard was born in 1883 in New Britain, Connecticut. He grew up in a loving and caring family. He was a kindred spirit with his mother to whom he often turned to for advice.

Howard was encouraged to develop his intellectual and literary skills. He was socially precocious, enjoying being around friends and family. His elementary school and secondary school experiences were extraordinary. He was truly intellectually gifted and very creative and inquisitive.

Howard graduated with honors from secondary school and was accepted at Princeton University. He excelled in college in every subject and with virtually everything he attempted. Howard made lifelong friends at Princeton, including faculty members. Despite a large number of friends, he never told any of them his secret; he was suffering from a heart condition.

Howard wrote several poems while attending college. His friends said that he went several months writing one poem or more before going to bed each night. Howard won the Baird Oratorical contest which was the highest literary honor at Princeton. He graduated with honors from Princeton with a Bachelor of Science degree. Howard then studied at Hartford Theological Seminary and at universities in Edinburgh and Glasgow, Scotland before expanding his studies in Germany. In 1906, he traveled to Japan to live and teach English at Waseda University, an independent research university in Tokyo. Howard remained there for about sixteen months, but his poor health required him to return home for treatment and care. When he returned home his health improved. He resumed his studies and was ordained in the Congregational Church and became an assistant pastor at the Asylum Hill Congregational Church in Hartford.

Howard wrote many papers, sermons, poems, and hymns. Even though Howard was very young, his health problems became worse; he suffered from bouts of fatigue and weakness. Physicians at Princeton confirmed that his heart condition was becoming grave. He was cautioned to modify his rigorous work schedule. Despite his illness and episodes of physical weakness, he was very active and productive. He was the Editor-in-Chief of the *Nassau Literary Magazine* and one of the editors of the *Princeton Tiger* magazine.

Howard's doctors were especially concerned about any extensive travel abroad. Despite the warnings, Howard felt compelled from a sense of duty to travel as a missionary. Representing the YMCA he traveled to India and Sri Lanka. He began working at the Foreman Christian College in Lahore, India (later the city would be in Pakistan) which was and remains one of the most densely populated cities in the world. While he was there he wrote extensively about the Indians and what was known as the Ahmadiyya Movement (based on the belief that Mirza Ghulam Ahmad was a reformer of the 14th century Hijra and not a prophet). Howard was in Lahore in 1918 at the height of the influenza pandemic. In the overcrowded city, several thousand people contracted and died from influenza. Howard became ill one morning and by the afternoon of the same day he was dead. He was only thirty-five years old.

Howard wrote and published many poems and hymns in his short life, but he is probably most remembered for his poem, ***My Creed***. It has been used for over one hundred years by thousands of people for various reasons but primary for motivation and reassurance. It has been printed in numerous books, magazines, postcards, greeting cards, graduation presents, etc. Howard wrote it in one sitting when he was on his missionary trip to India shortly after he finished college. He sent it to his mother who was so impressed with it that she sent it to the wildly popular *Harper's Bazaar* magazine where it was published. ***My Creed*** became an overnight sensation. Howard also published ***My Creed and Other Poems*** which included over 100 of his poems.

(References: *Howard Arnold Walter,* Dictionary-Handbook to Hymns, 1978, Donald Paul Hustad; *Howard Arnold Walter,* Ancestry.com. Retrieved 2015; *The Hartford Seminary Record, 1909 Entry.* Retrieved 2015; *Howard Arnold Walter,* hymntime.com. Retrieved 2015)

Warner, Anna Bartlett

Anna was born in 1827 in Long Island, New York, into a wealthy family. Anna had one older sister, Susan. When Anna was still a baby, her mother died and an aunt, Aunt Frances, came to care for the two girls. Their father, Henry Warner, was a successful New York attorney with several investments and financial holdings.

The wealthy lifestyle of the family was suddenly destroyed by the Panic of 1837, which devastated the family's finances. Much to the sadness and shock of Anna and Susan, the beloved family home at St. Mark's Place in New York had to be sold. The family moved to their summer home on Constitution Island on the Hudson River. The home was an old and small American Revolutionary War era farmhouse. With his finances in ruins, Anna's father resolved to become a farmer and live off of the land.

Anna and Susan wandered about the island together. It was during this time that Anna and Susan realized that they shared a love of stories and make-believe. They often made up stories as they walked around the island. One day as they were heading home from a day running and playing on the island, Susan announced to Anna that they should write their stories. And so they did. Anna began writing books and to her surprise earned some money, which the family desperately needed. She also created a children's game called ***Robinson Crusoe's Farmyard*** about natural history. Susan also began writing and eventually published ***The Wide, Wide World*** in 1851. The book became an overnight success, and at one time was second only to *Uncle Tom's Cabin* as the bestselling book in the world. Few people knew that Anna helped Susan write the book. Anna would publish thirty-one books and Susan over sixty books. However, many of their works were pirated, leaving them with little income from their books.

Several of Anna's books and poems were put to music as children's songs and church hymns. Her most famous and endearing work was the hymn ***Jesus Loves Me***, which became and remains one of the most well-known and popular Christian hymns in history and is the favorite hymn of children. Anna wrote the hymn in a room in the old farmhouse; she said the inspiration for the hymn came from her exploration of the island and her love of the natural world - God's creation is proof of his love.

Anna and Susan taught Bible study classes at West Point, which was located just across the river from the family farm, starting when they were young. They taught there for over forty years. The cadets grew to love the sisters and their gleeful attitude toward life. They were always singing songs while walking the campus of West Point. The story goes that cadets heard Anna singing ***Jesus Loves Me*** one day as the cadets filed into class. Thereafter, it was not uncommon to hear cadets singing the song.

Millions of people, especially children, sing ***Jesus Loves Me*** on a regular basis over 100 years after Anna wrote it. It is poignant to note that when the famous theologian Karl Barth was asked to summarize an essential doctrine of the Christian faith in simple terms, he said, "Jesus loves me this I know, for the Bible tells me so."

Anna's sister died in 1885 at age sixty-five. Anna continued to write books and hymns and teach Bible study at West Point until her death in 1915 at the age of eighty-eight. The family farmhouse was carefully relocated and is now a museum on the grounds of West Point Military Academy.

(References: *Susan Warner*, 1909, Anna Warner; *The Hudson River in Literature*, 1980, Joel Benton; *I Sing for I Cannot Be Silent*, 1997, June Hadden Hobbs; *Anna Bartlett Warner*, hymntime.com. Retrieved 2014; *Anna Bartlett Warner*, Hymnary.org. Retrieved 2014)

Watts, Isaac

Isaac was born in 1674 in Southhampton, England. His father, Isaac Watts, Sr., was a devout nonconformist who he insisted that his family adopt his views, also. This was not a popular position in England at the time because it ran contrary to the Church of England. His father was incarcerated twice for his nonconformist ways.

At an early age, Isaac showed a propensity and talent for rhyme and music, as evidenced by his response to a question about his habit of keeping his eyes open during prayers: "A little mouse for want of stairs ran up a rope to say its prayers." When his father became upset by Isaac's rhyme, seeing it as disrespectful, Isaac said to his father while being punished: "O father, father, pity take and I will no more verses make." There is some debate as to his father's reaction to this rhyme, but it is generally believed that he laughed and encouraged Isaac to make more rhymes.

Isaac attended King Edward VI School where he received a strong classical education, including learning Latin, Greek, and Hebrew. Because of his nonconformist views, he was not allowed to attend Oxford or Cambridge, even though he passed the qualification exams with high marks and was fluent in four languages. Instead, he attended the Dissenting Academy in Stoke Newington, England. After he earned a Bachelor of Arts degree, he was invited to preach at an independent church in London.

Isaac's fame grew and soon he was asked to help train other preachers, which he greatly enjoyed, despite worsening health issues. To help with his expenses and in order to receive assistance with his poor health, he lived with the Hartopp family at Fleetwood House in Stoke Newington for a short period of time. It was during this time that he met the Hartopp's neighbors, Sir Thomas Abney and Lady Mary. A strong friendship developed and for almost forty years, Isaac lived with them in Abney Hall, even after Sir Thomas died.

Abney Hall had spectacular gardens that were carefully maintained by the staff and Lady Mary and her daughter, Elizabeth. Isaac loved the gardens, also, and spent many hours walking on the Abney Hall grounds. It was there, he said, that he often found inspiration for his numerous books and hymns.

Isaac became a prolific writer, including his most famous work, ***Logic***, which was an influential text at leading universities such as Oxford, Cambridge, Harvard, Yale, and others. However, his public popularity grew primarily from his many poems and hymns. He wrote over 750 hymns, including many popular hymns such as ***Among the Princes, Earthly Gods***; ***And Will the God of Grace***; ***Behold the Morning Sun***; ***Come, Dearest Lord***; ***Give Me the Wings of Faith***; ***Joy to the World***, and many others. He was often called the "Father of English Hymnody." Several of Isaac's hymns are used today in a variety of Christian worship services and revivals. It is an interesting footnote that the poem ***Against Idleness and Mischief*** in his book of poems, ***Divine Songs for Children***, was parodied in the Lewis Carroll poem *How Doth the Little Crocodile*, which Lewis included in his book *Alice's Adventures in Wonderland*. The popularity of Isaac's poem is further illustrated by the fact that it was quoted by Dr. Strong, a character in Charles Dickens' famous book *David Copperfield*.

After an amazingly productive life, Isaac died in Stoke Newington in 1748 at the age of seventy-four. It is told that he was writing another hymn while in his final minutes of life.

(References: *The Divine and Moral Songs of Isaac Watts*, 1918, Wilbur Macey Stone; *Isaac Watts Remembered*, 1978, David Guy Fountain; *So Amazing, So Divine*, 1997, Hal McElwaine Helms; *The Poetic Wonder of Isaac Watts*, 2013, Douglas Bond)

Wesley, Charles

Charles was born in 1707 in Epworth, Lincolnshire, England. His father, Samuel Wesley, was an Anglican minister and a poet. Charles' older brother was John Wesley.

Charles attended Westminster School and later Christ Church, Oxford University. As a young man at Oxford, Charles wanted to explore his beliefs and his spiritual development, but he felt that he needed more than classes at the university to accomplish that, so he formed a study/prayer group with his fellow students in 1727. The group became well known and the ranks of the attendees grew rapidly. Charles' older brother, John Wesley joined the group two years later, in 1729, and thereafter took over the leadership of the group with his strong personality, elegant speech, intellect and overbidding belief that there was a more truthful way to worship God. Even though the prayer and study group flourished in some respects, the group was often the subject of ridicule by other university students, who referred to the group as the Holy Club. Some students took to calling the group the Methodists because of their tendencies to be so methodical in beliefs, studies, meetings, and actions.

Charles received a Master of Arts degree in classical languages and literature, but his heart was in theology and the spiritual life. Charles said his conversion occurred on May 21, 1738, with John's conversion occurring only three days later. Charles and John were very close, and their strong religious beliefs brought them even closer together, but they did not always agree on issues related to their beliefs. Charles, for example, did not want to break from the Church of England; he was ordained through the Church. However, they usually settled their differences.

It was shortly after his spiritual epiphany that Charles became inspired to write poetic hymns. He would at times sit for hours writing them, as the ideas flowed so fast that he could barely put them to paper fast enough. At one point he composed hymns at a rate of ten each week.

In 1739, Charles and John took their beliefs to the public in the form of an open-air ministry - preaching in fields, town squares, and other public open spaces. Over time, the movement they started became the origins of the Methodist denomination. Due to a chronic respiratory illness, Charles stopped open-air preaching and took a job at the St. Marylebone Parish Church. It was there that Charles continued his prolific hymn writing. Even during times of illness and worry, Charles could be seen up late at night writing. He found spiritual expression and soul-searching relief in writing hymns. Many of his hymns are legendary and are a true expression of his beliefs and a full illustration of his knowledge of literature, religion, spirituality, and hope. He wrote and published over 6,000 hymns. Some of his most popular hymns are ***Hark! The Herald Angels Sing; How Can We Sinners Know; Jesus! The Name High Over All; And Are We Yet Alive; Blest Be the Dear Uniting Love; Blow Ye the Trumpet, Blow***, and many others.

Charles died in London in 1877 at the age of eighty.

(References: *A Biography of Charles Wesley*, 1956, Gwen Hubbard Redford; *Charles Wesley: A Biography*, 2006, Gary Martin Best)

Westendorf, Omer

Omer was born in 1916 in Cincinnati, Ohio to a middle-class family.

He received a traditional education in local elementary and secondary schools. Omer did not distinguish himself as a young scholar, but he showed an early interest in and a talent for music. His interest in music strengthened as he grew older.

Omer earned a Bachelor of Arts degree in music at the Cincinnati Conservatory of Music, where he also received awards for his music compositions. He earned his Master's degree when he was only twenty years old.

After college, he took a position as choir director and organist at the St. Bonaventure Church in Cincinnati. The church's music program became famous throughout the United States, mainly because of Omer's talents and leadership. Under Omer's leadership, they performed many concerts and were invited to perform at numerous events around the country. They also produced several professional recordings.

While visiting Holland after World War II Omer became fascinated by the hymns he found there. He brought them home and translated them. He also rearranged them for his church's choir. From this experience, Omer founded the World Library of Sacred Music in the 1950s and formed the World Library Publications as a means to collect, publish, and distribute church music across the United States and worldwide. The origin of the publication company was humble; he started it in the garage of his home. The company's first publication was ***The People's Hymnal*** which became popular and brought in enough profits to allow the company to survive and later flourish.

Omer was a popular speaker and teacher of music and hymns. Also, he published the first vernacular hymn and service book, ***The People's Mass Book***, for Catholic liturgies as decreed by the Vatican Council II. Omer was a master of music but he also recognized that there are technical skills that musicians must master in order to fully develop. He believed that learning how to sight read music was important for musicians but also for anyone who loved or enjoyed music. For the musician, it was necessary to grow professionally, and for the layperson, it was another way to more fully enjoy music. Omer developed a unique way to teach sight-reading and it became so popular that he was encouraged to write about it. He published ***Music Lessons for the Man in the Pew*** to teach the art of sight reading choral music.

Omer received many awards and honors, including the National Association of Pastoral Musicians' *Pastoral Musician of the Year Award*. Among other influential publications were his hymns ***Where Charity and Love Prevail; Sent Forth by God's Blessing; Gift of Finest Wheat***, and his own favorite ***Shepherd of Souls, In Love, Come Feed Us***.

Omer worked until his health declined. While at home gravely ill, his family gathered around his bed and sang his favorite hymn. He died in 1997 at the age of eighty-one in Cloverdale, Ohio.

(References: *Omer Westendorf*, Liturgical Pioneers Pastoral Musicians and Liturgists. Retrieved 2015; *Omer Westendorf*, GIA Publications. Retrieved 2015; *Obituary of Omer Westendorf*, Ancestry.com. Retrieved 2015)

Whiting, William

William was born in 1825 in Kensington, England, into a wealthy family.

He received an excellent education and showed remarkable creative talent and intellectual acumen beginning at an early age. William loved music and poetry and is thought to have written poems when he was an adolescent. He attended school at Chapham Academy, where he excelled in all subjects. Later he graduated from Winchester College with honors. It was during his college years that his musical talents blossomed, as did his ability to compose music.

After graduating from college, William was offered the position of Master of Winchester College Choristers' School, a prestigious post for such a young person. While working at Winchester, he wrote several hymns and poems and he published two books, ***Rural Thoughts*** and ***Edgar Thorpe or the Warfare of Life***.

William is most famous for the hymn ***Eternal Father, Strong to Save***. The hymn became one of the most popular and well-known hymns throughout England. Every division of the Royal Navy sang the hymn on a regular basis; consequently, it became known as *"The Navy Hymn"*. It was sung at virtually every Royal Navy church service. Sir Winston Churchill had great admiration for the hymn and often said the verses brought tears to his eyes. The United States Navy adopted the hymn, also, and began singing it at church services. The hymn was one of President Franklin D. Roosevelt's favorites. So much so that it was sung at his funeral in Hyde Park, New York, in 1945. President John F. Kennedy, having served in the Navy during World War II, also loved the hymn. In honor of his life, the United States Navy Band played it while President Kennedy's body was being taken up the steps to the United States Capitol to lie in state after his death in 1963.

William worked at Winchester College for over thirty-six years, until his death at the age of fifty-three in 1878 in Winchester, Hampshire, England. During his years at Winchester College, he wrote several poems, hymns, and other musical compositions, but he will forever be known as the author of the immortal ***Eternal Father, Strong to Save***.

(References: *William Whiting*, Hymns Without Words, Retrieved 2014; *William Whiting*, The Hymnal Companion, 1940; *William Whiting*, Dictionary of Hymnology, 1907, John Julian)

Whittier, John Greenleaf

John was born in 1807 in Haverhill, Massachusetts. He had a brother and two sisters. The family lived on a farm with an aunt and uncle. All of the family members worked on the farm to scratch out a living. Almost all that was produced on the farm had to be used by the family to survive.

John was not suited for the manual labor necessary on the farm. The long days of hard physical work left him physically depleted and ill most days, primarily because he had uneven health and was physically frail. It was obvious to his mother and father that John was more suited for the intellectual world, so they did the best they could to provide him with reading material. There was not much of an opportunity to attend a public school because of the demands of the farm, so what John learned came from his own reading and studying. He became an avid reader. It did not matter what was available, he read it all. Other than an occasional newspaper, farm information pamphlet and books he read the few times he attended public school, he had very little else to read. However, John's family had a six volume set of books about the foundation and history of Quakerism. (It is unknown how or why the family acquired the six-volume set). He read and reread each of the books and was impressed with and influenced by the doctrines of the Quakers, particularly the doctrine of all men being created equal, which was the genesis of his later impassioned anti-slavery work and literature.

As John's love of reading expanded and he found that he had writing skills, or at least he enjoyed writing. He did not know if his writing was good or bad until he began reading poetry that was given to him by one of his friends. It was a book of collected poems by various authors. Not only was John inspired by the book, he also felt certain that he could write poems just as good as what he read. Encouraged by one of his sisters, John wrote, ***The Exile's Departure***, a poem his sister thought was excellent and illustrative of John's talent. Unknown to him, his sister sent the poem to the *Newburyport Free Press* where it came to the attention of the editor, William

Lloyd Garrison, who not only published the poem, he also wrote to John to encourage him to submit more poems. Only then did John learn of his sister's exploits with his poem.

Garrison became an influential person in John's life. He encouraged John to enroll in Haverhill Academy. John was reluctant at first, but his sisters and parents encouraged him to pursue his education; however, one significant obstacle was the cost of the private school. Now determined to attend Haverhill, John worked as a shoemaker and later as a teacher in a small school near Merrimac, Massachusetts. He saved almost everything he made at those two jobs, but he was still short of cash for tuition. His family came through for him, providing money from the farm for John's tuition, money that they really could not afford to give him.

John attended Haverhill Academy and in just two years completed all of the academic requirements to earn a high school diploma. Upon graduating, he was immediately offered a job at the *National Philanthropist* by Garrison. John had found his element. He was a gifted writer but also a talented editor. Garrison soon made him editor of the weekly *American Manufacturer,* a Boston publication. John loved his job and he could not believe how much money he was paid. He was generous in the amount of money he sent to his family to help them improve their quality of life.

In 1830, he became the editor of the famous and powerfully influential *New England Weekly Review* in Connecticut. Venturing out on his own, away from his family's influence and that of Garrison, John ran for Congress and lost in 1832. He was so physically and emotionally exhausted from his campaign and the effort to pay off his campaign debts that he collapsed and returned home. When he recovered, John reconnected with Garrison and together they became widely known for their strong opposition to slavery.

John continued to write poems and tried his hand at hymns. As a frequent contributor, he was instrumental in the success of the *Atlantic Monthly,* one of the most long-lasting and influential publications in the United States. One of his most famous poems was ***Snow-Bound,*** which to his surprise was purchased by thousands of people. It is estimated that he made over $10,000 from the poem, which was an unprecedented amount of royalties at that time. Also, some of his poems were set to hymns, because they were spiritual and inspiring and were widely popular. His most famous hymn is ***Dear Lord and Father of Mankind,*** which is in many modern hymnals. John was inspired to write the hymn after reflecting on the many talents that people possess only by the grace of God, the Father. He realized that his talent for writing was a divine gift.

John continued to write until the time of his death in 1892 at the age of eighty-five.

(References: *Works of John Greenleaf Whittier,* johngreenleafhittier.com. Retrieved 2014; *John Greenleaf Whittier: A Biography,* 1985, Roland Woodwell)

Wimber, John

John was born in 1934 in Kirksville, a small town in northern Missouri. He was raised in a family with no interest in religion or faith of any sort.

He attended local public schools without distinction, and he worked at various jobs in the small town, trying to earn money to help the family. After secondary school, John joined the Army and upon his return home, he floundered trying to find his place in the world, and with no help from his family. While he was in the Army he enjoyed music and became interested in the composition of music. Eventually, music became his main interest and companion.

John followed his love of music and used his musical talent to form the *Righteous Brothers* singing group, the same group that would later become the famous duo of Bobby Hatfield and Bill Medley.

His life changed in 1963 at the age of twenty-nine when he went with a friend to a Quaker Bible Study class. He was moved by the experience and felt that God spoke to him during the class. John said it was that experience that brought him to a life of worship. He attended Azusa Pacific College and majored in Biblical Studies. He later became ordained as a Quaker.

With an engaging personality, spiritual motivation, musical talent, and a true desire to help others, John became a traveling evangelist. He traveled the country giving inspirational messages at revivals. He brought several hundred people of all ages into Christianity. He preached occasionally at Yorba Linda Friends Church, and eventually became a member of the staff in 1971 as co-pastor.

In addition to being a gifted preacher, John was also an exceptionally talented singer and keyboard player. John felt that God wanted him to extend his ministry through music so that he would touch more people that way. So, he thought about becoming a full-time musician. In the meantime, in 1974, John joined with Peter Wagner to create the Charles Fuller Institute, an entity that helped Calvary Chapel churches grow their congregations. He parted ways with the institute and the Calvary Chapel congregations and after observing the "power of the healing word of God" he and Chuck Smith created the Anaheim Vineyard Fellowship, which focused on the healing power of God. As word spread about "miracles at the Vineyard" attendance steadily grew. When famous evangelist, Lonnie Frisbee, heard about the Anaheim Vineyard Fellowship, he contacted John about preaching one Sunday. Arrangements were made and Lonnie preached on Mother's Day in 1978. His reputation brought hundreds to the service. From that moment, the weekly attendance soared.

John's work and influence spawned thousands of churches across the United States and the world. His "Power Evangelism" sermons with a focus on the healing power of God brought him international fame. John embraced the word and power of the Apostles, modernizing their Biblical concepts into "signs and wonders".

Music remained important to John's beliefs, sermons, and prayer. He found influence in the power of lyrics and expressed that in the dramatic words of his hymns. His most popular hymn is

Spirit Song which is found in most hymnals. John also published several books such as ***Wonders and Church Signs and Growth*** and ***Power Evangelism***.

John's health declined after an accident when he fell and struck his head. While recovering from the head injury, he had to have emergency coronary bypass surgery. Complications from the fall and recovery from heart surgery limited his work. Nevertheless, he maintained a positive attitude. John died in 1997 at the age of sixty-three from a brain hemorrhage.

(References: *Power Evangelism*, 1986, John Wimber and Kevin Springer; *John Wimber: The Way It Was*, 2000, Carol Wimber)

Wolfe, Aaron Robarts

Aaron was born in 1821 in Mendham, New Jersey. His family was closely tied to the community activities and leadership of Mendham.

Aaron was a precocious child who was known in the small community for his cheerfulness and intelligence. His parents wanted him to be either a minister or a lawyer. After receiving an education at home, in church, and in the small local school, Aaron was accepted at Williams College, a small private liberal arts college in Williamstown, Massachusetts. Members of his local church had ties to the Williams College and they helped with his admission and tuition.

Aaron enjoyed the college life as well as the social life and activities at the college. He was a good student, earning his Bachelor of Arts degree, but he had to work while attending college so he could afford the tuition. This delayed the completion of his degree. It was during his time at Williams College that he developed an interest in philosophy and theology. After he graduated from Williams College, Aaron enrolled at the Union Theological Seminary in New York. He thrived at the seminary. He felt like his spirit was fully awakened by the environment at the college. While attending seminary he composed the hymn

Complete in Thee which was published in the book *Church Melodies: A Collection of Psalms and Hymns with Appropriate Tunes.*

Aaron was ordained by the Presbyterian Church of New York shortly after completing seminary. While looking for work, he was offered a job by the family of a friend that ran a school for girls in Tallahassee, Florida. He directed the school for three years; he loved the job. He felt that he was called by God to help the children grow intellectually and spiritually. Aaron was offered a job as a minister in New Jersey, which he felt like he could not turn down, but something happened that changed his mind and career. When he left Florida he put all of his personal writing material, including copious notes, books, hymns, and other material in a chest on board a ship at St. Mark's, Florida. It was too much material for him to carry with him as he made his way across the country to New Jersey. When he went to retrieve his materials he learned that the ship had been hit by lightning and burned. Everything he packed was lost or destroyed. Aaron viewed this as a sign that he should change his plans to become a pastor and instead continue his work with children. Consequently, he founded the Hillside Seminary for Young Ladies in Montclair, New Jersey which became his life's work.

Aaron wrote hymns and poems and other materials throughout his career. Seven of Aaron's hymns were included in the book *Church Melodies* by Thomas Hastings. Many of them are in modern day hymnals, such as the famous and popular ***A Hymn of Joy We Sing***.

After a brief illness, Aaron died in 1902 in Montclair, New Jersey at the age of eighty-one.

(References: *Aaron Robarts Wolfe,* Dictionary of Hymnology, 1907, John Julian; *A Parting Hymn We Sing,* 2012, Warren Shiver; *Aaron Robarts Wolfe,* Ancestry.com. Retrieved 2014)

Wolfe, Lanny

Lanny was born in 1942 in Columbus, Ohio. According to Lanny, he was born and raised in a middle-class family. His father was a railroad engineer and his mother was the daughter of a Methodist preacher and was the guiding light in his life. She instilled in Lanny a love of music and worship.

At age nine, Lanny started his music journey when he began taking piano lessons. When his piano teacher moved away, Lanny began teaching himself piano and music composition. At age eleven, Lanny was baptized. He has stated that his two loves came together when he was young: Christ and music. Also, he was influenced in junior high by his music teacher, Lois Newstrand, who played the piano and organ and directed the junior high choir. She encouraged Lanny to continue working on his music skills, and she invited him to perform at various events, furthering his confidence, competence, and interest.

Lanny's music and academic successes during junior high continued in high school, where he excelled in all subjects and music. He was offered a scholarship to Ohio State University, where he earned a Bachelor of Arts degree in business education. After graduating, Lanny taught public school during the day and attended graduate classes at night at Ohio State University, where he earned a Master of Business Administration degree.

Even while working and attending school, Lanny's music skills continued to expand, as did his interest in and love for music, especially gospel music. His music reputation grew, also, which led to him being offered a job to teach worship music at the Pentecostal Bible School in California. This experience helped Lanny recognize that it was music, gospel music, that he loved the most.

He went back to college and received a Bachelor of Arts degree and later a Master of Arts degree in music education from San Jose State University. Lanny was offered the chance to lead the music departments at several Bible schools affiliated with the United Pentecostal Church International.

For over twenty years, he has been the music director at South Texas Bible Institute in Houston, Texas, and he currently serves as CEO for Paradigm Music Productions. Lanny has won several awards for his music, including two Dove Awards for Song of the

Year and Songwriter of the Year. His song ***More Than Wonderful*** has won international acclaim, as have many of his hymns such as ***Surely the Presence of The Lord; God's Wonderful People; Whatever It Takes; One Day Too Late,*** and many others. He has been nominated eight times for Gospel Songwriter of the Year, and he has been named SESAC's Gospel Composer of the Year.

(References: *Lanny Wolfe Biography,* Paradigm Music Productions. Retrieved 2014; *Lanny Wolfe,* Absolutely Gospel Music, 2008, Daryl Williams)

Wright, Ralph

Ralph was born in 1938 in Ollerton, England. He was one of four brothers.

His father was an engineer and CEO of a mining company. His father was also a respected community leader, but it was Ralph's mother who helped him develop a love of reading from a variety of literature. In fact, Ralph said that his mother was his inspiration for writing.

Ralph's parents were devout Catholics. Ralph had an interest in the spiritual side of his life and at an early age determined that he wanted to be a monk. However, his oldest brother became a monk so Ralph decided instead to become an engineer so he could work in his father's mining company. A large number of math classes required to become an engineer, however, changed Ralph's plans. His skills were more in the literary domain, and he found that he loved poetry above all other types of literature.

He graduated from Ampleforth College and considered joining some of his friends in the British Army, but he had been offered a scholarship in the classics at Oxford University so his family and friends encouraged him to enroll at Oxford. Surprising everyone, Ralph joined the British Army instead. After basic camp, he was assigned to Malaysia to learn jungle warfare and other military tactics. He was considered a natural leader and the British Army encouraged him to remain there with the idea of future promotions through the ranks. Ralph was not unhappy during his British Army service, but he was anxious to expand his experiences.

After leaving the British Army he began novitiate and monastic training and was ordained a short time later. He returned to college and earned a Bachelor of Arts degree at Saint Benet's Hall, Oxford, and a Master of Arts degree in theology at the Catholic University in Switzerland. Ralph became a priest but found that his gift was in teaching and poetry.

He has published several books of poetry, including the bestselling ***Our Daily Bread***, and he has written over two dozen hymns. Many of them are in hymnals, including ***Sing of One Who Walks Beside Us***. His book ***WILD...Alphabet*** is a bestselling illustrated book of humorous stories. He has also published scholarly books, such as ***Praying the Psalms in Christ*** and ***The Rule of Saint Benedict***.

Ralph entered the Saint Louis Abbey in 1970 where he has lived and strived since. Currently, Ralph (Father Ralph) is the vocations director, teacher of moral theology and original poetry and the varsity tennis coach.

(References: *Father Ralph Wright,* Saint Louis Abbey. Retrieved 2015; *Ralph Wright,* Dictionary of Hymnology, 1907, John Julian; *Ralph Wright,* United States Library of Congress. Retrieved 2015)

Yamaguchi, Tokuo

Tokuo was born in 1900 in Japan. His family was a traditional Japanese family but Tokuo was interested in many aspects of religion far beyond what he learned at home and at the nearby temple.

Tokuo was introduced to Christianity by friends and was converted before he attended college. He enrolled in one of Japan's top education sites, Aoyama Gakuin University, a comprehensive educational institute which includes a kindergarten, an elementary school, junior and senior high schools, a women's junior college, and a university. It was established in 1874 by missionaries Dora E.

Schoonmaker, Robert Samuel Maclay, and Julius Soper who were from the Methodist Episcopal Church of the United States.

After earning a Bachelor of Arts degree in theology he was ordained as a pastor in the United Church of Christ in Toyohaski of the Aichi Prefecture. Tokuo remained there for over forty years. His sermons became legendary. People would travel several miles to hear him, and if a minister or theologian visited Japan from any other part of the world they often made an effort to attend one of Tokuo's worship services. Tokuo brought the joy and energy of music to his services. He loved hymns and he tried to embrace the spirituality of hymns as he expertly wove the messages of hymns into his sermons.

Tokuo was also a theology scholar. He translated ***The Journal of John Wesley*** into Japanese and published it in 1961. It was well received by the public and by scholars of John Wesley's works. Tokuo also translated other works of English theology into Japanese and received several awards for his translation work, including the prestigious Christian Literature Society of Japan's highest award for translations.

Tokuo wrote several poems and hymns. Some of his poems were also composed into hymns. Perhaps his most well-known hymn is ***Here O Lord Your Servants Gather*** which can be found in many hymnals and all Methodist hymnals.

Tokuo lived a long and productive life and frequently traveled between Japan and the United States. He was greatly troubled by World War II because he loved his country but was brokenhearted over his country's entrance into the war and was especially troubled by the attack on Pearl Harbor and other atrocities committed by the army of Japan. Tokuo and his congregation were at times harassed by the Japanese military during the war, but they continued to hold services and prayed for peace.

Tokuo remained active and involved in religious work and activities until his health declined. He died in 1995 at the age of ninety-five. He is revered by Christians around the world for his steadfast love of Christ and his devotion to his congregation and community of worshipers.

(References: *Hymns, Psalms, and Spiritual Songs,* 1990, John Knox Press; *Tokuo Yamaguchi,* Michael Hawn, UMC. Retrieved 2013 and 2015; *Tokuo Yamaguchi,* hymnsite.com. Retrieved 2015; *Tokuo Yamaguchi,* Portal Luteranos, March 26, 2014. Retrieved and translated by translate.com 2015)

Ylvisaker, John Carl

John was born in 1937 in Moorhead, Minnesota. He was born into a family with ties to academic excellence and legacies in colleges and universities. The Ylvisaker name is linked to the history of three colleges.

John was an excellent student, with an early love of music and a recognized talent both in writing and music composition and performance. After secondary school, John attended Concordia College in his hometown where he earned a Bachelor of Arts degree. He continued his studies at Luther Northwestern Seminary (now Luther Seminary), and he attended the University of Minnesota and St. Cloud State College. In addition to his college studies, John composed music.

John became a voice teacher and continued that work for four years; during that time, he performed music in different venues and wrote and recorded music. His love of music and his spiritual life brought him to the Lutheran Church of the Reformation in St. Louis Park, Minnesota, where he served as the music director for almost fourteen years. He also continued recording his original works, with eleven recordings primarily for the Lutheran Vespers radio broadcasts between 1967 and 1988.

Since 1988, John has served as president of New Generation Publishers, which produces worship resources for churches around the world. He has also produced SCAN, a radio broadcast for the ELCA that can be heard weekly on many radio stations in the United States and Canada. His work on the radio broadcast led to five Gabriel Awards for broadcasting excellence.

Despite his busy work schedule with the publishing house, performances, and other work, he still finds time to write songs. John has published over 1,000 songs and hymns. His most famous and popular hymn is ***I was There to Hear Your Borning Cry***, which has been sung around the world and is in most church hymnals. This beautiful ballad hymn is a love song to mankind from God. The creative and spiritual inspiration for the hymn evolved when he was working on a study series for the American Lutheran Church on baptism. He also wrote ***Mass for a Secular City***.

John's book ***What Song Shall We Sing*** became very popular. It combines traditional folk songs with hymnody. His most recent book, ***Borning Cry***, contains over 900 songs, including 120 of his own.

In 2012, John was the recipient of an honorary doctorate of humanity letters from Wartburg College for his life-long work.

(References: *John Carl Ylvisaker*, ylvisaker.com. Retrieved 2015; *John Carl Ylvisaker*, hymntime.com. Retrieved 2015; *Borning Cry*, 1992, John Carl Ylvisaker; *Word and World: Theology for Christian Ministry, Volume 12, Number 3*, 1992, Paul Westmeyer and Gracia Grindal)

References

1. Angelou, Maya. (1990). *Goodreads quote from Maya Angelou*. Random House.
2. Buck, Pearl S. (1931, 1958). *The Good Earth*. Washington Square Press, Simon & Schuster, Inc.
3. Carlyle, Thomas (1837). *The Works of Thomas Carlyle*, edited by Henry Duff Trail. Cambridge Press Publishing.
4. Collins, Suzanne. (2008). *The Hunger Games*. Scholastic Press.
5. Davis, Chad. (2015). *Hope is the Antidote for Fear*. Tiny Buddha.
6. De Becker, Gavin. (1998). *The Gift of Fear*. Dell Publishing.
7. De Cervantes, Miguel. (1605). *Don Quixote, Man from La Mancha*.
8. De Saint-Exupery, Antoine. (1943). *The Little Prince*. Houghton Mifflin Harcourt Publishing.
9. Ford, Henry. (1922). *My Life and Work*. Kessinger Publishing, LLC.
10. Frankl, Viktor. (1946). *Man's Search for Meaning*. Beacon Press Publishing.
11. Fulgham, Robert. (2004 edition). *All I Really Need to Know I Learned in Kindergarten*. Ballantine Books.
12. Furedi, Frank. (2007). *The Only Thing We Have to Fear is the Culture of Fear*. Spike Magazine, April 4, 2007.
13. Hazlitt, William. (1842). *The Complete Works of Michael de Montaigne*. Northcote, London.
14. Hillenbrand, Laura. (2014). *Unbroken*. Random House Publishing.
15. Hughes, Langston. (1959). *Selected Poems of Langston Hughes*. Random House of Canada.
16. Jiddu, Krishnamurti. (1928a). *The pool of wisdom. Who brings the truth. By what authority, and Three Poems.* Eerde, Ommen*: Star Publishing Trust. pp. 43–53.* OCLC 4894479. Saaremaa, Estonia*: jiddu-krishnamurti.net [web publisher].* Retrieved 2015.
17. Martel, Yann. (2001). *Life of Pi*. Random House of Canada.

18. Maslow, Abraham. (2012 edition). *A Theory of Human Motivation*. Start Publishing LLC.
19. Najapfour, Brian G. (2012). *The Very Heart of Prayer: Reclaiming John Bunyan's Spirituality*. Media Universe.
20. Silverstein, Shel. (1974). *Where the Sidewalk Ends*. Harper Collins Publishers, Inc.
21. Spinoza, Baruch. (1660). *A Short Treatise on God, Man and His Well-Being*.
22. Stanley, Charles. (2008). *Stuck in Reverse: Break Free from Fear and Disbelief and Enjoy the Good Things God Has for You*. In Touch Ministries Publishing.
23. Toffler, Alvin. (1995). *Creating a New Civilization*. Turner Publishing.

About the Author

Dr. Garry W. McGiboney is a nationally recognized for his work in education and psychology. He has a Ph.D. in psychology and administration. Dr. McGiboney is an adjunct professor at Georgia State University and deputy state superintendent of schools. He has made hundreds of presentations across the United States and is often a keynote speaker at state and national conferences. He has published over 30 professional articles and is the author of four books: *The Private Side of Public Education; Student Relations and Discipline; Lessons for Leaders and Governing Boards,* and *Crisis Management Planning*. Based on his work and research, he has been quoted in *Time Magazine, USA Today, Los Angeles Times, Wall Street Journal* and many other publications, including the international press such as *Le Devoir, Listin Diario, El Diaro, Japan Press,* and *Mato Grosso*. Dr. McGiboney has appeared on *CNN, A&E, Discovery Channel, National Public Radio, Nickelodeon Network* and many local and regional television and radio programs. He is the recipient of numerous awards, such as the NAACP Educator of the Year and National Association of School Psychologists Friend of Children Award, and others. Also, he was inducted into the University System of Georgia Board of Regents Hall of Fame for his career-long efforts on behalf of children.

87775565R00240

Made in the USA
Lexington, KY
30 April 2018